Oct 1, 1993

Inscribed with warm regards for Merwin Fleig a Hamilton County native. Hope you enjoy reading about our good(?) old days.

God Bless

Ed R. Anderson

Bittersweet Years
Smiling Through Tears

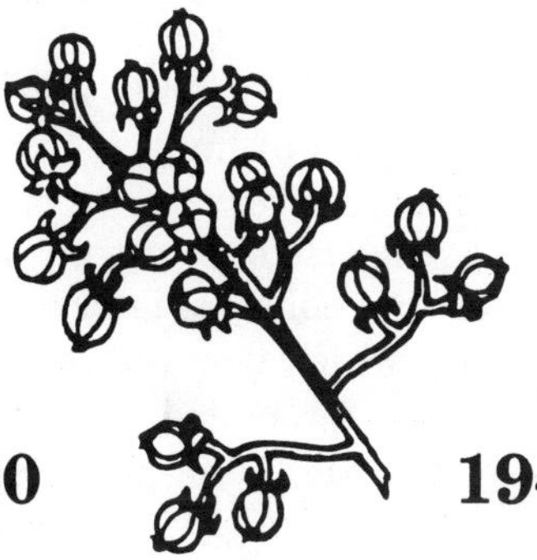

1920 **1941**

By Homer R. Ankrum

Published by Graphic Publishing Company,
204 North 2nd Avenue West
Lake Mills, Iowa 50450

DEDICATION

Dedicated to those wonderful school teachers whose tireless efforts adequately prepare their students for entry into the academic and non-academic world. To those teachers whose outstanding performance of duties mentally equips their trusted charges as best possible to meet the challenges of their chosen fields of endeavor, and cheers to those purveyors of knowledge who instill in their scholars a determination to "use what talents they possess, for the woods would not be nearly so melodic if no birds sang, except the best."

Praise be to those teachers who impart meaningful history to their students in order that mistakes of the past not be repeated. And plaudits to those in the academic field who teach their students to be honest - trustworthy; also to have compassion for their fellow human beings. Special kudos to those teachers who have encouraged their students to have a good sense of humor - for during trying times it can prove to be an invaluable asset.

Further dedicated to Alice Eikenberry, my wife Ellen, and Barbara Westervelt Seney. Alice, my college history teacher, for her inspirational teaching of history which inspired me to author two historical novels. Ellen, for her encouragement - untold hours of typing and retyping the manuscripts and exhaustive research assistance. And, last, but not least, Barbara Westervelt Seney, a college classmate, whose journalistic expertise and fantastic editing contributed heavily to the betterment of "Bittersweet Years - Smiling Through Tears."

Library of Congress Catalog Card Number 93-79072
ISBN 0-89279-082-2

Published by Graphic Publishing Co., Lake Mills, Iowa
Printed by Stoyles Graphic Services, Lake Mills, Iowa
Lake Mills, Iowa 1-800-458-2922
Mason City, Iowa 1-800-247-5986
Printed in the United States of America

CONTENTS

Preliminary

Chapters

BITTERSWEET YEARS

With the war for democracy over in 1918,
There was joy on every hand.
It was a time of milk and honey,
A time of plenty throughout the land

There were flappers in the movies,
The Charleston dance was born.
College boys wore big raccoon coats,
Coeds' locks at last were shorn.

The wealthy drank champagne from slippers
Others, white lightning and bathtub gin.
Lovers cuddled in Model "A" rumble seats,
Five dollar bills became known as a fin.

Then came loud rumbles from the East,
Stocks and bonds on Wall Street fell.
People jumped from tall building ledges,
Rather than face an economic hell.

Banks by the thousands closed their doors,
A Great Depression swept the nation.
No longer did factories prosper and hum,
Fifteen million people lost their vocations.

People stood patiently in long soup lines,
President and Congress offered no good news.
There was canvas on many house roof tops,
Cardboard on windows—in soles of shoes.

Hooverville shack towns and hobo camps,
Across the nation emerged and grew.
People slept outdoors and in nickel flophouses,
Dreaming of nourishing pots of stew.

Compassion for one another grew,
People didn't sit and mope.
Most banded together in strong resolve,
A new president offered hope.

President Roosevelt taught people to smile
Through tears and make jokes of their plight.
They took the bitter with the sweet,
Then marched off, a war to fight!

by H. R. Ankrum

FOREWORD

By Herb Plambeck

An author "extraordinaire," Homer Ankrum, a native of Webster City, Iowa, in writing "Bittersweet Years — Smiling Through Tears" paints a fascinating word picture of the trying period between the two World Wars. It was a brief time of prosperity to begin with, followed by a long nationwide period of depression, when millions lost their jobs, hunger and hardship gripped many, farmers lost their land, and countless families became homeless.

Those of us who lived through those difficult years will appreciate the author's first-hand observations and experiences, many of them bittersweet, some of them humorous, and all of them authentic. Readers too young to know the trials and tribulations of the '20s and '30s, and the resiliency of most of the nation's hardpressed citizens, will find Ankrum's work exceedingly interesting as well as historically accurate.

It is a story emphasizing the courage of the people of that era and their ability to subsist, educate their children, find some humor in adversity, and achieve a measurable degree of happiness into their troubled lives. Readers will smile at the often amusing experiences of the book's main character as he, his family, and his friends, cope with their stressful problems. Many, like myself, can relate to the author's writings as he captures state, national and international events—while adding a touch of bygone politics into some well-balanced, delightful local flavor.

Ankrum's initial chapter provides the reader with the feelings experienced by an elderly veteran returning to his childhood haunts and the flood of memories that come rushing back to engulf him. Readers participate in some thought provoking analysis, as the author explores the possible causes of the so-called "generation gap" that came to exist between youths and their elders during the Viet Nam War. Was the "gap" caused by unsettled world conditions after World War II, or from the difference in socioeconomic environment under which the two generations grew to adulthood? Both possibilities are explored.

For those born after World War II the author allows them to be the judge of whether the era was instrumental in causing the "gap." Ankrum takes them with him on an interesting trip down memory lane. To lighten the impact of serious reading, humorous and human interest anecdotes are skillfully interwoven into his writings.

Readers will love the many humorous and masterfully told adventures of a boy growing to adulthood during a period when people learned to grin when grimacing would have been far easier. They will share with him the dark days when depression stricken people were forced to sell their every possession to the offbeat cadence of the auctioneer's gavel.

Through Ankrum's intensive research and perceptive treatment of excellent material, readers will feel that now, or again, they are living through the boom years immediately following World War I, prohibition, the notorious gangster era, and the age of coonskin coats, rumble seats, and Charleston dancing flappers. Readers can virtually feel the terrible pangs of the Great Depression and the hardships endured by those who struggled through poverty, then saw the light at the end of the tunnel - only to be forced to stand helplessly by while their dreams were shattered by events leading to World War II.

Ankrum has succeeded admirably in the extremely difficult task of combining history, humor, and human interest into a superbly written novel. His writing is so unique that both young and older readers will find themselves laughing part of the time, possibly shedding tears at other times, absorbing interesting American history much of the time, and always wanting to read on to see what the next pages will unfold.

Inevitably, readers will also feel great admiration for Ankrum's genius as a writer based on the world of experiences he has had in peace and war, including earning a battlefield commission for outstanding combat leadership during the long, bitter World War II battle on the Anzio beachhead in Italy. Now a retired Lt. Col., Homer Ankrum first won literary honors when he authored "Dogfaces Who Smiled Through Tears", an outstanding chronicle of the hardships, heroics, heartbreaks and humor American soldiers experienced in World War II.

Those who have read the adventures of our GIs, known as "Dogfaces" in North Africa and Italy, will find "Bittersweet Years - Smiling Through Tears" just as interesting and captivating.

ACKNOWLEDGMENTS

First, I must give a great deal of credit to my wife, Ellen, for her research assistance—word processing of the writes and rewrites of the manuscript and her undying commitment to the completion of the book. Next, an expression of admiration and gratitude to Barbara Westervelt Seney, a fine journalist and retired magazine editor, who applied her outstanding journalistic skills to editing and re-editing the manuscript and making helpful suggestions.

A hearty thanks to George Drake for sharing with me many hours of joyful reminiscing while providing input on several historical and hysterically humorous anecdotes.

Deep appreciation is expressed to Nadine Lunning Dingman, historical-geneology researcher, for providing timely, expert research assistance. Without Nadine's assistance several interesting stories would have been incomplete or left untold.

Much appreciation is due Mrs. Gertrude Horan of Edison, New Jersey, widow of the great journalist and author, James D. Horan, for allowing me to use several photos from her husband's wonderful book, "The Desperate Years." Horan's book, published by Bonanza Books (Crown Publishers, Inc. New York) is one of, if not the greatest chronicles ever written on the Great Depression.

A special thanks to Editor Jeff DeYoung of the *Daily Freeman Journal* for research assistance—permission to use photos and reference material from that newspaper. I am very appreciative for research information provided by Walter B. Stevens, retired Editor of the *Fort Dodge Messenger* and to Maurice Stark for research assistance in the Fort Dodge area.

Enough praise cannot be given to Historian Arthur Fischbeck for his in-depth assistance in providing excellent reference material for stories and related photographs concerning the Mason City-Cerro Gordo County area. Also, a "well done" to Michael Kuhfus for research assistance in the Ellsworth-Radcliffe area.

I will be forever grateful for the research materials and photos provided by Major Jack Johnson, historian for the Military Historical Society of Minnesota. Also, the exemplary cooperation General Al Rolfes and Col. Lennie Jave rendered in helping me obtain research data from the Gold Star Military Museum at Camp Dodge, Iowa.

My appreciation is offered to Frank Holdmeyer, Managing Editor of *Wallaces Farmer* magazine, and his staff for their helpful research assistance and providing some excellent photographs. And, I am extremely grateful to Paul Troth, Mount Dora, Florida cartoonist, for his gracious providing of several hilarious cartoons that greatly enhance some humorous happenings.

Much gratitude is expressed to Mr. & Mrs. Lawrence Kayser and Mr. & Mrs. Larry Kayser for providing a base of operations during research travels in the midwest and helpful research assistance.

To the aforementioned and the people listed below the author gives his heartfelt gratitude—without your help the book would not have been nearly so interesting.

Samuel Ades
Mr. & Mrs. Curtis Anderson
Patricia Ankrum
Gordon Aasgaard
Elizabeth Gillis Bigelow
Wayne Brinton
Fay Kennedy Buckles
Robert Burton
Dan Cassidy
Mr. & Mrs. Dale Castle
Gus Dermand
Diane Dickey (Kellogg Co.)
Fred Eason
Herschel Flugstad
Paul Gauthier
Wilfred Groves
Mr. & Mrs. Elmer Hack
Derald Hanson
Gladys Kallem Hare
Phyllis Harned
Terry Johnston
Willis Knight
General William Krieger
Everett Ludley
Robert Manke
Bernice Sealine Lund
LeRoy Matteson
Warren Maxon
Wilbur McMurtry
Helen Forrester Mertz
Robert Mertz
Ruth Passwaters Neese
Mr.& Mrs. Robert Nelson
Carmalita Nichols
Lavon Kallem Peterson
William Pritchard
Stanley Quick
Lloyd Rinehimer
Mr. & Mrs. Leonard Samuelson
Bart Seney
Ann Reisner Smith
Mr. & Mrs. Ralph Shaffer
Doris Anderson Stearns
Lois Berglund Swanson
Weldon Swedlund
Janet Weaver (WHO Radio)
Fay Gillis Wells
Mabel Bonner Whaley
Mildred Jewet Zeihan

RESEARCH FACILITIES	ASSISTANCE FROM
Amon Carter Museum, Ft.Worth,TX	Melissa G. Thompson
Boone County Historical Society Museum, Boone,IA	Charles W. Irwin
Boone Public Library, Boone, IA	
Brown County Historical Society, New Ulm, MN	Muriel Jeske
Columbia Broadcasting System (CBS), New York, NY	Sheila Larkin
Ellsworth Public Library, Ellsworth, IA	Arlene Skartvedt
Fort Dodge Public Library, Fort Dodge, IA	
Gold Star Military Museum, Camp Dodge, IA	Gen. Al Rolfes
Hamilton County Historical Society Museum, Webster City, IA	Vernon Ratcliff
Jewell Public Library, Jewell, IA	Kris Koehnk
Kendall Young Library, Webster City, IA	Nadine Dingman
Lake-Sumter Community College Library, Leesburg, FL	
Mason City Public Library, Mason City, IA	Arthur Fischbeck
Minnesota Military Museum, Camp Ripley, MN	Maj. Jack Johnson

RESEARCH FACILITIES

Mount Dora Public Library, Mount Dora, FL
Newberry Library, Chicago, IL
Shenandoah Historical Museum Shenandoah, IA
State Historical Society of Iowa, Iowa City, IA
WHO (1040) Radio, Des Moines, IA
Wide World Photos, New York, NY

ASSISTANCE FROM

Cathy Caine and Mary Burley
David Thackery

Dale Castle

Mary Bennett
Gen. Mgr. Mark Halverson
Dan Bowden

REFERENCES

NEWS MEDIA

Daily Freeman Journal, Webster City, IA; *Chicago Tribune* (Newberry Library) Chicago, IL; *Mason City Globe Gazette,* Mason City, IA; *Sioux City Journal,* Sioux City, IA; *Minneapolis Star Tribune,* Minneapolis, MN; *The Des Moines Register & Tribune,* Des Moines, IA; *Fort Dodge Messenger,* Ft. Dodge, IA; *Council Bluffs Nonpareil,* Council Bluffs, IA; *Boone Ledger,* Boone, IA; *Ellsworth News,* Ellsworth, IA; *Stratford Courier,* Stratford, IA; *Wallaces Farmer,* Des Moines, IA; *Waterloo Courier,* Waterloo, IA; *Adams County Free Press,* Corning, IA; WHO 1040, Des Moines, IA

BOOKS AND PUBLICATIONS

"The Desperate Years" by James Horan (Crown Publishing Bonanza Books); "Plain Speaking - Harry Truman" by Nathan Miller; "FDR" An Intimate History by Nathan Miller (Doubleday & Doubleday); "Blood on the Moon" by Linton Wells (The Riverside Press); "Robert Kennedy and His Times" by Arthur M. Schleisinger, Jr. (Houghton Mifflin Co.); "A Treasury of Great Reporting" by Louis L. Snyder & Richard B. Morris (Simon and Schuster); "Spirit Lake Massacre" State Historical Society of Iowa; "The Great Crash" by John Kenneth Galbraith (Houghton Mifflin Co.); "The Hidden History of the Korean War" by I. F. Stone (Monthly Review Press); "The Midwesterner" by Robert J. Casey & W.A.S. Douglas (Wilcox & Follett); "The Sioux Uprising of 1862" by Kenneth Carley (Minnesota State Historical Society); "The Heritage of America" edited by Henry Steele Commager & Allan Nevins (Little, Brown & Co.); "Hamilton County Home Remedies" by Ruth Greiner Nail; "Old Cars" Pat Klug, Mgr. Book Division (Krause Publications); "Reflections of Britt, Iowa (1857-1957)" Britt Centennial Committee; "The Peoples Almanac" by David Wallechinsky & Irving Wallace (William Morrow & Co., Inc.); "Family Encyclopedia of American History" Bernard A. Weisberger, P.H.D., Chief Consultant (*Readers Digest*); "Encylopedias" (Americana & Britanica)

I
"THE GENERATION GAP"

It was June in the summer of 1990. The sun was peeking through the trees bringing a sparkling silvery glitter to fresh green leaves as its first warm rays served notice of the dawning of another beautiful summer day.

A lithe, elderly man, slightly bent of shoulder and grey of hair, walked with his miniature pinscher dog at a military gait toward a bridge that spans the Boone River as it winds its way through a quiet, typically small midwestern town.

The old-timer hadn't walked across the bridge since World War II and as he approached their habitat along the river's wooded banks, birds struck up a chorus as if heralding his return to the environs of his childhood.

Pausing at the bridge approach, he stooped slightly, with head held back, and peered through his bifocals at a bronze plaque affixed to the abutment. The plaque read, "Sgt. James E. Wedding, first man from Hamilton County to be killed in World War I."

Crossing the street he sat down on the opposite abutment and gazed down at one of his favorite old fishing holes. He observed bass and catfish creasing the water in quick short jerks, creating "v" shaped riffles as they foraged the shallow water for food.

There are many such small rural towns dotting the landscape throughout the United States. Life goes on at a slower pace; no one is exceptionally wealthy and modest homes, surrounded by tall trees, line the not-so-busy streets. Although frequently stared at, even strangers receive a cheery hello from the town's friendly inhabitants. Yes, the old veteran thought, Webster City is truly "Happyland."

To some large city dwellers, accustomed to daily hustle and bustle, the scene might appear to be one of peaceful solitude—even of boredom in some degree.

Approaching the bridge two young boys smiled and said good morning to the old citizen, then clambered hurriedly down the bank, pole and worm cans in hand. One of the boys appeared quite large for his age. Memories came forth of Robert "Bludge" Patterson, a round faced, powerfully built young boy, who loved life and everyone in it.

"Bludge" had been killed in action while fighting with the local National Guard Company in northern Italy during World War II. Slight tears welled in the old man's eyes and he found himself saying aloud, "Well, 'Bludge,' a lot of water has surely gone under the bridge since we sat over there back of Williams acreage and fished." Somehow the dog sensed his mood, for she lay exceptionally quiet, her head lovingly resting on his foot.

He remembered the day "Bludge" and he caught some frogs for fish bait at Fortune's slough (now owned by Jon Kayser), which was behind the old LaForge livestock rendering works about a mile down the river. For the moment, he was the boy, Hank, again as he recalled how he and "Bludge," with bait in hand, had hurried back to their favorite spot in search of catfish.

They had baited up and cast their lines well out into the center of the river. "Bludge" had hauled in a couple, but Hank wasn't having any luck. A half hour or so later, Hank finally decided to check his bait to see if the frog had got off the hook.

As Hank reeled in the line, it seemed to be going in a circle and finally led to the far side of a bush, obscure from view. "Bludge" walked around the bush and soon was howling with laughter. Hank hurried over to take a peek. There sat the frog, regal with head high, surveying the line and the river. "Bludge," who always had a fine sense of humor, still howling, said, "You better have a little talk with that frog, Hank, and get it worked out with him just who is going to be the fisherman and who is going to be the bait!"

Suddenly the old veteran's thoughts were interrupted by the laughter of young people about a block upstream. Soon he could see them in canoes, rented from Dean and Lois Lee's "Boone River Navy," coming toward the bridge—enjoying an early morning twelve mile trip down the beautiful scenic river, past Briggs Woods to the lower reaches of the Boone. Their trip would end near the site of the old Tunnel Mill, which was started in 1850 by Robert "Blue Jacket" Watson and served the settlers of the day until 1889.

As the last boat floated under the bridge, he arose slowly from the abutment, his legs a bit stiff from arthritis, pushed back his hat, scratched his head and thought, "Those young kids are like this beautiful day—just dawning, whereas for me and many others my age, life's twilight is rapidly settling in."

LIFE'S DAWNING

Youth like the dawning of each new day,
Is fresh and exciting in every way.
Like the first new rays of the morning sun,
Their life on earth has just begun.

For them each day is filled with zest,
For an entire lifetime awaits conquest.
There is no doubt in their youthful mind,
That a pot of gold they'll surely find.

No thought, no worry, no need to mope,
With all life's problems they can cope.
Daydreams they foster through the hours,
Never seeing the weeds - only the flowers.

Elders warn the young, life can be cruel,
Caution them to live by the golden rule.
But the young will live life in their own way,
Confident there will always be another day.

But wasn't it great when you felt immortal,
With a lifetime beckoning through open portals?
But wouldn't it be nice in many ways,
If you could store that energy for twilight days?

At the north edge of the city the Des Moines Street bridge had been dedicated to Marshall E. Crippen, the first serviceman from the city killed in World War II. The Second Street bridge, just to the north, had yet to be dedicated. He hoped somehow that the names of the canoers, or those of other young people, would never appear on a bronze plaque affixed to the Second Street bridge. As the last canoe faded from sight the old man mused, "Wonder how anyone could explain to those young people how peace can be maintained by fighting wars."

Remembering "Bludge" Patterson brought the old veteran's thoughts back to World War II and those with whom he had served. Many of his friends had been killed in action; others had died relatively young from wounds and physical stress brought on by the rigors of combat duty.

His energetic dog had sat about as long as she could endure inactivity so, with the day so beautiful, the old veteran decided to hike out to the cemetery to pay his respects to some of his wartime buddies.

Arriving at the Graceland Cemetery entrance, Hank stopped to look at a marble monument erected in honor of those who had served with the local National Guard Company during World War II. It would soon be fifty years since the local unit had loaded on trains to go to Camp Claiborne, Louisiana for a year's active duty training. With the Japanese bombing of Pearl Harbor December 7, 1941, their tour had stretched into nearly five years. Yes, the old-timer remembered all members of the unit, for they had come to be like family to him.

Further on he stopped at the grave marker of PFC Edwin J. "Phantom" Lemke. Lemke's daring feats during World War II would have staggered any man's imagination, for he had been proclaimed a "one-man army" and became a legend on the Fifth U.S. Army front in Italy.

The seemingly shy, withdrawn man had spent nearly as much time behind enemy lines as he had in front of them, destroying ammunition dumps, disrupting communications and creating havoc in the enemy's rear area. He had become an expert rifle shot stalking game along the Boone River for the dinner table during the depression.

The fabulous Lemke had been honored at the July 4th Independence Day celebration in Twin Parks just two years before. In a country where many have come to admire and honor movie heroes more than those of real life, it had been wonderful to see this quiet courageous man receive long overdue recognition for his heroic exploits.

At grave after grave the old veteran visited childhood friends who had served with him in the local National Guard Unit during World War II. Yes, the visit continued through more than twenty graves.

For awhile he just stood in silence among huge beautiful pine trees while the sun cast flickering beams through shadows on the military markers and flags of two of his childhood friends and wartime buddies—remembering the sorrow, grief and good times they had shared. Sgt. Donald Shelton had met his demise at the horrible battle of Cecina, Italy and PFC Truman Sharkey had fallen from a sniper bullet.

At last the old veteran raised his head and walked slowly and dejectedly from the cemetery. As he passed Hamilton County Hospital, the lights in the operating room brought him out of his doldrums, and he remembered the first time he had undergone surgery. It wasn't so funny at the time, but now he couldn't help chuckling a bit as he recalled one of his life's most embarrassing moments. The pre-World War II depression youths had a way of injecting humor into trying situations and this was no exception.

It had all come about in April of 1943, a month before the Allies launched their final offensive to destroy the German and Italian Armies in North Africa. Hank was still with the local Guard Company, and two rifle platoons from the company and two platoons of tanks from the lst Armored Division were out in the Tunisian desert.

They had been assigned to the Allied Forces Headquarters Advance Command Post of General Dwight D. Eisenhower to provide security at the headquarters and escort service for General Eisenhower and his staff during their visits to the front lines.

Hank, the now - old veteran, then a young platoon sergeant, had developed a suspicion that someone or something was following him. Upon further examination he discovered he had some protruding hide on his backside.

The doctor, assigned to care for Eisenhower and those in his advanced command post, diagnosed Hank's problem as hemorrhoids. The announcement was nothing he cared to write home about, but the good doctor had made him sorta proud when he said he was sending him back to an evacuation hospital to let an associate of his take a peek.

An ambulance wasn't immediately available, so the medical sergeant arranged for Hank to be taken to the hospital in a jeep. Within minutes the vehicle roared up to the aid station, its driver appearing confused that he had made it that far. He might have been qualified to change wheels, but from all Hank could tell, he certainly wasn't qualified to guide them.

Not until Hank had positioned his seat in the jeep did its operator inform him he was not a regular driver. Hank informed him he need not worry since, as an infantryman, he was not a regular rider. Hank did advise him he was a little sore in the sitting section and cautioned him to stick to the road with his load. From the reckless manner in which the driver handled the jeep it appeared he had received permission to drive through procrastination and not through vehicle familiarization.

They only missed one corner during the entire trip and most people wouldn't have detected this, since it was difficult to tell when you were on or off the road on the desert floor—but then Hank had the advantage, or disadvantage, of his handy-dandy hemorrhoid bump-detector device.

When the evacuation hospital, located in a weather-beaten adobe building on the outskirts of an Arab village, loomed in sight Hank breathed a sigh of relief, thankful for having arrived safely. Not being convinced it was safe even to sit in a parked jeep with the guy, he took his sick slip from the glove compartment and hotfooted on over to the hospital.

Reporting to the front desk, Hank was greeted by a big robust sergeant who said he hailed from "West by God Virgini!" Hank explained his problem and the jovial one said, "Son, yah all listen to me and I'll make ah star outa yah—might even get your name in lights!" After consulting with a doctor, the sergeant returned and told Hank he was in luck; they were doing some screen tests that very morning and he sent him to what he referred to as the "photo gallery."

Now Hank had never been exposed to the dubious delight of a barium enema before—but even if he had, he would have been unprepared for the experience. He was ushered into a small room where he was given a soap and water enema. With water being rationed (a quart canteen full each day while in the desert), this was more liquid than he had drunk in the past two weeks.

Hank's humor was coming back and while the medical corpsman was assisting him they discussed the next episode of what the West Virginian had referred to as Hank's screen test. Soon he was advanced from the sound effects department to the makeup room where the makeup artist injected a large container of liquified powder into his rectum to make him more photogenic.

While the hero with the hose proceeded to fill him up to the nose with tummy-touchup powder, Hank looked apprehensively about the room for photographic equipment. Seeing none, he developed a slight case of stage fright and when, for better or worse, he was about to burst, the medic told him to stand up and walk down the hall to the next door. There, he assured him, the test would continue. Hank thought surely the guy must be funning, but he was assured he was serious. He could see right then and there this test was going to be a trying experience and would reveal a lot of things, as all he was wearing was a split-tail G.I. hospital gown!

Hank counted to three, raised to his knees and slid from the casting couch. It was then he discovered how a balloon must feel when it reaches its air tolerance capacity. Contracting muscles he didn't know he had, he thanked the lad for all his influence and started down the hallway.

Walking with his knees as close together as the conformity of his body permitted, he advanced cautiously, one leg around the other like a tightrope walker. Actually Hank was in a more precarious position, for his danger could not be alleviated with a net. His entire performance could be ruined with a bump of a knee or a slight sneeze.

Meeting a few smiling nurses along the way did nothing to make his day. He tuckered and puckered and damn near went into convulsions trying to hold shut his split-tailed gown while trying to return their smiles. Somehow he made it to the set without getting things wet, and the technician leisurely photographed him in several poses until he was satisfied he had filmed him from his best angle. The photographer jokingly claimed he had a little problem with a mole on Hank's lower left cheek.

When the pictures were completed, Hank thought surely a toilet would be available in the same room, but the attendant directed him down the inevitable hallway. This he knew would be the deciding factor on whether he would be a star or stand—in—something!

Knowing the end was in sight, he threw caution to the wind and raced to the end of the hallway and through the door. From the look on his face any fool on a stool could see he had no time to waste. With clear sailing he breezed in, loosened the toilet from its base, and dashed out of the place before someone could decide they needed a place to store a garden hose.

Although he had endured more than he cared to discuss, he was told to stick around until the doctor could look at the end results. When his turn came, he was admitted to a room where he was told to lie face down on a table. Hank, of course, thought the doctor just wanted to sneak a better peek, but this just wasn't his day. He was given a thorough hand inspection and asked if he could feel anything. After Hank pushed himself back down from the ceiling, he said, "Hell, yes—would you please remove your wristwatch?"

Apparently the doctor thought Hank was a wise guy and, with that, he decided to prop him apart and needle him a bit—in the fanny that is. Before long Hank was numb in the rump and part of his anatomy ended up on the cutting room floor.

After resharpening his knife and taking two more swipes, the doctor let Hank relax for awhile. He then gauzed and taped him and said, "The hospital is so overcrowded with combat casualties that all I can do is send you back to your unit." The doctor then gave Hank some pain pills and instructed him to sit in hot water three times a day for a week or so. Hank, knowing sitz baths were impossible, displayed a weak grin and asked the Doc, "Will you consider giving me back my hemorrhoids?"

Hank hurried out the door as fast as the pain in his posterior would permit. While walking back to the jeep, he had a little talk with himself about riding back to the Allied Forces Advanced Command Post with old double-clutch Charlie at the wheel. With his fanny at stake, in more ways than one, he decided to pull his rank on the PFC and relieved him of his duties and drove the jeep himself.

They had almost reached their destination when the anesthetic wore off, and Hank's problems became deep-seated. Each pebble the vehicle struck felt like a boulder and before they arrived, he had slowed the jeep to the point that his co-occupant (he would never call him a driver) threatened to get out and walk for fear of being late for the next morning's breakfast.

The doctor at the aid station was surprised to see Hank return to the area after being reamed in the seams, but assured him he would be all right. However, when Hank told Mess Sergeant Frank Meller he had been instructed to sit in hot water, the Sergeant grinningly told Hank, "Just stick close to PFC O'Flaskagin. He's always in 'hot water;' all you have to do is bide your time and share the benefits." Of course "sitz" baths were not possible, and the next few days were plenty painful, but time quickly heals the youthful and, within two weeks, Hank had recovered fully.

By the time the old man had finished reminiscing about his hemorrhoid adventure, it was nearing noon and he was already headed down Bank Street back toward Twin Parks. His mind was too engrossed in memories to give even token thought to lunch. Hank was beginning to feel his age and, being tired, he sought out a park bench to rest a bit.

Looking around the old park, he noted many changes since the first of the century. Many of the tall stately elm trees that once graced and bordered the park had long since died from Dutch Elm disease. The red squirrel population, formerly profuse, had been drastically reduced, and the squirrels could no longer be seen leaping through lofty tree branches from street to street, never touching the earth.

The old majestic masonry bandstand and decorative water fountain, which had graced the center of the park, no longer existed. William Howard Taft, the nation's 27th President, had addressed the community's citizens from that very spot in 1911. That old bandstand had been the scene of many wonderful concerts played by the Happyland Municipal Band.

Maybe it is the air, the earth's magnetic pull, or old familiar houses and buildings, but for some reason when one returns to his childhood environment, suddenly names of people, faces and memories of long ago events come rushing back.

World War II had brought a tremendous surge of patriotism; virtually every house was the scene of tearful goodbyes as young men and women hastened to trains and buses to report for military duty. Many individuals volunteered, others went willingly when called—there were some, but very very few, shirkers.

Some of those young smiling servicemen never returned, while still others came back maimed for life of limb or mind. Yes, war had provided the people who lived around the park with their share of unhappiness. But the war had ended forty-five years ago and few of the people who walked about the park could remember the smiling young faces that never returned.

A mist filled the old veteran's eyes as he gazed across the street to the northwest corner of the park where the old Barnsdal Oil Station, operated by Kenneth and Howard Nichols, had stood in the pre-war days. In his mind he could still see Kenneth smiling and waving to him as he trudged past the station enroute to school. He was an intelligent man, fine athlete, a human charmer, and the possessor of a personality second to none.

Kenneth had married his college sweetheart Harriet Hale and a happier couple never existed. They thrived on goodwill and good deeds, both capturing the hearts of every kid in the neighborhood as they listened patiently to youthful problems and provided guidance.

Harriet presented Kenneth with a fine son just days before he was called up with the local guard company for World War II. Later, as Capt. Nichols, he rose to command his hometown company—loved and respected by his men.

In July of 1944, while a bloody battle raged at Cecina, Italy,—Germans had nearly encircled the company. Nichols, a fine tactician, promptly sized up the situation and ordered his men to withdraw quickly, then proceeded to order a withdrawal covering artillery barrage on the area they occupied. Without this barrage many more men would have been killed or captured.

Concerned that some of his men might not have got the word, Capt. Nichols went forward alone to conduct a search of the area. The lives of many were saved, but the courageous Nichols was killed by the incoming barrage. His son, Bruce, was too young to remember his brave father.

Tragedy had also struck the family that had occupied the stately old Forrester house, across from the southwest corner of the park. Earl and Emma Forrester's beautiful daughter, Lois, had married Lt. Vernon Wilke after he completed his flight training at March Field, California. A handsome, bright young man, Vernon was destined for a great future in the view of all of Happyland.

From early youth Vernon loved the old steam operated train locomotives, airplanes and, for that matter, anything mechanical. When time permitted, he could be seen sitting on his bicycle near the railroad station watching the huge behmoths of the rails.

Vernon was a studious individual and undoubtedly knew more about the functions of the locomotives than most engineers who operated them. The power of mighty engines appealed to him—small wonder he had joined the Army Air Corps.

Shortly after Lois and Vernon's wedding the Japanese attacked Pearl Harbor; war was declared and he was quickly dispatched to the Far East. Lois returned to Happyland where she later gave birth to their son, James.

Vernon performed his fighter pilot duties in an outstanding manner. His name was frequently mentioned in newscasts and he gathered many laurels for his courage and leadership abilities. He advanced rapidly to Flight Commander, and Lois was elated when word came that her husband had completed the number of combat missions established by the War Department. He would soon be rotated from India to the United States.

Lois' joy knew no bounds—her beloved husband would soon be back and young James would meet his father for the first time. Then a fateful message came—joy turned to sadness in the Forrester home. Capt. Wilke had died when the plane in which he was riding crashed while enroute back to the states.

Capt. Kenneth O. Nichols
Photo courtesy of Gene Marchi

Harriet Hale Nichols with son Bruce
Photo courtesy of Harriet Nichols

Harriet Nichols and Lois Wilke had much in common. They both grieved at the loss of their wonderful husbands, but both shouldered their grief, picked up their lives and went about the task of supporting and raising their fine sons. Harriet is now retired from her job as a school teacher in Akron, Ohio, and Lois is retired from her position at a Happyland bank. Neither Harriet nor Lois is bitter at their country, perhaps because World War II was fought for a just cause: retaliation against an enemy's unprovoked attack.

Capt. Vernon Wilkie
Photo courtesy of Lois Forrester Wilkie

Lois Forrester Wilkie with son James
Photo courtesy of Lois Forrester Wilkie

Vernon's favorite locomotive was engine No. 1180 on the Illinois Central Railroad line. Ironically it would be old engine number 1180 that would pull the baggage car bearing his remains back to his hometown—ironic yes, but fitting!

Capt. Wilkie's favorite engine brings his body home.
Photo courtesy of Lois Forrester Wilkie

Yes, he thought, there have been lots of changes in the old hometown and, for that matter, in the entire world. The country had passed into an era that came to be known as the "turbulent 1960s," and a so-called "generation gap" had developed between many of the youth of America and their elders.

Perhaps, the old man reasoned, one of the "gap's" contributing factors could have been the fact that there had been no lasting peace around the globe since before World War II. Constantly there were wars, rumors of wars, civil wars and revolutions.

After World War I the League of Nations had attempted to establish a state of Israel, but there were too many protests. However, after the terrible persecution of the Jewish people by the Nazis during World War II, the United Nations carved out a piece of Palestine that had been occupied by the Palestinians since bibilical times. Israel was born.

By 1962 Arab states in the Middle East had thrown off the shackles of European domination. Egypt attempted to seize control of the Suez Canal; Britain and France moved troops in to restore British control.

Israel, which had a strong lobby, had been armed to the teeth by the United States. While the Arabs were busy with the British and French, the Israelites joined the fracas and seized a goodly amount of Arab land, some of which remains in their hands today.

There have been wars, armed clashes and ill feelings among Israel, the Palestinians and most of the Arab neighbors ever since. Hostilities continue at this writing—with the United States, although badly in debt, still providing arms and monetary assistance to Israel.

As the old veteran sat on the park bench, Delbert "Del" Jahncke smiled and waved as he hurried back to work. Del was always a favorite of the old veteran.

As a young sergeant in the local guard company, Del, along with Martin Jacobson (both handsome, intelligent, stalwart young men), had volunteered for service during the Korean conflict. Jahncke and Jacobson had answered their country's call without hesitation and had performed their duties in an exemplary manner.

Corruption in President Syngman Rhee's South Korean government had brought about much dissension. Rhee refused to hold reunification elections with North and South Korea participating. North Korean communist troops invaded South Korea on June 25, 1950. The United States, along with the United Nations, interceded. Chinese forces joined with North Korea. After a see-saw battle, an armistice ensued; both forces, at this writing, remain squared off at the 38th Parallel.

The war over, returning Korean veterans received very few, if any, accolades for services rendered. However, they adjusted to civilian life with little or no problem. The Korean conflict came to be known as the "forgotten war." To date no monument has been erected in the nation's capitol to honor these veterans, although a movement is at last underway to do so.

Down in Cuba President Fulgencio Batista had been caught dipping his fingers in the national cookie jar for his personal use.

Realizing he would lose in the forthcoming election, he established himself as a dictator with the help of the military.

Pandemonium reigned supreme in the United States in 1959 when Fidel Castro led his Cuban revolutionaries in ousting Dictator Batista from power. Castro quickly nationalized Cuba's industries and agricultural interests. Many of these assets had been owned or controlled by Americans. Most of Cuba's population were at or near the poverty level.

Castro, like most dictators, became self-obsessed with power and greed. He failed to obtain recognition of many countries. To retain power he launched a series of inhuman atrocities that would have paled those of Batista.

The United States would not recognize Castro, although former President Harry Truman felt it should. A trade embargo was initiated, and Castro aligned himself and his country with the Soviet Union.

President Dwight Eisenhower's administration encouraged and supplied Cuban exiles in the organizing of a force to invade Cuba and wrest power from Castro. President John Kennedy, recently inaugurated, carried on with the plan but, without direct American combat forces support, the attack failed miserably and was handily repelled by Castro's supporters.

Russia sent military personnel and missiles, some with nuclear warheads, to Cuba. President Kennedy demanded that the Russians remove them and ordered the blockade of Cuba in 1962. Tension and fear of a nuclear war mounted. Russia finally acceded to President Kennedy's demands.

As the old veteran continued reminiscing, James "Jim" Gardner stopped and conversed for a spell. Jim, who was and still is very active in the American Legion, had joined the Navy during the Vietnam War.

The patriotic young Jim was proud of his service in Vietnam, although he was somewhat bitter about the lack of support servicemen received from the citizenry during that miserable, controversial war. A monument to the loyal Vietnam veterans was finally erected in Washington D.C. and some long - due acclaim is now being given to those who fought in that unpopular war.

With the end of World War II, Communism had got a strong foothold in many countries, and the newly-installed communist governments quickly nationalized their countries' industries and resources. Communism struck deep at American business and the American way of life. Containing communist expansion became almost a national obsession.

Senator Joseph McCarthy, Wisconsin, became chairman of the powerful Senate Investigating Committee. He had people literally looking everywhere, but in their underwear, for communists. A person couldn't ask a couple of friends to chip in on a bottle of vodka without someone jokingly calling him a communist.

Not unlike Korean negotiations, an agreement had been reached in Paris on reunification elections to be held in Vietnam. South Vietnam's first elected President, Ngo Dien Diem, corrupt and unpopular, had seized dictatorial powers.

Displeased with their dictator president, South Vietnam rebelled against the government, and communist North Vietnam came to the aid of the rebels. The United States and United Nations, again seeking to contain communist expansion, interceded.

Involvement in Vietnam by the United States began when President Dwight Eisenhower advised President Ngo Dien of South Vietnam not to hold elections agreed upon by both South and North Vietnam in the Paris accords. In 1960 President Eisenhower increased the number of U.S. military advisers in South Vietnam from 327 to 685. War erupted between North and South Vietnam and President John Kennedy increased the number of military advisers and military aid. The war escalated; advisers were increased. President Lyndon Johnson initiated combat involvement by the United States in February 1965 when he sent the U.S. Air Force into action. Ground forces were committed in March that same year.

College students protested and rioted from coast to coast. Some burned their draft cards, while others fled to other countries to avoid the draft. Some of the enemy's casualties were found to be civilians and thoughtless anti-war activists spat upon returning veterans, calling them murderers.

Jane Fonda, the actress, and Tom Hayden urged the Students for a Democratic Society into bloody riots. Jane Fonda went to North Vietnam and broadcast appeals to American pilots to cease bombing North Vietnam. Her antics were considered traitorous by a goodly number of veterans and others.

The rioting tore at the hearts of many veterans and those with staunch loyalty to the United States. They felt strongly that those who were laying their lives on the line in Vietnam should have the support and respect of the nation and that the rioters were giving aid and comfort to the enemy, thus prolonging the war.

Although most veterans did not object to peaceful demonstrations they did, as a whole, want peace through strength and honor. The difference in opinions became so pronounced it created a breach of mammoth proportions between millions of youths and their elders. In some instances the breach has not healed to this date.

By the time United States and United Nations forces were pulled out of Vietnam in January, 1973, the conflict had become the longest in American history. Were there other strong reasons why some college students, deferred from the draft while in college, had protested against the Vietnam War so violently and had taken every evasive action possible to avoid the draft, while still others supported the war, even volunteering for service?

Perhaps there were other compelling reasons for the behavior of some of the youths during the Vietnam War. Many of the parents, who had undergone the ravages of the depression, had known true want and sometimes hunger. Some became workaholics in their determination to ensure that their children were not deprived of anything that would make them happy.

A postwar baby boom, the likes of which the country had never witnessed, occurred in the years following World War II. There were millions upon millions of first-time mothers, and Dr. Benjamin M. Spock, a noted professor of pediatrics at Cornell University, seized the opportunity and published a book for new mothers.

Spock's theory promoted a flexible response to children's needs and happiness rather than corporal disciplinary action. The book sold like hotcakes in an unheated arctic igloo. A revolution on raising the little rascals soon prevailed, and Spock's book virtually became the baby manual for young mothers.

The spare-the-rod and spoil-the-child prophecy disappeared from the reservoir of American cliches. If little junior couldn't be cajoled or coerced into behaving himself, then so be it; he just tore hell out of things and vented his rage on all those about him. The hue and cry became, "Don't spank him; it will warp his personality."

The government of the United States had faced many difficult decisions following World War II. In its efforts to curtail communist expansion, the United States, time after time, found itself in the undesirable position of having to back the leader of the threatened country and being in control of that country's armed forces. Unfortunately President Syngman Rhee of South Korea, President Ngo Dien Diem of South Vietnam, and President Fuigencio Batista of Cuba, were all corrupt. Each had usurped dictatorial powers and was hated by most of the people.

But, if spread of communism was to be halted, support of these leaders of dubious character appeared to be the only choice. Then, too, many of these countries are sources of cheap natural resources and labor, both of which were readily exploited by United States business and industry. This is evidenced by the fact that it is difficult to find many items of American manufacture for sale in stores.

Did defending these corrupt leaders and their countries against communism cause the "generation gap" or was it the difference in the way the youths of the Vietnam era were reared? Let the readers form their own opinions.

The impact of the 1960s would be felt in other ways throughout the years to come. Another outgrowth of those turbulent years was tolerance toward civil disobedience, vulgarity and obscenities in public places, movies, books and other publications. All such acts became condoned under the guise of constitutional rights and free speech—upheld by the Supreme Court. Lawmakers became so embroiled in their pent up crusade for criminal rights that the rights of the general public and victims became secondary.

What a vast change in law enforcement, for before the 1960s, victims had more rights than criminals. Now a citizen or lawman shooting a criminal during the commission of (or fleeing from) an attempted murder, rape or felonious assault is subjecting him or herself to prosecution.

Even the obtaining of evidence has become a game of rules. If a cache of drugs or other criminal evidence is obtained without strict adherence to search warrant requirements, or if the lawman fails to advise the apprehended criminal of his array of rights, the felon, regardless of how heinous a crime committed, walks free.

Public funded attorneys are now appointed to vigorously defend confessed or caught-in-the-act murderers, rapists, drug dealers and perpetrators of heinous crimes—even after conviction through appeal. Then through legal maneuvering it is not uncommon for the criminal to be set free.

Protestors against capital punishment fight for the lives of murderers, while the families of loved ones suffer their loss without organized support. Is it small wonder that those who grew to adulthood during earlier times shake their heads in disbelief at changes in criminal law enforcement wrought upon American society?

Back in Twin Parks in Happyland, across the street the old-timer "Hank" could see the house where he lived during his teen years. Yes, times had been rough through the Great Depression, but, then too, there had been some joyful times. People had learned to live with far fewer luxury items—and without even some of the bare necessities. Many had felt the pangs of hunger. But one thing for certain: they were thankful for what little they did have. The young had been taught honesty and patriotism since birth, and, oh yes, they had learned discipline the old-fashioned way.

Somehow, Hank, the old veteran, was now glad he had grown to young manhood during that era, for he and his generation had learned to grin when grimacing was far more appropriate.

His eyes fell upon the old garage that had been used as a backstop for ball pitching practice. As he looked at the still-visible boards which had been used to splice those broken by wild pitches those many long years ago, suddenly the garage faded and his mind drifted back to the farm where he spent his early childhood.

II
SEEDLINGS

Hank, then a four year old, sat on the back porch steps of the family's large, saltbox shaped farmhouse. The sun was hitting high noon and reflecting from his blond hair onto a face that seemed to have an endless supply of freckles. His bib overalls, the past year's vintage, fell far short of reaching his ankles.

As he sat on the steps he made serious attempts to pick up a fishworm between his barefoot big and fore toe. This, he soon discovered, was no small undertaking and would require all the concentration he could muster.

Success achieved with his right foot, he launched off on an even bigger challenge—that of picking up the worm with his left. If he could accomplish this miraculous feat, he had visions of a career with no less an organization than the P. T. Barnum Circus.

Hank's fantasies about his future with fishworms ended abruptly when he heard his Father James Arthur's Dodge touring car come roaring up the lane. With him would be his Cousin Clinty, of whom his Mother Lucy so often spoke.

Clinty had just completed inhaling the town of Perry's last bottle of alcoholic spirits and of necessity was coming to Happyland because of its advantageous location on the prohibition day's booze run between Chicago and Sioux City.

The Temperance Movement, Prohibition Party, Anti-Saloon League, and Hank's Aunt Minnie had succeeded in adopting the 18th Amendment to the Constitution, thus banning alcoholic drinks on the claim that soldiers and workers must be kept sober if Germany was to be defeated. By January 16, 1919 a majority of states had ratified the amendment; total sobriety had been dictated, but would it prevail?.

James Arthur always contended the bootleggers were so thick in a tavern area north of Happyland called "White City" that the silly soup salesmen had to wear identifying lapel buttons to avoid wasting time attempting to sell booze to each other.

When James Arthur brought the horseless carriage up to a screeching halt near the back porch, a tall, handsome curly-haired man stepped down from the running board. He was dapper and neatly attired in a black suit with the coat draped over his arm. As Clinty approached the steps, he smiled broadly, his dark eyes sparkling.

Doffing his light grey homburg hat, he patted Hank on the head, then remarked in a congenial manner, "James Arthur, this must be your youngest son I haven't met as yet." Hank knew at once this was a man he was going to like very much.

Hank was too young to remember all of the conversation of that day, but it mostly concerned Cousin Clinty's exploits outfoxing Kaiser "Bill" Wilhelm with the aid of a couple of other fellows who went along for the ride, a Sgt. Alvin York, the one-man army, and a pilot named Eddie Rickenbacker, a proclaimed American Ace who had shot down twenty-six enemy aircraft.

One could easily conclude that if it hadn't been for Cousin Clinty, things wouldn't have gone nearly so smoothly for the Allied armies. Even in later years, Hank truly believed that historians had become a little confused and the Big Three were really the Big Four, consisting of President Wilson, Lloyd George of England, Georges Clemenceau, Premier of France, and Cousin Clinty.

It was immediately after hearing Clinty relate some of the flying exploits of Capt. Eddie Rickenbacker that Hank decided that his feathered friends didn't have a corner on flying. If a little old bird could fly, why couldn't he? Eddie Rickenbacker might have had something going for himself, but the guy did have some shortcomings—he needed a plane.

Hank decided to make a new discovery: that man could indeed fly without the aid of a flying machine and with determination, he sought out some high vantage point from which to launch himself.

It didn't take him long to discover the front porch rail was too high; he stung his feet too much when he landed. Like all good things, this flying was going to take a little doing and Hank reasoned that others had probably tried and failed for lack of determination.

Several days later, with sore feet, he decided to seek Cousin Clinty's advice. If anyone could help him attain proficiency in flight he felt reasonably sure it would be his all knowledgeable cousin.

After conversing with Clinty on the subject, Hank knew he had come to the right man. Clinty looked over the boy's sore feet, shook his head and told him he too had just about mastered the art of flying, but gave up due to his bunions hurting.

Clinty assured Hank that a four-year-old like him, with strong arms and good feet, would make out fine with some good flight training and a soft place for landings until reaching the advanced stages. Then, Clinty concluded, Hank could use tree limbs, the same as the birds.

Clinty and Hank sat on an old stump in the back yard for some time during the noon hour while Clinty gave him a few pointers on just how to flap his arms with his shirt sleeves unbuttoned to obtain maximum lift.

After Clinty was thoroughly satisfied that Hank had grasped the bare rudiments of flapping they proceeded to find an object of proper height with a soft landing place.

Several minutes later they discovered the rear wheel of the manure spreader—it would be just right. It was also parked next to a mud puddle, which Clinty reasoned would be perfect for breaking Hank's falls on unsuccessful flights.

Clinty cautioned Hank never to turn too much to the north as he might hit the grove of trees. After these final instructions, Clinty went back to his work and allowed Hank to continue his flight training.

Four hours later Hank, battered and sore, had not made one successful flight, and was covered from head to toe with mud and manure. Cousin Clinty finally returned and allowed as how Hank had tried enough for one day and muttered something under his breath about, "Enough for all time." Actually Hank thought he detected a humorous twinkle in Clinty's eyes, but somehow his cousin had managed to keep a straight face.

With his day's lesson completed, Hank ambled with pain and slow tortured movements to the house. His feet were killing him and the only part of his body not sore was his fanny and that was soon to lose its distinction.

While boiling water and scrubbing Hank, his Mother Lucy kept up a constant barrage of words about Cousin Clinty—the war affecting his head and those crazy Wright brothers who invented the flying machine. From that day forward Hank left all the flying to the birds and those equipped with the proper machines.

Children of that era were not exposed to television and the communication media of today. Did the youth of that period suffer from worldly knowledge inadequacy? Perhaps, but each day was a thrilling revelation through practical learning.

Yes, the youngsters of that era could be considered extremely gullible and they frequently were the butt of pranks initiated by their elders. Wholesome pranks provided laughs for the older people, down-to-earth lessons for the young ones, and amusing stories that the children one day would pass on to their own offspring.

Flying machines were not common sights at that time in the rural midwest. Howard Neel had brought the first airplane to Happyland in 1919 and only on rare occasions was one to be seen in 1924. Even then it usually was viewed from a distance as it winged its way through the sky to the larger neighboring city of Fort Dodge.

When Neel brought his plane to town, there hadn't been so much excitement since October of 1891 when, according to the local paper, millions of blackbirds passed over Happyland. The column of birds was estimated by Harold Hoozenphapper, or some such person, to be 200 feet high, 40 feet wide and some 20 miles long!

In the United States aviation and aircraft had its beginning with the first flights by Wilbur and Orville Wright at Kitty Hawk, N.C. During the following years the United States lagged in its development of military fighter aircraft. More than 6,000 Curtiss JN-4 Jennys were turned out by U.S. plants but, due to errors and confusion, none ever saw combat in World War I. American pilots used British and French aircraft principally.

Most of the American military aircraft were declared surplus after World War I and were sold for as little as $300 each. Many veteran flyers purchased the planes and barnstormed the country taking up passengers and stunt flying.

Above: John Pearson with his old biplane, at Elmhurst Airfield, Illinois

Photo courtesy of John Pearson

Right: Two dashing Mason City pilots—left to right, Charles Littlefield and Max Bruns.

Photo courtesy of Art Mason City Public Library Historical Collection

Aerial shows were all the rage at county fairs and celebrations. However, due to heavy demands it was difficult to schedule such events in small towns.

It was a thrilling day when Lieutenant Francis Senn came to Happyland. Handsome and dashing in his meticulously shined boots, whipped cord jodhpurs, leather flying jacket and colorful neck scarf, Senn brought a crimson flush to the cheeks of Happyland's most charming and beautiful women (in today's vernacular, "a slight case of the hots.")

Happyland merchants were elated when the jaunty self-professed aerial daredevil offered to bring his Flying Circus to town for a spectacular, the likes of which, Senn promised, the localites had never seen.

Senn's credentials, exhibiting outstanding war service, seemed uncontestable. To make his presence even more appealing, he laid claim to be a part of the famous Senn Family of Chicago.

There was no holding back when merchants were asked to support his show which was quickly scheduled for July 14, 1921. Of course, Senn did sweeten the pot a bit when he offered to take major backers up on a short ride.

By the next day Senn miraculously had been adopted by many of the town's elite as somewhat of a local hero. So it was that when he nonchalantly walked into Julius Bermann's clothing store, he was warmly welcomed. The purported flying ace's descriptions of the performance his daredevil squadron would give, slipped glibly off his silver tongue. Julius was totally aghast at Senn's description of the breathtaking performance to come.

Casually looking to one side, Senn spotted some of the more costly suits in the store and remarked they were far nicer than those carried in even the more exclusive stores he had visited in the larger cities. Julius beamed at the thought of such a worldly person delivering this high compliment and he soon had the handsome, broad shouldered, narrow-hipped aviator adorned in one of the store's finest and viewing himself in the mirror.

By now Senn was on a first name basis with Julius and talking to him as if they'd been friends for years. Lt. Senn said, "Julius, I'd like to buy this one and some accessories, but I can only write a check for $40. Can you charge the balance?" This honest admission of short funds gave Senn great credibility with Julius, and, of course, the deal was sealed.

The next day the great Senn approached Frank Leonard with a dejected look on his face. With a sad low voice Senn said, "Frank, I've fallen upon bad fortune. The propeller is broken on my plane; without it, I can't perform."

Frank consoled poor Senn and agreed to get him a taxi and even offered to accompany him to Mason City, where Senn said he could purchase a new propeller. Arriving at Mason City in late afternoon, Senn remarked it had been a long day and suggested they retire early and get the propeller in the morning.

At daybreak Leonard awakened to find Senn gone. He arose and, as he walked to the bathroom, he noticed a piece of paper on the dresser. A closer look revealed Senn had left a check for the taxi and the hotel room.

Upon returning to Happyland, Leonard learned that the check given Julius Bermann for the suit and other clothing, drawn on the First National Bank, Spencer, Iowa, had bounced. Bill Fastenow, the druggist and several other merchants were out money for worthless checks the convincing Senn had cashed at their stores. The check Senn had given Leonard was of no value.

Of course, there was no air show and the only flight Senn made was an unlawful one to avoid prosecution. But there would be other scams in Happyland, for most of the people in the rural midwest were trusting souls.

Hank's Mother was a hard working woman with a large family and the Father, always busy, rarely communicated with the young ones. Cousin Clinty, with his fantastic story-telling ability was always a source of knowledge and entertainment.

Cousin Clinty dances—cows enjoyed the performance

Cartoon courtesy of Paul Troth

In his early youth Clinty had mastered the art of soft-shoe and tap dancing. Possessing a fine voice he had all the attributes desirable in the entertainment world. Later Hank was to learn Clinty had in fact been a wonderful showman, but again his thirst for looney juice had been his downfall. He would find work with a vaudeville and become a main attraction only to have opportunity fade because of his affinity for drink.

One night as Clinty finished feeding the stock, Hank and his older brother (dubbed "Big Brother" by Cousin Clinty) begged him to dance and sing. A hired man at the time, Lou Taylor, played the harmonica.

Wearing his old work straw hat and using an old sledge hammer handle as a cane, he gave a thirty minute performance they would never forget. For a short while one could tell Clinty was not in a midwest barn, but miles away in his beloved vaudeville—tapping and singing his heart out.

The nearest town was Happyland which boasted a population of 6,641. Although Iowa had been a state since 1846, Happyland had been incorporated only since 1875. Hardly fifteen years had elapsed since 1910 when the bricks were laid to replace the gravel and dirt on Seneca and Second streets, the heart of business transactions in the community.

America's love affair with the gasoline driven vehicle had started to blossom and bloom during those years following the turn of the century and the era of the steam powered horseless carriage had begun to decline.

The first practical, dependable steam driven automobile to appear on Happyland streets was the old Stanley Steamer, developed by the twin Stanley brothers, Francis and Freelan. However, a French inventor Nicholas Cognat had built a steam powered artillery carriage before the American Revolutionary War back in 1769.

Steam powered automobiles were more powerful than one might imagine. Fred Marriot built up steam pressure in his Stanley racing car to 1,300 pounds per square inch, then sent it hurtling down the Ormand Beach, Florida track at 140 MPH, before his racer lifted off the ground and crashed.

Turn of the century Happyland residents were beginning to see more electric cars whizzing about town. Due to their carriage like appearance, early owners were frequently chided by townspeople with such remarks, as, "Did you forget to hook up your horse?" Among the popular manufacturers of these were Baker, Marlin, Columbia, Riker and Studebaker.

Of course men drove electric cars, but women who rarely were seen operating gas driven vehicles, seemed to favor the electric model. All Gladys Crosley and Sarah Jesse McMurray had to do was flip the power switch on and they were soon tooling around town. One could almost count the wheel spokes of electric cars as they moved around Happyland, but history reveals a special model was clocked at 132 MPH back in 1905.

In 1876 Nicholas Otto, a German, invented the first four stroke internal combustion engine—another German, Gottlieb Daimler perfected Otto's invention and he and Alvis Wolfmuller built the first marketable motorcycle. Karl Benz, a fellow countryman, built a crude automobile. But, in 1894 French manufacturers Panhard - Levassor, using Daimler's engine, built a dependable automobile equipped with a reliable clutch, transmission, accelerator and pedal activated brake.

There were several homespun cliches used around the turn of the century, such as, "There is more than one way to skin a cat." Not that people went around skinning cats, but it did stress a point. A rural counterpart of that witticism was, "In more ways than a farmer can go to town."

The cliche seemed quite appropriate during the early 1920s when one considered the broad range of transportation employed to convey passengers and cargo at that time. Never since has there existed such a broad diversity of individually owned primary means of transportation.

On a given day in a rural town one could see people riding horses or bicycles, driving horsedrawn buggies, wagons, bobsleds or sleighs. Others could be seen propelling about in gasoline engine driven tractors, trucks, automobiles, and motorcycles. Oh yes, and occasionally a steam or electric powered car would drive by.

1922 Steam powered Stanley Steamer
Photo courtesy of Old Cars—Krause Publications, Iola, WI

Detroit Electric Car Model 76
Photo courtesy of Applegate & Applegate, Annville, PA

The first gasoline driven American automobiles were manufactured in 1892 by Charles and Frank Duryea. Soon numerous automobile manufacturers sprung up all across the nation. Even mechanics and blacksmiths were building automobiles in their shops, family

Left to right: Leonard Clausen, Axel Swanson, and Carl Kane

Gunnar Herman & Friend with fine animal and rig

Photos to left and above courtesy of Lois Berglund Swanson

Paul Berglund with one-horse sleigh in Swede Bend, Iowa

Photo courtesy of Ellen Ankrum

James Arthur with bobsled

Photo courtesy of Mabel Bonner Whaley

Old time blacksmith shops did a lot of business—some even built automobiles.

Photo courtesy of Bernice Sealine Lund

Olaf Berglund, Stratford, Iowa with old-time garage and gas station.

Photo courtesy of Lois Berglund Swanson

garages and barns. By 1925 there were so many different manufacturers the proverbial farmer, if he could have afforded to do so, could have driven a different make to town each day for over two years without duplication.

By the mid-1920s Henry Ford's Model T was the most affordable automobile on the market, thanks to Henry's development of new assembly line techniques in 1913. General Motors was bending every effort to compete with its Chevrolet. Other popular medium priced automobiles seen cruising the streets were the Maxwell, Chalmers, Oakland, Dodge, Studebaker, Jordon, Locomobile, Buick, Oldsmobile, Case, Stearns, Chrysler, Flint, etc.

Dodge Touring Car—1926

Marmon—a Classic

Packard—What a beauty

Dodge, Marmon, Maxwell, & Duesenberg photos courtesy of Applegate & Applegate, Annville, PA Model T Ford photo courtesy of Model-T Times *magazine.*

Model T Ford (1924) the so-called "Doctor's Coupe"

Maxwell (1926)

Duesenberg (1922) Sporty and fast

Owning classic automobiles became a status symbol for successful business men. John Kamrar was one of the earliest owners of the vaunted Packard. Dr. W. W. Wyatt drove a Marmon and Walter Willson, Sr. a Lozier. Asa Drake steered about in his Paige with pride, and Weldon Helmick buzzed around in his Cadillac.

Automobiles and motorcycles were, and still are to many, prestige items. At family reunions back in the 1920s and 1930s the men and boys crowded around the newest machines, while the proud owner explained the fine technology.

While George Drake, one-time deputy sheriff, and the author sat discussing turn of the century automobiles and motorcyles, George recalled that it was around the mid-1920s when an astute articulate man named Arthur Grundy came to Happyland.

Grundy let it be known that he had just discovered a new low cost fuel for automobiles through processing ragweed, as hemp (marijuana) was commonly called in those days. Iowa was known to produce outstanding hemp, for much of the rope manufactured there was used during the Civil War.

According to Grundy, he conceived the idea for the new fuel while sitting on his porch back in South Dakota during an electrical storm. As lightning struck the ground, Grundy said he had marveled at all the electrical energy and finally came to the conclusion the energy entered the ragweed. With that, Grundy went on to say, he began in earnest to develop a machine to extract the energy from the ragweed plant for engine fuel.

The big oil companies, our hero allowed, would be deeply concerned about his new invention and would probably do anything to stop him. His portfolio was well organized, with an array of investment documents. He readily admitted, if the venture was to succeed, he would need more investors.

Mr. Grundy brought with him a pilot model of his processing machine with which he squeezed the ragweed and allowed its juice to drip into gallon jugs. Grundy soon had his plant in operation and a test engine installed on the second floor of a Seneca Street building in Happyland.

Several of the local elite nearly trampled each other in their haste to buy a stake in Grundy's enterprise. Grundy improved upon his pilot model and soon had his ragweed juice processing machine operating and a test engine running smoothly. Word of his new invention spread around north central Iowa like wildfire. He even demonstrated how hot his new fuel burned in a furnace.

Hearing of the new ragweed fuel, two successful Mason City businessmen decided to come to Happyland to take a look at the operation and consider purchasing stock in Grundy's company.

Grundy had installed a special carburetor in his automobile and was ready to demonstrate the efficiency of his new ragweed juice fuel. With the juice in the tank he gave a driving demonstration—his fuel performed magnificently. Who could doubt old Grundy after such a successful demonstration?

Being a little more skeptical than their Happyland investor counterparts, the prospective Mason City investors brought with them a chemist. On first look the ragweed fuel baffled the chemist, but he took a sample with him for laboratory testing.

Grundy didn't wait for the results of the test to come back, which showed that the secret of his ragweed juice fuel was the alcohol he was adding to it. No Siree, no one ever saw old Grundy again and ragweed went back to being rope making material and a surefire cause of hayfever for some people in Happyland!

The annual Old Settlers Picnic was held at Bells Mill, conveniently located for residents of Stanhope, Stratford, Duncombe, and Happyland. That year Cousin Clinty went along and there were thrills aplenty.

Father James Arthur was always ready to depart long before Mother Lucy and would complain loudly and vigorously that Lucy was taking too much time. She would invariably suggest he go warm up the car. Cousin Clinty always said James Arthur never wore out the old Dodge driving it; he just melted the damn thing down warming it up for Lucy.

A trip with James Arthur at the wheel was a spine tingling adventure. He was far more adept at driving horses than an automobile. He used about half the prowess he had attained with horses (a few of the same choice cuss words as well) when he drove the car. He would sit up front manipulating the steering wheel with gestures indicative of great skill.

On the day of the picnic, James Arthur, Cousin Clinty, Hank and "Big Brother" proceeded to the traveling machine which was parked in the center way of the corncrib, often used by farmers as a garage in those days.

When James Arthur asked Cousin Clinty to crank the engine, Clinty begged off saying his war injured elbow was acting up a bit. He started to explain but James Arthur, a little disgusted, told him if he didn't mind, he could spare the details—then asked Clinty to sit up front and operate the hand fuel choke while he cranked. Father turned the ignition switch to the on position and proceeded to the front of the machine to assume the cranking stance.

As James Arthur turned and walked away, Cousin Clinty, with a mischievous grin on his face, winked at the two boys and held his extended finger to his lips imploring their silence.

James Arthur, then in position, yelled for Clinty to pull out the choke knob, and commenced to perform the unpopular task, unaware that Clinty had deftly turned the ignition switch to the off position.

As James Arthur cranked, he bobbed in and out of view. After several tries, Cousin Clinty advised the machine motivator, "James Arthur you're getting a little too old to be playing peek-a-boo; you'd best be getting the machine started or we'll be late for the celebration." James Arthur stopped cranking to check for problems and, with that, Hank's crafty cousin turned the switch on; the engine started and James Arthur proceeded to warm up the car.

Knowing James Arthur was unhappy about the car cranking episode, Cousin Clinty kept up a steady barrage of conversation about the problem, concluding with sage advice that perhaps James Arthur's next wheeled conveyance should be one of those newfangled models he had heard were coming out with what he called, "self commencers."

James Arthur had the car warmed up pretty well (and the air too) when Mother Lucy arrived. It was a beautiful day and the touring car, with the collapsible canvas top down and loaded to capacity with human cargo and goodies, headed for Bells Mill with all occupants holding their hats as they roared down the road at the "breakneck" speed of thirty-five miles per hour.

Everything went well until they reached the long hill to Bells Mill Park. At this point they were coasting (quite frequently done to save gas) when another car came at them using the middle half of the road. James Arthur steered with agility but, a few curse words and several hectic seconds later, they were bounding across a ditch and through some low hanging tree branches. James Arthur swallowed his chewing tobacco, Big Brother bit his tongue and Hank's Mother allowed as how they never should have given up the harness team.

James Arthur was speechless for the first time in anyone's memory—Clinty surmised the tobacco juice hadn't settled too well in his stomach. Between gasps and gulps he allowed as how he had manipulated the steering wheel skillfully or the car surely would have hit a tree!

Cousin Clinty told James Arthur it took a lot more skill to sit in the back seat of the car dodging tree branches than it ever did to sit up front and drive—adding that, if the celebration was half as exciting as the trip, it was sure as hell going to be a thriller.

Fortunately Dr. Forest D. Hall and his son John were there and the good doctor treated Big Brother's tongue. Food had been strewn throughout the Dodge, but luckily some friends (the Gus Andersons, Oscar Elms, Ralph Jewetts, and others) shared their food and the outing proved to be a great success.

Bands were a must at each celebration—here the East Marion Township Band plays in Stratford.

Photo courtesy of Bernice Sealine Lund

Senator E. E. Cavanaugh of Fort Dodge, the principal speaker, told of ancestors crossing the plains in covered wagons, braving the elements and battling hostile Indians to settle the land, all to give their families a better way of life. Cousin Clinty couldn't resist saying, "If the pioneers ever had ridden with James Arthur in an automobile, they would have been happier than hell they had come west in a covered wagon." James Arthur gave Clinty a menacing look; then, unable to contain himself, he burst into laughter.

After the speeches were over, Cousin Clinty and James Arthur took Hank and Big Brother for a walk around the automobile parking area. Many of the proud owners of the fancier rigs, displaying pride of ownership, stood nearby or sat at steering wheels—eager to show off their automobiles.

Auburn (1928)—What a beauty

Stutz (1926) Wow!

Cord (1929) All ready—where is the chaffeur?

Pierce Arrow (1926)—Note headlights

Peerless automobile—A touch of class

Duesenberg automobile, by 1928 the choice of royalty.

All photos this page courtesy of Applegate & Applegate, Annville, PA

In addition to a few affluent people from neighboring small towns, there were goodly numbers of large city and out of state automobile owners at Bells Mill that day. Some of them were relatives of local residents—anxious to impress the less worldly locals with their new fangled machines. Hank and Big Brother were wide-eyed.

The local people were in for a treat that day and they crowded around the ultra, rarely-seen classic automobiles, such as the Auburn, Stutz, Cord, Pierce Arrow, and Peerless. Then someone drove in and parked a fabulous Duesenberg and he was almost mobbed. Everyone, except those in the front row, most likely had sore necks for weeks from stretching to get a better peak. Small wonder—for the Duesenberg was destined to replace the British Rolls Royce as the favorite of kings, queens, heads of state and those of exceptional wealth.

Clinty had, at each opportunity, been badgering James Arthur about his new Dodge not having a permanent lid (top) on it and some of the newer accessories. James Arthur became somewhat provoked at Clinty for asking each fancy car owner if his rig had a heater and self commencer (starter). James Arthur finally asked him to stop asking so damn many stupid questions!

There were also several new motorcycles at Bells Mill that day. Clinty said the speedy, maneuverable little cycles had come into extensive use during the World War by couriers carrying messages between commands. Some of the civilian cycles were equipped with sidecars to carry a passenger or cargo.

Harley Davidson had introduced the most commercially successful motorcycle manufactured in the United States in 1909, but the "Indian" followed closely. Of course, World War I veterans were among the most enthusiastic purchasers. It was a thrill indeed to watch Frank Sonnerholm and Robert Evans zoom around on their new machines.

Miner Haack (left) on 1910 Harley Davidson. Grandson Buddy Haack (right) on 1990 model.

Photos courtesy of Meyel Haack

Invariably the first question passed by an automobile or motorcycle enthusiast was, "How fast will it go?" With man's obsession with speed, automobile and motorcycle racing in Europe, as well as the United States, were becoming popular.

Research reveals the Duesenberg with its powerful engine had gained much respect when it won the LeMans Race in France. Barney Oldfield became the toast of racing enthusiasts when he set a new speed record of 131.724 MPH in his Benz engine powered racer.

The grand daddy of all auto races in the states, the Indianapolis 500, was born in 1911. Carl Fisher had bricks installed on the oval track and drew some 80,000 spectators. Ray Harroun finished the 500 mile race averaging 74.59 MPH with his Marmon Wasp. In 1924 the speedy Duesenberg took first place.

However, nothing seemed to diminish the popularity of Barney Oldfield, the old dirt racetrack driver who would go on to win the Indianapolis 500. When a young boy sat at the steering wheel of the family car pretending to drive he would most invariably proclaim, "Look, I'm Barney Oldfield!"

Hank and Big Brother were thrilled to see several motorcycles speeding around Bells Mill Park that day—some were climbing the steep hill. International motorcycle track racing began in England in 1897, had spread to France by 1904 and continued to gain popularity throughout Europe. Road racing was not generally allowed in the states, but oval track racing was held on dirt harness tracks or board tracks. The first race held on the Indianapolis Speedway was motorcycle competition.

Motorcycle riders meet at Stanhope, Iowa

Photo courtesy of Bernice Sealine Lund

Harley Davidson, Indian and Excelsior cycles were to dominate racing in the United States for decades to come. Stunt drivers began to emerge in the 1920s and afforded spectators a lot of thrills at county and state fairs and celebrations.

The trip home was uneventful, but later that night Cousin Clinty could be overheard telling James Arthur that if he didn't mind too much, he'd like to forego next year's celebration and as he headed up the stairway, he muttered something about it being a helluva lot safer fighting the Germans.

The morning after the Old Settlers Picnic Big Brother arose early—all he talked about was Barney Oldfield and automobiles. He sat most of the morning in the corncrib steering and practicing shifting the gears in the Dodge touring car. Shortly after noon Gus Anderson and his son drove up. Gus asked James Arthur to ride into Happyland with him and left Bud to play with Hank and Big Brother.

Shortly after the two fathers departed, Big Brother announced that he now knew how to drive an automobile and thoughtfully invited the two younger boys to take a spin with him. Arriving at the corncrib, Big Brother took on the airs of a mechanical genius and barked, "Pay attention and I'll teach you youngsters a thing or two about checking out a car before making a long trip." Bud gasped and said, "How far are we goin'?" Big Brother responded, "Oh, probably all the way to Highview (five miles)—depends on the gas!"

With the two young ones a respectable distance behind, the mechanically-minded one circled the car and delivered each tire a hefty kick. Then, after removing the radiator cap, he speculated, "She's about a cup low on water. We'll probably have to check 'er out again in Highview." Loosening and lifting one side of the hood he allowed the fan belt and spark plugs were okay.

After closing the hood, Big Brother told Bud and Hank they were too young to ride up front and ordered them into the back seat. Then, behind the wheel, he proceeded with a little more steering and gear shifting practice. Mimicking James Arthur, he announced, "I'm ready to crank 'er up now; you little kids sit still and behave yourselves or you can't go along!"

It was an awesome task to start the older automobile engines by use of a crank that protruded from under the radiator. The cranking could prove dangerous for engines frequently backfired causing a reverse spin of the crank, which often resulted in a broken arm. Then too, in one hundred degree temperatures a young man, freshly bathed and smelling like peach blossoms with his best after shaving lotion, could arrive at his girl friend's house giving off an aroma like he had just finished a wrestling match with Hogan's goat.

But luck, or lack thereof, was with Big Brother that day. He turned on the ignition, dismounted and proceeded to the crank. Then much to everyone's amazement (and the disgust of Big Brother, who later confessed he had hoped the car wouldn't start) the old Dodge engine started at the first turn of the crank.

Now Big Brother had watched James Arthur shifting many times, but evidently he had not observed closely enough for he must have placed the vehicle in second gear. With gas pedal depressed, he let out the clutch and the old Dodge lurched forward into the corncrib sliding doors. Fortunately the engine stalled with the doors resting neatly on the radiator and fenders. An automobile of the 1980s would probably have been demolished, but amazingly the old touring car, built like a battleship, didn't sustain a scratch. Big Brother, panic stricken, all but swore Hank and Bud to a blood-oath secrecy—threatening knots on their heads they couldn't untie.

Cousin Clinty and the boys had fed the hogs and had the cattle in the barn before James Arthur and Gus returned from town. Clinty, of course, had noticed the protruding automobile and pushed-out doors. He told Big Brother he had a good idea how the doors got that way, but said nothing to James Arthur. No doubt he would have moved the car and helped rehang the doors, but Clinty didn't drive.

The following morning James Arthur and Clinty went to the corncrib to get feed and James Arthur discovered the accident. Clinty didn't lie, but he did toy a bit with the truth when he allowed as how someone must have tried to take the car and didn't know how to drive! (Oh, how true!) James Arthur readily agreed and they soon had the Dodge back inside and the doors properly hung. Good old Clinty—he had again saved Big Brother from what he was sure would have been a fate worse than death!

It can be brutal in the midwest at the height of summer. There were no air conditioners in those days and for those who had no electricity, the only relief was a hand-held fan or a refreshing dip in the river or a lake.

Big Brother was a monkey see-monkey do type of individual and after observing Carl Elkin and Gerald Ratcliff, older neighbor boys, swimming in the river, he decided he had to learn to swim. However, James Arthur kinda put a damper on Big Brother's attaining aquatic prowess when he advised there would be no swimming the river until he learned to swim. Seemed a bit ridiculous to Big Brother, as most small towns didn't have a pool and the only pools he'd ever seen were in magazine photographs.

Of course, Big Brother went to Cousin Clinty with his problem. Clinty showed him how to manipulate his arms and legs to propel through water. Big Brother spent untold hours lying in the prone position on a long bench by the back porch flailing his arms and thrashing his feet.

After Big Brother thought he had mastered the art of swimming, he decided to try his newly-acquired skills in the stock watering tank. He had trouble keeping his head above water and at last, with several knots on his forehead from hitting the edge of the tank, he concluded the tank was too small.

Big Brother had been casting his eyeballs on a pond in the pasture, a favorite of the hogs, and when heavy rains came he was delighted. A couple of days later two neighbor boys, Elmer Timm and Edward "Bud" Anderson came over to play.

It was a hot summer day and Big Brother, wanting to show off his newly acquired swimming ability, announced he was going swimming in the pond. Elmer, not wanting to be outdone, advised that he too could swim and with that the youngsters all proceeded to the pond. Arriving, Big Brother again gave notice to Hank and Bud that they were too young to participate in one of his escapades. He told them to sit on the bank—then added all knowingly, "You little kids might drown, you know!"

Stripping off their clothing, Big Brother and Elmer entered the water. Actually their swimming exhibition was quite dynamic. The pond was really not deep enough and it was quite obvious, even to novices like Bud and Hank, that they were actually pulling themselves along on the bottom with their hands and arms. However, both of the older boys claimed to be swimming and neither Bud nor Hank dared dispute their word.

Each trip across the pond brought more mud boiling up from the bottom and after an hour or so the two would-be swimmers announced they had acquired sufficient skill to request their parents' permission to go to the river. When the two bathing beauties stood up and slogged their way to the bank, the only white parts of their entire bodies were their eyeballs.

Not being accustomed to swimming, they had not thought to bring along towels. Big Brother announced they each needed a washcloth and towel. Hank offered to run to the house and get some. At Hank's offer Big Brother paled so much that at the thought the mud on his cheeks appeared an ashen grey.

Big Brother was a person who consistently maintained the appearance of one having no fear of man or beast, but it was becoming more apparent by the minute he didn't consider his father to be in either category. Hands on hips he threw back his head in an authoritative manner and proclaimed, "No, I don't want to let dad know I've learned to swim yet; I'd rather surprise him. I've got a better idea." He soon had Bud and Hank scurrying to the grainery to fetch some empty gunnysacks from a storage barrel.

With sacks in hand, Big Brother and Elmer waded back into the pond, wetted them and attempted to wash off the mud and grime. Each wet sack application merely moved the mud from one spot to another. Worse yet, residue oats from the gunnysacks were now mixing in with the mud. It became readily apparent to the two swimmers that the churned-up mud in the pond might not settle to the bottom that day. After plucking oats from each other for a half hour or so, they at last decided that trying to clean up in muddy water was a hopeless task.

Suddenly Bud Anderson shouted and pointed down the road—a car could be seen approaching with dust from the gravel road boiling behind. Big Brother hunched low on the bank, mud oozing from between his toes. Elmer dashed back into the pond where he lay nearly submerged. It reminded one in later years of the old song, "Bull Frog on the Bank and the Bull Frog in the Pool," especially the part where one calls the other a green old water fool.

Now back out of the pond and onto the bank, the two aquatic champions assessed their naked plight in the light. Big Brother was visibily shaken. Standing at the pond's edge, he stretched his neck skyward like an ostrich and bellowed, "Can't go home looking like this; my Dad will kill me for sure!"

Elmer, who was by now black and white with a mite of pink from scrubbing himself with a gunnysack, wailed, "Hell, we just can't stand out here by this pond all winter!" Faced with the inevitable, the two swimmers donned their clothing. Once dressed, they started for home.

Big Brother, who was always real good at weaseling his way out of trouble, finally gathered a few of his wits and announced he'd clean up in the stock watering tank. Sounded like a good idea at the time. Circling around with the barn between them and the house, they successfully reached the side of the barn without being detected—so far, so good. After peering out from behind the barn and determining that the coast was clear, Big Brother made a mad dash for the tank.

Not having watches, none of the boys had known the time of day and, as fate would have it, James Arthur and Clinty came out the barn door to call the hogs for their feeding. Big Brother was skimming the ground halfway between the barn and the tank when James Arthur spotted him. His booming voice brought Big Brother to a screeching halt.

Then came the inevitable question, "Boy—where in the hell have you been?" That, anyone would be forced to admit, was a difficult question for Big Brother to answer. Big Brother peered out with panic stricken eyes through mud and oats matted hair—muddy water seeping through his shirt and overalls as it dripped onto his bare feet. However, he, who heretofore had been known to blind James Arthur with verbal footwork, could only respond, "I've le-le-learned to sw-swim now; now ca-ca-can I go to the ri-ri-river?'

By that time James Arthur had Big Brother by the ear and posed his second question, "Where did you learn to swim?" Big Brother pointed toward the pasture and finally blurted out, "The pas-pasture pond." To that James Arthur calmly responded, "If you're going to bathe with the hogs, then you might as well live with the hogs"—and promptly dispatched Big Brother to stand among the swine while they ate their food.

While Big Brother was doing his stint by the feeding troughs, Clinty went about the awesome task of softening up James Arthur's temperament a bit! Clinty, putting a hand on James Arthur's shoulder, said, "You know, James Arthur, there are always advantages in everything—just think, now if anyone ever says the boy isn't fit to sleep with the hogs, you can say he is!" James Arthur burst into laughter; the crisis had ended.

Mother Lucy, who had been watching from the house, met Big Brother at the kitchen door with two buckets of warm water, soap, wash cloths and towels. About an hour later he had cleaned up to her satisfaction and was allowed to sit at the table to eat his by then cold supper. James Arthur later relented and told Big Brother he could go to the river to learn how to swim, but only if he took lessons from Cousin Clinty and not from the hogs!

Each person has had experiences in his childhood that stand out as being most unpleasant. Cousin Clinty and Hank had one in common; both had a dislike for visiting Hank's Aunt Lydia (dubbed "Minnie Muchbucks" by Clinty.) Clinty accompanied James Arthur and Lucy to her house to be polite, but Hank only went along because of the applied force to his behind. He would hide under the bed, in the barn, cornfield, machine shed and even in trees, but sooner or later he would be found and dragged by the arm to the house, screaming in protest.

Describing Mother Lucy's sister adequately was as difficult as explaining how the chicken sexer at Murray McMurray's Hatchery could determine the sex of baby chicks. No one ever saw how it could be done. Aunt Minnie was a stately old maiden lady, scholarly, thrifty and, above all, an individualist. She was built like a locomotive with a touch of the Washington Monument thrown in for good measure.

Habitually Minnie wore high button shoes, a lace collar and a long dress even throughout the roaring twenties. She wore her hair in a high bun. Although it was naturally gray by this time, it was dyed to a brilliant red hue. Clinty staunchly maintained that if he hadn't known she was a member of the W.C.T.U. (Women's Christian Temperance Union), he would have sworn she dyed her hair by dunking her head in a tub of red wine.

A visit to her house meant repeated dissertations on working hard, saving, investing and, for Cousin Clinty's benefit, the futility of drinking liquor. She had carefully invested money, saved from her school teaching job, in land at the amazingly low price of fifteen to twenty-five dollars per acre.

"Going home," were the only thrilling words spoken during the course of an entire day, and Hank soon learned even those words were devoid of their actual meaning. The visit was truly a boring experience, but finally getting on the road to home was sheer hell.

As Clinty always said, "Old Minnie Muchbucks" never seemed to get down to the "nitty gritty" of how she accumulated her wealth until the visit was ending. This she divulged in what Clinty called, "living room talkin,' " "porch talkin,' " and "car talkin'!" All of this normally consumed, as a minimum, an extra hour. By the time they actually departed, Hank had slept on everything and everywhere except the dining room table.

During all of those visits Aunt Minnie only spoke of one subject that interested Hank, that being the American Indian. Hank, like most young people, was extremely interested and more than curious about Indians. He had heard Senator Cavanaugh talk about them at the Old Settler's Picnic, but he had never seen one.

When Minnie brought up the Spirit Lake Massacre, Cousin Clinty perked his ears as though he thought she was about to tell a story about a lake full of drinking spirits. Aunt Minnie was quite knowledgeable of local history, being a retired school teacher and an avid reader. She told her studied version of the Spirit Lake Massacre. The story was quite scary but extremely interesting. Her brief synopsis pretty well followed what has been documented by a survivor of the massacre, Abbie Gardner, and other historians.

Like an avalanche new settlers had slowly swept west and the United States Government coerced, duped and forced the American Indians into giving up the land to which only a few years before they had been ordered to retreat. With the Louisiana Purchase in 1803, the pioneers began crossing the Mississippi in increasing numbers. The Indians no doubt wondered, "When will it ever stop?"

The first sizable treaty acquisition of Indian land in the territory of Iowa came in 1830 when the Sioux, Sac and Fox, Omaha, Oto and Missouri Indians gave up the majority of their lands in western Iowa. However, they believed they could still use the land for hunting purposes.

With pioneers pushing from the east, the U. S. Government negotiated a series of treaties in the years 1832, 1836 and 1837. When the ink dried on the last treaty, the Sac and Fox found out they had ceded all their land in eastern Iowa.

More and more pioneer wagons poured across the Mississippi and in 1842 the U. S. Government was demanding more land to accommodate settlers. The Sac and Fox finally consented to sell the balance of their land in western Iowa and move to an Indian reservation in Kansas.

The area in western Iowa had first been visited by U.S. Army Captains Meriwether Lewis, William Clark and a small army detachment. Along the Missouri River, near some high bluffs, Lewis and Clark made their first contact with the Oto and Missouri Indians and held a council with them in July of 1804. Not far from that site now

Marion Shugart, Mayor of Council Bluffs, is made honorary Chief of Sioux Indians (1950) with title Chief Anuka San (Chief Bald Eagle). Left to right in photo: Chief John Sitting Bull, who fought at the Battle of the Little Big Horn alongside his father Chief Sitting Bull; Chief Howard Bad Bear, a veteran of the Battle of Wounded Knee; Ben Black Elk, a graduate of Carlisle Institute; Mayor Shugart; Mrs. Ben Black Elk. Ben Black Elk places a Chief's bonnet on the mayor.

Photo courtesy of Council Bluffs Non-Pariel

stands the city of Council Bluffs, Iowa. All reports described western Iowa as very favorable for settlement.

It was inevitable that settlers would soon be staking more and more claims in the rich, rolling lands of western Iowa, then considered the lands of the Potowatomi and Winnebago Indians. In 1846 an acquisition treaty was signed and the Potowatomi moved to the Kansas reservation and the Winnebagos in the area moved to Minnesota, still at that time the home of many Chippewa and Sioux tribes.

Now only the Sioux (in alternating strips across northern Iowa) and the Winnebago (occupying a forty-mile neutral strip of land across north Iowa) remained in that state. The neutral strip had been created to keep apart warring factions of the Sioux on the north and Sac and Fox on the south. However, when the Winnebagos had been driven from Wisconsin, they had been moved into the strip.

Winnebago Indians at Mason City reunion display old regalia.
Photo courtesy of Mason City Public Library Historical Collection

Needless to say, the Indians were not pleased—the land to which they were moved was not nearly so fertile as the Iowa-Illinois land for which they purportedly were paid around fourteen cents per acre. But it appears the Indians had little choice; it was that or face a losing battle with the whites. Sadly Hank and other people of his era were not to learn for several decades of the terrible injustice perpetrated upon the American Indian.

The Sioux were known for their courage in battle and the people of Iowa had not heard the last from them, for the Sioux in the northwest now possessed but a small sliver in what is now Iowa, but was then Minnesota Territory.

Further hostilities would later develop when Chief Sidiminidota, with his maverick Sioux tribe, contrary to the U. S. Government - Indian Treaty, had continued to remain with his tribe in the Spirit Lake - Lake Okoboji area in Iowa, in defiance of even the Sioux Council.

Unscrupulous traders still plied their trade with the renegade Sioux in Iowa. In 1847 a small party of Chief Sidiminadota's Sioux came to Trader Henry Lot's cabin near the juncture of the Boone and Des Moines Rivers not far from what now is Stratford. The purpose of the Indian visit was to trade for whiskey, trinkets, etc. Lot was away at the time; his wife panicked and his son ran into the woods where he died of exposure. Later Lot's wife died and Lot swore he would exact revenge. There would be many repercussions from Lot's actions in the years to come—read on.

In 1848 the last of the Winnebagos were moved from the so-called neutral strip to a tract of land near the mouth of the Crow Wing River in Minnesota. In a real estate speculator's dream, Minnesota Governor Alexander Ramsey negotiated a treaty in 1851 with the Sioux and Chippewa that ceded millions upon millions of acres in Minnesota and lands in what is now Iowa to the U.S. Government for $3,075,000 in goods and services. In 1852 the U.S. Government ratified the treaties, except for a five- million acre tract along the Red River in Minnesota.

Years later Henry Lot moved with his new wife and family to the vicinity of the Spirit Lake settlement. Lot and his stepson convinced Chief Sidiminadota to go with them on a hunt, during which Lot and his stepson murdered the chief. Disguised as Indians, they then went to the Chief's home, where they murdered all of his family, except for a son—left for dead. Maj. William Williams of the Fort Dodge Militia investigated and discovered that the dastardly Lot and his stepson had in fact committed the murders. Lot and his family escaped to California.

During the ongoing investigation County Attorney Granville Burkley asked the Indians to bring the chief's skull to Fort Dodge, and they complied. The thoughtless Burkley later took the skull to his home in Homer (then a thriving town of some 3,000 people), where he hung it in a tree. The skull fell out of the tree and he next nailed it to the side of his house. Infuriated, the Indians threatened to wipe out the Homer settlement. Throughout the years to come, Hank would never pass through Homer without remembering Burkley's cruel behavior.

In addition to the Lot-Sidiminadota altercation, a number of unrelated incidents stirred the wrath of the far-from-docile Sioux. Another cause of discord resulted from the non-payment of goods and services promised under the terms of the treaties consummated between Minnesota territorial Governor Ramsey and Sioux and Chippewa Indian tribes.

Back in Aunt Minnie's front room (as the living room was sometimes called in those days), Aunt Minnie was about to reveal her ulterior motive for insisting Mother Lucy and her family come to visit her that Sunday. She always set aside a few heavier tasks for James Arthur and Cousin Clinty for, as Clinty always said, "Old Minnie wouldn't spend one of her nickels to see the good Lord walk a tightrope."

Minnie halted her storytelling abruptly, held up both hands as if a great idea had just struck her and said, "Before I forget it, (she always began that way) I'd like to move the piano from the dining room into the front room. I think it looks better there."

Hank and Big Brother were furious. Here for the first time in their lifetime Aunt Minnie was talking about a subject that interested them; then when she got to the best part, she wanted to stop to move a piano she hadn't played for years.

Clinty turned to James Arthur and winked, then responded to Minnie's money-saving request, "Minnie, you shouldn't lift that heavy piano; I'll go get the neighbor lady to help you." From the look on old Minnie's face, it was clear she didn't appreciate Clinty's sense of humor, but James Arthur nearly fell off his chair laughing.

Minnie had almost regained her composure when Clinty tripped the trapdoor in her thinking compartment saying, "Minnie, we just moved the piano from the front room to the dining room last month because you thought it looked better there. Are you real sure it wouldn't look better in the upstairs sewing room?" Old Minnie Muchbucks summoned up her most devastating school teacher profile—Mother Lucy shook her head. Clinty and James Arthur arose—moved the piano and politely returned to their chairs to hear the balance of her story.

Aunt Minnie breathed a sigh of relief—her philosophy of a penny saved is a penny earned remained uncompromised. She smoothed out a mythical wrinkle in her apron, tilted her head back and continued.

It seems Inkpaduta, nephew of Chief Sidiminadota (or brother according to some historians) continued to remain in what is now northwest Iowa. He was now chief of his renegade tribe and was determined not only to avenge his uncle's death, but to halt movement of settlers into the area.

It had been a severe winter and Inkpaduta became further infuriated when settlers would not give his tribe more of their food supplies. During the years since the chief's murder, he had harrassed the settlers around Spirit Lake increasingly and good relations did not exist between the two factions.

In March of 1857 Inkpaduta and his band attacked the settlement killing forty-three settlers and taking four women captive. The nearest U. S. military forces were those of the U.S. 10th Infantry Regiment garrisoned on the Sioux reservation at Fort Ridgeley, Minnesota, some forty-eight horseback hours away.

The nearest militia was at Fort Dodge, Iowa. When word of the massacre arrived at Fort Dodge, a battalion of militia, under the command of Maj. William Williams was alerted. The battalion, consisting of Companies A and B from Fort Dodge and Co. C of Happyland, ill clad and in sub zero temperatures, force-marched over 104 miles to Spirit Lake. Happyland Militiamen had marched some 124 miles. (Co. E, 133rd Inf. Regt., successor to Happyland's old Co. C Militia would reenact that historic rescue march in June 1957.)

Capt. V. K. Brandt leads Co. E. 133rd Inf. troops in reenactment of Spirit Lake Massacre march.

Photo courtesy of Daily Freeman Journal, *Webster City, Iowa*

Undoubtedly Inkpaduta suspected the Militia would soon arrive, for he fled with his tribe toward the Dakota Teritory. The militia battalion buried the dead and gave aid to the settlers. They checked the surrounding area for Inkpaduta's tribe and guarded against further Indian attacks. The Indian agent ruled against close pursuit by the U. S. 10th Infantry or Militia, fearing Inkpaduta's braves would kill the women captives if attacked.

Their mission completed, the Militia Battalion commenced the long return march to home station through knee-deep snow. Capt. J. C. Johnson, commander of the Happpyland company, became separated from the main body during a blinding blizzard and died of exposure.

Sadly two of the women captives were killed by the Indians. The other two women were saved when a quick thinking Indian agent from the Sioux Reservation convinced friendly Indians to barter with Chief Inkpaduta for their release. MacKinlay Kantor gives a well researched account of the massacre in his book, "Spirit Lake Massacre."

When the militia returned from Spirit Lake, the sordid spine-tingling tale of the massacre had been told in detail by those who participated in the march. It had been a gruesome sight for the militiamen and an even more distasteful task had been the burying of the mutilated bodies of the victims.

It was only natural that settlers along the Des Moines River became a bit paranoid after Chief Inkpaduta's Spirit Lake Massacre. Even an eagle feather or tomahawk found in the woods could create speculation that tribes from the entire Sioux Nation were lurking behind trees waiting to relieve the settlers of their scalps.

With tales of horrors and rumors running rampant, the news was soon circulating that the Sioux were about to attack the local area settlements. Scouting parties were organized and dispatched to the northwest to warn of any impending attack.

On April 27, 1857 a scout, we'll call him Zeb, saw two blanket-wrapped figures about a mile away moving toward him in a southeasterly direction. These, Zeb deduced, were point scouts of a Sioux war party. Zeb, the story goes, even threw away a bottle of whiskey in an effort to lighten his load, then hightailed it back to warn the people of the impending attack—alerting cabin occupants as he hurried along.

Arriving back at the settlement, Zeb contacted Frank Mason and the militia. Claxtons were soon sounding, church bells were ringing and messengers were alerting those in town and surrounding communities.

Preparations for defense of the town immediately got underway. Settlers from north of the community came pouring in and as the news was spread south by horseback riders, those people too headed for town. It is said some outlying settlers departed in such haste they left cabin doors unlocked and food on the table.

As readers realize, word-of-mouth messages become more distorted with each transmission. So it was that shortly thereafter, rumor wags had the word out that Fort Dodge was under attack. Soon after the horseback courier reached the town of Homer, some ten miles away, settlers were fleeing the town by wagon, buggy, horseback and on foot. Another horseman brought word of the forthcoming attack on Happyland to the authorities at Boonesboro.

All alert procedures had been executed, cabins were barricaded and riflemen were in position with ammunition to ward off the attack when a detail of two scouts, well wrapped in blankets to ward off the chill, slowly walked up to the militiamen, then manning outposts. It was then that the militia came to suspect that old Zeb, the scout, might just possibly have mistaken the two blanket-draped scouts for Indians.

Bonebright cabin—Still preserved. Note antlers on side.
Photo courtesy of The Daily Freeman Journal, *Webster City, Iowa*

Reports of other scouting parties, returning from the area where Zeb had purportedly spotted the Indians, confirmed the belief that Zeb had indeed made an erroneous identity. These findings allayed fears of any pending Indian attack. However, by this time the Boonesboro Militia had already commenced their march to Happyland to aid in defense of the town.

By the time the Boonesboro Militia arrived, the community settlers were jubilant that an Indian attack was not imminent. The townspeople broke out their supplies of corn squeezin' liquor, and a bountiful feast was prepared. The Boonesboro Militiamen were treated to a party the likes of which they probably had never seen.

The Spirit Lake Massacre and old Zeb's two-scout Indian attack did serve a purpose; it pointed up the lack of federal troop protection. In 1858 the Iowa Frontier Guard was formed, under the auspices of the state, to beef up defenses against Indian attacks. However, it is doubtful old Zeb ever allowed an Indian blanket in his cabin after the ribbing he took over his erroneous "Indian sighting."

Although Iowa had no further serious Indian uprisings, Aunt Minnie related stories she had heard and read about the Sioux Indian attack on New Ulm, Minnesota. Settlers had been terrorized or under attack for nearly a week. She went on to say that some claim Chief Inkpadutah, who led his tribe in the Spirit Lake - Okoboji massacres, was also an instigator in the New Ulm raid. Further, some credence is given to stories that Inkpadutah was among Sioux leaders when the tribes wiped out Col. George Custer's 7th Cavalry in 1876 at the Battle of the Little Bighorn in Montana.

When the conversation about the Spirit Lake Massacre and New Ulm raid died down, Hank expressed his desire to see some real Indians. Aunt Minnie said the Mesquakie Indians at Tama, Iowa presented a Pow-Wow each year and that one was to be held soon. Continuing, she said, "Perhaps if you are a good boy your father might take you." James Arthur didn't seem to be too intrigued with the idea.

All the way home and until bedtime Hank carried on about Indians; then he dreamed about them all night. The next day he dogged his father's footsteps, talking about Indians and the "Wow-Wow" as he called it! At the supper table Hank finally got sidetracked from the Indian subject for a few minutes. Clinty, knowing James Arthur was a bit perturbed with Hank's ranting about red men, grinned and said, "James Arthur, I understand the boy wants to go to the Pow-Wow. Has he said anything to you about it?"

Patience definitely was not a virtue of James Arthur's, but he did have a good sense of humor. He had just taken a hefty bite out of one of Lucy's delectable pork chops, and at Clinty's last remark, he dropped his fork and almost swallowed it whole.

While staring at Hank, he shifted the parcel of pork to one side of his mouth with his tongue, and in a subdued bellow, blurted out,"Hank, if you'll just shut up about Indians, I'll take you to the damn Pow-Wow." Silence prevailed—Clinty grinned at Hank and winked.

Clinty taught Hank how to chant and, being a good tap dancer, he soon demonstrated the nearest thing he could to an Indian dance. With Clinty providing the rhythm beating on an inverted cream can,

Hank soon was dancing up a storm. Now he said, "All you need is a little practice."

For the next two days Hank drove all the earthworms in the barnyard a few inches deeper into the ground and all the cats stayed under the porch after he stomped on a tail or two. Clinty said he was doing fine, but needed a wee bit more practice on his ki-yi-yis.

By late afternoon Hank was convinced he was doing pretty darned well until Big Brother watched his dancing for awhile, smirked and said, "Hell, you don't even look like an Indian; you haven't got any eagle feathers on your head!" Then he showed Hank a picture of an Indian in a book.

Big Brother really hurt Hank's feeling and, of course, Hank went to Clinty with his problem. Clinty said he hadn't seen any eagles around lately, except those on the back of silver dollars—then hastily added that he hadn't seen many of those either. After giving it some thought, he allowed as how turkey feathers would be just fine.

It took a lot of doing, but Hank finally cornered a big tom turkey in the grainery. The ornery old tom was nearly as tall as Hank. After being eyeball to eyeball for awhile with the cantankerous bird, he began to realize he had about as much chance of getting a tail feather out of him as from the eagle on the back of a silver dollar.

But Hank was more determined than old tom realized and called his bluff. He grabbed him by the neck, wings flapped furiously and for a minute or so Hank thought the turkey was going to fly through the roof with him. However, after collecting a few spur scratches on his legs, Hank finally succeeded in relieving the irate bird of a couple of his tail feathers.

Mother Lucy shook her head, stopped what she was doing and applied iodine to the scratches. She then made him an elastic headband for his feathers. He didn't look very much like the Indian in the picture, but of one thing he was damn certain: he wasn't going to attempt to get any more feathers from that turkey!

It was a beautiful Sunday when James Arthur drove the family to the Mesquakie Indian settlement in the vicinity of Tama and Toledo to see the Pow-Wow. After much coaxing by Hank, Cousin Clinty finally had agreed to go along, but not until he had extracted a promise from James Arthur that there would be no more dashing through the daisies with the Dodge.

As they arrived at the Pow-Wow ground, the sun cast a golden glow through billowy clouds on the wickiup dwellings—dome-shaped structures created of bent branches with woven bark on the exterior.

Older warriors were now sitting in front of their wickiups at the edge of the ceremonial grounds with most of the squaws and children immediately behind them.

Mesquakie Indian brave in front of Wickiup (1926)
Photos courtesy of State Historical Society of Iowa, Iowa City, Iowa—Edward Rosheim Collection

Mesquakie Indian children by Wickiup (1926)
Photos courtesy of State Historical Society of Iowa, Iowa City, Iowa—Edward Rosheim Collection

With the first beat of the drums, Indian braves, bronzed and muscular, began emerging from wickiups. It was said some came from as far away as Kansas reservations.

The braves were an impressive sight as they entered the ring. Their buckskin jackets and trousers had been skillfully tanned and sewed, adorned with a radiance of colorfully dyed quill work and beads. Originally beads were made from seeds, and some of those were included in the bead work. When the chief entered the ring in his colorful war bonnet and exquisitely made regalia, the crowd marveled at the elaborate beauty.

Everyone in the audience enjoyed hearing the narrator tell the history of the Fox-Mesquakie Tribe as it had been passed down by the elders. He told how the Sac and Fox had merged after being driven from the north. Going on, the narrator said a battle between the Sioux and the Mesquakie had been fought on the very grounds where the Pow-Wow was now being held. He then told stories about the Black Hawk wars and the Indian attack on Fort Madison.

After the Sac-Fox sold their land, the Mesquakie had been moved to a reservation in Kansas. Unhappy, their tribal Chief Mamanwanika and a few braves set out for the Iowa state capitol, then in

Iowa City. Surprisingly they obtained an audience with then Governor James Grimes.

The Mesquakie had managed to save some money from their government allocations and presented this (purportedly $730) to Governor Grimes, saying they wanted to buy back some of their land. So impressed was the governor that he bought 80 acres himself, later turning it over to the Mesquakie. More money was accumulated by the Mesquakie in Kansas and their own 3,600-acre Indian settlement near Tama became a reality.

Sadly the narrator described how difficult it had been for the Indians when the white man slaughtered or drove the buffalo and other game west as they settled on farms and built fences. He said the Indian had suffered horribly from the wasteful wiping out of the herds by the white man.

History reveals that in 1800 there were an estimated 60 million buffalo in the plains area, but by 1867 there had been a massive reduction to 13 million. By the early 1900s only 1,000 of the magnificent beasts roamed the plains and all, except those in captivity, had disappeared from the plains states.

It was learned that some tribes used stretched buffalo hides to provide an outside cover on their wickiups. The Sioux and other tribes further west used buffalo hides to make their tepees, sleeping robes and clothing. Nothing had been wasted; even the buffalo hair was woven into rope, stuffing for cradle pads, gloves, moccasins, and many other items, including a crude type of ball. The horns proved useful and were fashioned into knives, tools and sleds.

Buffalo meat was cooked fresh and smoked for jerky; even the liver and intestines were eaten. The Indians considered the tongue and hump meat to be the most palatable. The buffalo's fat was used to soften pelts for tanning. Even "buffalo chips" were used for fires—a practice copied by the early pioneers.

Each dance presented had great significance to the Indian and was carefully explained by a narrator and in pamphlets provided. Warriors danced around an inner perimeter, while some of the women danced around the outside. Among the dances performed were the Dance of Eagles, the Friendship Dance, the Corn Dance, and the Bean Dance. Most of them centered around the harvest of crops or were in celebration of the successful hunt. With the dancing concluded, an exhibition of horsemanship was presented.

When the Pow-Wow was over, those present were given the opportunity to purchase an array of colorful dolls, blankets and trinkets which had been made for sale. Also, if desired, visitors were allowed to visit wickiups, which were far more livable than they appeared from the exterior. Some of the Indian artists had begun to dabble on

Above: Mesquakie Indians circle Pow Wow grounds—braves follow women (1926).

Right: Handsome Mesquakie Brave talks with white woman—1928 Pow Wow.

Photos courtesy of State Historical Society of Iowa, Iowa City—Edward Rosheim Collection

canvas. Their paintings were of people and animals; some seemed to have been conjured from visions.

All of the Indians displayed a genuine liking for the children. The older braves were polite, but were less outgoing toward the white elders. Small wonder since it had been only thirty-four years since the 1890 massacre at Wounded Knee, South Dakota, where the whites brutally murdered hundreds of Indian men, women and children.

James Arthur finally succeeded in rounding up the family and they headed for home. He had driven so well thus far that on the way Cousin Clinty couldn't help but compliment him on his newly displayed skill. However, Clinty's original premonition of the danger of making another long trip with James Arthur was soon to be proved correct.

As they passed Kurtz's corner and motored north on what is now County Road R-27 by the Moose brothers' farm, something hit the Dodge behind the left rear door with a resounding thud, turning it halfway around in the road. With that, Hank experienced the only thing that hadn't happened to him that day; he thoroughly wet his pants. Since he was sitting on Cousin Clinty's lap, his cousin received the dubious benefit of his excitement.

After further investigation, a horn-sized hole was discovered. Father James Arthur reasoned the machine had been gored by Hank and John Moose's prize bull. Cousin Clinty allowed from the location of the horn hole it was obvious James Arthur had the right of way and as they drove off, he mumbled something to the effect that the stupid damn bull should have known there was no room for him in the crowded car!

Bull ready for blind date!
Photos courtesy of Wallace's Farmer

This would be Hank's first year in school and it was time to purchase new clothing for the children, who had outgrown their wearing apparel during the past summer. Hank was pleased to receive new shoes, shirts, overshoes and a new jacket, but he was especially proud of his new overalls with pockets in the bib to hold his pencils.

When the clothing shopping was completed, James Arthur gave Hank his first dollar, a bright shining silver one. A dollar then was nearly the equivalent of fifteen dollars during the latter part of the 1980s. Like most young children in those days, his eyes lit up when he thought of all the candy he could buy.

Lovable Cousin Clinty consented to go along with Hank to the candy store. They looked over every case and barrel. Hank couldn't seem to decide which candy to purchase. Each time he was about to make a decision, he pulled the silver dollar from his pocket, looked at it, and then proceeded to the next delectable display. No doubt Clinty was becoming a bit disgusted, but he was a tolerant individual. At last Hank told Clinty he guessed he'd just keep his silver dollar to show it to the kids at school. Clinty laughed heartily, then took a nickel from his pocket and bought them each a candy bar.

III
THE HALLOWED HALL OF MUD HOLLOW

It was one of those beautiful clear midwestern September mornings. Summer has lost some of its botanical beauty but still steadfastly clings to its vegetative finery before yielding to inevitable forthcoming frosts. Another school year was about to begin. Throughout the rural areas across the nation, school teachers were arriving at small uniformly constructed, box-shaped structures each topped with a little bell cupola.

All "country school" teachers had more than a little bit in common. They had the inherent desire to pass along the learned word, and each faced the monumental task of giving formal education to students from first through eighth grades. Amplifying their task was the fact all instruction had to be accomplished in a one-classroom building.

Soon children in small groups, all with freshly scrubbed faces, could be seen walking down the dirt roads leading to Mud Hollow School (no pun). Those coming from longer distances had been joined by children living closer to the school. As they walked along they bubbled with enthusiasm, telling each other about their past summer activities and humorous happenings.

Arriving, Hank and others filed into the one and only "hallowed hall of Mud Hollow School," hung up their caps on the wall pegs provided, and proceeded to their pre-assigned desks—girls on one side of the room, boys on "tuther."

The pair of two-holers out back were not unisex. Segregation of the sexes was pretty well honored, except in the spring when each kid got

Boys play marbles at Mud Hollow School.
Photo courtesy of Doris Anderson Stearns

Some Mud Hollow students on playground.
Photo courtesy of Arthur Blue

his annual bowel system cleansing after being given a hefty dose of sulphur and molasses.

Most of the year students had to skip over mud puddles to get to the two-holers. At times when it was raining, it was questionable whether the trip was worth it as the patrons of the little buildings got wetter making the trip than they would have if they had thrown caution to the wind and wet their pants.

The younger kids hated to make the trip to the two-holers during bad weather and waited until the very last minute. Nearly everyone made it in time, but once in awhile some older boy would slip out from behind the schoolhouse and trip a desperate speeder enroute, then stand back, point at the poor soul and laugh.

Smoking had grown popular during World War I and a few of the older boys were soon experimenting with smoking cornsilk roll-your-own cigarettes in the outhouse. Big Brother decided he would participate in this adventure, but by that time the teachers in country schools had devised measures to eliminate the practice.

Big Brother and one of the neighbor boys were practicing the manly art of smoking one noon hour, when Caroline Gerber, the teacher, spotted smoke belching from the little half-moon-shaped hole on the side of the outhouse. Caroline quickly summoned one of the older boys to fetch a bucket of water. With pail in hand, she proceeded to the outhouse where she yelled, "Fire," opened the door and drenched the two puffers.

Hank wanted to experiment with this smoking thing, but Big Brother, four years his elder, apprised him of the fact that he was too young. Hank found out later that Big Brother wasn't considered old enough either when Hank let slip at the supper table that his brother had been caught smoking in the outhouse. Big Brother got a couple of knots on his head and later, always wanting to share a good thing, passed a lump or two on to Hank.

The head thumping Father James Arthur gave Big Brother and the bucket of water the teacher had thrown on him didn't dampen his smoking desire, but it did create a more cautious individual. Upon his suggestion the outhouse was abandoned as a smoker and he and some of the neighbor boys moved on to bigger things—namely the strawstack.

Alas, Big Brother's burning desire for cigarettes soon burst into flame. Upon the occasion of one of the smoking engagements someone became careless and an ash ignited the strawstack. They made a valiant effort to extinguish the blaze but, failing miserably in their attempts, they ran at breakneck speed through a grove of trees and around to the front of the house. Pretending to play hide and seek, the boys stayed within sight of their parents, who were sitting on the front porch.

In a short time the phone rang and a young lady Clinty had dubbed "Leather Lungs" was on the other end. Between gasps for air she advised James Arthur something was on fire in back of his barn. Everyone dashed out to look; James Arthur conceded that old "Leather Lungs" was surely right. By this time the strawstack was half gone and all anyone could do was stand back and marvel at the intense heat.

Big Brother proved that day that he possessed a certain quality of acting ability. His conjectures on the probable cause of the fire were fabulous. He spewed a constant barrage of possibilities as to what may have ignited the stack. Father James Arthur tried to explain how it could have happened several times and finally told Big Brother to shut up and let him think.

Cousin Clinty, the observant one, had seen the boys dash into the front yard. Later he said to Big Brother, "If your father had known how the fire started, your fanny would have glowed more brightly than the straw stack."

There are those who can prevail against adversity with smiles on their faces. One such man was the Hamilton County superintendent of schools, Ed Snow. In contrast to his surname, his face radiated the warmth of a bright sunny day. When Superintendent Snow visited Mud Hollow School, everyone greeted him with admiration that bordered on adulation. You see, Ed had lost both arms above the elbows back in 1875 when, as a not yet two year old he wandered onto the railroad tracks and the train wheels passed over him. Fortunate for Ed, the Illinois Central Railroad paid his education expenses. His wonderful wife, Alice, performed secretarial duties for him.

When checking instruction and curriculum Mr. Snow always smiled politely, greeted the teacher Miss Gerber and the class, then somehow crowded his slightly rotund, football tackle physique into an eighth grader seat.

Hoisting his suit coat upward, Supt. Snow extracted a pencil from his coat breast pocket with his teeth. He next maneuvered the pencil into a tight elastic band around the stump of his right arm. Using the same procedure he secured a notebook with his teeth from his inside coat pocket. Flipping the notebook on the desk, he turned the pages back with his pencil and was then prepared to make notations.

Even more amazing was Mr. Snow's marvelous penmanship, it was beautiful to the point of being artistic. If classes were proceeding well and to his satisfaction, he would sometimes draw a sketch of the school, a student, or an object while listening to the classroom routine. When the class was concluded he frequently gave the sketch to the teacher, a student or a friend. His sketches to this day are prized possessions.

Did someone drive him to the school? Of course not. Supt. Snow drove his own Model T Ford. Placing his foot on the crank, he spun it with a strongly driven right foot. He maneuvered the machine by placing the stump of his right arm into a socket on the steering wheel and down the road he traveled, a burden to no one. The great learned man was featured in Iowa Oddities—a rare, rare person and personality indeed!

Ed Snow as he appeared in "Iowa Oddities" in *The Des Moines Sunday Register.*
Photo courtesy of The Des Moines Register

Mud Hollow School was a little long on mud and a little short on extracurricular school activities. No school sponsored band or sports program existed. Lowell and George Garth did do a highly commendable job of beating out a marching cadence on water buckets. John Elm and Edward "Bud" Anderson could play the harmonica pretty well and Noble Johnson was a darn good whistler—that is, until he lost one of his front teeth during a fist fight at recess.

The only well organized sport was a lunch hour game called, "wee-wee in a circle." One of the older boys drew a circle in the field behind bushes and out of sight of the girls. The boy who could hit the closest to the center of the circle was the winner.

Elmer Timm, who was shorter in stature than most of his peers, always complained vigorously about the circle being too large, but the older boys refused to change from the standard measurement, which was derived by having the tallest boy in the class, Charles Howd, lie prone on the ground.

Disgusted and determined to garner a place among Mud Hollow's notables, Elmer could be seen attempting to drink the water crock dry about one hour before recess. That day he scored his first victory with a stream that some say would have loosened a brick in the county jail.

The big social event of the year in that locale was the annual box social held at the school. This event was a subject of discussion for months and was not a gathering to be taken lightly.

On the night of the big event an auctioneer, chosen by the ladies, would sell each box to the highest bidder. The name of the lady who had prepared the box of delicacies was kept a secret during the auction, but the Sir Lockinvar of the plowshare who purchased it was allowed to sit with the donor of the box and help consume its contents. Not only was the box social the premier social function of the year, its profits provided much needed reference books, school equipment, etc.

The school teacher, Caroline Gerber, worked for weeks with the children on their parts in the production, which might involve recitation of a poem, playing a musical instrument, singing, reading aloud or acting in a short skit.

The school board, consisting of five people who could read, write and argue, arranged for a small stage platform to be built. The women of the neighborhood prepared a stage curtain from sheets and clothesline and as one could say, the stage was set for the box social.

"Big Brother" had been selected to recite a bit of prose. He had protested, screamed, beat his head on the wall and said several words he wasn't supposed to know, but with his Sister Mabel's and Cousin Luella's perseverance and patience, he had memorized three stanzas by the end of the first week. The only problem he had was the fact he was unable to recite them.

Big Brother had been changed from left-handed to right-handed and for this the fabulous county superintendent of schools, Ed Snow, blamed Big Brother's stammer. Big Brother was beset with woes about prose.

When the big night arrived, everyone squeezed into the touring car and set forth for the schoolhouse. Dismounting from the horseless carriage, Big Brother, the poet laureate of the cow manure set, threatened to bolt and run, but Father James Arthur grabbed him and he came along into the school, protesting and screaming all the way.

The program started with much pomp and ceremony and proceeded like a Broadway production. Finally the curtain was closed to allow preparation for recitals and skits.

Big Brother was next on the program, but had he not been sitting between his two older brothers, Al and Bill in the front row, it was certain he would have bolted out the door. When his name was announced, they catapulted him onto the stage.

Big Brother turned to face the audience. He had the look on his face of one who had just reached the two-holer after a stiff dose of sulphur and molasses and had found the door locked and the little building occupied.

The poem had one phrase that went, "The green grass grows all around on the ground." With a look of defiance, Big Brother launched into his saying session. He was doing just fine until his older brothers started heckling him from their conspicuous front row seats.

Big Brother looked at the stove, ceiling, kerosene lamps and his feet, but finally glanced painfully at his older brothers. His next few words went like this—"An- an- and— the— d- dr-dreen- an-an-and da-da- dr-dre-dreen drass drows all around on the da-da-ddd round —DAMN IT!" With that he ran off the platform. Thus ended the stage debut of Big Brother.

Actually he was the star of the entire program. He drew more laughter and applause in three minutes than Charlie Chaplin, the silent movie comic, ever did in the course of an old three-reeler.

Time had arrived for the highlight of the evening, an organ recital by Doris Anderson, a very talented young girl. She proceeded with calmness and dignity to the stage, seated herself at the pump organ and addressed the sheet music.

Unbeknown to the teacher, some of the older boys (believed to have been Charles Howd, Edward Timm, Leo Gramblin, and Arthur Blue) had caught and placed some mice in a loosely tied paper sack inside the organ.

With the first ripple of the keys, there was a rustling of paper and a scratching sound. Then mice came scrambling out of the organ. Wild tigers couldn't have wrought more pandemonium. Within two seconds women in the front two rows had vacated their seats and were standing on chairs and desk tops.

Quick thinking Newt Paige opened the door and after the entire animal kingdom representation had departed, the men pried the women down from the ceiling and the program resumed.

With the end of Doris Anderson's organ recital the acts were concluded and the auctioning off of the box lunches began.

Cousin Clinty saw a box which he said he was certain belonged to a pretty widow lady who was visiting in the community. Clinty bid and bid and bid again until at last he was the proud possessor of the beautiful box.

Who do you think was the preparer of the box? None other than the woman Clinty had nicknamed, "Leather Lungs." The talkative woman was so verbose she almost gave up breathing to attain more rapidity of speech. Clinty whispered to Mother Lucy, "Of all the damn boxes I could have bought, I had to buy the one prepared by a woman who was vaccinated with a phonograph needle!"

At Clinty's request Hank was invited to eat with him and the one with the built in bagpipes. There was plenty to eat as old "Leather Lungs" had a bad case of indigestion and, from the way her stomach growled Clinty expressed fear she was going to give birth to a batch of pups.

All the way home Clinty stretched his long legs to get the kinks out of his knees. He complained of the crowded condition at the small desks and said his desk partner had to be at least one ax handle and a plug of tobacco across the beam. In today's vernacular it might be said Clinty ate a one "bun" dinner. But, he always had something good to say about everyone and allowed as how she was a darned good cook and had real pretty elbows!

During harvest season a farmer's day began at daybreak and rarely ended before nightfall after stock had been fed and cows had been hand-milked.

Of course, the women, having worked hard all day, still had the evening meal to prepare and serve and dishes to wash by hand.

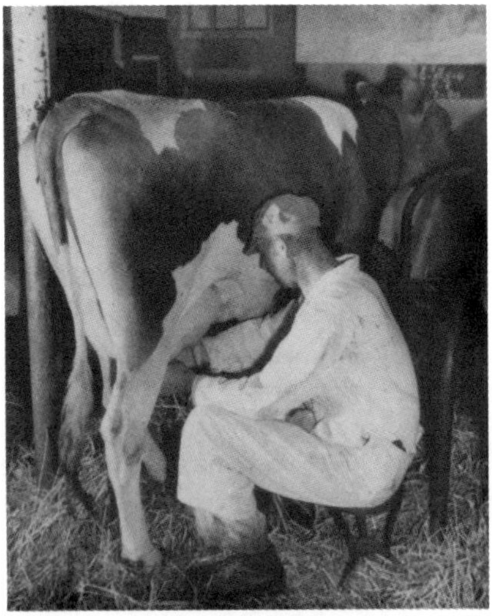

Hand milking cows
Photo courtesy of Wallace's Farmer

Separating cream from milk. Note fancy electric powered separator.
Photo courtesy of Wallace's Farmer

Women prepared wonderful meals on these stoves.
Photo courtesy of Wallace's Farmer

Hand washing clothes for a large family was a back-breaking task.
Photo courtesy of Wallace's Farmer

Without the huge combines and cornpickers of today, corn harvesting often continued through Thanksgiving.

It might be added that the wives also had a backbreaking job during harvest time. As frequently happened, especially during corn picking season, each man would get up at earlier and earlier hours in order to get a team hitched up and be ready to dash out to the field at the crack of dawn. This meant wives were fixing breakfast for each man and the children at varying times. The women might just as well have been short order cooks in one of Happyland's restaurants.

In addition to tending crops, virtually all farmers raised cattle, hogs and chickens. Banks often made participation in these extra ventures a prerequisite for obtaining a loan.

Eggs and cream were often bartered at stores for sugar, flour, salt and other staples. Each farm wife tended the chickens, raised a large garden and canned meat, vegetables and fruit to feed her family during the long cold winter months.

Most farm wives raised sizable flocks of chickens.

Photo courtesy of Bernice Sealine Lund

Anna Hanson and daughter feeding turkeys (1927).

Photo courtesy of Ellen Hanson Ankrum

Oats and wheat were cut with a binder which made them into bundles by tieing binding twine around a clump of grain stems. Bundles were hand stacked in shocks, later to be hauled by horse-drawn hayracks to a steam engine operated threshing machine, equipped with no-choke sieves invented by Charles Closz and manufactured at his factory in Happyland.

A thresher blower created a large stack of straw for horse and cattle bedding, and the grain was placed in bins for storage to be used for stock feed or transported to the grain elevator for shipment to mills.

Hay for the animals was cut with a side arm mower, wind-rowed with hay rakes, then usually hand pitched and hauled loose in hayrack wagons to the barn. There the hay was placed in slings or hayforks and elevated by rope and pulley into the haymow on the upper level of barns, where it was convenient for feeding stock.

Farm tractors were still quite rare before 1925, and many farmers plowed fields and tended crops with horses. Although cultivating corn with horses was a slow and monotonous task, man's only duty in the process (except for turning the team around at the end of each row) was to sit on the steel cultivator seat and guide the blades around the stalks. Amazingly, most horses could turn the cultivator around and position themselves astraddle the next row without man's guidance.

Corn was planted with use of a horse-drawn planter and was picked by hand and thrown into a wagon. Corn on most farms was then taken to corncribs where it was shoveled or lift-dumped into a horse-powered elevator, which carried it upward to roll off the end into the crib.

Many farms did not have elevators and on those corn had to be shoveled by hand into the crib, a backbreaking job to say the least! Hand-operated corn shellers were frequently used to shell the corn for the fowl.

Farmers constantly argued over whose crop yield was biggest and corn pickers bragged incessantly about the number of bushels they could pick in a day. Payment by the bushel spurred corn huskers on to a torrid pace. When the pickers got together on a Saturday night at the billiard parlor, it became a standard joke that a helluva lot more corn was picked in the poolrooms than was ever picked in the fields.

Contests were held at the county, state and national levels, and the fluid-like motion of the top pickers was a sight to uphold. Like the ambidextrous basketball players who can pour the ball into the basket with either hand, they were truly professional athletes in every sense. By the time one ear hit the backboard, another was on the way.

Brothers Bill and Al always picked at top speed in attempt to outdo each other. Cousin Clinty, with his aching bunions and not-so-strong or so youthful hands, could never reach the coveted goal of 100 bushels per day. His best was near sixty.

The merits of using a pick or hook were often argued. The pick fit in the hand with a protruding steel point, while the hook consisted of a leather strap across the palm with two upward protruding hooks. Both were used to shred the husk from the corn; the husk was then snapped from the ear to be thrown in the wagon.

For several evenings, Clinty made much to do about fashioning a combination hook and pick, which he said would double his speed in the field. Both Bill and Al scoffed at the idea, while James Arthur just shook his head and grinned.

Hand picking corn was a laborious task.
Photo courtesy of Bernice Sealine Lund

Corn elevator in action—note horses providing power.
Photo courtesy of Bernice Sealine Lund

With his somewhat crude invention completed a few days later, Clinty arose early, immediately hitched his team to the wagon and, when chores were finished, he was quickly on the way to the field.

By the time the brothers were on their way up the corn rows, Clinty was a couple of hundred yards ahead. The corn rattled off the backboard and his team and wagon moved forward at an unbelievable pace. Both brothers increased their picking tempo, literally attacking the ears, but their Cousin Clinty continued to widen the gap.

By 10 a.m. Clinty drove his brim-ful wagon past the brothers headed toward the corncribs. Bill and Al scratched their heads in astonishment. Clinty ate a leisurely dinner and as the brothers were coming in with their loads, Clinty laughed and waved, enroute to the field for another load.

That afternoon by 4:00 Clinty pulled up to the boys with another full load, halted and yelled, "What's holding you guys up; you both got sore arms or something?" Both dashed over, looked at the well husked full load and returned to their wagons shaking their heads. That night at the supper table Clinty made much to do about how, with his new invention, he had shown the young upstarts a trick or two. In the course of the conversation, he asked James Arthur if he could get a few days off to go to Des Moines and file for a patent. The brothers moped through the entire meal and had very little to say—their egos shattered.

The next morning Bill, Al and Cousin Clinty proceeded to the barn to hitch up their teams. It was then Cousin Clinty took them over to his wagon and showed them how he had placed three saw horses in the wagon bottom and covered them with planks. The crafty Clinty had picked only a third of a wagon load and had picked every other cornstock in his dashing performance.

Cousin Clinty always managed to keep something going to lighten the cares of the day. One night at the dinner table he told about one of his World War I experiences in France where he had seen people wagering sizable sums on the sport of cock fighting. Hank's creative Cousin with the knowledgeable noggin' told how gamblers wagered money on the outcome of the battles between the Sir Galahads of the setting hen set.

Brothers Bill and Al listened intently to Clinty's conversation about the chicken house gladiators and decided to train one of the roost roustabouts in the specialty of spurring. Clinty advised against the venture, but they proceeded to devote much of their spare moments to their feathered protege. The chosen perky little perch ruler soon became so fiesty he dominated the entire barnyard. Any man, beast or fowl that came near him was immediately challenged and greeted with a flurry of wings and flying spurs.

There was no natural gas in those days, and kerosene stoves were not designed for large family cooking. Most farms had no electricity and used oil-burning lamps and lanterns. Electric stoves and refrigerators were luxuries of a few city dwellers. The first power plant had been built in Happyland in 1890 at a cost of $14,400 but, even with a large plant nearby, few farms had electricity.

Iceboxes were rare on farms and lack of freezers meant volumes of food canning and preparation of large meals each day on wood or coal-burning cook stoves. Fires were often started with corn cobs.

Mother Lucy was preparing to do some baking and, with none of the older boys around, James Arthur hurried out to gather cobs. He approached the feeding lot where the fearsome fowl was filching corn left over from stock feeding. Being unaware of the rooster's spurring specialty he nonchalantly went about picking up cobs, oblivious to the seriousness of exposing his sitting section.

As Father James Arthur told the story later, with gestures and gems from the unprintable English language, he heard a thrashing of wings behind him and could see a shadow bobbing up and down on the ground.

Shortly after the wing-waving episode, he said, he had wondered how the Zublin and Garth Up River Ice Co. delivery wagon had got off its town route and out into the country—for he had a sensation like six ice men were alternately shoving ice picks into his behind.

The story was completed at the supper table as James Arthur polished off the last leg of the John L. Sullivan of the top roost. The fight had ended with James Arthur's hand firmly around the rooster's neck and then Lucy popping him in the pan!

James Arthur with famous cob basket
Photo courtesy of Mabel Whaley

All during the meal Cousin Clinty sympathized with James Arthur about his punctured protrusion. While the Father sat tenderly on his tailbone, Clinty ate the wishbone and suggested that, with all of James Arthur's experience and the natural ability of the fighting flock in the henhouse, they should go into the business of training fighting cocks. James Arthur didn't seem to "cotton" too much to the idea and told Clinty that if it was all the same to him, he'd just as soon sit on it awhile.

Hank's family lived about two miles north and a half mile west of Kurtz's corner. This he learned at an early age from his Father's telephone conversations instructing people on how to reach their home.

A single community telephone had been installed in the Happyland post office in 1881 and twenty-four placed in businesses. By the turn of the century some city residences had telephones, but farm installations had progressed slowly.

Father James Arthur never did trust the telephone alone to carry the message and put one hundred percent of himself into each conversation. Cousin Clinty said when James Arthur called the nearby neighbors, they could have heard him just as easily from the back porch—and that he used the telephone only because he paid the bill on the damn thing.

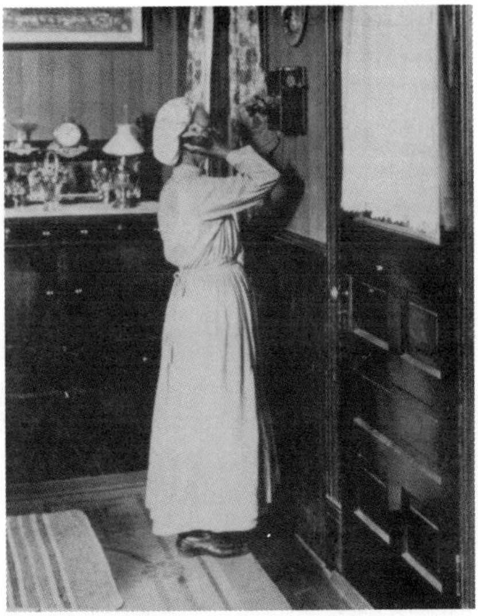

Old time telephone
Photo courtesy of Wallace's Farmer

Despite the popularity of automobiles, many people couldn't afford one and still used horses to pull their passenger buggies as well as cargo wagons. The city square, replete with the official city scales, bustled with activity each Saturday with wagons parked by farmers who had taken grain to the elevator.

Horse hitching posts were still to be found in the town's business district in the early 1920s and, as Weldon Helmick, a councilman said, "Much resistance was encountered in 1927 when an ordinance was adopted to remove the sturdy old posts."

To go into Happyland was one of Hank's early day thrills and when Cousin Clinty hitched up the team to the wagon to haul grain to the town elevator, he couldn't help him enough.

They sat high up on the wagon seat—Cousin Clinty and Hank—singing or whistling and clucking "gid-dap",—"whoa!" and all that stuff at the beautiful team. Hank envisioned they were in a P.T. Barnum Circus parade as they rode along. At times Hank could have sworn the horses had elephant trunks. Clinty would mock a steam calliope and into the town they'd roll.

On one of those glorious trips they started home late. Clinty had bought Hank an ice-cream sundae at Pappas Ice Cream Parlor and, no doubt, somewhere along the line, a bottle of spirits for himself.

As they reached the outskirts of town, they drove past the old National Sewer and Tile Co. plant situated at the extreme west end of the town's main street, and headed up by Henry Teget. Cousin Clinty told Hank that a man in the factory would blow a whistle if he would just yell loudly enough, "Blow the whistle."

When they reached a designated point Clinty said, "Yell now and yell loud!" Hank yelled, "Blow the whistle!" until he thought his eyeballs would rotate and when he neared exhaustion, wouldn't you know the whistle did blow. Cousin Clinty got quite a laugh out of the episode, but Hank thought he was just amazed at his fine performance.

Several days later Hank rode into town with his Father and Mother in the touring car. Going home he waited until they arrived at the same spot and started his lung bursting yell, "Blow the whistle." He kept this up until his Father, in disgust, said, "Son, what in the hell ails you?"

Hank told his Father the story and as usual, all he got out of either of his parents was, "Clinty's been at it again!" A year or so later Hank learned the whistle was a work whistle blown at seven o'clock each morning, twelve noon and six o'clock in the evening.

Although this was in the mid 1920s, Iowa was still in its infancy. The lack of ditches and adequate drainage caused the thinly graveled road to the farm to be virtually impassable during the spring thaw and rainy periods.

Farmer grades road with improvised grader.
Photo courtesy of Wallace's Farmer

When the road became frozen and deeply rutted, people from cars traveling in opposite directions would dismount and, with boards carried for the purpose, bridge one car out of the rut while the other passed through. That summer the county road crews had cut drainage ditches in some of the rural roads—and Clinty averred that to be progress of some sort or another.

A wave of new inventions had swept the globe. An Italian, named Marconi, had invented the radio which was by far the most exciting. When Mr. Grigg Elkin, a neighbor, invited the family over to listen to his new wireless Atwater-Kent, everyone was thrilled beyond imagination.

The wireless was displayed prominently in the Elkin living room on a beautiful black walnut table. It looked like a black metal box, with more knobs than even Clinty had ever seen. Mr. Elkin showed everyone the dial which had numbers on it for each station. On top sat a horn similar to those on the old phonographs. For better reception he said he preferred to use earphones.

Everyone stared in amazement as Mr. Elkin, with unheard of skill, manipulated the knobs. First there was a lot of screeching; then suddenly music could be heard coming out of the horn. Listening to a radio for the first time was truly a historical event for everyone who lived during that era.

Atwater Kent radio with speaker horn
Photo courtesy of Everett Ludley

Arborphone radio with classic RCA speaker (1920s)
Photo courtesy of Everett Ludley

In the field of aviation progress continued at a rapid pace during the early and mid-1920s. Pilots and manufacturers in several nations reached for new and greater horizons. Everyone was talking about airplanes and the impact they would have upon the world.

Balloons had long been used for transportation and observation, but more exciting things had been happening in aviation. During World War I, airplanes, then described as heavier than air craft, had begun to play a serious role. Pilots and their planes were assigned to the U.S. Army Signal Corps and proved extremely valuable for observation and reconnaissance. Aircraft were armed with machine guns for aerial combat and were used for the first time to drop bombs on enemy troops and military installations.

Before the war ended the first airmail was flown from New York to Washington, D.C. on May 15, 1918. By September 8, 1920 routes had been established from New York via Cleveland, Chicago and Omaha, to San Francisco, and by 1926 numerous cities had been added to the list.

The first transcontinental flight had taken place in 1911 and took 49 days. Then in May of 1923, two U.S. Army pilots flew non-stop across the United States in 27 hours.

Earth had yet to be circumnavigated by aircraft—Britain, France, Italy and the United States were in a race against time vying for this prestigious accomplishment. At last eight U.S. Army Air Service pilots in four pontoon equipped Douglas Cruiser airplanes stood poised and ready to make the trip. The flight departed Seattle, Washington April 6, 1924 under the command of Major Gerald Martin.

The pilots faced a grueling, dangerous trip for their scheduled route would traverse the treacherous cold arctic sea. During the flight American destroyers stood by to provide logistic support and render assistance as needed. That assistance would be needed for word was received April 30, 1924 that the plane carrying Major Gerald Martin and a man named Harvey had crashed: a search was initiated, but the two pilots were not to be found. It would be ten days after the crash before Martin and Harvey would complete their on-foot journey out of the arctic wastelands!

Few reference books cover this first around-the-world flight of the U.S. Army pilots. Even less is recorded about a Tokyo based Associated Press reporter, Linton Wells, who became a part of that historic flight on one leg of the journey. Fay Gillis Wells, an acquaintance of the author, provided this interesting story about her deceased husband. The author felt compelled to share the story with readers.

Linton Wells was waiting on board the U.S. destroyer Ford when the first trans-Pacific flight, then consisting of three U.S. Army planes carrying six very tired pilots arrived May 17, 1924 at the northern Japanese Island of Paramushiru. It had been six weeks since the flight departed Seattle.

Reporter Wells had a wonderful interview and with some difficulty got his story off to Associated Press. When the around-the-world flyers departed for Tokyo, Wells traveled by destroyer and train hoping to join the flyers there. He found them being lavishly feted at the Imperial Hotel. There he became better acquainted with the flight commander, Lowell Smith, and other pilots Leigh Wade, Erik Nelson, Leslie P. Arnold, Henry Ogden, and John Harding, Jr.

The next leg of the journey would take the flyers to Calcutta, India. Reporter Wells struck out by ship, train and whatever. Due to airplane mechanical problems, Wells was able to overtake the flight in Calcutta where he again interviewed the pilots. There he was to leave the flight and return to his Tokyo office.

Wells had jokingly asked flight commander Smith if he could ride in one of the planes. Impressed by Wells' dogged determination to cover the flight, the Flight Commander dashed off a wire to General Mason Patrick, Chief of U.S. Army Air Services, to ask permission for Wells to ride in a plane with Leigh Wade and Henry "Hank" Ogden. No return wire was received so Wells was squeezed into a cockpit with Ogden. They sat on a board placed on the seat to gain added width, their heads protruding above the cockpit.

Since the pilots needed rest and sleep, Linton Wells proceeded to give speeches for them, refueled, etc. Several stops later after flying through unbearable heat that raised temperature in the cockpits to 156 degrees, with on-ground temperatures of 130 degrees they finally arrived in Karachi. The faces of Wells and Ogden were badly sunburned; their lips looked like lobsters. A Reuter reporter, in a tongue-in-cheek news release, reported that a stowaway, Linton Wells, had been found on a plane.

The first around-the-world flyers (U.S. Army pilots)

Photo by Linton Wells; Courtesy of Fay Gillis Wells

In Karachi Smith received a wire stating in no uncertain terms that Wells was not to accompany the flight. Another wire soon arrived from Tokyo firing reporter Wells for disobedience of orders. The pilots bade Wells a fond farewell and took off on their cross-country flight to northern Scotland.

Two adventurers, Linton Wells and Fay Gillis Wells celebrate 50th anniversary.
Photo by Leigh Wade, round-the-world flyer; courtesy of Fay Gillis Wells

Wells, without a job, decided to continue his journey and struck off for Rome. The flyers had many problems, but so did reporter Wells. He hitched rides on trains, tramp steamers, and any other mode of transportation he could find. Nearly broke, he taught some workers on a steamship how to play poker and relieved them of $194.

Arriving in Rome, Wells tried to land a job as a reporter. Failing to do so, he decided to do some free-lance reporting. Using obsolete press credentials, he convinced Benito Mussolini, the Italian Premier, to grant him an interview.

The aggressive reporter Wells asked Mussolini how he thought Italy would fare under Fascism. Mussolini ranted and raved, then closed by saying that he would renew the glories of ancient Rome and regain Italy's rightful place in the sun. Shortly thereafter secret police raided the room rented by Wells and found in his notes derogatory remarks about Mussolini. The secret police gave Wells the choice of jail or a plane ticket to Paris. Of course, Wells opted to go to Paris, but he had already collected some good stories.

Wells wired a friend for the loan of $200. Upon arrival in London via Paris, he landed a job with the "New York Herald Tribune". He was soon assigned to cover the Prince of Wales (David Windsor) on his 1924 trip to the United States. He became quite friendly with the prince during their steamship trip. Wells obtained some wonderful stories about the man who later became King Edward VIII and subsequently abdicated his throne to marry Wallace Simpson, an American divorcee. When the trip ended, the Prince of Wales presented Wells with a gold cigarette case inlaid with diamonds and rubies forming the letters E.P.F. Edward, Prince.

Meanwhile Lowell Smith and his army flyers reached Seattle, Washington September 28, 1924. In 176 days they had successfully completed the first flight around the world. The plane carrying Leigh Wade and Henry Ogden had developed a broken oil line and crashed in the North Atlantic ocean. But they survived, picked up a replacement plane at Labrador and finished the flight. Oh yes, reporter

Wells would see his pilot friends again when they were welcomed by a howling crowd at Mitchell Field in New York.

Wells would also team up with Leigh Wade and accomplish the first non-stop trip across the United States in an automobile. They departed Los Angeles in a Packard in early July 1925. They arrived in New York, a distance of 3,965 miles, 167 hours and 50 minutes later. They had one flat tire, that while they were crossing the desert. Wells put a dolly under the axel and changed the tire while in motion. Thus forward momentum was never halted.

Fay went on to say that Linton Wells' thirst for adventure never seemed to be quenched. He and Edward S. Evans, a Detroit millionaire, established a new round-the-world record of 28 days in 1926, traveling by automobile, steamship, train and plane. The previous record had been set in 1913 by John Henry Mears when he made the trip in 35 days plus.

No one had flown over the North Pole, and flying over the frozen mass would certainly test the mettle of the most courageous men. At that time were a plane forced down for any reason in such an area, chances of its occupants surviving would have been nil. Temperatures often drop to the level of fifty degrees below zero and the ice extends for thousands upon thousands of miles.

Rear Admiral Richard E. Byrd and Floyd Bennett, his co-pilot, undoubtedly had several reasons for choosing the month of May to challenge mother nature's frozen wonderland, but one plus factor could have been twenty four hours of daylight each day.

Byrd already had conquered broad expanses of water in 1921 when he crossed the Atlantic Ocean in a dirigible. On May 9, 1926 the news was flashed around the world that Byrd and Bennett had successfully flown over the North Pole. People could only wonder what daring feat of aviation would come next.

Meanwhile back on the farm Christmas that year was to be a wonderful and memorable occasion for Hank. He accompanied his Father on one of those infrequent bumpy rides to town in the touring car. When they entered Mason Hardware and Harness Shop, Jesse Mason grinned at Hank from ear to ear. He then put an affectionate hand on his shoulder and took him back into the harness shop portion of the store. There he presented Hank a dog sled harness, adorned with shiny brass studs, for Buster, the family's huge male Russian wolf and stag hound.

Hank thanked Mr. Mason with tears in his eyes; he was too choked up to express in words what he would have liked to have said. Mr. Mason was a kind man, who had great love for children and animals.

Going to Mason Brothers Hardware was always a wonderful experience. It was quaint by modern standards with long rows of box-like

Mason Hardware Store—note ladder on right.
Photo courtesy of Willis Knight Collection

cubby holes almost to the ceiling. Hank always marveled at the ladders with rollers, which could be moved along the shelves from the front to the rear of the store.

When a customer needed something, the Mason brothers knew just exactly which compartment contained the item and would roll the ladder straight to it. If a child promised to be real good, the brothers would sometimes allow him to ride the ladder for a few feet. This was more thrilling than an airplane ride would be in later years. Hank would cherish the memory of the Mason brothers the rest of his life.

Rare indeed was the farmer who didn't have at least one dog. Most dogs would allow a visitor to go to the door and knock, but proceeding further was not advisable even if the dog appeared friendly. Man's best friend would often bring in the cattle for milking and protect domestic animals and his family with its life.

James Arthur had purchased their Russian wolf and stag hounds from a former neighbor, Carl Bauer of Kamrar. They had the grace and even greater speed than most greyhounds and were far larger. The male, Buster, weighed 140 pounds and the female, Fannie, well over 100 pounds.

The two dogs became legendary in the community for their tremendous speed; they could easily catch jack rabbits. During the winter months Hank would walk to the edge of a cornfield and wait for the powerful dogs to catch rabbits and bring them to him. Quite often they would bring at least two, which Hank carried to the house for cleaning and dressing.

Alas, someone who knew of the hunting prowess of the two dogs and their fabulous speed stole Buster, the huge good-natured male. Hank cried for days thereafter and Buster's sister, Fannie, was so distraught she couldn't eat.

Although Jack Ziegler, a Happyland policeman, devoted many hours to a search for Buster, his efforts yielded no success. Eventually James Arthur decided Fannie would be happier away from the farm and let Cousin Luella and her husband take her home with them. She did start eating but never would be her happy self again.

Shortly thereafter James Arthur came home from a sale on Saturday afternoon with a cuddly mixed breed puppy in his arms. Hank, thrilled beyond belief, took the little bundle of joy and dashed for the house to show Clinty and the rest of his family his new dog. Clinty put the appraisal eye on it and allowed as how the pup's mother was a German Shepherd and the father had been in town for a week with the carnival. Hank promptly named the puppy Jack.

Oh, what a precious puppy he was. Hank played with it, slept with it, and would have set a plate for it at the table if his mother had allowed. As it grew its police dog build became more pronounced, but it had thick beautiful black curly hair, tan chin and chest and tan stripes down its rear legs to its tan feet—what a beauty he was.

On the national scene President Calvin Coolidge showed no concern for the farmer. American agriculture was on an economic toboggan—it had been off to a good start, had rounded some perilous curves, but was soon to find itself in for some rough sledding.

The most noteworthy accomplishment of prohibition had proved to be the curtailment of the use of grain to produce alcoholic beverages causing a loss for the farmer and the shift of profits from distillers to organized crime.

Jubilance of the non-imbibers soon subsided for the American public merely shifted their preference to home brew and rot gut. In New York where 15,000 saloons had existed, an estimated 32,000 "speakeasies" (illegal bars) sprang up. Crime bosses had seized the initiative and liquor, called "rot gut," by some, had continued to flow.

Lack of compassion shown by government toward the farmer was beginning to take its toll. Farm land and crop prices that had begun to drop in 1924 continued their downward spiral in 1926. Making ends meet on a farm became more and more an exercise in futility.

There just was not enough money to go around and James Arthur's eldest sons, Bill and Al, were driven to seek other employment in areas of the economy not yet so badly stung by the recession.

Although James Arthur now had a Fordson tractor, he and Clinty could no longer keep up with the work, and crop prices would not support the hiring of additional help. If he was to continue farming, James Arthur was rapidly coming to the conclusion that he must attempt to find a smaller farm.

IV
GOURD HEAD GRAMMAR and THE COUNTY SLAMMER

On the local scene cold, strong winds, driving heavy snow out of the northwest, brought the midwest under the seige of a terrible winter. Under normal winter conditions the children walked the nearly two miles to school, but as conditions worsened during that 1925-1926 winter, roads became impassable for automobiles, and huge snow drifts made even walking extremely difficult.

Wind had driven the snow so hard it was packed in drifts, well above the fence lines. James Arthur discovered he could drive diagonally across the field direct to the school with the bobsled without barbed wire fences posing a danger to the horses.

At last, during the latter part of February, a break in the weather came. Clinty and James Arthur started moving horse and tractor-drawn farm implements to a farm located some one and a half miles south of Happyland. On March 1, 1926 the last of the household goods was moved to their new home.

On the day of the move there was excitement aplenty. Although the house was an old one, it was near enough to Happyland to have electric lights one turned on and off by merely pushing a button. James Arthur did insist on keeping a few kerosene-burning lamps since neighbors, Gus Stein and James Scott, advised winter ice storms sometimes snapped the electric lines.

There were few farms with electricity, a ratio of one to ten, until the Rural Electrification Administration (REA) was created in 1932.

Farmers then formed a sort of cooperative and strung their own lines. But it was to be after World War II that virtually all farm homes would be electrified.

Speakeasies, where one could drink the better illegally smuggled-in alcoholic beverages, existed in the larger cities. In the rural areas bootleggers sold raw alcohol, white lightning and homebrew to those suffering from thirst.

Young people with good jobs, or those whose parents could afford luxuries, wore raccoon coats, drove open top roadsters with rumble seats. Jazz was the music of the day and Charleston was the "in" dance. Clara Bow was the "it" girl. Mary Pickford, Douglas Fairbanks, Sr., and Rudolph Valentino were the dramatic movie stars; Charlie Chaplin, Harold Lloyd and Buster Keaton were the top comedians, and Tom Mix still headed the list of cowboy stars.

Crime was on the increase in the big cities and Al Capone, the infamous Chicago gang boss, was well on his way to becoming a multi-millionaire.

Nearly everyone liked baseball and their idol was George Herman "Babe" Ruth. The "Sultan of Swat," as Babe came to be known, had begun his career with the Boston Red Sox as a pitcher, and an outstanding one at that, but because of his hitting ability, he had switched to the outfield.

The mighty Babe soon hit a record 29 home runs in 1919 and was traded to the New York Yankees. In 1920 he poled 54 round trippers. Crowds soared and in 1923 the Yankees built a new "Yankee Stadium," soon to be called, "the house that Ruth built!"

Ruth continued literally to belt the covers off baseballs and was now the most colorful player in the game. However, Lou Gehrig, a younger teammate of Ruth's, was now playing first base for the Yankees and the two were setting a torrid pace at the plate.

On the football scene, Harold Edward "Red" Grange, "the gallopin' ghost from Illinois," had played his last season of college football. At Illinois Grange scored five touchdowns in as many carries against Michigan, with runs of 15, 44, 56, 67, and 95 yard runs.

Bill Tilden squeaked by Bill Johnson to remain the top tennis player and a girl by the name of Helen Wills topped the women on the courts. Bobby Jones was the most talked-about golfer and Jack Dempsey was world champion heavyweight boxer.

Getting back to the local scene, the switch from Sodbuster School (Mud Hollow) to the city's South Building Grade School (Clinty promptly dubbed it "Gourd Head Grammar") was quite a transition. South Building Grade School, huge compared to the Mud Hollow one-room school, provided separate rooms for each grade.

South Building grade school with cylindrical fire escape
Photo courtesy of Willis Knight

Clinty marveled at the ingenuity the school board had exercised in coming up with the name, South Building. It was obvious, Clinty averred, that they could have been more original since he had seen at least twenty mud puddles on the playground, and the building had pigeon manure all over the roof.

A few of the boys were trying to emulate the world's great champion Jack Dempsey's prowess with their fists, and to Hank it seemed like every bully descended on him during his first weeks of school. The thought crossed his mind that if he could just find a kid he could whip, he would just tie him to his bedpost and get up and thrash him soundly every hour on the hour!

After absorbing several beatings, Hank became concerned and, as usual, took his problem to his Cousin Clinty. Clinty related a few of his own experiences and allowed Hank should take his short course in alley fighting, designed to make one rougher than a wood hauler's fanny, in ten easy lessons.

Each night after school, Hank received a lesson from Cousin Clinty. The course was not designed for compliance with Marquis of Queensberry rules, and Hank gleefully dreamed of the utter destruction he could wreak upon his lesser trained tormentors.

Cousin Clinty deduced Hank could not complete the course satisfactorily without more practical application of lessons learned. Big Brother volunteered to assume the role of sparring partner and obligingly beat hell out of Hank each night in the furtherance of his younger brother's fisticuff abilities.

Hank's boxing homework increased to such a tempo that his fights at school almost became a pleasure; in fact he was beginning to like the ones at school a whole lot better!

However, Cousin Clinty's clobbering course did help. One day during the noon hour, a larger, heavier boy decided to feed Hank a knuckle sandwich. Hank threw Clinty's training into play and was making out quite well until the older boy decided to wrestle.

Hank was soon pinned and the bully was rubbing and banging his head into the pebbles. Suddenly the boy on top flew backwards. Lawrence Kayser, who was on his way back to school, had the ruffian by the collar. With the two boys on their feet, Lawrence explained to the bully that Hank was too small to wrestle with him.

The kid looked big to Hank—real big—almost big enough to play tiddle-de-winks with manhole covers. Hank allowed as how he'd best blind the kid with a bit of the footwork he had mastered while taking Clinty's clobbering course. As Lawrence Kayser related years later, the footwork exhibition took on the appearance of someone trying to play hopscotch and scrape gum off his shoe soles at the same time.

At any rate the footwork must have had somewhat of a hypnotic effect on the kid as he just stood and stared at Hank in amazement. Perhaps he thought Hank was giving him a free tap-dancing lesson. The kid became so engrossed that he didn't notice Hank bringing up his most devastating uppercut punch from all the way down by his shoelaces. Blood spurted; the kid allowed as how he'd best take time out or ruin his clothes and departed for the boys' room.

Lawrence Kayser as a star quarterback

From that day forward Hank idolized Lawrence, who went on to be a star basketball and football player in high school and later starred in basketball and tennis at Grinnell College.

Hank was winning more fights than he was losing. His adversaries decided fighting him wasn't all pleasure and another phase in Hank's transition from Sodbuster School to Gourd Head Grammar had been completed. Hank was now allowed to sneak a slide down the South Building's long cylindrical fire escape with all the other kids during lunch hour—that is, if he brought his own slippery waxed bread wrapper to sit on.

Summer finally arrived and Hank and Clinty's Sunday afternoon activity was often a long leisurely walk along the Boone River as it wound its way through Briggs Woods Park. The area presented a vast change from the fields around it. Once you were within the forest you were in a nature wonderland of beautiful wild flowers, berries, and animals, along with an abundance of hickory nuts and walnuts, free for the picking.

Clinty and Hank sat for many an hour observing the daily activities of the bird and animal inhabitants. They usually frequented the same places. Clinty had advised that the birds and animals would soon recognize them and come to understand they meant them no harm.

Clinty's comparison of human nature and characteristics with those of birds and animals was fabulous. He steadfastly contended that each human trait could be readily associated and identified with one of birds and animals.

As they sat in the serenity of the woods, basking in the sunlight, Hank thought deeply of Clinty's words. There was, he knew, much truth to the comparisons he made and, in future years he couldn't resist placing people in their proper categories in accordance with their animal and feathered counterparts.

Clinty and Hank would sometimes walk across the field to the Neel farm, without doubt the most beautiful in Hamilton County. Howard Neel, Happyland's famous flyer, had set up a makeshift airfield in the pasture. He gave rides and even provided the first commercial flying service in that county when he flew Dr. Guy McCauliff to administer treatment to a patient at Rolf. It was a big thrill to see the old biplanes up close and watch them take off and land.

Happyland was soon to have an air show, as Ray Shiflett's Flying Daredevils were coming to town. The entire family went to watch the performance. Cousin Clinty asked Frank Bossert, the grocer, if he and Hank could watch from the top of his building and, with permission granted, they were soon on the roof.

What a performance it was. For thrills, it topped everything Hank would see thereafter. Clinty said the mock air battle the troop presented was very much like those he had seen in World War I.

Planes of that time were highly maneuverable. With two wings they were a spectacular sight in their close turns, wing-overs, barrel rolls, climbs and dives. Developers of most later planes were to sacrifice maneuverability for speed.

But, the most impressive feat was performed by a member of the troop, Nervy Murphy, believed to have been an American Indian.

While the plane flew very low over the business district buildings, he walked the wings and was all over the plane. Then, in the grand finale, he hung by his knees from the wheel axle of the under carriage as the plane roared only a hundred or so feet above the buildings.

The courage of Nervy Murphy and Ray Shiflett was remarkable; they were absolutely without fear. Ironically Shiflett would not meet his fate in the air, but on the ground. At the Neel farm that same day, Shiflett, while cranking the plane by whirling its propeller, stepped into a chuck hole, fell forward into the whirling blades and was killed—a sad ending for a very brave man.

Now living near town, Hank soon discovered he was within walking distance of the Isis Theater where silent "moving pictures," as they were called in those days, were shown. After a little coaxing, he was usually able to convince Cousin Clinty to take him to the old three-reeler cowboy shows on Saturday afternoons. Cousin Clinty

Tom Mix with his horse Tony (advertisement, Ralston-Purina Company)

Advertisement—courtesy of Ralston-Purina Company

knew all about cowboys and he told Hank he himself had been one until his mother sold the cow.

Talking pictures were yet to be invented and an organ player supplied the accompanying mood music. Hank always persuaded Clinty to sit with him in the front row to read the on-screen sub-line dialogue for him, which disgusted his cousin no end.

Clinty finally told Mother Lucy that Hank insisted on sitting so close to the screen that he was having difficulty deciding if he was at the movie or in it. He jokingly threatened not to take Hank again if Lucy didn't give him some beads or something to take along to trade with the Indians.

Hank's quest to emulate the celluloid cowboys became an uncontrollable obsession that grew with each trip to the weekly movie. Many of the kids who attended did so for entertainment alone, but to Hank his ten cents was a down payment on a continuing course needed for his future occupation.

As summer sped by, the chill could be felt in the early morning air, the once beautiful rows of green corn stalks were maturing and turning yellow, large gardens were being harvested, and beef cattle and hogs were being butchered.

Farmhouses were busy with women canning food for the cold winter months ahead. Often neighboring women would get together—easing the boredom of the task and allowing them to share garden crops, gossip and conversation about interesting events past or to come.

School normally started the day after Labor Day while the county fair was in full swing. On children's day, families made a big to-do about going to the event together. Hank enjoyed the acts most when Happyland's own Black family, billed as the LaTona Troupe, performed on the high trapeze. Their pretty little daughter, Mildred, was in Hank's class at school.

When Happyland aerialists Frank, Bernard, Ruth, and Beatrice Black ascended to the high trapeze, a chill went up the spines of spectators. Unlike most other aerialists, they used no safety net to break accidental falls. Audiences were held spellbound with their death-defying performances.

Then too, all members of the Black family seemed to possess unique flexibility of joints and spine. They performed with unusual agility in acrobatic - contortionist acts, literally tying themselves in knots like human pretzels.

Audiences would gasp as Frank Black stood on a cigar box while accomplishing a reverse back bend, culminating when he touched the box behind him. Herb Black and Frank, his brother, were without doubt two of the greatest contortionists that ever lived. Herb would sometimes pretend he couldn't get untangled and his fellow performers would roll him around the stage. Small wonder he was widely acclaimed as "the human serpent."

The LaTona Troupe, children and all, toured the midwest throughout the summer months performing at celebrations and fairs. The children of the troupe members, when not performing, spent untold hours in rigorous training, designed to perpetuate the act for the enjoyment of generations to come.

Back in Happyland Herb and Bessie Black's children continued their training routine almost daily in the backyard of the Black home on Seneca Street, weather permitting. Francis, Harvey and Richard would become aerialists and Mayabelle, Mildred, Marjorie, and Marion would carry on the acrobatic - contortionist tradition. Mildred and Marjorie occasionally performed as aerialists. Mrs. Black handled the bookings and always kept them busy throughout the summer. Amazingly enough, the LaTona Troupe aerialists in the years to come would continue the dangerous tradition of performing without nets.

No one ever tired of these performers, for they constantly introduced new routines involving clown acrobatics and contortionist acts. They also introduced a "Trick House" routine, and children and adults alike roared with laughter at their hysterical antics.

Black Family performers reunion—1941

Photo courtesy of Daily Freeman Journal

LaTona Troupe (1930s)
Photo courtesy of Mildred Black Pringle

Mildred Black practices on trapeze (1930s).
Photo courtesy of Mildred Black Pringle

Those who weren't talking about the fair were discussing the forthcoming heavyweight boxing title match. September 22, 1926 finally arrived and Mr. Grigg Elkin invited James Arthur and his family over to his farm to listen to the Jack Dempsey-Gene Tunney ten-round fight on the wireless radio.

The fight, which was the first to gross over a million dollars, was held in the outdoor Philadelphia Municipal Stadium. Midway in the fight it started to rain and on a wet mat, Tunney, a younger, more agile and more scientific boxer, outclassed Dempsey by decision to become the new World's Heavyweight Boxing Champion. Hank surmised that Tunney, being in World War I and all, like his Cousin Clinty, just might have taken Clinty's "clobbering course."

Farm people had multi-party telephone service in those days. To reach the party called, the operator would ring one long ring and one short ring, or one long ring and two shorts, etc. One day the phone rang with three longs and a short. Knowing this was their ring, Clinty picked up the phone.

On the calling end a man announced, "This is Willobee. I've lost my job. How do I get out to James Arthur's place?" Clinty had known Willobee from years before and unwillingly gave him directions, concluding with, "You can't miss it; there is a crow sitting on a fence post right by the lane."

Willobee soon could be seen driving up the lane in his touring car. The radiator was steaming, and he was exercising such violent control over the machine that it came to a screeching halt within inches of the gate. Hank was to find out later why Willobee had driven so close to the gate. There were two predominant factors involved: one, he didn't see too well and, two, he wasn't a believer in long walks.

Cousin Clinty quipped, "Well, James Arthur, they say it's an ill wind that blows no good, and the wind must be sicker than hell today to blow a 'no gooder' like Willobee all the way from Des Moines."

When he got out of the car, Willobee grimaced until Hank thought he would surely pop his eyeballs and it looked as if he was trying to stretch getting out from behind the steering wheel into an all day job. As he finally stepped from the running board, it became apparent that he was more than a little portly above the pelvic section.

James Arthur's Cousin Willobee was not a tall man, being about five foot six inches, but he weighed in at about two hundred pounds. His most prominent features were a flowing white beard and a bald head that glistened in the sunlight as he walked up the sidewalk to the porch. The next fascinating aspect was the wide belt he wore low on his hips under his potbelly—this in addition to a pair of extra strong suspenders!

Hank never hesitated to ask Cousin Clinty the "why for" of anything, as he was always reasonably sure he would receive an answer. That night, as they sat on the porch, Hank asked Clinty why Willobee wore the strong suspenders in addition to the belt.

Clinty grinned, brushed some imaginary wood chips from his overalls, then took another whittle with his knife at the willow whistle he was making for Hank. After taking one more whittle, Clinty's answer was forthcoming. He said he had it from a reliable source that Willobee had experienced a trouser tragedy of sorts several years back while waiting on a corner for a street car back in Des Moines.

Seems Willobee had sneezed so violently that the buttons popped off his trousers, and the trousers had dropped to the pavement. Women standing in the line had screamed, drawing the attention of a nearby policeman who damn nigh arrested Willobee for indecent exposure. Concluding the story with a whimsical tongue-in-cheek grin, Clinty went on to say, "From that day forward, Willobee has worn double protection to forestall any further problems with his 'tricky' trousers!"

As the days went by, Willobee's laziness began wearing on the fibers of James Arthur's patience. Both Clinty and Hank were deriving no small amount of pleasure in knowing that the lazy one, who knew no fear except for death and his tricky trousers falling down, was drastically slipping in popularity.

Nothing seemed to encourage Willobee to get his Chevrolet radiator fixed and go up the road, as he had threatened to do many times.

Lucy was so kind she couldn't tell Willobee to leave and her wishes prevailed upon James Arthur.

Hank finally came up with a scheme he felt certain would launch old Willobee into lunacy and out of the house. He then sought out Cousin Clinty to see what he thought of his plan. Cousin Clinty said it sounded like a hot idea and agreed, if properly implemented, the scheme had merit.

Having completed the chores, they proceeded to the house and ate the dinner Lucy had ready and waiting. Hank always enjoyed his Mother's cooking, but he could hardly wait for the meal to be eaten that night.

Dinner completed, each member of the family went about normal activities. James Arthur had to go across the road to see Charles Nelson, the neighbor, and everything seemed to be falling in line, far better than Hank had anticipated.

Cousin Willobee arose from the table and, as usual, made for the best rocking chair with the newspaper. He sat down, adjusted his bifocals, which were thicker than his Chevrolet's windshield, and went about reading the paper, which was the heaviest task he had accomplished all day.

While Clinty and Hank sat on the davenport the one with the weak eyes and tricky trousers read everything on each page of the Daily Freeman Journal, down to and including the crossword puzzle and the delivery address stamped on the cover sheet.

The paper completed, true to form, he slid his glasses up on his forehead, put his feet up on the edge of the chrome ring that circled the center of the pot bellied stove, then leaned well back into the rocker. Hank looked at Cousin Clnty who gave him such an assuring look that his confidence soared.

By now the wiley one was emitting flute-like snores that were disturbing even Jack, the dog. Up until this time, the rabbit chaser had been sleeping blissfully behind the stove with a happy look on his face like he had just cornered fifty of the little carrot eaters inside an orchard fence.

Hank gave old Willobee about ten minutes to get his tuba in tune with the flute he was already playing. Then he launched his orneriness offensive, which was designed to drive Willobee off his rocker.

Hank proceeded to the woodpile and procurred a neat stack of kindling which he had previously chopped from wooden shingles, recently removed from the barn. With stealth and skill Hank sneaked past his Mother, still busy in the kitchen, and was soon back in the dining room. Willobee remained asleep with his feet on the stainless steel stove rim.

Carefully Hank opened the stove door, piled in the dry fast burning kindling and successfully closed the door. Willobee smacked his lips, repositioned himself, but didn't open his eyes. So far—so good!

After placing the wood in the stove, Hank stood on a chair and opened the damper on the stovepipe. He then hastened to resume his place on the davenport beside Cousin Clinty. As they waited for the stove to heat up, Clinty assured Hank he would turn off the damper if any danger of fire existed.

Results were not long in coming; within minutes the sides of the stove were beginning to glow and the heat was extending into the stainless steel rim upon which Willobee was now resting his to-be-toasted "tootsies."

Afraid Willobee's feet would get too hot, Cousin Clinty rocked the chair slightly and Willobee partially awakened. Feeling the heat, he yowled like a coon dog in cockleburs and shot out of the rocker.

Once on his feet, Willobee received the full impact from his hot shoe soles and went into a dancing exhibition no one would have dreamed he was capable of performing. At times he patted the floor with his feet as fast as a trap drummer playing the popular tune, "Hold that Tiger," and the next moment he appeared to be trying to suspend himself in midair in an attempt to keep his feet away from his hot shoe soles.

Cousin Willobee defies gravity.

Cartoon courtesy of Paul Troth

Cousin Clinty told Willobee it was just plain inconceivable because he, himself, had tried for years to originate a new dance step and now with no apparent effort Willobee, in his first attempt, had come up with the all-new "Hot Sole Shuffle," the first dance to combine ballet, tap and the Charleston.

Lucy quickly decided it was well past Hank's bedtime and sent him to his room, knowing full well that peace and tranquility would return to the scene during his sleeping hours.

This newly arrived Cousin was not overly fond of children and, being more than a little mischievious, Hank didn't contribute much to good relations. Willobee's main interest in life was his car, and he spoke incessantly on the subject.

Willobee apprised James Arthur of the fact he was having a mite of a malfunction with his move-about-machine and said as soon as he could earn a few dollars he would get the raderator (radiator) fixed on his Civerolay (Chevrolet) and then he would go down the hard road and find a good job.

James Arthur became less talkative as the fall wore on and began sitting alone evenings as if in deep thought. Lucy, usually a happy person, had quit smiling as frequently and even Clinty appeared to be more serious. Hank would later learn that the nation had suffered its worst major stock market crash since World War I, and farm prices had declined drastically.

President Coolidge continued his support of big business, reducing taxes for corporations and those in higher income brackets. Not unlike the 1980s, billions of dollars were spent making loans to other countries to pay for American goods exported to them.

Labor unrest had begun to ferment in the east. Low wages and sweat shop conditions had caused an upsurge in union activities. Pennsylvania coal mine workers, who labored under terribly unhealthful, dangerous conditions, finally had won some concessions from owners and in 1926 ended a strike that had started in 1924.

Textile workers, many of them foreigners who could not speak English, had been exploited for years by shops and mills. They became fed up with conditions and walked out of two botany mills in New Jersey. Strikers became so violent police had to use tear gas bombs and fire hoses on them.

Mergers and consolidations became very acceptable. The biggest combinations occurred in public utilities and before Coolidge left office, nearly two thirds of all electricity produced in the United States was controlled by six corporations—a comparable situation, it would appear, to ownership of natural gas interests today, though not quite so extensive.

The Chicago Board of Trade controlled the world's largest grain market and even today its traders hold the farmers' fate in the palms of their hands. It was and still is not in the farm fields that the farmers' future is decided; it is in the Board of Trade where the trader reaps the preponderance of the rewards for the grains harvested.

Henry Ford's ingenuity in mass production had spilled over to other industries and commodities, such as fine clothing and radios, became more accessible to the average worker. With prosperity, more credit was given to consumers and installment purchasing had become widespread.

At the national level personal gain, much as in the 1980s, was proving too strong a temptation for those with big industrial, commercial and political interests to resist. President Calvin Coolidge was so strongly behind big business that he continued to shun the interests of the farmer.

With the farmers' purchasing power dwindling, business in small towns spiraled downward. Eventually the highly industrialized east and larger cities throughout the nation would feel the pinch. The seeds were being sown for the "Great Depression."

Farmers were and are very independent people, with most farms still primarily owner-operated by families. They would help each other during haying and threshing seasons, but shied away from membership in any major organization designed to bring them the lobbying capability needed to sway legislative votes in matters of vital importance to agriculture.

Lacking cohesiveness, the farmers' voices were heard only as individuals, and thus they created very little impact on legislation. Yes, an attempt at organization had come about when the "National Association of Corn Growers" was formed, but few farmers joined and it lacked the all encompassing strength and lobbying necessary to gain legislative attention.

A prominent Happyland man, C. H. Richeson, was elected president of the National Association and had visited Washington, D.C. in 1926 to confer with President Coolidge and leaders in Congress about farm problems. Richeson pointed out to the President that never in the history of the nation had land values slipped down so rapidly as in the past five years, despite the prosperity in the country as a whole. (Does this remind the reader of the United States during the 1980s?)

Although Mr. Richeson made a marvelous presentation and impressed President Coolidge with his fine grasp of the situation, it became obvious the President and legislators were unconcerned since nothing appreciable was done to improve the farmers' lot. James Arthur said Mr. Richeson might as well have directed his appeal to

Willie Sipmore, the town's undisputed booze-guzzling champion. At least old Willie, he quipped, could have influenced the demand by upping his daily consumption of corn squeezings.

The year of 1926 would stand out in the memory of all Happyland residents. During the fall bank after bank throughout the midwest closed its doors. Rumors concerning the possible insolvency of local banks had been running rampant for several weeks, and a steady stream of depositors waited in line to withdraw their money. Bankers advised people not to take their money out or the banks would fail. James Arthur unfortunately was one who did not remove his deposits.

Happyland residents were appalled when on December 1, 1926 the Hamilton County State Bank failed to open due to heavy withdrawals. On December 2nd the First National Bank closed its doors for the same reason. The First National Bank would reopen in 1927, but the Hamilton County State Bank would remain closed.

Christmas of 1926 was not nearly so joyful a season as it had been in the past. Gifts were not quite as plentiful. However, the entire family was home and the adults at least made a pretext of being reasonably happy.

As if everyone in the area hadn't suffered enough from the bank closures, on January 13, 1927 a terrible fire struck the Happyland business district. It destroyed four business buildings and the Isis Theater, which caused near panic for Hank and other kids, as their cowboy shows were cancelled. However, even during the fire the old Isis Theater continued to provide thrills—not make believe, but the real thing.

Hank was spending the night with his friend, Marvin Baxter, and Marvin's mother took them down to the fire. Hank's brother, Bill, and Marvin's father, Vern, were on the roof fighting the fire. Little did they realize how dangerous it had become to the firefighters. Later they were to learn that Vern Baxter, an electrician with the municipal electric line department and a courageous volunteer fireman, had proceeded across the roof with a hose when weakened roof timbers gave way.

As Vern dropped through the hole in the roof, he instinctively spread his arms to break his fall. He could feel the flames below licking at his rubber boots and rubberized trousers. In no time at all he felt hot rubber heating up in his boot liners; death he knew was only minutes away if he wasn't rescued soon. Hot, black smoke emitting from the hole was engulfing him and searing his lungs.

Nearby Hank's brother, Bill, and Ted Christeson, also a volunteer fireman, heard Vern's shouts and hastened to his aid. Vern attempted to pull himself up, but as he tried to do so he felt the boards under his elbows loosen. If more of the roof structure were to give way, he knew he would drop to his death in the blazing inferno below.

Ted and Bill, carefully crawling on their stomachs, worked their way to either side of Vern and were able to grab the nearly unconscious man under his arms and pull him from his date with death.

Dragging Vern to safety, they quickly removed his fire boots, wrapped him in a blanket and helped him down the ladder. Although he suffered a few burns from drips from the rubberized boots and trousers, his worst problem was smoke inhalation. However, with a little rest he was soon back on the job.

In the weeks to come, James Arthur and Clinty worked harder, and Big Brother and Hank pitched in to the best of their ability. There was no more burning of coal; instead huge stacks of wood provided heating fuel. There were very few store-purchased groceries, and Lucy's garden provided most of the food needed to subsist.

Everyone in the family was thankful that James Arthur had purchased and paid for a radio, for this was the primary source of entertainment. Clinty, whose morale couldn't be kept down for long, was soon laughing, joking and telling stories in an attempt to raise the spirits of everyone around him.

While Al Capone was masterminding his gangs in Chicago, Happyland was having its very own crime wave. The town was having a mite of a problem with bootlegging and nearly every week some ne'er-do-well was picked up by the long arm of the law for the sale of alcohol, moonshine or homebrew and ended up in the county "slammer."

Throughout the entire prohibition period, Hamilton County professed dryness, but for each person arrested for drinking alcoholic beverages, there were scores who could have been. Happyland police could no more enforce the prohibition law than those in major cities. The town had its fair share of people who liked to nip at the nectar. However, if a Hall of Fame for Alcoholic Imbibers is ever created in Happyland, Willie Sipmore's elbow-worn jacket will undoubtedly occupy a prominent place in a glass encasement.

Willie was nearly six feet of compressed muscle, having done an inordinate share of hand-spading drainage ditches in Hamilton County. Even when consuming illicit beverages, old Sipmore was always an affable person. He was handsome in a chisled-feature sort of way and possessed a broad smile radiating from beneath a shock of prematurely greying hair.

However good natured, Willie did have a tolerance point and when pressed far enough by the pugilistically inclined, he was known to engage in a bit of fisticuffs. Many was the tormentor who, carrying heckling a bit too far, ended up being sent to dreamland via one of Sipmore's hamhock like fists.

So it was that, lovable as he was, Willie Sipmore on rare occasions was arraigned before Justice of the Peace Louis Cantonwine and sent to the old county jail for a bit of repose after clobbering someone in the nose. During one of Sipmore's short stints in the county lockup, a human interest adventure of sorts occurred.

George Drake, who was at the time employed in the county engineer's office and later became deputy sheriff, still enjoys telling the story he dubs "Boozenick's Folly." Only the names of the persons involved have been changed, George quips, "to protect the innocent!"

Throughout the prohibition years, druggists continued to stock alcohol as disinfectants and for medicinal purposes. It wasn't uncommon for some drugstore's legal stock to end up in the stomachs of illegal imbibers. One enterprising druggist, Henry Boozenick, engaged in this extra activity in Happyland.

Short of legal supplies and as an expedient, Mr. Boozenick occasionally resorted to replenishing store stock from illegitimate sources. Somehow the city and county preservers of peace got wind of an incoming shipment of unauthorized alcohol.

With the drugstore staked out, the lawmen waited and, sure enough, shortly after midnight a truck arrived at the alley entrance to Boozenick's drugstore. Two men dismounted from the truck; Boozenick opened the door and, as they prepared to tilt-roll a fifty-five gallon drum through it, the local lawmen descended with raised revolvers. They proceeded to take old Boozenick and the two men to the city jail where they were booked for illegal possession and bootlegging. Of course, all met bond and were quickly released.

Storage of the alcohol posed no small problem, for it was too large a container for the one-room, two-cell city jail; the sheriff's office was too small, and open storage at the courthouse was out of question for such a highly prized quantity of lunacy liquid. Someone finally came up with the brilliant suggestion of storing the drum in the second story of the county jail. The second story hadn't been used since several prisoners playfully lifted up one corner of the rotting roof while some stalwart citizens were walking by.

While the lawmen struggled up the stairs with the heavy drum, Willie Sipmore and two other inmates, one a small-time burglar from Fort Dodge and the other a local bootlegger, looked on with no small amount of curiosity. Willie asked if he could give them a hand, but they adamantly declined his offer. The prisoners doubted the barrel contained oil, gasoline or kerosene, and, in light of the secrecy of the lawmen, they reasoned it must be evidence of some sort. In muffled voices they all blurted out in unison, "Booze!"

With the task completed, the lawmen closed the upstairs door, locked it and departed. Curiosity was killing the trio. At last the burglar confided he was certain he could open the lock and soon had it picked. The bootlegger hurriedly obtained a tin cup from the jail kitchen; they tipped the barrel and removed a sample.

The bootlegger sniffed the cup's contents, but of course Willie was called upon to administer the expert taste test. Willie took a gulp and his eyeballs almost rotated in opposite directions. He gasped and was speechless for a few seconds while his cohorts anxiously awaited his verdict. At last he wiped his lips, leaned back, popped his tongue, grinned and proclaimed, "Alcohol—damn good stuff; let the festivities begin!"

"Now to hide the stuff," Willie commented. Willie, a quick thinker, hurried to the kitchen, grabbed a gallon pickle jar, emptied its liquid contents and substituted alcohol. Willie said later it kinda softened the alcohol and gave it a nifty tang. In short time the three were getting slightly pickled on pickle cocktails.

George Drake said no one suspected the trio had been into the barrel as the second story was always found to be locked. However, it wasn't unusual that someone would slip a pint of booze through the bars from outside the jail. It was obvious that morale had reached a high point for incarcerated residents, since no one seemed concerned or posed questions about when they would be released.

Of course fifty-five gallons is a heap of alcohol—far more than the trio could drink during their stint in jail. All things being as they were, the bootlegger's mind naturally evolved around plying his old trade—no need to get rusty, you know!

There was no fence around the jail at that time, so it wasn't long before the prisoners were calling friends over to the window and offering to sell them alcohol at bargain basement prices on a "bring your own empty bottle" basis. Business flourished and time passed rapidly as they listened to ball games on the radio during the afternoon and partied at night.

The trio had been out of jail for some time when the druggist's trial came up on the court docket. While the accused was ushered into the courtroom, lawmen were sent to pick up the evidence. Having lifted the drum earlier, they were fully aware it would tax their strength. They hoisted it up with such force they damn near threw their vertabras out of place and the drum through the roof.

Examining the drum, the lawmen found it empty, and even the fumes had mostly evaporated from the open bung. Sadly the lawmen rendered their report to the judge. Mr. Boozenick and his attorney grinned from ear to ear when the judge dismissed the case for lack of evidence. Another amusing episode in the history of the old jail had been relegated to history.

Anecdotes surrounding the old county jail could fill a book. Affable George Drake, who worked in the county engineer's office for many years prior to becoming a deputy sheriff, remembers the old county jail with a fondness normally reserved for an old friend.

Vernon K. "Bud" Brandt and the author sat reminiscing with George about the hilarious happenings at the old jail. Bud had succeeded George as deputy sheriff under E. R. "Rap" Lear after World War II when George stepped down from the job.

Brandt twiddled his fingers a bit, smiled and suggested to George, "Tell him about the haircut incident!" George howled with laughter, slapped his leg and shouted, "Yeh, that was a good one!"

Continuing, George recalled that Sheriff Blair came to the county engineer's office near noon one Saturday morning and asked him to accompany George Hurst, who did some barbering on the side, to the jail while he clipped an inmate's hair. They proceeded to the jail. Once the two Georges were inside, the sheriff, as was the practice, locked the jail door and returned to his office.

Seems an urgent call came in from a farmer near Kamrar demanding the sheriff's presence immediately. Sheriff Blair strapped on his revolver, dashed out the door and was soon motoring south. In his haste, he completely forgot the two Georges still in the jail.

Heavily engrossed in solving a crime, the sheriff gave little thought to the jail. No problem, he had delivered groceries to the prisoners that morning and they had their own kitchen to prepare meals. There was no need to worry about fires either. If one should occur, it would be no problem pulling the bars out of the windows with the fire truck. On one past occasion, a farm lad had hooked a log chain to a window bar and pulled out a corner of the jail to free his brother.

Meanwhile, the court house closed at noon and employees went home. When Hurst finished cutting the prisoner's hair, there was no immediate concern that the sheriff would not return, but by one o'clock the situation, as George Drake allowed, was becoming a mite serious.

By mid-afternoon, the two wrongly incarcerated citizens were getting desperate. They made futile efforts to gain the attention of passersby using the cut-across sidewalk through a small park to the rear of the jail. Thinking back, George laughingly relates how they shouted such phrases as, "We're locked up by mistake—go call the sheriff and tell him to get us out of here!" Their pleas for help only drew snickers and grins. At last, throats sore and lungs exhausted, they sat down and played checkers with the prisoners to pass the time.

Arriving home late for his dinner, Sheriff Blair was greeted by his wife. She informed him the chief of police had been calling all afternoon. The sheriff quickly gave the chief a call. The chief advised him he had a drunk for the jail and since the two city cells were occupied, he needed to transfer one of his prisoners to the county jail. The word "jail" struck the sheriff's mind like a bolt of lightning and he blurted out loud, "Oh, my God, the two Georges are still in jail; I'll call you back!"

The two Georges had already shared the prisoners' cooking by the time Sheriff Blair arrived, but as George Drake says, "The experience provided me an interesting story to tell all my life about how I did time in the old county jail!"

Then too, one had to give the local bootleggers credit; they were an ingenious lot. Roads between towns were yet to be paved; muddy roads during the thaws and rain-seasons were virtually impassable and long trips by wagons and buggies were extremely slow. The railroads provided a far less time-consuming mode of transportation. Farmers leaned heavily on earnings from cream and eggs to augment crop income, and timely shipment to avert spoilage was imperative.

Rail passengers were subjected to frequent stops, even at the smallest of towns, to pick up riders, as well as drop shipments of

Trains picked up cream and eggs (Herschel Flugstad, boy far right; Ole Flugstad, third from right).

Photo courtesy of Herschel Flugstad

mail, parcels and even cream, milk, eggs, and, occasionally, a crate of chickens. Thus, a slow train for many years was called a "milk run."

Old-timers tell the story of how each morning John Clabaugh trudged with a large hand cart to the Chicago and Northwestern Inter-urban and Cripple Creek Railroad depots to pick up drop shipments of produce. With produce loaded he pulled his load down the brick main street to the produce station on Seneca Street, often waving to policemen Jack Ziegler, Jim Silvers, and Dick Carpenter sitting on the bench in front of city hall, as he trudged on down the street.

One day as he wheeled the cart, he noticed a lid to a cream can ajar. Clabaugh stopped, removed the lid to reposition it and, in doing so, glanced inside. The can's contents provided proof positive that bootleggers, as a whole, were indeed an ingenious lot for the cream can contained alcohol.

Clabaugh wiped mythical sweat drippings from his brow, not knowing how long he had been hauling contraband under the very noses of the local law enforcers. In later years he could laugh about the experience, but at the moment he, as a law-abiding citizen, was terrified. Needless to say, that was Clabaugh's last milk run! He decided he'd rather be on the right side, and nearer to the law. He started a candy and cigar stand at the court house and doubled as the custodian for the rest of his working years.

Then too, a few of the boys liked to gamble with the cash exchange cubes (dice) and, lo and behold, the police raided a house on February 7, 1927. Wouldn't you know the lawmen caught a big city slicker, George "Sonny" McIntyre, from Fort Dodge running a dastardly crap game (heaven forbid) for eleven of the localites? All this lawlessness right smack dab in the middle of Happyland on Main Street.

The professor of the fine art of shaking the galloping dominos was fined $300 for his crime. This event gave the people something big enough to provide gossiping material if nothing else happened for a month.

It seemed inevitable that sooner or later someone would succeed in flying non-stop across the Atlantic Ocean. There had been three attempts. In 1926 a French pilot, Rene Fonck, crashed in New York in a gasoline loaded plane before leaving the ground. Then on April 26, 1927 two Americans, Noel Davis and Stanton Wooster, were killed when their overloaded plane crashed during a New York test flight. Next, May 8, 1927 two Frenchmen, Charles Nungesser and Francois Coli, took off from Paris and vanished over the North Atlantic.

Two top-notch flyers, Clarence Chamberlin, and a young lad from Little Falls, Minnesota, Charles A. Lindbergh, were among those now working neck and neck to become the first.

Lindbergh had logged a lot of flying hours as a barnstormer doing stunts, walking plane wings and taking up passengers. He then had become one of the nation's first airmail pilots, flying between Chicago and St. Louis.

The daring young pilot wanted desperately to try for the $25,000 prize being offered by Raymond Orteig, a wealthy French hotel owner, for the first non-stop flight across the Atlantic. With the backing of some St. Louis businessmen, Lindbergh bought a Ryan monoplane, named it the "Spirit of St. Louis" and made a record-setting flight across the United States.

In his Spirit of St. Louis Lindbergh took off from New York City May 20, 1927 and earned the love and admiration of the world when he landed at Orley Field near Paris, France May 21, 1927, after thirty three and one-half hours in the air. His spectacular flight did much to raise the morale of midwest people momentarily, for they all considered him one of their own.

There were more thrills when it was announced that Lindbergh would be in Mason City August 28, 1927 at the dedication of the new American Legion-Chamber of Commerce Airfield. A few Happyland people journeyed to the event to see Lindbergh, as well as a big blimp and a flying demonstration by the Army Air Corps flyers from Selfridge Field, Michigan.

Charles Lindbergh was the first to fly the Atlantic and he rightfully was due the laurels. However, Clarence Chamberlin and

Above: U.S. Army dirigible at Mason City during Lindbergh visit.
Right: Charles Lindbergh arrives at Mason City Airport shortly after Atlantic flight.

Photos courtesy of Mason City Public Library Historical Collection

U.S. Army planes at Mason City Airport day of Lindbergh visit.
Photo courtesy of Mason City Public Library Historical Collection

Floyd Barlow, Clear Lake, Iowa made first flight in Cerro Gordo County Iowa. He built the plane.
Photo courtesy of Mason City Public Library Historical Collection

Charles Levine would soon accomplish the feat flying from New York to Germany. Loss of time in preparation for the flight had denied them the honors of being the first to fly the ocean. Other flights were then made from California to Hawaii, from there on to Fiji Islands, then to Sydney, Australia.

By that time the Associated Press was pretty well keeping people informed of national and world events. However, in small rural communities local newsworthy items were best obtained at the barber shop, blacksmith shops, beauty parlors, and pool halls or by listening in on telephone party lines!

The cylindrical peppermint stick-striped barber pole was still displayed by all barbershops. Originally the pole had been used to advertise that the tonsorial parlor (as barbershops were called years ago) did bleedings, which for some reason were thought to be beneficial to people's health. Or perhaps to some the purpose was to lower the blood supplies to ward off vampires.

Although barbershop quartet singing had steadily declined after the turn of the century, occasionally a trio or other group would break into harmonizing. Customers still gathered more local news in barbershops than was ever published in the newspaper. Waiting chairs in a long line were always full. If a chair wasn't needed for a waiting customer, it was occupied by someone waiting to swap yarns or tell anecdotes involving practical jokes.

Harry Maxon's Barbershop had the most chairs and naturally yarn-swapping was always best there. Another favorite hangout for old-timers who wanted to spend the day was Shorty Hanson's Blacksmith Shop. In settings of this type MacKinlay Kantor, Happyland's Pulitzer Prize winning author, gathered much material for his books listening to the old Civil War veterans tell hair-raising stories of their adventures.

Swapping yarns and playing practical jokes were probably the most popular forms of entertainment during Iowa's early years. The laugh-provoking prank was rarely, if ever, used to harm someone; rather it was designed only to evoke laughter and brighten what otherwise could have been just another dull day. The one who had been the butt of a good practical joke was often the most frequent teller of the story at yarn-swapping sessions.

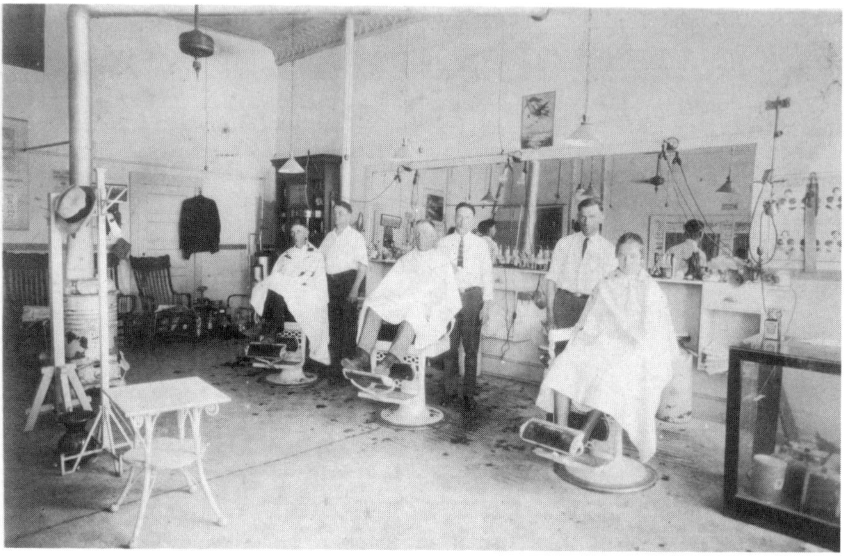

Harry Maxon's Barber Shop—best yarn-spinning place in Happyland (Harry Maxon at front chair).

Photo courtesy of Warren Maxon and sister Helen

One of Harry Maxon's favorite stories involved James Arthur and Clinty. Seems they were visiting with "Shorty" Sinn in his candy-pop store located in a small frame building a few doors away from Harry's Barbershop. As the mischievous trio enjoyed a bottle of soda pop, they came up with a brilliant practical joke to pull on Harry.

James Arthur proceeded to Ralph Tucker's Jewelry and Watch Repair Shop, explained the prank and enlisted Ralph's help in getting Harry out of the shop for a few minutes, which would allow time for them to set the stage. It was mid-afternoon and Ralph, doing his part, dropped by Harry's shop and insisted he accompany him to Steve Dermand's new cafe that had opened in May, 1927 for a cup of coffee. Since no one was in his chair, Harry consented to go with Ralph.

Harry always parked his car in front of his shop and while he was out for coffee, Clinty and James Arthur deftly sneaked up with two jacks and placed them close to the inside of both rear wheels of Harry's Model T Ford, then jacked up the car until the tires were barely out of contact with the street. With the old high pressure tires

Steve Dermand's Cafe—1927

Photo courtesy of Gus Dermand

used then, it was extremely difficult with the naked eye to see that the tires were not touching the brick street.

Returning to the barbershop, Harry finished the day, then headed to the Model T for a pleasurable drive home. After shifting into gear, he applied pressure to the gas peddle and waited for his dependable machine to respond. The car roared, vibrated and shook, but remained stationary. Harry dismounted and walked around the car. He said later, "Everything looked all right, but the damn thing just wouldn't move."

After trying repeatedly to start the car and knowing all the garages were closed for the day, Harry finally gave up and walked to his home on West Second Street, admittedly carrying on a conversation with himself all the way about clutches, wheels and cars in general.

Harry learned later that moments after he departed James Arthur and Clinty had dashed out and removed the jacks, departing for home wretching with laughter, looking forward to telling Harry about their prank the following day. Harry never told the story but what he added, "Hell, they missed the best part!"

The next morning Harry had hurriedly walked downtown and proceeded to Fred Kayser's Ford Garage, less than a block east of his barbershop. After he explained his problem, Fred sent his son, Lawrence, to fetch a mechanic. The vehicle fixer then grabbed his toolbox and followed Harry back to his Model T.

Upon their arrival the mechanic told Harry, "Start 'er up and we'll see what she'll do." Harry started the car, placed it in gear and revved up the engine, then floored the gas peddle, expecting the cantankerous thing to vibrate and shake as it had the previous afternoon.

To Harry's complete surprise the car lurched forward; the mechanic leaped out of the path and the vehicle careened to the left, barely missing another car to the front. In all the excitement Harry said he had forgotten to take his foot off the gas peddle and damn nigh drove into the First National Bank building on the far side of the street. Jesse Mason was just opening up Mason's Hardware Store next to the bank. Jesse told Harry later that when he saw him bolt across the street with his car, he figured he must have cut an awful lot of hair the day before—being so anxious to get to the bank with his money.

Of course, sports was one of the prime topics of conversation in the barbershops and interest in boxing had reached a new fevered pitch. Boxing heretofore had been considered a sport of the rowdies and looked down upon as barbaric by many people. Gene Tunney, with his smooth boxing style, had brought a bit of science and finesse to the fight game, making it a little more palatable for those wanting to see something other than a bloody brawl.

The night of September 22, 1927 Jack Dempsey, seeking to regain his title from Tunney, crawled into the ring at Soldiers Field in Chicago in front of 105,000 spectators, the largest crowd ever to assemble for a boxing match. The younger Tunney was the odds end favorite. Now many Americans, who had considered Dempsey a brawler, ironically came out in favor of him because he was considered the underdog.

Listening to the fight direct from Soldiers Field on the radio was tremendously thrilling. The roar of the crowd rose and faded because reception was not all that good. By then too many radio stations were in operation and one minute you were getting the fight and the next music. The two fighters were introduced and soon the fight was on.

Dempsey was not doing so well until one of his crashing blows brought Tunney to the canvas during the seventh round. Dempsey failed to go to a neutral corner and the referee adamantly refused to start the count.

Some argue that from the time Tunney was down on the canvas until the referee had reached the count of nine, fourteen seconds had elapsed. Thus the long count became boxing legend. Tunney with his youthful strength went on to win the fight on points. The great Dempsey was never to regain his championship.

On the day of the Dempsey-Tunney fight the mighty Babe Ruth hit his 56th home run of the season. September 27th Ruth hit one home run and the following day hit two more to tie his record of fifty nine. In the last game against the Washington Senators he poled his record-breaking 60th home run. Lou Gehrig was the first to congratulate Ruth. Gehrig had batted .378 that season, hit forty-seven home runs and driven in a record 155 runs. Gehrig was voted the most valuable player of the year, and the great Ruth was happy for his younger teammate and congratulated him.

The day of December 7, 1927 was to be a big one for Hank. His second grade teacher had decided her class should present a play. They had been practicing fifteen minutes a day for quite some time for the big event.

Students were asked to use their ingenuity on creating the visual and sound effects. There were no cowboy parts, and Hank knew from the start he would not get a starring role. However, he had hoped to be chosen as an extra. The skit was a drama about a little girl lost in the woods. Jane Willson, being one of the cutest girls in the class, got the starring role.

It was supposed to be a moonlit night and Ralph Burton, the tallest kid in the class, was chosen to stand on a chair and hold up a piece of round gold cardboard to simulate a moon. Then, to be lost in the woods one has to have trees and all the others in the class stood around with their arms held out like branches, while the teacher selected the tree cast.

As everyone knows, to have a really spooky night, you have to have an owl. Bill Vance outhooted the balance of the second grade and naturally he got that part. Bill Powers did a fair to middlin' job of making a noise like a squeaky branch and soon captured that role. On a scary night, the wind must be whistling through the trees. Marvin Baxter's father was an electrician and he rigged up a fan with tinfoil streamers to simulate the wind and, with several boys whistling, the sound effects were quite realistic.

Then came the thunder part and after a couple of practice sessions on Mother Lucy's washtubs, Hank finally convinced the teacher to let him play that part. Of course, no one could compete with Clare Powers for the lightning effects. Mr. Francis Powers, Clare and Bill's dad, owned a hardware store and Clare brought two five cell flashlights to school. He gave a brilliant performance playing the light up and down the gold crepe paper that was hung from the ceiling.

By the end of the first week of Hank's practice at home on the tubs, he had about driven Clinty up the wall. Clinty told Lucy he was about to call Hank's teacher and ask her why in the hell she couldn't have a play about a snowstorm and get away from all the damn racket.

On the day of the play the second grade class, oblivious to the weather outside, was conducting the big production. Hank was inside a wall locker ready to beat on the door to simulate thunder when the play was halted abruptly. Superintendent John Smith had sent out a message announcing school was being dismissed immediately as an extremely intense snowstorm was moving in.

In those days there were no school buses to transport students. Not everyone had radios or telephones, and, of course, the smaller towns did not have broadcasting stations. Weather reporting was not as sophisticated as it is today and parents had no way of knowing how terrible the storm would be, or even that students were being dismissed early.

Hank started homeward, having little or no concern for the heavy snowfall. As he approached the old Catholic Mercy Hospital on the southwest corner of Des Moines and Ohio Streets, there were no longer buildings to break the wind. Wind velocity increased and at times there appeared to be a wall of snow, virtually solid, blowing almost horizontal to the ground.

Hank stopped occasionally, crouching low and turning away from the wind to catch his breath. By the time he ascended the hill on the far side of Brewer Creek, he was on flat ground and the full impact of the storm was coming straight toward him. It then became a struggle just to stay on his feet.

Ditches were full of snow and only a few times, when the wind subsided, could he catch momentary glimpses of the electric and telephone poles, assuring him he was still on the road.

As he reached the halfway point between the Harold Entriken and George Groves farms, Hank's eyelids were covered with ice, his overshoes filled with snow, his body numb from cold, and he was completely exhausted from stepping through the huge drifts. Dropping to his knees, he laid down thinking he would go on as soon as he was rested.

Mrs. Vern Baxter, concerned about Hank, called his Mother to inform her that her own son, Marvin, was home and that school had been dismissed. After receiving the call, Mother Lucy immediately located Cousin Clinty, and he hurried up the road to meet Hank.

How long Hank lay there is unknown, but he awakened to feel his dog, Jack, nuzzling his neck with his nose. Soon Cousin Clinty was at his side. Hank's face was raw and covered with ice, and the snow had nearly covered his body.

Clinty picked him up, opened the buttons on his sheepskin coat and held him close to his body as he carried him the remaining distance home. When they entered the house, Hank's Mother Lucy was in tears. She carried Hank to the stove, put his feet in snow, a remedy used often in those days, and changed his clothing. After a short while his feet stopped burning and he quit shivering.

In the course of the conversation Mother Lucy informed Hank that his Father was having difficulty convincing the dog to bring the cattle and horses into the barn. Hank, knowing Jack normally would do anything in his power for him, arose, put on his coat and overshoes and went out with Clinty to see if he could help.

Proceeding to the edge of the barn several times with Jack, Hank told him to "fetch." The dog soon reacted and was off through the blinding blizzard, traveling less than ten feet before disappearing from sight.

Then came the long torturous wait. Almost an hour elapsed before the first cow loomed into sight and walked slowly into the barn. In the next few minutes they were all to follow, one by one. Jack had been forced to chew on their legs until they bled to keep them moving, but he had brought them all to the barn.

Another thirty minutes or so elapsed before he had brought all of the horses in safely. Jack was a black dog with tan markings, but he was now completely white, except for his bloody paws which were built up with ice. It was plainly visible that each step he took was painful. The courageous animal must have been moving from instinct and smell as his eyes were virtually closed from frozen ice.

James Arthur picked up the dog, his face reflecting true love for the brave animal as he carried him to the house. Holding the shivering dog in his arms with tears streaming down his cheeks, he repeated over and over again, "He saved all of them! We would have been ruined without him!"

Hank was too young to realize just how important the livestock was. The economy for the farmer had been steadily worsening and James Arthur, like many, was feeling the terrible financial strain.

Loss of human and stock life that day was horrible for many, and the family felt fortunate indeed that all members were safe and the livestock had been spared. Memories of that horrendous blizzard would be etched forever in the minds of those who experienced it.

The Ben Goehring family, farming four miles north of Happyland, suffered the tragic loss of their daughter, twelve year old Juanita, who froze to death attempting to walk home from a stalled car.

In addition to the terrible blizzard, the years of 1926-1927 had produced some great historical events with giant strides taken in radio, aviation, automobiles, movies, and sports. Most notable of course, was Charles A. Lindbergh's non-stop flight across the Atlantic.

So many new radio stations had been established that broadcasts were beginning to overlap frequencies, and the government had to step in and establish controls in 1927. Rudolph Valentino, the "Great

Lover" idolized by millions of female fans of the silent movies, died in 1927. Over 100,000 people lined up at the funeral parlor to view the body. Around one hundred people, primarily women, were injured in the confusion.

Warner Brothers produced the first movie with sound, a "talking picture," in 1927. Al Jolson was the star of "The Jazz Singer" in which his voice was heard singing three songs. A new era in movie production had been introduced and the American public loved it.

On the world scene Adolf Hitler's book, "Mein Kampf" (My Struggle), written while he was in prison for his radical efforts to overthrow Germany's government, had been published. Hitler used economic problems brought on by the Versailles Treaty to stir the wrath of the German people against the Jews.

Hitler's book was being used as documentary proof that the Jews were behind many of Germany's problems. He professed, "I am now convinced that I am acting as the agent of our creator by fighting off the Jews; I am doing the Lord's work." First he would liberate Russia from Jewish influence, then tend to France. On Christmas of 1926 he blasted the Jews saying, "Christ was the greatest early fighter in the battle against the world enemy, the Jews."

After the conclusion of World War I, November 11, 1918, the Germans had been forced to sign the Treaty of Versailles with both sides knowing full well the terms spelled economic suicide for Germany.

Although the Deutschlanders had established the required democracy after World War I, the Treaty of Versailles contributed little or nothing toward its survival. The world would soon know that a country with a sick economy was ripe for dictatorship.

Benito Mussolini was well entrenched in the Italian government; Joseph Stalin had succeeded in having Leon Trotsky expelled from the Russian Communist Party in 1926 and Hirohito had succeeded his father as Emperor of Japan. All were events that would contribute much to alter radically the lives of the young children of that era.

On the local scene James Arthur didn't have to worry about his money: the closed bank had assured him it would take that worry off his hands.

Cousin Willobee had discovered he wanted no part of show business if it meant doing the "Hot Sole Shuffle"— and the Isis Theater, destroyed in the huge business district fire, was being remodeled, and bigger and better cowboy talking pictures were in the mill.

V
BOOM AND BUST

Across the nation 1928 was ushered in with much frivolity. In Happyland the fire whistle was activated at midnight. Several explosions could be heard, even from nearby farms. James Arthur said it was young people exploding fire crackers left over from Fourth of July, but Clinty maintained the noise was a result of friends uncapping homebrew to which Willie Sipmore had added too much yeast. Let the good times roll!!

On the world scene the depression had struck in European industrialized nations from Scandinavia south to Italy. Most of the U.S. economy remained prosperous and, enticed by the opportunity for a better life, thousands upon thousands of additional Europeans had migrated to the United States during the years 1920 to 1927.

Many, who hoped to engage in agriculture, arrived in the midwest only to find the fabled pot of gold no more than a pot under the bed. But somehow, with the help of required immigration sponsors, they did find a window from which to throw the pot.

Back in those days ethnic groups were allowed to live among themselves if they desired; that was long before civil rights legislation dictated racially mixed neighborhoods. The immigrants pretty well went to like ethnic communities in both urban and rural America since this made overcoming the language barrier and finding work far less difficult.

Most of the immigrants were hard workers and eventually did well in their adopted country. Many possessed valuable skills, but some were unable to find work in their areas of endeavor. Unlike the Hispanics of the late 1900s, the old-time immigrants did not complain about language barriers. They simply applied themselves and, for the cohesiveness and solidarity of the United States, they learned English.

Many learned their new language by participating with their children who were in school. When the children studied their reading and spelling homework, the parents took advantage of the situation and studied along with them. In essence the child was teaching the parent.

Immigrants had many barriers to overcome in the United States, even in small ethnic communities. Oh yes, they could always find someone who spoke their own native tongue, but that sometimes contributed to difficulties in mastering the English language.

Today there are incidents of record wherein Hispanics have filed suit against cities because a police dispatcher couldn't understand an emergency call in Spanish. Sounds ridiculous when one questions how many dispatchers are bilingual in their country of origin.

Norwegians had settled in Stanhope, Lehigh and Story City. Kamrar had a predominant Holland-Dutch, German populace; Stratford and Boxholm were havens for Swedish immigrants and Woolstock had a goodly number of French families. Earlier arrivals spoke a mixture of their country's language and English, which came to be dubbed "Pidgin English," understandable only to those in the locale who spoke the foreign language and had been in the states for sometime.

There were serious problems with these language barriers, but, then too, there were humorous happenings. Let's take the example of Nels Hanson, who immigrated with his family from Sweden in 1927. When Nels moved to the Stratford community he knew but one English word, that being banana. Now banana is a good word, but as Nels later recalled, "It was so damn seldom I got to use it!"

Like many other immigrants, Nels worked hard and in a couple of years, in addition to grain farming, he had accumulated a sizable herd of hogs and pigs. His hogs matured well, were a picture of health and their coats glowed from the feed formula he had concocted. All this was long before the advent of "Wayne's Pigtail Curler" and other highly nutritious foods.

Nels was feeding his healthy swine in a barn on the "Big Andrew Johnson" farm in the community of Swede Bend when a non-Swedish speaking neighbor came by to make his acquaintance. Observing the healthy animals, the neighbor managed through gestures to convey to Nels that he was asking what he was feeding the hogs.

Nels had progressed far beyond his first word "banana," and summoned his best efforts in Swedish and English to explain that he had yeast in a barrel along with ground corn, oats and milk, which he let ferment.

Not knowing the word yeast (yast in Swedish) Nels tried to come up with the American version of fermenting (jasar in Swedish). However, in Nels's Pidgin English mixture, the word came out something like "jayses."

Nels, of course, noted the perplexed look on the face of his new acquaintance. In later years he recalled the neighbor sort of grinned, tipped back his straw hat, shook his head slightly and said, "Yeh!" After more exchange of belabored pleasantries, the man mounted his automobile and drove down the mud lane.

A short ride up the road the neighbor dropped in at the Albin Anderson farm. Alighting from his automobile, he hurried up to Albin hardly saying hello before blurting out, "Boy, that new Swede is really a religious nut; he thinks he's got Jesus in the barrel helping him fatten his hogs." Of course, Albin asked him what Nels had told him and, understanding Swedish, Albin easily understood where the confusion developed.

Containing his laughter until the neighbor departed, Albin jumped in his car post haste and hurried over to tell Nels the story. Nels roared with laughter and, in later years, it was one of his favorite tales to tell at social gatherings.

Albin Anderson thinking about Nels Hanson's pigs!
Photo courtesy of Helen Anderson Nelson

On the local scene, the Snyder-Kayser Ford Garage ushered in Henry Ford's newest wheeled conveyance, the Model A Ford. The newer Ford was the successor to the Model T "Flivver" as an affordable car for the American public.

The old Model T had served millions of people well over the past fifteen years. Many people were leery about the Model "A" as it had a new fangled floor gear shift and one of those fancy "self-commencers" (starters) that Clinty was always talking about.

About that time, some of the local girls were going through a "Peeking Tom" trauma of sorts. Terror struck Happyland when repeated reports came to the police station that a guy was leaping up and looking into girls' bedrooms. There were obvious clues such as: the guy had extra strong legs and did possess a certain amount of

Fred Kayser sits in twenty-millionth Ford sold—Ford Garage employees and friends surround him.

Photo courtesy of Lawrence Kayser

levitation ability as he was purported to suspend himself in air long enough to take two peeks. It was inevitable that someone would hang the moniker, "Leapin' Tom", on him.

With such a definitive description, it wasn't too long before the long arm of the law virtually reached out January 28, 1928 and caught a sixteen-year-old boy between a leap and a peek! Word was

"Memories of a Former Kid" cartoon by Bob Artley

Cartoon courtesy of Bob Artley

soon out there'd be no more leaping and peeking in Happyland—No-siree-bob!

There had been too many "goings on" of late in Happyland and the Parent Teachers Association decided to put its foot down—and it did. A central meeting was held on the subject, "Safe-guarding the Morals of Our Children."

Mrs. Ima Dogooder, we'll call her that, announced there were too many parties and that movies were keeping the children out too late. This made some sorta sense as "Leapin' Tom" had been caught looking in the windows after dark. Good thought—everyone in the room applauded!

Then, too, the police probably found candy and gum in Leapin' Tom's pocket, for the meeting revealed the average child had too much money for candy and gum. What caused Tom to leap and peek was decided right then and there: the girls were starting to dress too scantily.

Police caught Tom between leep and a peek.

Cartoon courtesy of Paul Troth

This statement didn't really make sense. If the girls were so scantily dressed in public, why was it necessary for the leaping one to look into bedroom windows? However, research does reveal that a vast change in women's clothing had taken place. For example, in 1910 a woman's complete costume took nineteen yards of material and in 1928 little more than seven yards were needed. At any rate, by today's standards, the youth of that period dressed like they were competing in a Sunday school class style show.

The Isis Theater had been reconstructed after the terrible December 1926 fire. Movies were getting longer and better and so were the cowboy tricks. However, due to his financial difficulties, Hank's attendance had to be curtailed severely. Ten cents would buy enough flour to make several loaves of bread.

At last the Westerns were nearly all talkies, and Clinty breathed a sigh of relief for Hank was no longer pestering him to go along to read the brief printed dialogue at the bottom of the screen.

A record with the sound was played along with the movie. However, it was difficult to get the sound synchronized perfectly with the film. Not too bad a problem—but it did detract from realism when the hero told the villain to put up his hands after he had already shot the dastardly one and he was lying on the ground.

Clinty would sometimes give Hank a dime from his meager resources to attend the movie. This was with the stipulation that Hank give Clinty his money's worth by telling him all the best parts. These long narrations disgusted Hank's mother and sister, and they would have gladly settled for a penny's worth. Clinty didn't do much to help matters when he consistently accused Hank of leaving out the best parts. Dale Castle of Shenandoah recalls that three brothers alternated going to the movie on Saturdays, with the one in attendance giving a detailed report of the movie when he returned home.

As spring progressed, politics started to heat up since the primary elections were coming in May. Most people expected the Republicans to win in the November general elections, for with a Republican in the White House and that party holding the legislative majority, business and industry had continued to ride the waves of the biggest economic boom in the country's history.

Happylanders loved to argue and election years always provided an outlet. One would have surmised that a mistake had been made and the old proverb about Maine should have been, "As Happyland goes—so goes the nation."

In the end at the convention Alfred E. "Al" Smith was the Democratic nominee. He, at that time, was the governor of New York state. Smith had upset tradition when he became the first Catholic to be nominated as candidate for president by a major party.

Another first took place May 11, 1928 on the day of the Democratic nomination. Although television had not been perfected, a station in Schenectady, New York telecast Smith's nomination. However, England was still out ahead in television development since that same year John Baird transmitted the first color television program from London.

On the Republican side in Kansas City on June 12-14, Herbert Hoover easily became the presidential candidate. He had served as a commission chairman and administrator for President Woodrow Wilson during World War I. More recently he had been Secretary of Commerce during President Warren Harding's administration.

In all, the summer of 1928 was somewhat like the calm before a storm, with less political campaign activity than was normal. But not too long after the primaries, a few staunch Iowa Republicans were beginning to have doubts about the state's native son, Herbert Hoover, because he came out against a bill that would have helped the farmer.

As November approached, all one heard discussed were football games, the price of crops and the coming general election. Arguments raged in Steve Dermand's Cafe and the Little Chicago Cafe. In the drugstores the clientele at the soda fountain pretty well consisted of Republicans, except at Channers Drug, where the party line affiliations were somewhat a mixed bag, so to speak.

The Republicans quite often compared the educations of Democratic candidate Al Smith and Herbert Hoover, the dean of all Republicans. Smith, the Republicans would chortle, only had a high school education while Hoover was a Stanford University graduate with a mining engineering degree. "Big deal," retorted the Democrats. "Is the government going into mining? What experience does he have at the helm of government? Smith is a four-time governor of the country's biggest state."

Republicans then told how great an administrator Herbert Hoover was, and much bragging was done about his feeding destitute people in Europe during World War I. Much to-do was made about Hoover being Secretary of Commerce under President Warren Harding. He was credited with helping to keep the economy strong. Political arguments in Happyland became quite heated when Frank Lund, who had bolted the Republican party, and auctioneer Val Wehrheim argued politics in Dermand's Cafe. Their booming voics caused the chickens at McMurray's Hatchery some one-half mile away to consider bolting their nests!

Although Smith was said to have suffered the loss of votes due to his being Catholic, Iowa was not a state that placed that much emphasis on the religious preference of a candidate—unless he was a heathen. The rumor was circulated that Al Smith had connections with the Ku Klux Klan, which of course was dreamed up as a campaign smear.

There were those who strongly opposed Smith's wanting to repeal prohibition and allow the sale of alcoholic beverages. Mother Lucy was one of them. Hoover, on the other hand, was a Quaker and against imbibing in alcohol in any form. One had to wonder just how the minor league bootleggers in Happyland could make such a good living in a booze-dry town. Rarely a week went by that the newspapers didn't carry an item about a bootlegger transferring his residence to the county jail.

It was obvious Hoover had the backing of big business as campaign funds were easily raised. Riding on the "shirttails" of prosperity, Hoover stated, "In no nation are the fruits of accomplishment so secure!"

Meanwhile, back on the farm everyone had discovered Willobee was not only lazy, but he had all the traits necessary to make others contemplate jumping off a cliff in hopes the guy would follow.

Hank, desperate to see Willobee leave, resorted to strong measures and carefully concealed molasses in Willobee's work cap. To put it mildly, all hell broke loose. Willobee wasn't too sweet on the idea but, considering his bald head, the prank hadn't caused him a problem of great magnitude. However, after the "Sweetening of Willobee," James Arthur gave Hank the job of pulling the cockleburs in a three-acre recently-harvested garden, which seemed to have an endless supply.

Hank was called from his weed pulling chores the following day to help load the hogs for transport to the local stockyards. The hog sheds were long buildings with narrow aisles down the centers. On both sides of the aisle were doored compartments for farrowing brood sows. The truck driver promptly backed the truck up to the shed door and placed a loading ramp through the opening into the aisle.

Actually the loading process was quite simple. James Arthur would stand in the aisleway just in front of the truck ramp to divert brood sows and other hogs he desired to keep to his right through a stall and back out into the hog lot. When a hog approached that he wanted to sell, he would stand aside and allow it to run up the ramp into the truck.

Big Brother and Hank always had the task of driving the hogs into the hog shed, then out of the end stalls into the aisles and up to the point where the hogs were to be separated. They had just about completed the roundup except for an old sow and several gilts. The old sow was blocking the stall door when Hank spotted a pitchfork with the handle broken off lodged safely behind a wall board. His mind

The old sow raised sizeable litters of larders.
Photo courtesy of Wallace's Farmer

immediately conceived an idea, which both brothers considered extremely worthy of implementation.

Big Brother grasped the pitchfork and gouged the old sow, not hard enough to penetrate the skin, but enough to get a wonderful response. She let out a shrill "Oink! Oink,!" lowered her head and some 500 pounds of ear-flapping pork moved down the aisle like a runaway locomotive.

Father James Arthur, true to their belief, was planning on saving this sow, for she produced sizable litters of larders. He stood, legs spread, in front of the loading ramp prepared to head her off.

She reached the ramp going full tilt and drove her head between James Arthur's outspread legs. Without breaking speed, she hoisted him up onto her back and sped up the ramp toward the truck—James Arthur astride, facing the rear, still yelling out commands as if someone could stop her. From the look on his face, one could readily see hog bustin' was definitely not his cup of tea.

The old sow reached the top of the ramp and the small gate in the truck box with James Arthur still astraddle. Had the stage been set for this performance by a professional stunt man, the results could not have been better.

The top of the truck box opening was only a couple of inches higher than the old sow's back. As James Arthur reached the truck box, the boards above the opening very neatly slid him to the end of the sow's back and set him down with a thud on the loading ramp. He breathed a sigh of relief, gathered his wits, stood up, surveyed himself and the area around him, then shouted, "Now I wonder what in the hell got into that old sow?"

Later at the supper table, Cousin Clinty congratulated James Arthur on his sowmanship. He then said with all his sow "bustin'" ability, he might want to consider joining the Buffalo Bill Wild West Show he had seen back in 1901 in Happyland. Although a bit sore and stiff, James Arthur did manage a weak grin when Clinty averred that, after a little practice, he just might be billed by the circus as the only man ever to ride sidesaddle on a sow.

Although Walter Willson, one of the town's founders, had succeeded in bringing the railroad to Happyland in 1869, few of the town's inhabitants had ever ridden on a train. However, most of them did dream of some day taking a trip—most likely to a big city like Chicago.

About the only small town people who were frequent travelers to the big cities in those days were the local stockbuyers. Occasionally the buyers would take one of their outstanding stock farmers along on the glorious trip—as a fringe benefit of sorts! Of course, James Arthur wasn't a big enough producer to be invited on one of those magnificent sojourns to the Windy City.

The stockbuyers and their guests always rode in a special car attached to the train transporting the stock. There, in somewhat subdued splendor, they rumbled along the tracks playing poker whilst telling some of the latest off-color jokes and impressing first-timers by reminiscing on the high points of past trips.

So it was that when the big beef and pork barterers returned to Happyland from the big city of Chicago, they were heroes in their own right—especially when they attended the next sale at Wehrheim's or Marvel's sales barn. The worldly ones were surrounded quickly by those of the younger set, who waited to hear tall tales about big city life. Anxious to oblige some of Happyland's less sophisticated citizens, the stockmen embellished their stories and let them grow both in magnitude and intensity with each trip.

The stockbuyer gained even more stature by standing back, appearing just a tad aloof and too worldly to tell about such minor adventures, and allowing the stock farmer to do most of the talking. He would interject only when the stock farmer didn't put across a salient point. Good psychology—right? By the following fall the stock farmer was damn nigh ready to give the stock to the buyer just to make the trip.

Naturally it had to come out that the stockbuyer was on a first name basis with practically all of the big shot city slickers at the stockyards. With this announcement, the buyer nods a little and gets a sly grin on his face. This alone would have been enough to thrill the stock farmer even if they hadn't gone out on the town!

Of course—but of course—the stockbuyer always took the farmer to one of the fancier "speakeasies." While enroute to the speakeasy, the taxi driver is making such over-the-shoulder remarks as, "You might even see Al Capone, the big crime boss, there." Then talking kinda confidential, out of the corner of his mouth, the driver lets slip that Capone might own the place, but warns them, "Ya gotta be hush - hush about things like that!"

Going on, the stock farmer tells how they arrive at a dingy building and proceed to the door, where they rap out a signal. A guy opens a small portal and they go in. The stockbuyer prompts the farmer, "Not until I gave the guy the secret password!" (The farmer gets a little flushed—he had left out one of the best parts.)

Continuing, the farmer tells how the stockbuyer slips a guy in a tuxedo a ten spot and they are soon seated at a table right smack-dab down in front of the stage. How about that! The stockbuyer sticks out his nicely rounded stomach, leans back, nods, then returns to chewing on his cigar.

The farmer tells how they order a couple of Scotch whiskies, smuggled in from Canada. Little strong for him, so he switches to champagne. By now the stockbuyer is getting a mite disgusted about the farmer leaving out important details and interjects again, in an authorative voice, "from France!"

From the stock farmer's descriptions no one present had ever seen anything like that speakeasy, even if they had been to Des Moines, Sioux City or Omaha. The exhuberant farmer goes on to describe the plush red carpeting, red satin drapes, and a beautiful mahogany bar so long he allows as how the bartenders should have been on roller skates.

Then the farmer starts to tell about the meal and, at that point, it becomes obvious the younger men don't want to hear about food. Sensing this, the stockbuyer breaks in and prompts the farmer, "I'll bet they'd like to hear about the girls." A chorus of "yehs" arise from the crowd—then shouts of, "Now we're getting somewhere—tell us about the girls."

The stock farmer comes through with flying colors. His descriptions of the chorus girls are pictorially vivid; nothing is left to the imagination. At this point the stockbuyer breaks in and comments, "Hell, that was nothing; tell 'em about the peep holes."

By now the young unworldly ones are beginning to get up a sweat visualizing the strippers and the cry was, "Yes—gowan—gowan; what the hell did you see behind the peep holes?"

About that time things are at a fevered pitch. The stockbuyer pulls out some of the fancy long Cuban cigars he had purchased in Chicago and hands the stock farmer one. Removing the fancy aluminum cylindrical covers, they both calmly light up while tension mounts in the crowd.

The stock farmer, sensing he has more than the mild attention of his audience, takes a deep pull on the cigar, then continues. By the time he finishes telling what he saw behind the peep holes, the younger men damn nigh have to go over to Zublin and Garth's ice house and sit on the ice to keep from scorching their underwear.

As the election banter accelerated on radio and in the newspapers, Cousin Clinty and James Arthur arose to every politically related argumentative occasion. Cousin Willobee stated that he, like Lucy, was for the Republicans. This alone was nearly enough to swing Mother Lucy over to the Democratic side for the first time.

Lucy never would forgive the Democrats for wanting to repeal liquor prohibition. James Arthur was an unwavering Democrat, not because he was an extremely thirsty man, but because he believed the Democrats, at the time, would do more to help the farmer and working man.

From all anyone could tell, James Arthur and Lucy might just as well have stayed away from the polls in election years, but each respected the constitutional right of the other to select the candidate of his or her choice.

During the election year of 1928, James Arthur started the political campaign early in hopes of swaying Lucy over to his way of thinking, and he all but stood on the dining room table delivering long and forceful speeches. On one occasion, he stood up so fast to stress a key point that Clinty had to remind him he had his hand in the butter dish.

At any rate James Arthur flung himself into the flamboyancy of politics with vigor, if not with wisdom, and the more excited he became, the more delighted Lucy appeared. With each good point he stressed, Lucy would nod approval and when she quit nodding, he craftily switched the subject. By election time he was certain he had achieved success this time.

Lucy had a way of appearing subdued. She was mild of manner and, in a way, projected a kind of timid reaction to most things. Underneath it all she had staunch convictions of her own and was not one to be easily swayed. "Hell," Clinty once told James Arthur, out of earshot of Lucy, "she's so dead set against alcohol in any form she has to turn her head while wood alcohol is poured into an automobile radiator as anti-freeze."

On the day of the general election, Lucy put on her best dress and hat while James Arthur patiently waited to drive her to the polls to cast a ballot for the candidates of HIS choice.

Normally James Arthur was warming up the car and honking long erratic blasts for Lucy when she was late, but this day he was a picture of charm and grace. He told her to take her time and opened doors politely. Lucy didn't even have to resort to asking him to warm up the car in advance. When they drove away, it was kinda nice to watch them since they appeared to be in the courting stage of their lives again.

Returning home after the visit to the polling place, James Arthur drove up to the garage like he had just been assured the job of Secretary of the Department of Ground Hog Breeding or something. Securing his newspaper, he turned on the radio and sought a bit of repose while waiting to hear the news of his favorite candidates winning the election.

When he attained sufficient serenity and blissful composure, Lucy walked into the room and announced in her quiet way, "We might just as well both have stayed home from the polls." James Arthur asked, "Why?" She then revealed that she had voted Republican. It was at this time that the house vibrated with such intensity everyone feared another crack would develop in the ceiling plaster.

Republican nominee Hoover won the popular vote by a margin of over six million votes and won the Electoral College vote 444 to 87. Although Smith polled victories in twelve major cities, this was not enough to change the result. Then too, southern states that had voted Democratic since the Civil War had gone over to the Republican side.

When the news of the Republican victory came out, James Arthur proclaimed over and over, "Now the farmer is doomed!" Little did he realize how correct his statement would become.

Throughout 1928 the economy seemed to be gaining a little strength in the midwest. The federal government was encouraging even more speculation in industry.

Local retail businesses were also experiencing a much better year. The Charles Closz Co., manufacturer of threshing machine sieves, had reorganized and added employees, and there was talk of starting production again at the tile plant. Even James Arthur had a better year and was able to purchase a 1928 Chevrolet, which had one of those "self-commencers" Cousin Clinty was always talking about.

There were a few things looking up in the medical world. Scottish bacteriologist Alexander Fleming had discovered penicillin, a new drug with which to combat severe infections. However, its broad use was hampered as supplies could not be stored for more than two days.

Penicillin would save the lives of or heal thousands upon thousands of wounded soldiers during the latter part of World War II. Northern Research Laboratory, Peoria, Illinois, would discover an overripe watermelon would provide a storable culture for penicillin. How many millions of people worldwide owe their lives to this miracle drug would be difficult to estimate, but the number would be astronomical.

Overall, you might say, the year 1929 was greeted with enthusiasm by people in virtually all walks of life. Why shouldn't everyone rejoice, for in just a couple of months Herbert Hoover, the big filler of billfolds, would be inaugurated into office?.

With all the ballyhooing that had gone on before the election, those who had followed the government's advice and invested in stocks were convinced that, by the end of the year, it would take six men and a good sized boy to carry home their earnings.

For the superstitious and psychic, the "Rose Bowl" football game New Years Day 1929 should have provided some insight on things to come. Roy Riegels, California's center, recovered a fumble, then ran like hell toward the wrong goal. Fortunately his teammate, Benny Lom, could outrun him and finally dragged him down before he could cross the opponent's goal. Before the end of that year, a lot of people would be wishing Hoover had run the wrong way when he was called to the inaugural podium.

By 1929 organized crime was much better organized than was the government. Prohibition had been a boon to the acquiring of illegal capital. Then too, the crime bosses didn't have many problems getting rid of inefficient help. No red tape, no waiting for the next election—just take the bungling S.O.B. out and shoot him.

With a strong foothold in Chicago's gangland, Al Capone pretty well controlled bootlegging and the protection rackets. Occasionally some power hungry tough guy would challenge Capone's authority, but rarely did the person get to enjoy his wealth very long before he went to his grave. "Bugs" Moran was such a man.

On February 14, 1929 four members of Capone's gang, two in police uniform, raided an illegal liquor warehouse. With seven of the Moran gang backed against the wall, Capone's fake cops riddled them with bullets. Then came the amazing escape. The two mobsters in uniforms marched their two cohorts in civilian clothes, hands above their heads, out past curious witnesses and zoomed off in their automobiles, never to be identified or apprehended for what was to become known as "the St. Valentine Day Murder."

Back in Happyland, toward evening on February 24 huge snowflakes started falling and when the night of February 25 ended, eighteen and one-half inches of snow had accumulated.

Grader clearing snow (1929).

Photo courtesy of Wallace's Farmer

Just getting from the house to the barn and stock lot to feed the animals was a major chore. Snow was drifted nearly over the window tops on the north and west sides of many houses. All outside doors were packed with snow and ice. Clinty finally squeezed through a window and cleared snow from the door, then shoveled a path to the barn.

Farmers shovel bobsleds through to Woolstock for supplies (1929).

Photo courtesy of Helen Whilty

Naturally there was no vehicular travel on rural roads or city streets. With no school for a couple of days, Hank and Big Brother had been bounding around the house like centipedes on a pogo stick. When Mother Lucy found out city streets were cleared, she told James Arthur and Clinty to get the children to school in the bobsled and get them there fast. Of course, James Arthur and Clinty complied with her wishes.

Summer of 1929 came forth with all its glory. Seeking to gain additional income, James Arthur purchased a hay baler. Hank had the job of poking baling wires through slots in heavy wooden blocks to the opposite side of the baler where James Arthur tied the wires at the correct tensity. When the bales emerged from the end of the baler, they were in neat storable bales weighing around eighty pounds each.

On days Hank was away, Willobee was supposed to do all the chores except for the milking of cows. However, this proved to be wishful thinking as Willobee never performed up to the required level. This disgusted Hank no end.

One afternoon the hay baler broke down and James Arthur motored into town to get the baler part welded. Hank proceeded to the garage and, sure enough, there was Willobee tinkering with his car again instead of doing his assigned work.

It was when Hank disturbed Willobee while he was working on his car that he became most enraged. Hank deduced that if he could just heckle him enough, Willobee would surely go get himself a job and move on. With that in mind, Hank headed for the garage to launch another orneriness offensive.

Willobee was working with some pliers and when he laid them down, Hank deftly snatched them and hid them in a partially emptied nail keg. Unable to find the pliers, Willobee was reasonably sure Hank had hidden them. He flew into a rage, grabbed Hank and threw him into the stock watering tank, which was conveniently located beside the garage where he was working.

Dripping with water, moss and a desire for revenge, Hank crawled from the water tank and began thinking of ways to drive the one with the well drawn-up trousers out of his machine motivated mind.

James Arthur and Lucy were both industrious, hard working people and as time went by, they became a little more than displeased with Willobee's laziness. He expected Lucy to cater to his every whim. James Arthur had got him a job helping neighbor Herman Onken with haying, but in a day or so he complained of a sore back and quit.

Willobee enjoyed most sitting on a bench on the south side of the garage sleeping and sunning himself. He would sit by the hour snoring and ignoring jobs James Arthur had assigned him. He always had an excuse for not working and, as Cousin Clinty said, when it came to work, Cousin Willobee had more stalls than his father's livery stable in Perry.

Later that afternoon, as Hank headed for the stock lot to feed the animals, he noticed Willobee sleeping exceptionally comfortably on the bench—the sun glistening on his shiny head and white beard.

The thought of Willobee being so comfortable while Hank did chores bothered the young one no end.

In those days farmers were allowed to feed their hogs food residue mixed with ground grain. As Hank stirred the hog slop, as it was called, with a long paddle, edibles such as tomatoes, bread, biscuits, and grain floated majestically to the top of the barrel. Suddenly Hank felt a strong urge to throw a bucket of the mixture in old Willobee's face.

The idea appealed to him so much he could no longer resist it. Hank proceeded to sneak, bucket in hand, to a concealed vantage point near where Willobee sat head back, mouth open, his whiskers fluttering like a butterfly in the breeze with each snore. On nimble toes Hank maneuvered from the front of the garage to a spot directly in front of Willobee, bucket raised and poised for discharge.

Everything went fine until Hank thought of how wonderful a day it would be if he could be successful slipping him the sow soup without being caught in the act. It was then that Hank broke into uncontrollable muffled laughter and became so weak he was momentarily incapable of delivering the slop to its target. However, after taking time to recall the many problems old Willobee had caused him, he aroused his anger sufficiently and gave the old geezer the geyser, floating biscuits and all, right smack dab in the kisser—wow!!

The look on Cousin Willobee's face was priceless as the slop sloshed on him. Parts of soggy biscuits, oats and corn were caught in

"The Slopping of Willobee"

Cartoon courtesy of Paul Troth

his beard and his glasses were covered. Old Willobee bellowed like he had just been beaten out of a job testing mattresses in Miami, Florida.

Hank didn't stop to view any additional results. He beat a hasty retreat around the corner of the garage while Willobee contemplated how in the world a stock feeding barrel fifty feet away could have fallen on him.

By the time Willobee collected his senses, Hank had streaked across the yard, hid the bucket and quietly sneaked through the front door. He then sat down in a chair and continued to read a magazine and eat cookies as he was doing the last time Mother Lucy had seen him.

Well-slopped Willobee waddled to the house and Hank could hear him babbling to Lucy something about being bushwhacked in the beezer with a bucket full of soggy biscuits. He demanded Hank be given every punishment short of being dangled from a dirigible by his toes or beaten with a board full of bridging spikes.

Mother Lucy cautioned Willobee about making such strong accusations. She told him Hank couldn't possibly have been the guilty party since he had been sitting in the living room, eating cookies and reading a magazine.

What a wonderful sight it was! While ranting and raving, the one with the tricky trousers pointed at Hank with one hand, plucking hog food from his beard with the other. Willobee finally stopped screaming about Hank, buckets and biscuits, heated some water, bathed and changed clothing.

When James Arthur came home from town, Hank listened from outside the door as his Mother told his Father about the "slopping of Willobee." For the first time Hank realized his Father and Mother had a good sense of humor for they couldn't contain their laughter.

Later, as usual, Willobee complained to James Arthur about Hank. More than a little agitated, James Arthur asked him, "How could he sneak up in front of you without being seen?" Willobee then had to admit he had been sleeping. When James Arthur learned he had not completed his work assignment, he literally seared the seams in Willobee's underwear with a verbal barrage that would have melted a blast furnace.

James Arthur made it clear to Willobee there would be no more snoozing sessions during chore time and that he would have to start pulling his share of the workload. With this Willobee showed evidence of extreme duress and suddenly discovered he had enough money to get his radiator soldered.

James Arthur allowed him to fill the tank with gas and let him take two five-gallon cans of extra fuel from the storage barrels. Lucy gave him some of her "saved-back-for-a-rainy-day" egg and cream money. Willobee allowed as how he was going to visit his Uncle Raymond, who had a good job with the railroad at Sioux Falls, South Dakota.

After twice circling the barnyard like a whirlwind to test the car's performance, Willobee steered his Chevrolet down the lane toward the road. He hadn't driven for a couple of years and when he came to the end of the lane, he misjudged the corner and neatly decapitated the mailbox.

Another whirlwind, other than Willobee, descended on the area a few days later when Cousin Clinty and Hank stood on the porch watching ominous clouds approach from the west. Suddenly a huge whirling mass of dark clouds could be seen forming, then a black funnel reached earthward. Clinty shouted, "Cyclone," the name given tornadoes in those days.

Tornadoes were, and still are, the scourge of the middle United States. Their strong, whirling winds kill and maim people, destroy buildings and wipe out the fruits of a farmer's labor—his crops! Now the funnel could be seen heading directly toward a neighbor's homestead some three miles away, uprooting everything in its path. After the tornado passed, James Arthur hastily drove Clinty, Big Brother and Hank to the farm to see if they could be of help.

Approaching the farm, they could see the house was still intact, apparently undamaged. However, the barn, corncrib and other outbuildings were in shambles. Most of the trees had been uprooted, shorn of their branches.

A group of people stood around one tree pointing. Moving closer, they could see a wheelbarrow hanging some four feet up the trunk, its axle impaled in the tree. Then they saw an even more impressive oddity; oat straw stems had been driven endways into the bark.

Of course, the conversation drifted to the strange behavior of tornadoes. Some of the men were discussing a tornado that occurred near Madrid a few years back where several people were picked up and deposited in a field, alive!

Research reveals the tornado victims were members of the Hans Hanson family who had but a short time before emigrated from Sweden. Jennie Hanson Richardson, a daughter of Hans and Anna Hanson, now of Riverton, Wyoming, gave this account.

The family was living on a farm near Madrid at the time. They were unfamiliar with tornadoes in Sweden, but had been instructed in evasive actions they should take in the event of one—such as going to basements, cellars or below ground door-covered storm cellars, which frequently doubled as storage for fruit and potatoes.

It had been an unusally hot April 6 in 1922. They were all tired and had retired early. Sometime later an extremely violent storm descended on the calm night. Thunder shook the house; lightning bolts creased the sky and in jagged strikes severed nearby trees. All of them bolted upright in their beds.

Hearing a strange roar, Father Hans warned that tornadoes made such a noise as he leaped from the bed, heart racing, and dashed to the window. Through lightning flashes against an almost purple and white sky, he spotted a huge funnel-shaped cloud rapidly coming toward the house. He was in deathly fear for his family; somehow he must get them to the storm cave if he was to save them.

Hans shouted at the top of his lungs, "Get up everyone—get up quick. We have to go to the cave!" Then Mother Anna yelled, "Jennie, get your brother, Arthur. We have no time to lose!"

By this time Hans and son Hugo were unlocking the door. Jennie recalls that, as she ran down the stairs with brother Arthur, she could hear her father shouting, "Lie flat on the floor; it's too late!" There was a horrible noise like a hundred simultaneous claps of thunder.

The ear-shattering blast was the last thing Jennie remembered until she awakened in a field some half mile from where their home had stood.

In the still of the now-cool night, she thought she heard a voice—anxiously she waited and listened carefully. Sure enough, she heard it again and this time she recognized it as that of her brother Arthur. She thought to herself, "At least one other member of the family is alive; now there is hope for the others." Her hopes soared when she heard her brother Hugo calling her name. He and her father Hans were some fifty or so feet away. Then tears of joy flowed when they all discovered Mother Anna and sister Agnes a short distance from them. All of them had landed in pairs as they were in the house. One horse was discovered to have gone along for the ride and found to be in excellent condition.

By the time a neighbor, a Mr. Bryant, arrived on the scene with a lantern, golf ball-sized hail was falling, pelting their bodies. Someone had called for medical help and their family doctor, Dr. Gamble, plus another doctor and two nurses soon arrived.

The Hanson's night clothes were covered with dirt and blood from cuts and bruises. Hans and wife Anna were taken to the Lutheran Hospital in Des Moines. Anna was found to have back injuries and Hans' eye had been injured. However, both would recover. Jennie lost two front teeth.

Their hard-earned stock and poultry were gone except for a few embarrassed de-feathered chickens and Nellie, the flying horse. A few badly damaged photos and Father Hans' checkbook were returned to them. Remnants of possessions were found up to fifteen miles away. The Madrid Bank had Hans' checkbook on its bulletin board for a long time, with a caption: "This is proof that a bank is the only safe place to keep your money!"

People rallied to help clear the debris; the family was split up to live in four homes until the parents were out of the hospital. Hans did get a crop in that spring. A thrill? Derald Hanson of Stratford, born later, said, "After the tornado, it took a lot to thrill anyone in my family." Small wonder!

Hans Hanson family—a flat tire was a mild problem after tornado.
Photo courtesy of Jennie Hanson Richardson

By this time Hank's Big Sister was taking on the shape and looks of a young lady and had arrived at the age where Cousin Clinty and her older brothers were getting much delight from teasing her about boys. Clinty would ask her when she would marry, whom she would marry and in general question her about various potential suitors.

The friendly jesting continued throughout those years and Clinty kept Big Sister in a dither about boy friends, in particular about a neighbor's hired hand who definitely liked her. Clinty succeeded in exhausting her good humor completely only once. This came about when Clinty told the guy that Big Sister was really quite fond of him, but she had said he (the hired hand) must be bashful as he never dressed up and properly came calling.

Cousin Clinty charged him up like a battery and informed him the family would be making homemade ice cream that afternoon. He told the elated prospective suitor that Big Sister liked strong men and he would really impress her if he were to crank the freezer without help until the ice cream was frozen. With that Cousin Clinty grabbed Hank by the hand and they went home—not, however, until Hank had been sworn to secrecy.

Mother Lucy completed preparing the ice cream ingredients for freezing about five o'clock that afternoon. Clinty made much to do about placing the freezer to the north of the house and out of the sun. He finally got his way and the freezer, ice and other items were placed strategically at a spot where the Beau Brummell of the barnyard couldn't miss them.

The hero for the day must have been standing with his nose pressed against his window because the freezer had hardly touched the ground when his foot hit the top front step. Clinty looked at Hank, winked and gave him his all-knowing smile.

Old Lover Boy turned up the drive, his feet throwing rocks like a Mack truck, and charged on to the scene like Tom Mix, the silent movie star, on a villain fencing off a water hole and nothing, but nothing could ever top that.

The prospective suitor wore a blue serge suit and had shined his shoes to a brilliant glow. He even wore a white shirt and tie. He ambled up to the group, grinning like a coon dog eating taffy and announced proudly to Big Sister, "See, I'm not as bashful as you thought I was." Big Sister looked at him as if the ballast had shifted in his brain. Clinty gave him a sly wink and flexed his arm indicating muscle and strength.

Lover Boy, with the agility of a tiger, moved in on the freezer and announced, "The rest of you guys might just as well sit down and relax; I'll handle this!" In his eagerness to get to the freezer first, he hadn't paused long enough to remove his coat and hat. He grabbed the freezer handle in a style that must have been reminiscent of Billy the Kid slapping leather to draw his six gun and in one fluid-like motion he was on the freezer and churning.

Now, if the reader has never turned the handle on a homemade ice cream freezer on a hot July day, he probably won't appreciate the next few paragraphs quite so much. The feat compares favorably with changing fifty car tires, using a hand lug wrench, without stopping. But Lover Boy left no doubt in anyone's mind he planned to do the entire job himself.

A few minutes later, sweat pouring from his nose like water from a leaky shower head, he was thoroughly drenched. Clinty told him he would spell him for awhile while he took off his coat. The hero looked up at him like a kid when someone threatens to step on his all-day sucker and said, "Hell no, you just want to take a turn at the freezer."

After a few more minutes, the "Beau Brummel of the Barn Yard" did have to stop long enough to take off his coat, but when he did, the look of defiance on his face gave notice of the destruction he would wreak upon anyone attempting to take over the task.

The ground was pulverized where he shifted like a grape stomper to get into a better position. Cousin Clinty chided him about stopping to take off his coat and, hearing this remark, the churning champion just churned all the harder.

The last few hundred turns on old freezers were usually the toughest, and Clinty asked old Churnin' Charlie if he wanted to stop while he added more ice. The hero of the day looked up and saw Big Sister, then gasped, "Just put the damn stuff in while I'm churnin'."

As the hour wore on, our hero gained on the project, but his fluidly smooth turns were slowly reduced to pushes and jerks as his face became grey and red alternately. Then tragedy struck; one of his suspender buttons broke off and he was now faced with a possible exposure problem.

However, he was unflinching in his determination and had almost completed the freezing of the ice cream when the second suspender button popped loose. The loss of the second button made it appear that he wouldn't be able to finish the task successfully. He was now holding up his trousers with one hand, his knee planted solidly atop the freezer bucket. Clinty volunteered to hold the bucket fast, but all he received from old Lover Boy was a low guttural growl.

The feat Big Sister's prospective suitor accomplished undoubtedly has never been duplicated. When he finished, he looked like he had been run through a barbed wire fence, been trampled by bull elephants, held prisoner in a sauna bath, and forced to swallow fifty peach seeds whole with castor oil. To say the least, he didn't appear flush with victory.

The ice cream was good and the handle turning hero, despite fatigue, did eat exceptionally well; however, he looked a mite peaked. He had stopped perspiring but had taken on an aroma equivalent to that emitted by a half dozen billy goats after a rain.

After consuming six or eight dishes of ice cream, he announced he was a little tired and best be getting home to bed. When he departed, romance was the furthest thing from his mind. He had no doubt come to the conclusion: if ice-cream churning was a part of courtship, he didn't want any truck with it!

On the national scene, large corporations and businesses had been encouraging employees to buy shares in their companies for sometime. Why not, thought many employees? This way they received a piece of the profits. Of course, the big business moguls had ulterior motives, for if one owns a part of the firm, the person is less prone to strike or demand higher wages.

So obsessed were employees with getting a portion of the big business profit pie that many people committed their lifetime savings along with a healthy chunk of their paychecks. Some even borrowed to buy stock in their employer's company or in others who offered stocks on the market. Why not? Hadn't President Hoover predicted the day would soon come when poverty in the United States would be abolished for all time?

No one had stopped to think that when the small business man or salaried employee put nearly all his money, after living expenses, into stocks, there would be very little left over for purchase of merchandise.

Committed as they were to installment payments and their investments in stocks, people simply didn't have the money to purchase manufactured goods. There was a decided downswing in purchase of new automobiles, radios, etc. Christmas sales dropped in 1928. Stores were overstocked and warehouses were bulging with wares their companies were no longer able to sell.

The bubbles started bursting—no longer was it just those engaged in farming and agricultural supplies who would suffer. On October 24, 1929 at the New York Stock Exchange 12,894,650 shares hit the for sale market counters.

So fast and furious came sale requests that stock market workers collapsed from exhaustion as they tried to process transactions. The country's largest bankers attempted to head off the market tailspin and restore calm. However, their efforts to bolster up the sagging market were to no avail.

If there was doubt about the health of the nation's economy, it was expelled. On October 29, 1929, "Black Tuesday," the bottom fell out of the market and this proved to be the crowning blow to the country's long financial boom. Over 16 million shares were sold for any price they would bring with many millions more dumped through brokers and markets coast to coast.

Appreciating the amount of money involved, by 1990 evaluations, would be difficult due to the growth of the nation in both population and inflation. But it would be safe to say losses by investors overall would have been upwards of 10 trillion dollars in today's economy. In a country of 75 million people, one can readily visualize how horrendous the blow was to the economy.

Then too, let us not forget that money at that time was on the gold standard and was not just printed and distributed as it is today. It

Wall Street the day of the stock market crash.
Photo courtesy of Gertrude Horan—from James D. Horan Collection

was backed by gold, stored in Fort Knox or elsewhere, for exchange on demand.

President Hoover stood fast in his resolve not to help the farmers or other working people. Of course, he was a millionaire by age 40. How he had earned so much money, even as a brilliant mining engineer working in China and Europe and as a Secretary of Commerce and a government administrator, still had many people perplexed.

James Arthur and Clinty's predictions had come true, for Hoover seemed to care little about the plight of the common man. Clinty maintained Will Rogers, a lovable actor-comic from Oklahoma, had Hoover pegged right when he said, "The money was appropriated for the top (big business) in hopes it would trickle down."

As 1929 drew to a close, the curtain not only came down on the economy, but also on a fabulous era in sports. Down through history the 1920s will no doubt continue to be heralded as the "Golden Age of Sports." With more people able to afford to participate, either as players or spectators, interest grew rapidly from the so called "sandlot" to professional level.

Everywhere one looked after school hours and on weekends youngsters and young men could be seen playing baseball, basketball or football. Television was yet to be perfected and radios were not plentiful until the late 1920s. Sports seasons were not intermingled and a far greater percentage of people actively participated than do today.

Schools were not consolidated; even the smaller high schools had baseball and basketball and most had football and track. Rare indeed was the town, no matter how small, that did not field a semi-professional baseball team.

Above: Nearly every town had a baseball team (Stanhope team pictured).
Photo courtesy of Bernice Sealine Lund

Right: Stratford Highschool football players (left to right) Harold Richardson and Lester Carlson. Uniforms offered little protection.
Photo courtesy of Jennie Hanson Richardson

Inspired by the school's athletic teams, even boys in the grades held the high school team members in high regard. The lower grades had their own unofficial sandlot teams. The basketball backboards were fine, but the school's playground was gravel and every kid who played tackle football had skinned-up knees and elbows.

Hank decided to set up a football field in the pasture and invite his school chums to come out to play. Cousin Clinty helped lay out the field and since he had no regular chalk to mark the ten yard lines, he substituted ground corn hogfeed.

It was a beautiful day for the game. Ralph Burton, Bill and Clare Powers, Virgil Gage, Marvin Baxter, and a host of others, had arrived by 9 a.m. Hank could hardly wait to show them the fine regulation grass field.

The field was obscured by the barn and as they rounded the corner, Hank's heart sank. Fifty porkers stood calmly eating up the ten-yard stripe markers. The pigs were hastily rounded up. Clinty saved the day by pacing off ten yards each time the ball changed hands. Both Marvin Baxter and Clare Powers fell in pig manure and they were the stars of the day, for no one wanted to tackle them.

The mighty "Babe Ruth," had hit a record sixty home runs in 1927 for the New York Yankees. Throughout the 1920s he and Lou Gehrig, a teammate, dominated the baseball scene. In 1928 the Yankees swept the World Series. Ruth batted a phenomenal .625, hitting three home runs in game four. Gehrig batted .545 with four home runs in the series.

The great Rockne, who had popularized the forward pass in 1913, was now coaching his old alma mater's team at Notre Dame. His teams had become the tops in the nation. During 1924 his backfield, dubbed the "Four Horsemen" and consisting of Stuhedreher, Miller, Crowley and Layden, became legendary and remain so today.

But no college player, or professional for that matter, will ever outshadow the awesome Harold "Red" Grange, "The Galloping Ghost from Illinois." He had cast his name in bronze in the annals of football history. No one as yet has ever bested his record of five touchdowns in five carries and sixty five years has elapsed at this writing.

Jack Dempsey, "The Manassa Mauler" who started his career fighting bare knuckle in Colorado mining town saloons for contributions and bets, had successfully defended his World's Heavyweight Boxing Champion title in 1923 knocking out Argentina's huge Luis Firpo, "The Wild Bull of the Pampas," in the fourth round.

Dempsey, as mentioned earlier, was defeated by Gene Tunney in 1926 and 1927, but his rugged fighting ability will never be contested. There are those who still maintain the second fight against Tunney would have belonged to Dempsey had he gone to his corner, as required, before the count could begin. His failure to do so prompted the referee's famous long count.

Bobby Jones became the Babe Ruth of golf and Bill Tilden dominated the tennis courts. Helen Wills became the first woman athlete to become a celebrity. In 1927 she won the British singles championship, which in itself gave her acclaim as world champion.

Basketball, invented in 1891 by James Naismith, a YMCA instructor from Springfield, Massachusetts, had come a long way since it was played inside a cage—without backboards and with dribbling not allowed. Basketball provided a sports outlet during cold winters since it could be played indoors.

Although basketball players continued to be called cagers, during the 1920s the cage was eliminated, backboards were added, dribbling was allowed and a new sport soon swept the nation. Most high schools and colleges had teams and even a few professional clubs were emerging.

Hockey, which had long been popular in Canada, was another sport inspiring enthusiasm in the United States during the 1920s. Professional teams were formed in New York, Boston, Pittsburgh, Detroit, and Chicago. By the 1927-28 season hockey was drawing big crowds in the east. The New York Rangers defeated Montreal, Canada in a heroic effort to win the coveted Stanley Cup— an amazing feat in so short a time, indeed.

Not only were universities producing outstanding athletes, but all across the country high schools literally seemed to have them coming out of the woodwork.

Each town had its sports heroes and they were idolized by the local fans. Such Happyland basketball and football stars as Louis Nichols and his brother Kenneth, the France brothers (Melford and George), and Raymond Ades will never be forgotten for their prowess on the basketball court and football field. Raymond Ades went on to the University of Iowa while the others played at (Lombard) Knox College, Galesburg, Illinois, a relatively small school which, amazingly, fielded some of the finest teams in the nation.

Oh, yes, there was Orville Eckstein, one of the greatest all-around high school athletes of the era. Like the great American Indian Jim Thorpe, Orv could play any popular sport. He was a fine football and basketball player and could belt the baseball over the fence either right or left-handed. As a sidelight, in high school he threw the old-style javelin 156 feet in track. There are still people around who will testify he literally broke one in half, whipping it so fast when he launched it in the air. Later Orv would take up golf and be equally proficient in that game.

Then let's not forget the speedster, Raymond Burns, who held the state record for the 100-yard and 220-yard dash. In 1926 the great Raymond Ades, an all-stater, kicked one of the old pumpkin end footballs eighty nine yards. Ades was also an all-state basketball player. And he also played a bang-up game of baseball.

Although sports were in their heyday, banks were not and they fell like ten pins. In 1930 an additional 1,300 banks failed. There was no federal (FICA) insurance to protect depositors—those who had money in the banks were to see nothing or only an insignificant portion of their deposits returned.

There was no bailing out of the banks by the government and American taxpayers, as was done in the late 1980s and 1990s. It was downright hardcore hardship. America's confidence in banks, bankers, stock brokers, and yes, even the government, was shattered.

What were people to do? Newspapers carried the news of people who grew so despondent that they jumped from tall building windows and committed suicide in other ways.

VI
DEPRESSION DILEMMA

As the winter of 1930 began to cast its most somber shadows across the depression-struck nation, the dreams of most Americans had been shattered with the cruel reality that it could be a long time before economic normality would return to their country, if ever!

Of course there had been monumental lessons learned, one being that those of "old wealth," (handed down from family member to family member) were not infallible in their judgment. Many of their ivory towers teetered and in chain reaction toppled when the bastion that was Wall Street came tumbling down.

It was most difficult for those of extreme wealth to adjust to being penniless for they had long led pampered lives and many of them had never endured want, hunger or a day of backbreaking labor. By contrast, those of meager means had known few luxuries and had learned to subsist without those amenities that the rich considered necessities. They had become experts at squeezing the maximum livelihood from hard-earned dollars.

So it was that former tycoons in the business world, high salaried executives, top notch engineers and lawyers stood in long lines at Salvation Army shelters, soup kitchens and unemployment offices, rubbing elbows with people whom they might well have snubbed just a few months earlier.

Even in Happyland most of the unemployed were bitter, feeling their government had misled them on the severity of the depression. Very few trusted the country's elected officials and President Hoover was rapidly rising to the top of the list of villains.

The previously much-hailed humanitarian Hoover continued staunchly to oppose any government program or legislation to put people back to work or implement welfare relief. Sadly, many of the beneficiaries of such help would have been those who helped pay the taxes that had been used to purchase the food and medical supplies Hoover had doled out to needy Europeans during and after the war.

Industrialists, whose businesses continued to thrive, made fantastic profit margins by setting high production quotas, dropping wages and demanding that employees work longer hours. However, there were some compassionate employers, mostly operators of smaller enterprises, who established shifts and shortened the work week, which did allow more people to continue working. A 1930 survey of 1,026 industries indicated 126 had given wage increases while 900 of those reporting decreased compensation to their employees.

Those who were working part-time sometimes made out reasonably well. Many younger men and women, both single and married, moved back home with parents. Even in Happyland people, who were not related, doubled up in houses and apartments.

There are those who attained great wealth during the depression, even in small towns. Those who had their money in safe investments and were fortunate enough not to have lost it in bank closures sometimes profited by the misfortune of others.

Out of jobs, many people were unable to make payments on their homes even when owing as little as $300. Rather than let the houses go back to the lending agency and receive nothing, they sold to shrewd investors for say $500, feeling at least they had $200, which at 1930 prices would buy a lot of groceries.

Those who lived during the 1970s and 1980s, when inflation grew by leaps and bounds, would find prices during the Great Depression ridiculously low in comparison.

Hamburger, on special, sold two pounds for 25 cents, a loaf of bread 7 cents, flour in 49-pound bags $1.75. Beans were 10 cents per can—two for 15 cents on sale, beefsteak 26 cents per pound, and butter 30 cents per pound. Oleomargarine was soon on the market for 10 cents a pound. To satisfy strong dairy interests, Iowa law required that margarine be sold without color. As a result most people colored their own to make it more appealing to the eye. Ice cream, made with pure cream, was 20 or 25 cents per quart.

Reasonably priced living quarters were usually available in most small towns with rooms renting for $5 to $10 per month, apartments $10 to $15 per month and houses $15 to $25. Women's dresses could be purchased for $3 to $5 and a good suit for $15. However, to those who were broke, the price was immaterial for they had no money with which to buy.

Dr. Harry Kunkle's mother, Mary, was postmistress at Rinard, Iowa during the 1930s when postage for a first class letter was three cents. Strangely enough, Harry and wife Isabel recall that one man accused her of getting a rake-off as postage shouldn't be that high!

The Salvation Army, just as it is today, was always there to help people without fanfare and media acclaim. Its efforts drew the praise of those who lived through the depression and most of those thankful people continue to contribute without hesitation to that wonderful organization.

When Salvation Army and municipal shelters were filled to capacity, those who could afford to do so slept in flop houses, the worst of which went for as little as ten cents per day. Sometimes as many as three people chipped in to pay the dime, then slept in three eight-hour shifts on filthy mattresses in stacked wooden boxlike cubicles.

Still in all, those who slept in flop houses were living like kings compared to those sleeping in unheated warehouses, makeshift tents, cardboard boxes, tunnels or under bridges. Luxury for many was a cardboard box over a sidewalk coal chute grate where their cold numbed bodies could be warmed by steam escaping from coal boilers and pipes.

So it was that millions of men and even a few women rode boxcars and hitchhiked while traveling the country hoping to find employment. Hobo jungles sprang up in wooded areas along railroad tracks, usually by streams at the outskirts of the smaller towns.

Happyland's hobo jungle was located on the west bank of the Boone River below the Zublin and Garth ice harvesting dam. Fishing was good there—so Hank and Clinty often fished the same spot as did the hobos. No one ever felt unsafe—the hobos at all times were congenial. Carp, although quite bony, were plentiful. All the hobos needed to catch them was some chalk line and a treble hook. Bait—carp loved cornmeal doughballs and farmers certainly didn't care if a few ears were taken from their fields.

During the summer the hobos slept in the open-air or in lean-tos constructed from tree branches with roofs of scrap canvas, castoff tarpaper or anything that would shed water. Most of them headed for a warmer climate before cold weather settled in—some on freight trains—others hitched rides with a sympathetic truck or automobile driver. Travelers then could pick up hitchhikers without concern for their lives.

Hobos, who couldn't find work for food and shelter with a farmer or someone else, suffered a terrible existence. Hank, during the early morning hours, would often see them coming from Wehrheim's or Marvel's sales barns and even from the shelter of stock-loading chutes along the railroad tracks. A few could be seen emerging from open church vestibules.

There were no Salvation Army soup kitchens in Happyland; they existed only in larger cities. Bakeries gave out three-day old bread, rolls and other baked goods. Grocery stores usually let the "traveling men", as the hobos liked to be called, have aged milk and produce for food spoiled more rapidly in those days since preservatives were not added. Most restaurants saved leftovers which were placed in clean containers—these the hobos considered a special treat.

Each jungle had a huge pot in which to make stew. Most of the "traveling men" would offer to work for food in any form. Of course,

Britt, Iowa hobo jungle (1934). They shared the stew.

Photo courtesy of Darrell C. Schaper

many who could afford to do so gave them money or food while others allowed them to pick vegetables from their gardens. From what they accumulated a hobo stew was created and cooked in the big pot for everyone to share.

Hobo Drum Corps marches in Britt, Iowa.
Photo courtesy Darrell C. Schaper

Hank's Mother Lucy always gave something to the traveling men—food from her garden, canned vegetables, bread—sometimes eggs from her henhouse. On one occasion she even washed clothing for two boys from New York who were searching for work in Iowa. Her standard comment: "If you ever can afford to do so, help someone else in need."

Strangely enough, the hobos rarely stole or robbed. Most of them were men of honesty who would gladly work if given the opportunity. Naturally there were some "no goods" who brought problems to the hobo jungle, but the honorable inhabitants had unpleasant methods of dealing with criminals.

Let the reader be apprised there is a distinct difference between a hobo and a bum. As the old-time travelling men quickly explained, "A hobo will work - but will not pay for transportation." Britt, a beautiful north central Iowa town, is still the scene of a colorful "National Hobo Convention," an annual event held on the second Saturday in August—great fun!

Chicago came to have a reputation worldwide as a city of gangsters. Some World War II veterans will remember that even in North Africa when the city of Chicago was mentioned, an Arab youngster would respond, "Gangster!"

At the height of criminal activities during the depression, the most notorious gang leaders had to have appropriate nicknames if they were to gain any worthwhile notoriety. A brief review reveals Al "Scarface" Capone, Francis "Two Gun" Crowley, "Big Rudolph" Duringer, "Bugs" Moran, Jack "Legs" Diamond, etc. Perhaps this was a throwback to the old days when gunslingers, the likes of William "Billy the Kid" Bonney, roamed the west.

Lest the reader develop the opinion that life was dangerous to the average person back in those days, it should be explained that the gangster of that era would probably qualify for a sainthood of sorts in comparison to the criminals in the hardcore drug-crazed segment of society that existed at the time of this writing.

Honesty was still held high on the list of desirable virtues by most people, even during the depression years. Like James Arthur and Lucy, people in rural areas rarely, if ever, locked their doors and if they did, it was with a standard lock, the key for which could be purchased at any hardware store.

Rural people tended to keep the criminally-inclined on honest pathways. Horse and cattle thieves, murderers and rapists had been ceremonially hung on the spot well past the turn of the century.

Barbara Hansen, Paton, Iowa, cites an example of honesty to be found in a small rural town of the 1930s. Tommy Jack, a cattle farmer on a large scale, had lost a good deal of money when the banks closed in 1926. He had accumulated a sizable herd. Some animals he had raised himself; others were range cattle he had purchased from Nebraska and the Dakotas for final feed-off before market.

After the bank failures, Tommy never believed in banks and kept his money hidden at home. He had just sold a sizable number of cattle and went to the Paton Bank where he cashed the check, some $10,000 or more.

Placing the cash in an old sock, Tommy walked out to the sidewalk where he became involved in conversation. While talking and stooping over to tie his shoelace or something, he absentmindedly laid the sock on the hood of a car.

The conversation concluded, Tommy and his friends strolled on down the street to conduct other business. He had been gone for some time when someone noticed a sock on a car hood. To their surprise, they learned it was full of money. Knowing it was probably Tommy's money they dashed down the street, found Tommy and returned it to him. At this writing such honesty would be front page news!

During the depression era a person could go for a stroll after dark in downtown New York or Chicago with very little fear of being raped, mugged, robbed or murdered. Today most people would be courting disaster were they to venture into some of those same areas after dark and, yes, even during daylight without an attack dog or weapon.

Drugs have brought extreme change to our country and are responsible for an epidemic of heinous murders, rapes, abductions and sexual assaults of even little children. Some youths of good parentage and background are known to commit murder for hardcore drugs.

There were gang wars in the 1920s and 1930s, but the gangsters of that era didn't stalk the common man on the streets. Alcohol is considered a drug, but it was a rare, rare instance, in those days, when man killed to satisfy his own personal craving for a drink.

Movies continued as the favorite affordable entertainment throughout the depression. Those who could afford it usually attended at least one movie a week. The silent movies had been great, but with sound, they were even better.

With the invention of the first magnetic recorder, called the "Blattnerphone," better sound synchronization was achieved, greatly enhancing realism in movies. It was inevitable that someone would soon produce a dynamic war movie, for the sound effects and filming technology were by then available.

In 1930 "All Quiet on the Western Front" was a milestone in realism and, ironically, directed by a Lewis Milestone. This was the first and last movie James Arthur ever took Hank to see. Perhaps its vicious presentation appalled him.

The story featured seven young German students, whose schoolmasters goaded them into joining the German Army during World War I. It forcefully brought home to James Arthur and Hank what Clinty, and others like him, had gone through during their wartime service.

With unprecedented drama, fabulous settings and the superb acting of Lew Ayres, Slim Summerville and Ben Alexander, the picture took the glamor out of war and brought it down to its true level of horror and reality. Hank would never forget the final scene when the sole survivor of the original seven reached out to catch a beautiful butterfly and was killed by a sniper bullet.

Students of military history have learned that a strong Allied attack was launched after word had been received that an Armistice would go into effect November 11, 1918. Casualties were heavy and history buffs who have read or seen the movie, "All Quiet on the Western Front," couldn't help thinking of that useless waste of life and wonder why such an attack was ever allowed.

Youngsters, young men, and non World War I veterans learned through the viewing of that great movie the full horror of war. Little did they realize that at that very time in Germany, Adolf Hitler, along with the NAZIs (National Socialist German Workers Party), was actively plotting the overthrow of the democratic government of President Paul von Hindenburg, which would be a prelude to World War II.

Hank and other youngsters would have been far more impressed with the scenes had they known that many of them would find themselves squared off with the Germans in such battles as those at Anzio Beachhead and Cassino, Italy, locked in the noise, destruction and hell of a stationary front similar to that depicted in "All Quiet on the Western Front."

Those families on farms continued to eat fairly wholesome meals. During the winter months they consisted mostly of canned meat, vegetables, fruit, and potatoes. Food staples purchased in town were sparse commodities—especially sugar, spices and flavorings. A banana or an orange was a coveted gift, usually restricted to such special occasions as holidays and birthdays. Homemade ice cream, fudge and taffy were rarely-made delicacies. Could times become any rougher? They could and they would!

It was a thrilling day indeed in 1931 when Happyland's first municipal swimming pool was completed at a cost of $18,805. Many years before a dam had been built by volunteers on White Fox Creek in Kendall Young Park to make a place for swimming. It had long since been washed out by floods and since raw sewage went into the Boone River, the advisability of swimming in it was questionable.

The city council allowed children free admission on Wednesday mornings. It was a smart move, for that same year the city's largest plant, Knapp Monarch, an appliance manufacturer, closed its doors and moved to St. Louis leaving two hundred more unemployed. Few were left who could pay admission.

On one of those first free admission days a cavalry regiment from Fort Des Moines, out on a march, came by the Twin Parks, which bordered the pool area. They were an impressive sight on their beautiful horses, sabers and all.

It was an extremely hot day and the cavalrymen looked longingly at the nice pool. The soldiers allowed the curious young boys to pet their horses and, of course, all of the kids were extremely thrilled when they unsheathed and showed them their sabers. Few of the youngsters had seen a cavalryman except in the movies. Hank, for the first time, had serious thoughts about being a soldier. Hearing of Hank's interest, Clinty soon had him practicing the manual of arms and foot drills with his bee-bee gun in the back yard. Roger McIntosh, an enterprising classmate, gave Hank a job selling the "Saturday Evening Post" door to door, and Mrs. Charlie Nelson hired him to mow and rake her lawn. The two jobs netted him enough to buy a few things and attend a movie now and then.

Old time cowboy movies were patterned after western novels by Zane Grey or other authors seeking to capture the adventures of the old west. In all ways they pictured the hero as a law abiding person of high morals who was out to help the oppressed.

True, those films did not project the realism of today's movies, but they did send young viewers, like Hank, away with a wholesome respect for goodness and a feeling that they had an obligation to help their fellowman, and, of course, combat evil in all forms.

Unfortunatly, the tragic fate of the American Indian at the hands of the white man rarely was brought out in movies until after World War II. Of course, the cowboy's life and activities were grossly magnified and in movies the Daltons and Younger brothers turned up in situations they had never experienced and in locations where they had never been.

If he was ever to learn the tricks necessary to become a cowboy, Hank felt he best continue his movie lessons. The Isis Theater films with synchronized sound were getting better. One Saturday movie would stand out in his memory forever—not the movie so much, but the events to follow!

The most outstanding trick came about when Hoot Gibson in the white hat was being chased by three bad guys (always in black hats) across the plains and ultimately through some woods. At the height of the chase Hoot rode under a tree, reached up and grabbed a limb and swung neatly out of the saddle; meanwhile his horse galloped out of sight into the bushes.

When the last of the trouble-causing trio loped under the tree, the peerless pinto rider leaped from the limb and knocked tail-end Charlie from his charger and, to put it mildly, literally eliminated him from the balance of the afternoon movie.

In the production of the old westerns there appeared to be an unwritten code—no two villians could ever be portrayed as having the ability to overcome one hero. So it was that the two remaining desperadoes sped off into the sunset to bushwhack some sodbuster's eighty-year old grandmother or do some such easy task.

With this latest caper fresh in Hank's mind, he headed for home anxious to try duplicating the action. Immediately he saddled Judy, the Indian pony, and carefully surveyed the orchard for a limb of suitable size, height and strength to serve as the scene of his first tree trick triumph.

Having located the tree of his choice, Hank practiced the leap from the saddle onto the limb until he was able to duplicate the hero's performance quite proficiently. Then, disguised as a pony express rider with saddlebags full of gold and mail, he made sure he had the minimum required three gun slingers on his trail and headed into the orchard at full gallop, head down, hat hanging on his back from the chin strap.

Now, the one who was playing the part of the cowboy's dog effectively for that day's production had gone through many an ambush and chase with Hank. However, pow-pow gun sound effects had always been used.

Hank had purchased a cap pistol and the real bangs altered the scene enough that he would have been wise to have called off production for the day.

At the report of the cap pistol, Hank's loyal dog Jack thought his master was being harmed and with a mad, barking dash attempted to head off the horse and stop her. The horse veered and it became apparent it wasn't going to be necessary for Hank to stretch up to grab the limb, as he had originally planned, for the one he was heading for on the new course was chest high.

Approaching the limb at a speed far greater than intended, Hank could do nothing but hold his arms and hands outstretched to cushion the impact.

It was fortunate indeed that the limb was smaller than the one Hank had chosen for the stunt or he would have been boothill-bound for sure. The limb was small enough to bend quite easily, but strong enough not to break with his weight.

When the horse reached a point where she and Hank parted company, he found himself relying on the limb as his sole means of support. Holding on with all the strength he could muster, he soon found himself and the limb headed in the direction opposite that of the horse.

For the next few seconds Hank looked like a runaway pendulum on a grandfather clock, as he swung to and fro crashing into smaller branches. He harvested more apples in those few seconds than some itinerant fruit pickers could have garnered in a day.

When the limb stopped whipping, Hank fell to the ground amidst a heap of green apples, his breathing momentarily halted by the impact. The dog apprehensively licked Hank in the face as he lay on the ground unable to raise a hand or utter a word.

In a few seconds with his breath restored, Hank raised himself from the tree's apple crop and slowly dragged himself to the house.

The horse by this time was grazing in the yard unconcerned with the calamity that surrounded her.

While Hank's Mother applied iodine to fifty scratches, more or less, Hank explained what had happened and then proceeded to the davenport for rest and recuperation. Later, feeling better, he ambled out to help Clinty pick up the bushels of green apples that littered the ground.

James Arthur was a bit concerned when he came home that afternoon, wondering why Lucy had picked so many green apples. She announced, "I'm going to can some; they make such wonderful pies."

For the next few days apple pie, apple cobbler or apple crisp was a part of each meal except breakfast. Cousin Clinty finally got Hank in a corner and explained cowboy heroes really don't perform all the daring doings depicted on the screen and that professional stunt men usually take over the tricky parts.

Clinty decided to play it safe and suggested to Hank that if he had his heart set on being a stunt man, he would surely appreciate his going next door to the George Groves farm since they had a pear tree, and he could sure as hell use a little variation in desserts.

The day Hank played "Arnold the Apple Picker" instead of "Dry Gulch Dan" kinda dampened his desires to become a cowboy for a few weeks.

A popular comic strip in the newspaper at the time was about Tarzan of the Apes. The story intrigued Hank and after getting the book from the library, he threw himself headlong into a few of his adventures. The tree bit in Tarzan's performance was dangerous all right. Tarzan usually swung on grapevines but, by substituting a rope, Hank found the stunt was far easier than duplicating some of the feats performed in the Westerns.

Extras were hard to come by and a playmate of long standing (we'll call him Fearless Freddy) got a mite tired in the legs after a day sitting in the treetop, playing his inevitable role of the ape in the productions.

Freddy's parents finally got word of Hank's episode as "Arnold the Apple Picker" when their son complained about shortness of breath (from chest thumping) and scratches sustained when he missed a branch and fell face first into a gooseberry bush.

Fearless Freddy's parents decided this play acting had gone far enough and, in addition to tiring their son, could also get a little dangerous. They promptly withdrew him from bit parts before he could be torn apart, took him out of the bright lights and put him on a new bicycle.

Freddy made it clear he was through bungling in the jungle and allowed as how he would a whole lot rather go back to being the bad guy in Westerns. Cousin Clinty said the boy had real talent and would probably have had a promising future playing the part of the ape, but went on to say he did have a helluva time overcoming his tendency to dive into things.

That fall crop prices continued their descent to unbelievable lows; corn brought seven cents per bushel and oats five cents. Cousin Clinty, James Arthur, Big Brother and Hank finally got all the corn picked before Christmas. Many people found it unprofitable to hire hand corn pickers and left it standing in the fields. Farmers were paid a measly $3.00 per 100 pound weight for hogs.

When woodpiles became depleted and no more trees could be located, free for the cutting, many farmers resorted to burning corn in their space heaters and furnaces. It was a terrible tragedy that this should happen when people in the cities were starving. Still, on the federal level the politicians refused to give aid.

DEPRESSION CHRISTMAS

A farmstead stood at the side of the road,
Its clapboard weathered and worn.
Inside the house a woman stood,
Her apron tattered and torn.

She stood at an old wood burning stove,
While dabbing at a tear in her eye.
She was too proud to allow her family to see
That sadness had caused her to cry.

The Great Depression had taken its toll,
But she had never been one to complain.
The bitter she had taken, along with the sweet,
But now in her heart there was pain.

With coming of spring she knew she must move
From her house at the end of the lane.
A lifetime of work had been for naught,
All labors had been in vain.

For the banks had failed to open their doors,
And crops stood in the field.
For the cost of having grain harvested
Could not be paid from the yield.

But when she turned to face her family,
There was a Christmas smile on her face.
Let's all be thankful we're alive and well,
And God is still in his place.

by H. R. Ankrum

There was some talk of Big Sister having to drop out of school, but Mother Lucy would not hear of it. It was finally decided that education had become extremely important and they would make every effort to see that she would be able to finish high school, especially since she would graduate the next spring.

The banks and creditors continued to pressure James Arthur to pay off his promissory notes. Finally, in deep trouble themselves, they called for immediate payment wihout regard to due date. James Arthur, like most others, was down the ladder so far that his credit wouldn't allow him to buy a turtleneck sweater for a termite on a yearly installment plan.

The closeout farm sale was a sad spectacle which was being repeated at farm after farm all over the midwest. Attendance was usually good, but most of those present were there for lack of something better to do and for the free coffee and sandwiches served midway in the sale.

Many people came to sales to get an indication of what their items would bring in a forthcoming sale of their own property. Then too, the auctioneer, Val Wehrheim, always told a few funny jokes and some farmers drove miles to stand in a compost pile, braced with their backs against an icy cold wind, strictly for the entertainment.

Farm sale
Photo courtesy of Connie Samuelson

Father James Arthur held up pretty well during his sale as the auctioneer's chant brought five to ten dollars for cattle, one to three dollars for calves, five or six dollars for wagons, and two dollars for the family's wonderful sleigh. It was plainly visible his composure finally was slipping as the auctioneer pounded the gavel and proclaimed the last item sold.

Father James Arthur walked slowly to the house, through the door and out again on the side porch. Hank found him there with tears streaming down his cheeks, repeating over and over—"Thirty-five years for nothing."

James Arthur had gone out into the world at age twelve to earn a living for himself. He had always been an honest, hard working man, who had taken in numerous relatives when they were down on their luck and somehow had managed to feed and shelter them as well as his own immediate family. It tugged at Hank's heart to see him beaten into the ground by a force against which he could not retaliate. James Arthur was self-schooled, had been a tough disciplinarian, and was somewhat of a "diamond in the rough."

Although Hank didn't fully understand the impact of what was happening, he did sense life would never again be the same for his Father or the family. Somehow he wanted to be alone.

With head down, Hank walked slowly out the door and crossed the yard. As he looked down at his tattered overalls with knee patches on knee patches and shoes long due for replacement, he could not conceive of times becoming worse, yet from his Father's display of emotion, he knew it just might be possible. As he crossed the barnyard, he felt a moist nose nuzzle his hand. His dog Jack must have sensed his sadness and was urging Hank to share his sorrow.

Approaching the barn, he could see men loading trucks with horses, cows and calves. Clinty, with tears in his eyes, was helping. When a man came to the manger for the Indian pony Judy, Jack growled in defiance and Cousin Clinty turned his back in anguish. At this point Hank was no longer able to control his emotions and he sought solace in the hayloft where he could allow his tears to flow freely. He had fed many of those animals since their births, and they had come to be like part of the family to him.

Clinty soon could be heard coming up the haymow ladder. Weldon Helmick, who had purchased Judy, had seen Hank crying and told Cousin Clinty Hank could keep her. After telling the boy that, Clinty put his hand on Hank's shoulder, sat down beside him and explained that everyone in the family was alive and healthy and for this all should be happy. He went on to remind Hank that he still had his horse and dog and that a good soldier faces each day with a smile on his face. With Clinty's encouragement, Hank felt like he was now ready to face the future.

That spring Big Sister graduated from high school and it was a proud girl who marched down the aisle and across the stage to get her diploma. When she departed for the school she had her hair beautifully curled, wore a lovely new dress and as Clinty said, "She looked pretty as a picture."

Schools of higher learning had moved west slowly during the development of the United States and though a high school diploma is now considered a mediocre educational achievement, history records the first high school commencement in Happyland was held June 24, 1881 with only four girls graduating.

Most parents in the midwest had not been given the opportunity for education beyond the eighth grade and, for this reason, felt a deep sense of pride in fulfillment of their dreams through the accomplishments of their offspring. Everyone in the family was proud that she was the first in the family to achieve that goal.

The family moved to Happyland shortly after the sale, and Father James Arthur was fortunate enough to find an acreage along Brewer Creek and close to the Boone River. The acreage had a nice barn with stalls for Judy. It was a break that they had been allowed to keep her as she could be used to plow and cultivate the garden. Mother Lucy was not one to complain and could stretch a dollar further than anyone could imagine. She was to perform the impossible during the lean years to come.

Turmoil, depression and strife were not conditions solely reserved for the United States. Shattered economies were being experienced in Europe, the Far East and, for that matter, around the globe. The stage was rapidly being set for a military scenario that would rock the world. The key players now were jockeying into position for attainment of power beyond their borders—possibly world conquest.

Japan, long seeking to rid the Far East of Western influence, had invaded China's Manchuria. Their better equipped and trained forces soon over-ran Manchuria. The word "over-ran" is used to describe the action as the vastness in both population and land in China precluded complete control.

Germany's economy had gone from inflationary recession to depression. Adolf Hitler, whose armies would launch World War II, was gaining popularity with the NAZI party and German industrialists.

In Italy I1 Duce (the leader) Benito Mussolini was well entrenched in the leadership of the Fascist party, had abolished Parliament and was now the uncontested dictator of Italy. He had established a strong Fascist police force and personally exercised total dictatorial control over all phases of government, banking and labor.

Back in Happyland, James Arthur was doing somewhat better than he expected. He still had his haybaler and, surprisingly, with Clinty and Big Brother's help, he was getting enough jobs to turn a profit. Some locales in the midwest and western states had suffered a drought and grasshopper problems. Consequently farmers in those states were badly in need of hay.

Robert Nelson, then living in Kansas, now a retired railroad civil engineer, recalls that Kansas not only had clouds of dust to contend with, but also clouds of grasshoppers. Ravished from hunger, the pests descended on vegetation eating everything they could ingest.

Grasshoppers were so thick they formed a slippery film on the roads causing thousands of accidents.

Nelson recalls how they put poisoned grain around the edges of fields hoping the grasshoppers would eat it. When fall came all most farmers had was a little wheat, a little corn, alfalfa and milo (sorghum), the hoppers had taken all other crops. Continuing, Nelson states, "The pastures were dry and provided no feed for livestock. They baled wheat straw and poured molasses on it so that the livestock would eat the straw." Most farmers, he remembers, pretty well lived on eggs and milk that winter.

Not one to sit back and mope, James Arthur took hay in payment for baling, then filled orders for bales to be trucked to the drought areas. Not large profits, but they did pay the rent and utilities, though nothing was left for frills.

Meanwhile Hank and Big Sister helped Mother Lucy in the garden. Big Brother and William "Bill" Bashford did a lot of hunting and supplemented the meat supply. Hank and neighbor boys, Clifford "Tip" Van Doren and Eugene Bashford, picked berries at Briggs Woods and Frank and Shad Huddleston allowed them to gather nuts from their grove. Hank, Eugene and Frank Bashfield caught fish in the Boone River, which still had quite a plentiful supply of catfish and bass. Still Hank never found the hole his Cousin Clinty described where the fish were so thick and aggressive one had to go behind a tree to bait the hook.

Clinty allowed as how Jack was the best hunting dog he'd seen since his coon dog, "Old Blue". He said, "Old Blue was so good that when I wanted a coon pelt, all I had to do was set out a board the length of the pelt I wanted, and he would bring one back that just fit."

With a whimsical smile on his face, he concluded the story saying, "Everything went fine until one day my mother set the ironing board on the back porch and Old Blue went out hunting a coon to fit it and he never came back!"

Jack was a fabulous hunting dog and when fall came Hank and Big Brother, now fifteen years old, did a lot of rabbit and squirrel hunting. There were always game and Mother Lucy's chickens for the table. Of course, without Mother Lucy's garden, meals would have been far less nutritious. James Arthur finally purchased a milk cow and milk and butter supplies became ample.

Occasionally while hunting or fishing Hank and his friends would see the fabulous Scoutmaster Murray McMurray with his Scout Troop on a field trip along Brewer Creek or the Boone River. Yes, Hank and his friends would have loved to belong, but they couldn't afford the membership much less the uniform. But, it appeared to be much fun as the Scouts were taught about nature and camping out in the woods.

Murray McMurray was one of the founders of scouting in the mid-west, having formed a troop in 1913. Although a very busy man with banking: first operating a bank and later "McMurray's Hatchery," he spent untold hours building fine character in his charges. Many of Murray's scouts went on to become the stalwart citizens of the community. MacKinlay Kantor paid the great man high tribute in his book, "God and Country." John McMurray, his son, was to take over the proud McMurray tradition as scoutmaster, succeeding his father in 1950—with brother Charles as his assistant.

McMurray's Hatchery went on to gain nearly worldwide notoriety—shipping fowl to many corners of the globe. Occasionally celebrities, like the movie star Robert Taylor, who raised chickens as a hobby, would pay visits to the hatchery to purchase common or exotic chickens.

Robert Taylor and wife Ursula Theis visit McMurry Hatchery (Taylor third from left in front row, wife to his right).

Photo courtesy of John McMurray

Somehow James Arthur and his family managed to subsist at a time when malnutrition was becoming more than a small problem throughout the United States, a country that had always known abundance. During this period an estimated two million people drifted from one place to another looking for work, and food lines became ever longer. Hobos were quite expert at soliciting food. They put marks on fences, gates and trees, indicating to other traveling men that a family usually gave something.

By this time Hank was getting up in the world and had been to Boone, Fort Dodge, Highview, Woolstock, and the city dump—and had found out the Happyland grain elevator was not the tallest building in the world. It was, however, the highest thing in town, except for old Willy Sipmore on Saturday night.

Speaking of old Willy, there was one morning when he nearly swore off the bottle for good. However, most people would have made book he was referring to switching to drinking his pulverizing potion from a pitcher instead of the bottle.

It seems Willy had engaged himself in a booze fighting contest the night before and had licked a pint, up to and including the squeezings from the label. Stomach on fire and his head spinning like a cork in a whirlpool, he headed for home. He approached James Arthur and Lucy's house. Somehow it must have looked like home to him, and he proceeded to the back door.

All of the family members had retired except James Arthur, who was talking with the neighbor across the street. Everything had been serene up to that time and little did anyone realize this would be any different than the normal peaceful night in Happyland.

After all had settled down to a night's sleep, old weaving Willy staggered into Mother Lucy's bedroom. Willy gasped a sigh of relief, marveling that he had made it so many blocks. He then sat down on the edge of the bed and proceeded to take off his shoes and socks.

Lucy didn't awaken completely, she later said, and drifted quickly back to sleep thinking it was James Arthur coming to bed. Old Willy finally mumbled a few incoherent words that sounded like he was trying to blow out a candle with his mouth full of marbles, and it was then Lucy awoke and realized it wasn't James Arthur.

A few seconds later a blood-curdling scream pierced the quiet night. It sounded like someone was being given an enema with battery acid.

By now everyone in the house was awake and Jack, the dog, growled and bolted down the stairs to the first floor, bouncing off the wall and slipping on the waxed hardwood floors as he rounded the corner at the bottom of the steps.

James Arthur had just come home and by the time everyone else arrived on the scene, he had an armlock on Willy and was taking him to the door, while Jack was sinking his teeth deeper into Willy's leg with each step he took. Mother Lucy had scratched poor old Willy's face until he looked like he had been picking gooseberries out of a thorny bush with his teeth.

Cousin Clinty said he watched Sipmore as he departed the premises and said that, with all due respect to Red Grange, the famed football player from Illinois, it was the greatest exhibition of open field running he had ever witnessed. Clinty said old Sipmore rated high despite the fact he had dropped a few points by debarking a tree as he weaved down the driveway enroute to the street.

From what Willy told James Arthur later, he didn't remember all the activities of that eventful night, but he did allow the nectar he was drinking must have had a wildcat in the bottom of the bottle. Willy lived to be eighty years old, maintaining to the last that he would rather battle six dozen rattlesnakes and a pink elephant than have one more encounter with Lucy.

Hank still enjoyed cowboy movies, but his primary interest had now shifted to sports. More kids were available in town to form teams, and every spare moment was spent practicing or playing the games that were in season.

Playing baseball in the vacant lots behind Fred Heyer's garage at the corner of Superior and Pleasant streets was wonderful and, caught up in the fun of it all, Hank, Sam Ades and several other boys frequently played until dark, not even going home for supper.

Arriving home one night, Hank discovered his Mother Lucy and Father had gone up to Aunt Minnie's—what a break, he hadn't been asked to go along!

Swede Bend country school (near Stratford) baseball team. Left to right: Mike Waller, Arvid Anderson, Vernon Anderson, Carl Berglund, Iver Carlberg, Bill Hayer, Junior J. Sundine, and Bertil Carlberg.

Photo courtesy of Helen Anderson Nelson

Boys playing ball—looks like the dog calls the runner safe.
Photo used with permission of Kellogg Company

Hank made himself a couple of sandwiches, drank a glass of milk and, his appetite still ravishing, proceeded to the old icebox and looked for something sweet to round off the meal. His eyes fell upon it—a large bowl of pudding—wow!

He didn't bother to get a smaller bowl as he felt certain he could eat it all. The pudding tasted sorta flat, nothing like Mother Lucy had ever made before. Simple, thought Hank—they still had a cow, just add a little sugar and cream. Somehow he couldn't quite adjust the ingredients just right, but he kept on adding more sugar and more cream. By the time Hank finished the bowl, he wasn't sure he felt as good as he should have and while listening to the radio, he could hardly hear the program over his burps and belches. His dog Jack finally arose and left the room.

When his Mother arrived home, he met her at the kitchen door and quickly blurted out, "Mom, don't make any more of that pudding; it tasted terrible." Mother Lucy shook her head quizzicaly, then asked, "What pudding? Show me the bowl."

Hank went to the kitchen sink, retrieved the bowl and showed it to her, adding, "I ate the whole bowl. I hope you're not angry." With that Mother Lucy howled with side-splitting laughter. A few minutes later, when she could bring herself to speak, she made the amazing announcement to a perplexed Hank that he had just eaten her entire supply of corn starch. She had prepared it to starch the shirts and blouses the following day. Hank would never put on a starched shirt again without remembering that hilarious experience.

The Hamilton County Fair, like those in most rural counties at that time, was one of the highlights of the year. On the serious side were the competitors vying for prizes awarded for the best crafts, baking and crops. For the sports minded there were baseball games, horse racing, greased pig catching, foot races, and even the never-to-be under-rated hog calling contest. Providing glamor for the fair were the carnival and the "free acts."

Motorcycle racing and stunt riding were becoming extremely popular at fairs. Whenever motorcycle racing was discussed during the 1920s and 30s, the names of Joe Petrali, Jim Davis and Miny Waln were sure to surface. Top billing in stunt riding still went to the great Putt Mossman.

Few Happylanders had the opportunity to see Putt Mossman, but many were thrilled to watch Whitley "Whit" Hemingway and Carlton Crosley doing impromptu riding exhibitions on the schoolgrounds. Revving up their engines they would streak between the basketball backboard uprights, their cycle handlebars missing the 4"x4" posts by only fractions.

Of all motorcycle enthusiasts Whit was, and still is at this writing, one of the greatest. Hardly a weekend went by when he and Carlton were not to be seen whizzing around. Riders of the fast, maneuverable machines were considered daredevils, and rightfully so, especially during that period as loose gravel roads and chuckholes in streets offered ample opportunities for spills.

Carlton Crosley and Whit Hemingway—a couple of daring dudes.
Photo courtesy of Whit Hemingway

The author and Whit sat in the latter's law office in Happyland, where the author had come to reminisce a bit about Whit's long association with motorcycles. Motorcycle memorabilia is displayed tastefully in his office. He holds trophies for six Iowa amateur championships—covering years from 1940 to 1963.

Whit, a modest person whose mannerisms - measured and deliberate speech closely resemble that of the great movie star James Stewart, drawled, "What would you like to talk about first?" The author responded, "Why don't we start from your early days of cycling?"

Still an extremely handsome, well-preserved man at seventy-seven, Whit settled his tall 6'3" athletic frame back in his plush executive chair, grinned broadly while clasping his strong powerful hands behind his neck. The following interesting stories resulted from the conversation.

Whit was not quite thirteen years of age when he and his cousin, Carlton, pooled their fifteen dollar savings and, without the knowledge of their parents, purchased an old Indian motorcycle.

Driver's licenses were not required back in those days but, being skeptical of obtaining their parents' approval, the boys hid the machine out in a friend's barn across town. Of course their parents eventually learned about the purchase, but by that time both boys had become quite proficient in operating their coveted possession on nearby country roads.

Scarcely a year later the two young cyclists were no longer content with their old slow machine. They yearned for more powerful models. At last they located a couple of second-hand machines within the funds they could raise, and Whit was soon the proud owner of a 1924 Harley-Davidson and Carlton, an Indian Chief.

Carlton became enamored with stunt riding while Whit was obsessed with speed and racing skills. With mounting frequency Carlton strove to emulate the great stunt rider, Putt Mossman. It was while exhibiting his ability to operate his Indian Chief, standing upright on the seat using no hands, that Carlton became a legend in impromptu dismounting. In his enthusiasm, while performing the "Look Ma, no hands routine," he had completely forgotten a swale extending across Des Moines Street between alleys, created to provide better storm drainage.

Whit recalls that when Carlton hit the dip, his cycle went down, he went up and soared in a somewhat modified swan-dive down to the brick street. Whit professes to this day he will never forget the look on Carlton's face when he and his motorcycle parted company! Carlton was embarrassed and more than a little angry when he picked himself up off the bricks and checked for broken bones. Finding only abrasions and contusions, the gutsy Carlton mounted his cycle and zoomed away, still having a self-berating conversation with himself.

Perhaps it was Carlton's stimulating flight off his motorcycle seat that led him to the conclusion there were more thrills to be had in flying. Selling his motorcycle for $75 he used the proceeds to convince an instructor at the Fort Dodge airport to give him flying lessons. Amazingly, at sixteen, Carlton became the youngest pilot in Iowa when he soloed after two lessons.

In 1931 the enterprising Whit, noting there was no Indian motorcycle dealer in Hamilton County, wrote the company and asked if he could be the dealer. Although he was only sixteen years old the company (evidently ready to do anything to boost sales) appointed him as their agent. Laughingly, Whit recounts, "I purchased a new Indian Scout 45, but I wasn't successful in selling any more motorcycles!"

Sometime later Whit acquired an Indian Pony, a small cycle and a rather beat-up Harley-Davidson, which had been driven under the back end of a truck. With hard work he put it in an excellent state of repair. He then was able to compete in both the class 45 and class 80 events at races.

As the number of contestants and spectators dwindled during the depression years, the American Motorcycle Association (AMA) started a new class "C" competition consisting of stock motorcycles competing in all sorts of competition in addition to dirt tracks. Introduced was so-called tourist trophy races, which unlike European time trials, were somewhat like scrambles or the present day motorcross without all of the highrise bumps.

But Whit had a problem—how could he get both cycles to the races? At last he was able to con his good friend, Bradford "Brad" Mason into riding the slower cycle. However, Brad couldn't keep up with Whit's powerful machine and Whit, somewhat disgusted at poking along, took remedial action and towed him. With Brad sitting on the Indian Pony at the end of a fifteen foot clothesline, Whit zoomed around automobiles to the race while Brad held on for dear life!

Whit nearly folds with laughter as he recalls that Brad was not all that pleased with the towing system. After a couple of trips Brad intimated Whit should get someone else to have the dubious pleasure of accompanying him on his trips.

Amazingly Whit continues to be intensely enthusiastic about motorcycles. He has four, and only recently had ridden in road runs in England and Florida. When asked if competing wasn't a bit dangerous at his age, he quipped, "Not as dangerous as riding on the highway." As for Brad Mason, he doesn't say too much—only that he's still not ready to let Whit tow him to a race again! But wait—more later about Brad and Whit.

Whit Hemingway—prepared for race.
Photo courtesy of Carlton Crosley

A short time after the 1931 Hamilton County Fair, tempers flared, fists flew and the air was filled with naughty words. Throughout the midwest the government had sent veterinarians to test cattle for tuberculosis. Those cattle found to be afflicted by the disease were ordered destroyed without reimbursement to the farmers.

Depression-stricken farmers, who had weathered the first rounds of foreclosures, now were faced with disaster for, in many instances, their milk cows were the only things keeping them solvent. Of course, the farmers knew the diseased cattle had to be destroyed, but they had anxiously looked to the government for some type of assistance to help in their losses. As usual, none was forthcoming.

Farmers now were fighting desperately to stay afloat in a financial quagmire that seemed destined to pull all of them under. Something had to be done to draw nationwide attention. In an attempt to do so, they grabbed their pitchforks and formed picket lines at their farms to stave off the veterinarians sent to do the testing.

On September 22, 1931 Iowa National Guardsmen were dispatched to Tipton to perform the distasteful job of forcing the farmers to accede to the testing. Fortunately the guardsmen encountered only verbal harangue. There was no violent resistance. The guardsmen would be called to Burlington October 22 of that same year with the same mission. Most of them were sympathetic with the farmers, for Hoover again had shown no compassion even for his fellow Iowans. Would they vote for him again?

On the national scene, on October 24, 1931 the slippery Al Capone fell into a trap from which he could not wiggle free. The government's Internal Revenue Service nailed him for income tax evasion. It seemed odd since he had been taking in illegal millions for years and had not been convicted for those offenses. The judge sentenced him to eleven years in prison, but only fined him $80,000, hardly a week's profit from his purported earnings.

Meanwhile Happyland residents learned in October, 1931 that, not unlike events in the big cities, things could get a mite rough between alcohol venders in Happyland. Harold "Hob" Jones, one of the town's most notable distributors of distilled spirits, had been murdered. Hob's body had been found two miles northwest of Happyland.

Brother Al's Cities Service Station (1929)
Photo from author's collection

Stanley Quick's gas station, Stratford, Iowa. Left to right: Charles Quick, LaVern Johnson, and Stan Quick. Note one of first electric pumps in Hamilton County, Iowa.
Photo courtesy of Stanley Quick

Hob traded at Hank's older brother Al's gasoline station and was quite brazen about displaying the products he peddled. Once while Hank was hand pumping gas into the old style glass cylindral tank from which the fuel was dispensed, he had glanced over to see two pints of alcohol openly laying on the seat beside the now deceased bootlegger.

The word was out that C. E. "Red" Porter from Belmond, one of Hob's competitors, had attempted to hijack thirty gallons of alcohol from Hob. Hob had resisted and "Red" had killed him. At the time the rumor had it that Porter dragged Hob's body around behind the car to make it look like a gangland-style slaying. Porter fled the state and was not apprehended and brought to trial until twenty years after the murder.

The entire nation was shocked when it learned on March 1, 1932 that Charles Lindbergh's twenty-month old son, Lindbergh's namesake, had been kidnapped. It appeared that "Lucky" Lindbergh, as he had been dubbed after becoming the first man to fly the Atlantic, had run upon the worst kind of bad luck.

Ransom had been demanded and paid, but the child was not returned. It was with much sadness that the Lindberghs and the world received the news that the child's body had been found in the woods a short distance from the Lindbergh home.

Bruno Richard Hauptmann eventually was captured after passing the ransom money. The ladder used to commit the crime and the balance of the ransom money were found in his house. He was convicted, but it would be April 3, 1936 before he would be executed.

The kidnapping led to the adoption of much tougher kidnapping laws. The Lindberghs later had several more children, but they were never to recover from the loss of Charles Jr. The great man was to have somewhat of a troubled life thereafter. Hauptmann never confessed to the crime and his wife, at this writing, is still trying to clear his name, professing that a person staying with them at the time committed the crime and immediately left for Germany.

On May 21, 1932 the perception of women's achievements was given a dramatic boost when Amelia Earhart, a beautiful young girl from Atchison, Kansas, became the first woman to fly the Atlantic Ocean alone. Earlier she had been the first woman to fly the Atlantic as a passenger. Amelia became a heroine worldwide.

Cousin Clinty had long talked of the bonus World War I veterans were promised and had never received. A bill was passed in 1922 to provide the bonus, but payment had never been authorized. Now desperate veterans were clamoring long and loud for the bonus. They had served during the war for a pittance while most of those at home prospered.

Bonus Army Camp

National Archives photo courtesy of Gertrude Horan

Bonus Army Bank

Photo courtesy of Hearst Corporation

In May 1932 angry veterans from all over the United States assembled in Washington D.C. Some came on foot and others hitchhiked while still others rode boxcars. Few had automobiles. They occupied make-shift wooden-canvas structures and tents in camps not far from the capitol in what was called "Bonus City." They were hoping to focus national attention on their cause and gain the support of Congress.

When Hoover and Congress did nothing for seven months, the veterans grew impatient. They occupied old federal buildings that were being razed. When police attempted to remove the veterans from the buildings, confrontations ensued. Washington superintendent of police, Pelham G. Glassford, himself a retired general, tried desperately to restore control. He and the Salvation Army, with resources available, helped feed the bonus army.

Finally the by-now enraged veterans touched off the worst riot in American history to that date. Glassford himself was injured, but he continued to attempt to restore peace and to prevent his officers from using their guns. The situation deteriorated. The marchers received only token sympathy from President Hoover. Hoover directed General Douglas MacArthur, then U.S. Army Chief of Staff and later Commander of Allied Forces in the Pacific during World War II, to commit regular Army troops to quell the riot and drive the veterans out of their makeshift camp.

Major George Patton, later to become General George "Blood and Guts" Patton of World War II, showed the veterans the same compassion that he showed the enlisted men who fought under him in World War II—none! He personally led the final charge.

Major Dwight D. Eisenhower, who would later as a general become Commander of Allied Forces in Europe over Patton, was one of the officers participating in the infamous military action.

When the troops arrived on the scene, the veterans smiled and waved to them; then all hell broke loose. What a sad, sad day it was—tear gas was used heavily on the veterans, some of whom were still suffering from the effects of being gassed during World War I. Then a saber-bayonet charge was launched with tanks lumbering along behind. The veterans, of course, fled. Some tried to retrieve their meager belongings but were forced to flee without them.

A three-month-old baby died of gas inhalation. A small boy tried to return for his pet rabbit and was wounded in the leg by a bayonet. It is doubtful that Patton saw (or would have cared) that one of the men whose tent was burned, Joe Angileno, had been awarded the Distinguished Service Cross for saving Patton's life during World War I.

The vicious attack was a terrifying answer to men's pleas for what was rightfully due them. Ironically, many of the sons of men in that

General MacArthur at the scene—U.S. Army troops oust Bonus Army.
National Archives photo courtesy of Gertrude Horan

Troops tear gas Bonus Army veterans.
Photo courtesy of Gertrude Horan—James D. Horan Collection

bonus army would die in World War II fighting under Generals MacArthur, Patton and Eisenhower—all of whom participated in that glorious feat of arms against their fathers.

Attorney General Mitchell stated that troops were called out at the request of superintendent of police Glassford. Glassford vehemently denied it. Hoover commented, "The challenge to authority had been met!"

Cousin Clinty had wanted to go to Washington, but of course he could not afford to do so, and Mother Lucy had begged him not to ride boxcars. When he heard the shattering news on the radio, tears welled in his eyes and he arose and quietly went out for a long walk.

In Happyland not only the veterans were unhappy about the terrible economic conditions that prevailed. It was during the latter part of August that year when Charles Esters (better known as Chic Middleton) and his wife sat in their ramshackle house near the end of Happyland's Division Street, discussing their lack of finances.

School would be starting soon and their two boys needed clothing, but they couldn't pay their electric bills—much less their other debts. Chic decided if they were going to continue eating and living indoors they'd have to rob somebody or something since he couldn't make a living performing odd jobs. Chic had been reading some cast-out newspapers and detective magazine stories about Bonnie and Clyde, Ma Barker and her family, and others. To Chic these publications had become sort of, "do it yourself manuals."

Now the biggest question was what to rob and, like the criminals Chic had been reading about, they needed a plan. Thus began the criminal life of Happyland's own Ma and Pa Esters.

For starters, Ma and Pa Esters decided they'd have to pull off the job locally. They didn't have a dependable car and, even if they had, they didn't have the money to buy gas to get out of town. It didn't take long to figure out they lacked enough experience to rob banks—too risky.

The local stores were having a rough time making ends meet, and no one carried enough cash around to make robbing an individual worthwhile. City Hall, with all its utilities collection money, would have been a good target. However, Pa Esters quickly ruled out the city hall because the police station was in the basement. It was like Clinty always maintained: a smart criminal wouldn't bother to come to Happyland, even if the localites took up a collection to finance his trip.

At last Ma and Pa Esters agreed robbing the county treasurer's office could yield the best return; there would be license and tax payment money in the vault. The planning began. They knew the heist couldn't be pulled off during court house hours for the office of high sheriff, Charlie Blair, was just down the hall.

Initial plans called for abducting the county treasurer, J. K. Fear, and making him go to the court house to open the vault. After casing Fear's neighborhood, they discovered that Fear's son Raymond had a dog—so much for that plan. Next they checked out the deputy treasurer, Herschel Swanson. Swanson worked part-time at the local theater and came home late—now they were getting somewhere.

If Ma was going to be of any kind of a self respected accomplice, she also needed a gun. Pa Esters had heard Robert Ambrose had one for sale. Sure enough, Ambrose had one—Pa told him he'd buy it, but wanted to try it out a few days first—Ambrose consented and even gave him some cartridges.

They decided good robbers needed masks. Ma measured them up. Of course, the masks had to be shoulder length, for Pa was the only Negro in town and would be easy to identify.

With the masks completed, on August 26 Ma donned some of Pa's clothing and they were ready for the caper. Well after dark, the pair proceeded to the Swanson residence where they hid out in the tall grass by the garage. It must have been kinda romantic lying there in the grass, but romance was the farthest thing from their minds. Swanson came home, but his wife was with him. Not wanting to abduct two people, they decided to wait until later to make their move.

The night of September 1 they returned to their spot by the garage. Shortly after midnight deputy treasurer Swanson drove into his garage. As he stepped out of his car Pa Esters accosted him with the gun. Ma proudly waved her gun around a bit just for side effects. Since it wouldn't be halloween till the following month, Swanson couldn't help wondering what in the hell was going on. This sort of thing just wasn't supposed to happen in Happyland, but he was thoroughly convinced he wasn't still at the movie.

Pa Esters ordered Swanson to drive out on a country road, while he and Ma stood on running boards on opposite sides of the car. Pa must have thought Ma would catch a cold, so he made Swanson stop and let her inside.

After directing Swanson to turn left at the Monroe farm, he ordered him to halt. Swanson told him he didn't have any money, but Pa Esters let it be known he wanted the money out of the treasurer's vault and asked how much was in there. Swanson told him about $1,000—sounded worthwhile so Pa Esters directed Swanson back to town.

Parking by Washington Central School on Prospect Street, Pa had Ma watch the car while he and Swanson went to the court house. They were soon back with the money. Swanson had changed from his office clothing when he went to work at the theater. Ma, most probably overcome by motherly instinct, must have felt kinda sorry for Swanson and handed him his good cothing when he and Pa returned. Pa wasn't used to the newfangled machine Swanson drove and

Hamilton County Court House—scene of big heist. (Note, built at cost of $37,837.17—the 17¢ was probably for O'Malley's Hotel in rear.

Photo courtesy of Daily Freeman Journal

Swanson, fearing he'd be shot, showed him how to start and operate his car. They left Swanson standing on the curb as they jerked and bounced up the street with his automobile.

Pa Esters let Ma off in the 1400 block of First Street—she walked on home while he drove west of town. At Kurtz's corner he turned north, stopped, abandoned the car, and headed for home. Arriving, he and Ma counted the loot—$1,113. Being a bit tired after such a long day, they both retired for the night.

The following morning Happyland was bustling with rumors. Some speculation had it that one of the notorious gangs had struck the criminal blow. But the robbers didn't fool old Sheriff Blair—no-siree-bob. Blair figured it had to be someone local—how else would they know to tell Swanson to turn left at the Monroe farm! "This," deduced Blair, "was a dead give away!"

The amount of $1,113 isn't much at this writing, but then it was more than three years wages for most laborers. The Bureau of Criminal Investigation was called in, and a couple of top flight sleuths, agents G. M. Abernathy and Guy B. Smith, were dispatched from Des Moines.

Pa Esters had promised his wife part of the loot. About three days later he gave her $378. She burned her mask, but for some reason she buried her money in the garden with Pa's mask nearby. Meanwhile Pa had gone to Des Moines and with $105 had bought himself a dependable used car. Guess he didn't like driving other people's cars under such stressful conditions. He also opted to spend another $5 for insurance.

Then Pa gave Ma an additional $15 and the boys $10. Ma dashed right down to city hall and paid the electric and gas bill—probably didn't want a bad credit rating. By now Robert Ambrose was demanding pay for his gun or the return of the weapon. Ma Esters hustled right over with the gun. She thanked Mr. Ambrose—said her husband hadn't fired it, but felt they no longer really needed one.

In the meantime a few people were getting a bit suspicious. In addition to the car, Pa had taken on somewhat of a Robinhood role and had purchased some gifts for a friend. Someone reported Pa Esters had been spending quite a bit of money when only a few days earlier he had been flat-broke.

The Des Moines sleuths brought Ma and Pa into the station. They had found the mask and $378 buried in the garden. At last Ma broke under the strain and confessed. When accosted, Pa steadfastly maintained his innocence. But at the trial Pa was sentenced to twenty-five years and Ma ten. Sadly enough, they were apprehended before they could become the first Happylanders to have their photographs displayed on the post office bulletin board.

In those days you could believe what the judge said when he passed sentence for heinous crimes and murder. The criminals weren't out of confinement and on the streets one to five years later. The "Great Court House Robbery" was relegated to Hamilton County criminal history.

How does one describe the feelings brought on by the impending primary elections of 1932? Certainly one cannot describe the feeling as joy, for joy connotes happiness and with economic conditions as they were, how could anyone feel happiness? Perhaps apprehension would be a better word, for all but the most diehard Republicans were ready for a change in political leaders and legislators.

Normally all Republicans in the midwest are verbose in displaying their political fervor and singing the praises of their party's achievements. But those who attempted to sing that year proved to be a bit off-key. Perhaps Hoover was a good man, in the sense of morality, and was even sincere in his thinking, but he had been placed in a position of leadership, which certainly appeared not to be compatible with his area of expertise.

The campaigning of the Democrats got off to a quick start. Al Smith, who had been the loser in the last election, again threw his hat into the ring, knowing this would undoubtedly be his swan song if he failed. Franklin Delano Roosevelt, now the popular governor of New York, was not sitting this presidential election out and was ready to seek the nomination, along with others including the Texan John Nance Garner.

Never had the Republicans been so desperate. They were even trying to draft Calvin Coolidge out of retirement. However, those in tune with the nation's thinking would no doubt have gambled that only a resurrected Abraham Lincoln could have won the election for the Republicans.

The nomination of Hoover as the Republican candidate seemed inevitable, and the Republican convention, held in Chicago June 14-16, was almost mechanical. Perhaps there were other viable candidates, but no doubt they were wise enough not to commit political suicide by being pulled into a hopeless cause.

At the Democratic convention that same June in Chicago, there were tense moments with spirited speeches and strong challenges for the nomination. Al Smith somehow had underestimated Franklin Roosevelt's energy and tenacity. There had been a grueling campaign with Roosevelt matching his quite boisterous opponent blow for blow. In the end Smith did not take kindly to his adversary when support for Roosevelt began to surge at the convention.

Then just before the nomination, Roosevelt supporters had the organist play the song, "Happy Days Are Here Again," which later would become the theme song of the "New Deal."

The first vote showed leading contenders Roosevelt with 666-1/2 votes and Al Smith 201-3/4. Roosevelt did not have the required majority. In the votes that followed, Roosevelt's tally moved up, but it wasn't until the fourth vote was taken that Roosevelt triumphed. Only Smith refused to release his supporters to cast their votes for Roosevelt.

In July of 1932 strenuous measures were taken to prevent the complete collapse of banks and businesses in Happyland. Depositors were asked to pledge that they wouldn't withdraw their money. Shops remained open, except during banking hours. Elmer Reisner, then superintendent of the electrical power and water plant, remembered that people came to city hall to get change, which was available from money collected from utility billings.

The Farmers National Bank reopened and remained so. The First National Bank reopened July 20, but it would close permanently in November of that year. James Arthur had little to lose, for his earnings were day-to-day and not of substance. He, like many others, did most of his business in cash.

September arrived and it was baseball World Series time. The third game of the series was scheduled for October 1, 1932. Hank sat glued to the radio; it was between the Chicago Cubs and the New York Yankees and the game was in Chicago. During batting practice Ruth and Gehrig had knocked 18 balls into the far stands. Chicago fans had given Ruth a rough time. One could hear the crowd roar disapproval of him.

When Ruth came to the plate in the fifth inning, he pointed to centerfield. His next feat became legendary. He sent the ball sizzling through the air to the spot where he pointed—it fell near the distant flagpole. The jeers of the fans turned to cheers as Ruth received a standing ovation.

Even the radio announcer gasped and was so excited he could hardly narrate the event. Next at bat the great Lou Gehrig followed Ruth and sent another home run into the stands.

Sports gave some relief to depression weary hearts, but when the games ended, poverty still prevailed. Mother Lucy's standard

Lou Gehrig congratulates Babe Ruth after called shot home run.
Photo courtesy of Wide World Photos

response to complainers was, "Cheer up; tomorrow things will be better!" Clinty always agreed with her, but with reservations. As he frequently said, "Lucy, hundreds of tomorrows have gone by since you began saying that—sooner or later that tomorrow has got to come!" Little did either realize a new deal was in the offing and things would become better—but not much or soon.

VII
NEW DEAL - BIG DEALS

As the time for the fall presidential election approached, James Arthur campaigned for Roosevelt with all the strength he could muster, delivering forceful persuasion everywhere except Mother Lucy's henhouse, although one rooster did seem to be crowing a little more than usual. Strangely, James Arthur made little attempt to sway Lucy's vote that year; perhaps he sensed she had endured enough from Hoover.

Roosevelt was for repealing prohibition and made no bones about his stance. During the 1928 election campaign, people who drank had been low key about their imbibing preferences, while others seemed to have learned that those who wanted liquor could always obtain it at a price.

Roosevelt was far more knowledgeable on the campaign trail than his opponents had realized. He could be likened to a modern day computer, storing vast resources of facts and figures. When the Republicans introduced mudslinging into the campaign, Roosevelt somehow managed to intercept their snide remarks and build them into a pedestal, thus gaining greater stature with the people.

His oratory was delivered in a calm, clear and concise manner that appealed to most everyone. Perhaps his most important attribute was his sincere concern for the common man. Despite his polio-afflicted legs, he exuded power, confidence and the knowledge necessary to cope with a sick economy.

Entire families gathered around radios to listen to Roosevelt speak. He bombarded the nation with new programs, steeped with innovative approaches to the country's problems.

Hoover reluctantly had gone along with his fellow Republicans in initiating a National Reconstruction Finance Corporation. However, in the implementation, aid was primarily reserved for big business. This trend seemed to have prevailed even back during President Warren Harding's period (1921-1923) when big breaks were given to two oil tycoons by allowing them access to federal oil reserves. Ironically, Herbert Hoover was then Secretary of Commerce. Research does not reveal that he made any strenuous objections when the following events took place.

Albert B. Fall, Harding's Secretary of the Interior, convinced Harding to remove the oil reserves from Navy control and turn them over to his office. Fall accepted a payment of $233,000, and the "Teapot Dome" in Wyoming was leased to Harry Sinclair's Mammoth Oil Co. The California Elk Hill's Reserve was leased to Edward L. Doheny's Pan American Petroleum and Transport Co. for $100,000.

Ultimately Fall went to prison, but Sinclair, who had initiated the bribe, escaped punishment. However, the Supreme Court cancelled the leases in 1927, and Sinclair was later imprisoned for contempt of the Senate and jury tampering.

Because of clever handling of the affair, President Harding's vice president, Calvin Coolidge, succeeded him in office, garnering strong farm belt support. Hoover remained unscathed by the incident.

In a famous radio speech, Roosevelt endeared himself to the common man by denouncing Hoover's trickle down theory. Roosevelt advocated allocating some of the Reconstruction Finance Corporation funds for loans to small business men, farmers, workers, and home owners facing foreclosure, as part of the "New Deal."

Hoover, still with the backing of big business leaders, continued with his prophecy that prosperity was just around the corner. By then most people would have bet that all they would find around the corner was a sharp cliff and that the only good times they would see would be in the hereafter. It was the same song Hooverites had sung in the last election, but this time there were no curtain calls. Sadly, in a few appearances Hoover was greeted with tomatoes and eggs, and some of the radicals shouted, "Hang him—hang him."

Franklin Roosevelt and his running mate, John Nance Garner, won the election by a landslide. When the votes were in, Roosevelt had amassed 22,800,000 votes to Hoover's 15,750,000. Electoral college voting margin was even higher, 472 to 59. Hoover had carried only six New England states.

Mother Lucy made no comments on how she had voted, so one might deduce that, for the first time since women had been granted the right to vote in 1920, she had voted the Democratic ticket. Even Hamilton County went Democratic for the first time. However, all were just as poor the following morning as they were when they went to bed on election night.

One man, Guiseppe "John" Zangara, a disgruntled unemployed mill worker, could have changed history. Roosevelt and Anton Cermak, Chicago's mayor, were in Miami, Florida riding down a street lined with spectators. Zangara crashed through the crowd and, shouting loudly about unemployment, fired his pistol. His aim was altered by a woman, but his shots wounded several people and killed Mayor Cermak.

Implementing his "New Deal" had to wait until Roosevelt's inauguration, but he had been laying the groundwork for months. It had been policy that a President wait a few months before making any substantial changes—but, to Roosevelt, that would have been wasting time and time was of the essence.

When President Roosevelt took office March 4, 1933 there were over two million homeless people drifting around the country, 15 million unemployed and millions not making a living wage. Although it was rough in the small towns, it was far worse in the large cities. There were few people who had enough yard space for a large garden and damn little could be grown in cement cracks. Bank failures had continued at a hectic pace with 5,100 failing in 1932.

President Roosevelt went to work in the White House like there was no tomorrow. Swiftly and with purpose, he ordered all banks closed while bank examiners made thorough audits to determine solvency.

In a marathon of action Congress passed an unheard number of bills. A Federal Emergency Relief Administration (FRA) was established and a National Recovery Act (NRA) was adopted. A new law authorized the President to regulate banking and reopen banks. Along with this portfolio of action came the Agriculture Adjustment Administration (AAA) providing relief to the farmer, and the Tennessee Valley Authority (TVA) to provide cheap electricity for farms, homes and industries.

Food relief was starting to come in, but many people were too proud to take handouts. Mary Ann Bygrave reminded the author of the depression era cliche, "I'm one of the poor genteel—too proud to beg, too honest to steal!" However, everyone was starting to realize the "New Deal" Roosevelt had promised was not just a change of dealers in the "penny ante" poker games, a luxury recreation then sweeping the nation.

The Agriculture Adjustment Administration had implemented its plan to reduce crop curtailment, bring about crop parity and provide means of refinancing farm mortgages. Work soon began on several large dams in the Tennessee River Valley. That hard pressed area received some relief and, additionally, the huge dam that was to create an electricity supply to manufacture war supplies for World War II.

Above: WPA project—Jefferson Gym under construction *Photo courtesy of Gus Dermand*

Right: No doubt this one-handed man was happy to have WPA work.
National Archive photo courtesy of Gertrude Horan

The work relief program, by then the Works Projects Administration (WPA), was putting some of the jobless back to work. Although the program was scoffed at by many people, it was beneficial to Happyland through the erection of an exceptionally well-constructed gymnasium and several other projects.

Much of the ridicule of the program was the result of assigning too many men to one job, thus giving the appearance of several loafing. However, many of the men became construction contractors and workers on the roads and buildings of the future. The object, some people forgot, was to put as many people to work as possible. Had most of the funds been spent on materials, there would have been very little left to put in the workers' pockets. At least the WPA helped them retain some dignity while performing useful tasks for their communities.

The Wagner Act of 1933, allowing workers to organize under unions of their choice, was having an impact on the hourly wage workers' paycheck. When the blue collared workers' wages increased, the white collared employees' salaries also climbed.

The Rural Electrification Act (REA) brought electricity to many farms. In some instances, farmers installed the poles and strung the wire under the supervision of qualified electricians.

By 1933 the horseless carriage had virtually replaced the horse and buggy, and it was well it had for a horse could hardly negotiate most of the streets in town without breaking a leg. Street potholes were so numerous after a rain each bird in town had its own private bath.

Signs of the time were evident everywhere one looked. Rain water was leaking through roofs into many homes, and some roofs looked like patched trouser knees with scrap canvas covering worn-out shingles. Sometimes tin cans were flattened out and nailed down to stop leaks. When windows were broken, many families couldn't afford to replace them; thus, in addition to cardboard in the soles of their shoes, they now had cardboard in the windows.

Erick Anderson cut huge stacks of wood for the long winter.
Photo courtesy of Lois Berglund Swanson

Wood had replaced coal as fuel for most stoves and furnaces—that is, if the family could afford it or had a friend who would let them trim or cut down a tree.

Those without wood or coal often went down to meet incoming trains, not to watch and wonder at the engines' might, but to throw off coal at night as the train made their runs between Happyland and Fort Dodge.

Hank would long remember the morning he arrived at school to receive terrible news about a good friend and classmate, one of the nicest kids in school. He lived with his family in one of the apartments created in the abandoned Catholic Hospital. The tall, handsome, well-built boy had lost a leg to a coal car wheel while

Train gets underway to Fort Dodge.
Photo by Vernon Wilkie, courtesy of Lois Forrester Wilkie

attempting to get fuel to keep their apartment warm for his younger brothers and sisters.

From the beginning food had been a problem for the larger portion of the population. By now savings not lost in bank closures had been depleted and everything except bare essentials had been sold for little or nothing.

Being without money has a certain effect upon people and, since Hank was people, it was having that certain effect upon him. Paper money had become something he remembered the older people discussing. If someone had asked him, "Right quick describe a dollar bill," his memory at that point could not have risen to the occasion. He sought out Cousin Clinty, and advice was soon forthcoming. Clinty suggested he apply for a newspaper route.

Clinty informed him all he had to do was to make application, be assigned a route, deliver the papers, collect from customers, pay for the papers and keep all the money left over. Sounded really good, and Hank daydreamed of standing in the basement on the second rung of a stepladder up to his fanny in dollar bills.

With high heart he headed for the "Des Moines Register and Tribune" manager's office to pick up his first papers and a sackful of money to buy bubble gum and licorice to chew while on his route.

Success seemed inevitable. Why hadn't he thought about applying for one of these easy money-making jobs before?

The paper boss was all heart and encouragement. He wasted a whole minute telling Hank there was no opening and pointed to the application form. Hank took a form, headed home, envying all those boys who were picking up papers and preparing to go out on their routes.

After questioning a few people, Hank discovered paper routes were hard to get and he was cautioned he would probably need someone with a little influence to recommend him for the job. When Hank advised Clinty of this problem, Clinty averred, "Hank, you've come to the right man; I have about as little influence as anyone in this town!"

Hank was a little more persistent than the paper boss had anticipated, visiting the office each night after school. It was obvious the paper boss was developing a bit of a trauma at the peak of their interviews. When Hank walked through the door, the media distribution tycoon would turn alternately purple and red and say odd little phrases in a muffled voice.

The end of the long wait finally came when the manager, through clenched teeth, informed Hank that a route was open and it was all his if he would just stay out of the office, except to pick up his papers and pay for them. Hank picked up his collection book (delivery list he was to call it later) and his papers and hurried out of the room like a newly elected PTA president going to preside at her first meeting.

The delivery of the papers went okay, but the revelation of problems was to come on collection day. Twenty-five percent of Hank's customers said they hadn't cashed their checks, and twenty-five percent needed change for a mythical five-dollar bill. As for the balance, he had to do everything but arm wrestle with them to get his money. Those rare individuals who could pay on his first collection attempt did so with much flair and dignity. Hank guessed they were pleased to see a bill they could afford to pay.

By the end of the month, Hank had gathered an extensive amount of executive know-how, walked fifty miles (which was to stand him in good stead in future army service), been chased by no less than thirty dogs, had twenty discussions with old people on the "Townsend Plan" (a plan that would put a chicken in every pot and a car in every garage) and collected enough money to have the soles replaced on shoes he had worn out trying to collect for past delivered papers.

Top profit on the job would have been around a dollar and ninety five cents but, considering those that didn't pay or moved out during the night to avoid rent payment, he usually ended up with little more than a dollar.

Hank stood in some yards so long trying to collect Cousin Clinty cautioned him against wearing his red spiked blue jeans for fear some dog might mistake him for a fire hydrant!

It wasn't long after he acquired his route that Max Maxon, a veteran "Daily Freeman Journal" paperman, showed Hank how to fold his papers into a flattened square, tuck-in style. This he found saved time since he could pitch them from the sidewalk to the porch.

Over confidence must have overtaken him somewhere along the route. Mrs. Grossgood, a quiet mild person and one of his favorite customers, wasn't too happy with his newly - found method of spreading the news since she had developed a kink in her back, or something while plucking her paper out of the perennials.

When Mrs. Grossgood came out on the porch, Hank thought she was going to give him some of her delicious cookies, which she had done before. Then in her mild voice she said, "Hank, I did not subscribe to the Slingsville Gazette. Day old news I can tolerate, but I don't like wet newspapers." She then told Hank he was getting his money right where she got her paper and, with that, she threw twenty-five pennies out into the yard.

When Hank arrived home he told Clinty about his experience with Mrs. Grossgood. Clinty laughed and told him he shouldn't be complaining since the purpose of the route was to pick up a little change.

Selby Poultry Co. had built a new $75,000 plant and had moved its operation from Britt to Happyland in 1930. The factory was the most impressive in Happyland after the Monarch Appliance factory closed. Although wages were quite low, without Selby's a lot of people would have had to fashion a tin bill and pick worms with the chickens.

The wages for feather plucking at the fowl factory was then five cents per bird, but when the chips were down, the feathers flew and the town became renowned as a place for the birds—to be plucked that is.

But, still in all, it was difficult to eke out a living plucking chickens although the pay had increased since 1931 when workers were getting only three cents per bird.

Big Sister's studious efforts in high school had paid off, and she now had a job in the office at Selby Poultry Company and was contributing to the support of the family. The family moved to a better and more modern house by Twin Parks. The house had a central heating furnace that burned coal or wood. By then some of the old Iowa coal mines were operating again and the cost of coal dropped. A combination of Iowa coal and wood kept the house much more comfortable than the one where they lived previously.

During winter months fifteen degree below zero mornings proved a test of a paper boy's heart. The pleasure of the day was lost in wading the snow on unplowed streets and unscooped sidewalks. The creaking sound of hard packed snow and ever-present ice underfoot made a tingling feeling creep up his spine in the early morning hours.

One exceptionally cold morning Hank's alarm clock rang and for the first time he truly resented getting up to carry his papers. Putting on his warmest clothing and Clinty's felt boots inside his overshoes, he glanced over at Big Brother sleeping comfortably and thought a few unkind things about the guy who created paper routes.

With heavy heart he headed toward the newspaper office seven blocks away. The streets were entirely deserted and there were no lights in any of the houses along the way. Arriving at the newspaper office, he found its doors closed as tight as the teats on a terrified tomcat. The office was dark and not a living soul was in sight.

Hank's alarm clock had never failed, so he reasoned he could call the paper boss, get him out of bed and down to the office, and thereby earn his undying gratitude. With this in mind, he proceeded to the Willson Hotel, about a block away, to use the telephone.

Hank asked the desk clerk if he would mind if he borrowed the phone and the guy gave him the typical hayshaker humor saying, "Hank, you can borrow it if you bring it back!" After arousing the night operator and giving her his boss's name, he leaned back and waited for the telephone to work wonders. The thought even permeated his brain his boss might be so grateful that he would assign him a different route where collections were not so difficult. After all, he could be saving him from losing his job!

Soon the boss answered the phone. Hank told him he was late and that it was time to come down and give out the papers. Hearing that, the boss man growled like a bulldog with his hemorrhoids caught in a vise and shouted, "What the hell is the matter with you, Hank? Do you have insomnia at your tender age?" After several incoherent statements, Hank gathered from the sketchy conversation that his paper boss thought he should go back to bed.

Something told him that all was not right with the hour and when he glanced at the clock on the wall, the hands pointed clearly to three o'clock. As he rounded the Miller Drug Store corner, he looked hurriedly at the big city hall clock, and it confirmed the hotel clock's time. He then trudged the half mile home so hot under the collar that it felt to him like a warm summer day.

When he got back to his bedroom, he checked his alarm clock and found it to be nearly two hours off. He then knew Big Brother had set the clock forward as one of his practical jokes.

Hank didn't say a word but went straight to the utility porch where he procured a bucket, filled it brimful of water and returned to the bedroom. David must have got about the same thrill out of working old Goliath over as Hank did in the moment to follow. In one magnificent effort Hank gave his Big Brother the dubious benefits of the water smack in the face, then streaked across the hall into Big Sister's bedroom and locked the door.

Peering through the keyhole, he could see Big Brother staggering to the hallway door with the agility of a drunken ostrich standing in a hammock. He halted abruptly at the door, without doubt thinking Hank was hiding around the corner waiting to douse him with another bucket of water.

Pondering awhile, he apparently decided that speed was his most reliable source of safety and he didn't just peek or peer around the corner, but bobbed his head out and back with the lightning thrust of a king cobra's strike.

Upon assuring himself Hank wasn't hiding in the hallway waiting to empty half the town's water tower on him, he deduced that his brother had run into Big Sister's room. This he confirmed when he checked and found her bedroom door locked.

Big Brother stood in the hallway, out of his head with anger, first orating like an evangelist with four bad wisdom teeth and then speaking to Hank in the mild tones of a funeral parlor director consoling the bereaved.

When all else failed to bring Hank out of the bedroom, Big Brother, in syrupy sweet words, told Hank he knew he had done wrong in setting forward the alarm clock, and begged Hank's forgiveness and invited him to come back to bed.

One thing Hank knew for certain: his brother wasn't beating knots on his head with the door between them. Big Brother, by now dripping and cold, eventually stopped muttering to himself, found some dry blankets and went back to bed.

Hank waited another half hour to be sure his brother was sound asleep, then departed for the paper office, knowing that at least some of Big Brother's anger would subside before he returned.

Although Hank thought he was having a tough time of it, the young men and women of that period had a much more frustrating life, for their opportunities for steady employment were almost nil. Those graduating from high school were extremely depressed for even those with college degrees were still roving the country seeking work of any type.

Young people wanting to marry were in a hopeless situation. Fortunate indeed were those whose parents could afford to send them to college. There were very few scholastic or athletic scholarships, and part-time jobs to supplement scholarships were scarce indeed.

Many of the youths dropped out of school to earn money to help support their families in any way they could. Big Brother was one of those. The number of unemployed workers was still well over fifteen million and more than six million were on state or municipal payrolls under federal programs.

President Roosevelt had come up with a means of helping young people, whose numbers in hobo camps had begun to grow. Under a youth rehabilitation movement, the Civilian Conservation Corps (CCCs) was formed.

Thousands of young men joined the Civilian Conservation Corps. Big Brother and Sterling Bonner, Big Sister Mabel's suitor (both members of the local National Guard Company) were among them and were stationed at Boone, Iowa.

The CCCs, a quasi-military unit headed up by regular Army and reserve Officers, worked on reforestration projects and built park buildings and facilities. The Ledges State Park at Boone exhibits evidence of the fine work of CCCs. Before being disbanded, the Civilian Conservation Corps provided work for three million American youths across the United States.

General Charles L. Bolte, who was then an Army captain, commanded a CCC unit. He would advance to become Vice Chief of Staff, United States Army and Commander of NATO Forces in Europe. The list of CCC men who went on to great accomplishments would probably fill a thousand page book.

On the local scene, Hamilton County had voted dry, but Iowa as a whole voted to repeal the eighteenth amendment. Legal beer returned to Happyland April 18, 1933. After the council had a special meeting, licenses were issued.

The first day beer was placed on sale in Happyland the pool halls and taverns were overflowing with people who hadn't bellied up to a legal bar since World War I. "Bottoms up" became a phrase not just reserved for Doctors Lewis, Crumpton and Galloway when they were positioning patients for hemorrhoid inspections.

Cousin Clinty and James Arthur made the excuse of going downtown for baling wire on the first day beer went on sale at Charlie Alexander's pool hall. Arriving, they were faced with the sidewalk jammed to capacity with experienced and inexperienced suds swallowers.

Willie Sipmore, Tip O'Flaskagin and Pat O'Kettlebelly were first in line when the doors opened. Charlie Alexander stood behind the bar, somewhat apprehensive about whether the brew would be pleasing to the palates of the most noteworthy imbibers in Happyland.

It was a memorable occasion. The three champion indulgers sauntered over to the bar and assumed stances befitting those with experience. Even a novice could tell Willie Sipmore was the only one with any appreciable pre-World War I drinking skill just by observing the way he placed his right foot on the brass foot rail, right elbow resting on the bar, and his firm, yet relaxed grip on the mug handle. Even Clinty, a semi-professional, conceded Willie was a true "pro" and always exuded class.

While the bartenders were filling customers' glasses with beers, bootleggers were filling their glasses with tears, for the legalizing of their product would surely necessitate radical changes in their standard of living. They would suffer a devastating loss of income.

There were many unforseen changes that had to be made in Happyland after prohibition was repealed. In the issuance of licenses the city council overlooked the fact that the public toilet in the basement of the city hall had but one stool and one urinal. Most taverns and pool halls had single service facilities.

All the tavern toilet lines became a mite too long and younger guzzlers learned how toilets came to be known as restrooms, for by the time a patron finished battling his way to the head of a line, he damn well needed a rest. With the novices drinking a picnic (one-half gallon) of beer, things got fairly precarious and those who were unaccustomed to drinking homebrew became a bit more than desperate for toilet facilities.

Nobody was deeply concerned when two of the town's top ranking imbibers, Tip O'Flaskagin and Patty O'Kettlebelly, had to give up their spots in the line at Alexander's pool hall and dash for another facility. However, when a councilman reported back to the city council that he had spotted Willie Sipmore, who had the best burden-bearing bladder in town, headed for Warneke's Royal 400 Gas Station with a despairing look on his face, it became obvious something had to be done. A second urinal was quickly added in the city hall men's room.

Iowa's government was always deeply involved in legislation innovatively designed to save its citizens from themselves and their follies. While most states authorized liquor by the drink, Iowa steadfastly maintained one should be required to buy liquor by the bottle. To add further to the confusion, a partially empty bottle could not be transported in a vehicle.

Most taverns and night clubs served what they called "setups," which were soft drinks to which the patron illegally added his own booze. This left the imbiber with only two recourses: drink the whole damn bottle or risk arrest by transporting the balance home, even in the trunk of an automobile.

Speaking of automobiles, by 1933 they were not only a prestige item, but people who could afford gas for a leisurely Sunday drive were becoming a rarity. Many had sold their automobiles to get money for food, while other automobiles stood elevated on blocks in

Fred Eason with stripped down Model T to get better mileage and cheaper license. Some states licensed by weight.
Photo courtesy of Fred Eason

Cars like this 1933 Cadillac caused big excitement.
Photo courtesy of Dale Castle

garages or backyards—owners couldn't afford even the license. One could purchase a used automobile in fairly good operating condition for $35. A youth who could get permission to use the family car was the envy of his peers.

It was 1933, the height, bottom or pits of the depression—whatever you wish to call it. Chicago had decided to host the World's Fair, the Century of Progress. The fair was highly publicized, everyone wanted to attend, but few could afford to do so. Sally Rand, a beautiful fan dancer, became a household word. There were songs, poems and even some off-colored jokes generated about her dance. But, compared to today's swimsuits, she might as well have been clad in "long john" winter underwear!

It had been a couple of years since Bradford "Brad" Mason had been clothesline towed on a motorcycle by his pal, Whitley "Whit" Hemingway. Whit had now planned another adventure. He and Brad would save their money and attend the Indianapolis 500 races—then on the return trip take in the World's Fair. Transportation would be cheap—Brad would ride on the back of Whit's motorcycle. Whit was a convincing person—the temptation was great! Yes, it would be another adventure Brad would have just as soon forgone.

It was a happy day when the two adventurers mounted Whit's Indian pony. The little Indian held up surprisingly well under their nearly six foot four inch frames and purred along like a kitten all afternoon and night.

It was at Crawfordsville, Indiana at nearly six o'clock in the morning that the engine started banging and clattering like it had tin cans for pistons and they were playing leapfrog. The Indianapolis 500 wasn't until 10 a.m. and, in a desperate attempt to make it, Whit and Brad parked the cycle and tried unsuccessfully to hitchhike. Unable to catch a train or bus, they attempted to trade the motorcycle for a Model T Ford, but found no takers.

At last a kind-faced gentleman gave them and the Indian pony a lift in his pickup truck to a maintenance shop in LaFayette, Indiana.

While the repairman attempted to fix the motorcycle, Whit and Brad caught some badly needed sleep by cramming themselves into the back seats of junk cars stored in a lot behind the mechanic's shop overlooking the Wabash River.

After several hours the mechanic advised them he didn't have enough experience balancing flywheels and agreed to take Whit into Indianapolis on the back of his motorcycle to get the flywheel balanced. Whit rode on the tandem seated cycle holding the Indian Pony crankcase and lower assembly on his lap—no small task.

After the motor was repaired, the disgruntled pair started back for Happyland. Did they stop in Chicago to attend the fair? Of course not, they were nearly flat broke. All they could afford to do was ride past the fair grounds.

The youths had gone without sleep for so long that they had a difficult time staying awake but, with no money for food or room rent, all they could do was ride on! Nine miles from home they spent their last twenty-five cents for gasoline at Blairsburg and rode miserably on into Happyland. By then the only race on their mind was one to a bed to get some badly needed sleep.

Whit grins broadly as he relates that, from that day on, when either he or Brad hears the song, "Back Home Again in Indiana," and the vocalist comes to the phrase, "On the banks of the Wabash far away," their minds drift back to that time long ago when they slept in the old cars along that famous stream.

Whereas Whit and Brad's trip to the World's Fair had brought pain—another Iowan, Marvin "Duke" Nelson of Fort Dodge would vault to fame. In 1930 Duke had won the Canadian National Exhibition Marathon Swim at Toronto, Canada over a field of 173 of the world's best swimmers. He completed the 15 mile swim in seven hours, forty-three minutes and thirty-six and one-fifth seconds.

The Amazing Duke Nelson became a first-time repeater when he won the marathon during the World's Fair of 1933. While competing in the William Randolph Hearst Swim Duke set a world's 15-mile record in seven hours, twenty-two minutes and ten and three-fifths seconds. Duke repeated his win in 1934. He was the greatest of the great—the world's champion!

Duke had another record in mind—he wanted to not only swim the English Channel, but he was determined to swim across—then back! But World War II interceded. There are still many people around at this writing who would have bet forty acres of fat cattle and held the stakes in their mouth he would have done it! But, Duke had to be content with training U.S. Navy "frogmen."

It didn't take a clairvoyant to predict Brad didn't want to go on any more motorcycle trips with Whit for awhile, but a certain aura has always surrounded those who can make predictions. Never is the supernatural more popular than during a depression era. People who are destitute often reach out for any source that can or will predict a brighter future.

Since the start of the depression, all across America mysterious women and psychics in increasing numbers peered into crystal balls, read palms or cards and foretold problems or wonderful futures for the less fortunate. Strangely, enough of the predictions came true that even the most skeptical were impressed.

Further enhancing superstitions were the strange happenings that occurred after the removal of the Egyptian boy king, Tutankhamen, from his tomb in 1922. Media attention had been given to an inscription taken from the tomb, which read, "Death shall come on swift wings to who toucheth the Tomb of Pharaohs." During the years that followed fourteen people, who in some way were connected with "Tut's" removal from the tomb, would meet their demise in unnatural ways.

Hank could never afford to consult a crystal ball reader; he didn't have enough money, although he had seen them in front of their tents at the county fair. But he could have used some advice as he needed to take quick action—he was badly in need of cash.

Summer vacation couldn't come soon enough to suit him; at least the warm weather offered a little more opportunity for employment. Hank continued his paper route and helped Father James Arthur when he had baling jobs. Every spare moment he spent practicing or playing baseball with the neighborhood kids' team. When a whole day was available, they went to the fairgrounds with a sack lunch in hand and played from morning until supper. Hank, who had become a pitcher, followed the St. Louis Cardinal team avidly and now hoped someday to pitch like Jerome "Dizzy" Dean.

One of the jobs his Father helped him obtain was extremely overrated. In fact, if one were to describe it without undue verbosity, one could say, "It stunk." The two-week job did require a specialist of sorts, but a strong back and a poor sense of smell were really the two most desirable prerequisites.

Mr. Fred Hahne owned and maintained a sizable herd of pure bred Aberdeen Angus cattle and was in need of help in putting the animals in top condition for a big sale to be conducted at the fairgrounds. He also published the "Aberdeen Angus Journal," and Hank hurried to the Hahne Printing Co. to apply for the position of responsibility and trust.

The job could be described as that of assistant to the head herdsman, and Mr. Hahne emphasized the extreme importance of his cattle attaining peak show condition. When it came time for Hank to make his pitch for the job, he related his previous experience in the care of milk cows on the farm and Mr. Hahne allowed that it was the same stuff and the only difference was quality and quantity. After a short debate, damn short, Hank's pay was set at ten cents per hour.

Hank reported to the head herdsman, Mr. Mathews, the next morning at six o'clock and was given a brief orientation. Mr. Mathews asked him if he knew how to run an Irish dump truck. Hank responded in the affirmative and was assigned his very own wheelbarrow. He then gave Hank a pitchfork and a shovel, showed him what he was to move and where to pile it.

His first duty was to haul hay and feed to the aisle way to the front of the cattle. He was made to understand that he was not allowed actually to feed the cattle since that was skilled labor.

Hank was soon introduced to his next job which involved the other end of the livestock; with that he was launched on the manure removal program. Now Hank knew cattle ate a lot and that all of this food was not retained in their systems. Pure bred Aberdeen Angus cattle, he soon learned, had a highly sophisticated two part system—the front being a highly efficient hay baler and, the rear a highly underrated sewage disposal plant. A short time later it became evident to Hank that, between winding his Mickey Mouse wristwatch and wheeling manure, he had at last found a full-time job.

The bovines had been fed in an orderly fashion and in sequence from one end of the barn to the other, but their manure production timing was synchronized like Cousin Willobee's work schedule; they didn't have one. Hank moved right and left, as the duty call sounded, with the speed and dexterity of an all-American halfback, but it was impossible to anticipate the location of his next job.

When Hank discussed the problem with the head herdsman, the man was sympathetic, but it was easy to tell from his dissertation that he felt cattle defecation had built the nation. Hank dropped the subject as, literally speaking, his work was piling up on him.

By six o'clock that afternoon the cattle were beginning to smell like humans and Hank was beginning to smell like cattle. Hank was so tired he felt like sleeping with the cattle, but it was doubtful the head herdsman would have approved, for he would have spoiled the appearance of the herd.

Hank headed for home taking shortcuts over fences, through open fields, alleys, and the Twin Parks, doing his best to avoid meeting people. Actually his main concern should have been that some overly zealous gardening enthusiast might smell him and throw him into his compost pile.

Mothers must have terrific compassion for their children, for Mother Lucy did not disown Hank when he arrived on the home scene. However she did have him take off his clothes and wash up before coming into the rest of the house. After he bathed everything but his left tonsil, Mother Lucy concluded that he now smelled like a human being and it wouldn't be necessary for her to go to the grain elevator to get some corn to feed him.

When the neighbor lady, Mrs. Earl Forrester, asked Hank what kind of job he had, Hank was kinda embarrassed. Cousin Clinty sensed his predicamemt and explained to Mrs. Forrester that every program and job nowadays had an abbreviated title such as W.P.A., CCC, FBI, etc. and that Hank worked with the ROFM program. When she asked what kind of job that might be Cousin Clinty replied, "Remover of fecal matter!"

The job lasted two weeks and Hank earned a dollar a day, but the fringe benefits (odors) went on for ten. The auctioneer was former Iowa Governor Nelson Kraschel. The cattle brought good prices; in fact, one bull calf brought over seven hundred dollars, an unheard-of price during those times. Really Hank was quite proud as on one occasion he himself might well have sold for one hundred fifty dollars, based on scent alone, if a nearsighted farmer hadn't finally put on his glasses.

The two-week stint with Fred Hahne's Aberdeen Angus cattle firmly convinced Hank that he didn't want a lifetime job as a substitute for bovine diapers.

Aberdeen Angus Bull—1935 Champion
Photo courtesy of Wallace's Farmer

Aberdeen Angus herd feeds on a cold day.
Photo courtesy of Paul Gauthier

Progress in aviation came in leaps and bounds—planes had become more dependable and were becoming faster and faster. Pilots continued to accomplish feats which heretofore had been felt impossible. It was a race against time to shatter past records and to set new ones.

Wiley Post, a pilot extraordinary, had risen from barnstorming fairs to win the Bendix Speedway trophy in 1930. He set a scorching pace for planes of that era cornering the pylons on the treacherous course.

Post's search for adventure and aerial conquest led him to lay plans for circumnavigating the globe. He and Harold Gatty had departed June 23, 1931 and eight days later July 1, 1931 had completed the trip.

Now Post had another goal, that of being the first person to fly solo around-the-world. Some interesting sidelights about Post's historic flight were gleaned years later from one of Post's closest friends. It all came about while the author and his wife sat at the Thanksgiving Day dinner table of Nina Sinisi (the widow of the great Associated Press correspondent Edmund Chester) at her beautiful Chesterhill Estate in Mount Dora, Florida. Most people at the table were reporters or writers and many had another thing in common—they were former aviators.

It was not coincidental that the conversation would evolve to airplanes—embracing such old-time notables as Lindbergh, Amelia Earhart Putnam, and Wiley Post. Fay Gillis Wells had been one of the pioneer women pilots in America and had developed a close friendship with both Amelia Earhart and Wiley Post. Fay was prodded by the author to tell some of her early day flying adventures, how she came to take up flying and her association with Earhart and Post.

Fay's eyes lit up at the very mention of airplanes for aviation was one of the top loves of her life. Her sister Beth spoke up describing Fay as a person completely devoid of fear. Also, she was one not content with just flying; she was obsessed with aerial acrobatics and other feats that fulfilled her yearnings for adventure (perhaps because she had been born in Minnesota, also the home state of the great Charles Lindbergh.)

Their father, Julius Howells Gillis, a noted metalurgical engineer, and their mother, the former Minnie Irene Shafer, a concert pianist with the Minneapolis Symphony, had in 1925 enrolled their two beautiful daughters, Fay and Beth, at Michigan State College.

Fay was a mere sixteen years old—too adventuresome a person to be content with a life teaching English and physical education. After three years she had decided she needed a more exciting life and quit school and moved in with a high school friend in New York City—then found a job as the banquet cashier in the Commodore Hotel. Beth remained in college.

When Fay's father learned of her move to New York he was very unhappy and said he didn't want her living in the big city away from family members. He soon convinced her to join him in Canada where he was building a huge gold smelter for Noranda Mines. Fay wasn't alone at the mine; there were 600 men—but she was the only unmarried woman. (Fay mischievously allows she's known plenty of women who would have jumped at such an opportunity!)

The smelter completed, Julius returned to the United States and not long thereafter accepted a fantastic job in Russia. He sat Fay down—they had a long discussion. He told her she must decide on a career or return to college. Fay, without hesitation, said she would like a career in flying. Julius consented and she was soon enrolled in the Curtiss Flying School, taking lessons from the great test pilot and instructor, John "Sonny" Trunk.

Three weeks after Fay soloed, Sonny invited her to fly with him in an experimental plane, an over-powered Curtiss Fledgling. Fay accepted. She asked her father and Beth, who had by now graduated from college, to come out to the field and watch the flight at the Curtiss-Wright Airfield located in Valley Stream, Long Island, N.Y.

As Beth said, they put that airplane through the supreme test—flying close loops, barrel rolls, wingover and screaming power dives. But, at last they went beyond the plane's strain tolerance, the engine fell out and the plane started to disintegrate. So close to the ground was the plane that from the end of the field Fay's father and Beth saw only one pilot bail out. Had Fay gone down with the wreckage? They didn't know.

Hearts in throats, they hurried to the area where they saw the chutist descend and discovered both pilots had bailed out. There was Fay, a whimsical half-hearted smile on her face with her chute entangled in branches. She did assure them that, miraculously, she was uninjured. Firemen soon arrived with an extension ladder and helped her down. Beth recalls that for some reason people wanted to touch Fay. Perhaps it was because they wanted to be assured she was alive or maybe it was for superstitious good luck!

Small wonder sister Beth and her father hadn't seen Fay jump from the plane, for she had indeed had a close call. The plane had been upside down when she jumped—she couldn't find the rip cord to open her parachute. "No need to count to ten before I pulled the cord," Fay says, "I was little more than four hundred feet above the ground when I found the rip cord." But, as Fay jokingly says, "my chute opened and I landed in a tree—so it didn't matter!" Fay was taken back to the airport and put in another plane and flew with another instructor—this was expected to allay future fears. The quick flight did ease the tension. Sonny was hit by a part of the plane and spent three weeks in the hospital recovering.

Fay, at age 20, became the first woman to join the Caterpillar Club, an exclusive group of flyers who've bailed out of planes to save their lives. (Chutes were made of silk back in those days—so is the strand used by caterpillars to lower themselves to the ground.)

Curtiss Aircraft executives noted her courage and flying ability and the next day after the jump gave her a job traveling around the country lecturing on the safety of flying. It was during these trips that she made the acquaintance of and formed a lasting friendship with Wiley Post, Amelia Earhart and many other notable flyers.

Fay Gillis—first woman to parachute from crashing plane.
Photo courtesy of Fay Gillis Wells

Fay Gillis—first woman to fly a plane in Russia.
Photo courtesy of Fay Gillis Wells

In 1929 Fay joined with Amelia Earhart and other women pilots to form a flying club. Invitations were sent out to the 117 licensed women pilots. Amazingly 26 attended the first meeting, Amelia Earhart among them; 99 responded to the application letter—thereafter the organization was called the Ninety-Nines.

In the fall of 1930 Fay and Beth joined their father in Moscow. Fay worked as a correspondent for the "New York Herald Tribune," while Beth worked for the "New York Times." The Russians were reluctant to let Fay fly. But, her persistence finally paid off—they later allowed her to fly a Soviet plane—thus she became the first American woman to pilot a plane in Russia.

So impressed were Russian pilots with her flying ability they invited Fay to accompany a three-man crew to deliver the first commercial Russian airliner, for the airline company from Tashkent to Kabul, Afghanistan. The flight was supposed to be a 37 hour trip, but she laughs as she recalls it took 19 days with 40 forced landings. The

Fay Gillis with "99 Club" friends. Left to right: Annette Gibson, Fay Gillis, Amelia Earhart and Margaret Cooper.

Photo courtesy of Fay Gillis Wells

plane's radiators leaked like sieves and had to be soldered at every stop. Her father was extremely upset, but his anger subsided somewhat when she arrived back home in Moscow by train—bringing with her melons, grapes and vegetables which, at that time, were unobtainable in Moscow.

Wiley Post was now making final arrangements for his second flight around-the-world and, knowing Fay's adventuresome spirit, cabled her to arrange his fuel dumps in Novosibirsk, Siberia and then they would fly to Vladivostok where she would help him refuel. However, the keepers of the record books said, "No way"—another pilot in the plane would jeopardize Wiley's solo record. Although she would be riding in the rear without controls or communications, in the end it was decided she best abide by the official ruling. Fay, however, did accede to Wiley's wishes and established fuel and resupply points for his flight across Siberia.

Fay later was advised she was fortunate she couldn't accompany Post on the flight. Without communications with him during the prolonged flight, she might well have been asphyxiated from the heavy gas fumes in the tail of the plane behind the gas tanks. Again fate had stepped in to save her.

Fay waved a fond farewell to Post as he flew off on the next leg of his journey. The great airman waved back, and Fay said a few silent prayers as he disappeared from sight.

Fay Gillis with Wiley Post

Photo courtesy of Fay Gillis Wells

Refueling and supply arrangements made by Fay proved flawless, and the daring Post again flew his way into international aviation history. He had started his flight July 15, 1933 and on July 22, 1933 he had accomplished his goal—the first person to fly solo around the world. He had logged 15,596 miles in 7 days, 18 hours and 49 minutes.

Fay would later have an opportunity to accompany her friend Post on a not quite so successful a journey! More about Fay later.

Back in Washington, D.C., Roosevelt was to face many problems during his tenure of office, but now, while he was throwing his heart into combating the depression, tragedy was literally tearing the bottom out of the nation's wheat basket.

During and after World War I, the United States provided wheat to many nations. Anxious to share in the profits, farmers had plowed up millions of acres of heretofore grasslands. Now the price was being paid, for terrible wind erosion set in.

On Armistice Day, November 11, 1933, huge black clouds emanating from the plains of Oklahoma, Kansas, Nebraska, and the Dakotas, drifted across the eastern half of the nation—laden with what was once good wheat-producing soil and cattle range land.

Dust storm on the way.
Photo by Conrad, courtesy of Charles F. Roach Collection

Dust storm descends on Midwest town (1935).
Photo by Conrad, courtesy of Charles F. Roach Collection

Wilbur McMurtry was living with his father and mother in Wichita, Kansas. His father was erecting oil drilling rigs around Lyons in Rice County. Wilbur recalls his father calling one night telling his mother that he woundn't be home. His mother asked, "Why?" The father responded, "I can"t see to drive the car the dust is blowing so hard—in fact I can't see the light on the pole across the street!"

When snows came to the midwest, they were of grey color. Still more dust came, and soon the snow in the ditches was so black it looked no different from the fields.

People from the dust bowl were a sad pitiful lot—half starved, dirty and miserable. The soil kept blowing until some smaller houses and out buildings were banked with it. God, how those people suffered. Being hungry was one thing; now their source of income also was gone.

With gaunt pale looks on their sand-driven faces, they loaded on to anything that would carry them and headed out—to where they did not care—any place had to be better than that godforsaken part of the country.

Cowboys follow cattle seeking food in Oklahoma Dust Bowl—note ribs on cattle at lower left.

Photo courtesy of Gertrude Horan from James D. Horan Collection

Most migrated farther west, but some came to areas east of the Missouri River. California was jammed with them and shack towns, called "Hoovervilles," sprang up on the outskirts of towns where the poor souls weren't welcome.

One desperate "Okie," as they were called, engaged himself in a nickel stakes pool game in Happyland, seeking to win a little money.

Someone jokingly heckled him when he was shooting. He became livid and pulled a switchblade knife as he said in his Oklahoma drawl, "That's not funny; all I have in this world is this twenty-five cents, and I have a family to feed." Hearing that several people, none wealthy, tossed in a quarter apiece and urged the man to take the money. The man, his face flushed with embarrassment, finally took the cash and hurried out of the room with tears in his eyes.

Hoovervilles like this one at Bakersfield, California sprung up across U.S.A.
Photo courtesy of Wide World Photos

When would the dust stop blowing? Not until 1935 and it would leave millions of acres of wasteland, which would require more than a decade to restore.

While the western states were suffering the worst drought in recorded history, oldtimers in Mason City could have told the upstarts a thing or two about drought breaking.

It seems back in 1894 some twenty or so young men, seeking to escape the heat of metropolitan Mason City, then a growing town of 4,000, planned and participated in a three-week outing at nearby

Clear Lake, not far from the old Oaks Hotel, in what was called the Mars Hill site.

It was soon discovered that nearly everyone in the group played a band instrument and, of course, a band was soon organized. H. I. Smith, then president of Mason City's First State Bank, being accustomed to the title of president, was elected to that office, and Harry Keeler was named director. The first concert proved a huge success, drawing a fine crowd of young ladies from an encampment a short distance away.

A long dry spell had left farmers desperate and praying for rainfall. The "Mason City Globe Gazette" centennial edition states: "Whether out of displeasure for the unholy noise and discord of the band or from the delight of soothing harmonies, one will never know, but the heavens let loose the floods and it rained for two days. The long drought was broken and from that day forward the group was dubbed 'The Rainmakers Band.' The Rainmakers Band later became Mason City's official band."

Down near Stratford the immigrant Swede Nels Hanson, the one who spoke little English and had difficulty explaining how he raised such fine hogs, was not having drought problems; however, he was having a mite of difficulty with the secondhand Fordson tractor he had purchased.

Farms in Europe were much smaller than those in the United States, and only a very few farmers had tractors. Nels had cleared some bottom and second bottom land along the Des Moines River. The land was rich, and he still used horses much of the time to save fuel money. The land held moisture well and he had prospered even during the drought. When he did use his newly-purchased tractor, it frequently bogged down in the mud during rainy weather.

Now, there were but few women who drove automobiles in those years, much less a tractor. Back in Sweden operation of such vehicles by women just didn't occur. With the tractor bogged down in the mud and no hired man or other male around, Nels needed help and wife Anna responded to his pleas for assistance.

Nels jockeyed his 3/4 ton pickup truck into position and affixed a log chain from truck to tractor. This accomplished, he seated Anna on the tractor and showed her how to depress the clutch, which she did. He then pulled out the hand throttle and told her how to release the clutch when he commenced pulling with the truck.

Anna understood and complied; the tractor bucked and tires ground into the mud as Nels poured the gas to the truck. At first it appeared the tractor would not be freed; then the tractor gained traction and lurched free of the by-then deep rut.

Now Nels had neglected a thing or two and had not shown Anna the brake. With the lurch forward, slack developed in the log chain and it came unhooked. Anna did a fine job of manipulating the steering wheel or she surely would have hit the back of the pickup.

With tractor moving along at good throttle, Anna did the only thing she could do—she steered it in circles, some wide, some small. She even mastered driving with one hand as she frantically waved and shouted for help and all that stuff. Nels tried to shout instructions, but they were drowned out by the roar of the engine. The entire episode took on the appearance of an old Mack Sennett Keystone Cops silent movie comedy with Anna shouting and waving her hands while Nels tried desperately to catch up with the tractor.

The ground was quite level and Anna didn't appear to be in any danger as long as she steered the tractor in circles—and that she seemed to have mastered. At that point, the humor of it all struck Nels and he howled with laughter as Anna continued to circle the field like a buzzard, waving and shouting as she steered in erratic circles. When Nels told the story in later years, everyone was laughing so hard by the time he finished they forgot to ask whether Anna turned the ignition switch to the off position or ran out of gas! One thing for certain: Anna never volunteered to do the fall plowing, but she did learn to appreciate the humor of her adventure.

Throughout the years 1930 to 1934 the entire country had been besieged with groups of non-depositors removing other people's deposits from the banks. The "Daily Freeman Journal" contained lengthy columns, two or three times weekly, about vicious killings and the names of John Dillinger, Ma Barker, Clyde Barrow, and Bonnie Parker became household words. Teller cage tappers toured the country picking up thousands of dollars as they went along.

Kate "Ma" Barker was somewhat of a homebody and pretty well stayed there except when she went to the bank. She always took her four sons along so they could save time by doing their banking as a family. Then, too, they didn't have to go all that often because they always made pretty hefty withdrawals.

None of them had accounts in the midwest banks where they did business, but that didn't pose too much of a problem. The boys just showed the tellers the new guns their mother had given them for their birthdays, and the tellers gave them the money anyway.

In 1933 the Barker family had headed south for a brief repose and warming of bones. Renting a house at Weirsdale, Florida, the family settled down for what might be called a vacation from crime. Ma Barker's family could have taken a lesson from Ma and Pa Esters' mistakes when they pulled off the "Great Court House Caper" in

Happyland. Like the Esters, their downfall came from activities in the backyard.

According to Jack Evans, a former deputy sheriff, now living near Mount Dora, Florida, Sheriff Melvin "Pokey" Williams said the Barker boys became a little bored, caught a pig, tied a rope around it and trolled it behind a boat on the nearby lake. When alligators came to get the pig, they shot the reptiles with a submachine gun.

Now, not everyone has a submachine gun and, of course, hearing the firing, neighbors just naturally came to take a look. They realized something was terribly wrong with their new neighbors and quickly called the law.

Ma Barker and her son Fred were killed in a shootout that followed. Arthur "Doc" Barker was sentenced to life and was killed while attempting to escape. Lloyd would be killed by his wife in 1939 and Herman had committed suicide in 1927. Before the law had narrowed in on all of the gang, they had killed at least ten people and had illegally taken over three million dollars from banks.

Meanwhile Clyde Barrow and Bonnie Parker, a couple from Texas, had quite a love affair going. Bonnie seemed to miss Clyde so much she couldn't tolerate having him out of her sight. So when Clyde went to work robbing cafes, banks and filling stations in the southwest, she sorta tagged along and when he got a mite busy, she just pitched in and helped out on the various jobs.

Eventually they got quite busy and Clyde, knowing work was hard to find and all, just up and gave his brother and sister-in-law a job helping out during the busy season.

Bonnie ended up being captured and Clyde was killed in 1933. A movie was made about the widely publicized lovers. Before the law ended their career, they became known as one of the most vicious families in American history, having sent over thirteen victims to their graves.

John Dillinger was a guy, Cousin Clinty always advocated, whose mother should have knocked in the head and sold the milk. However, she lived until he was three years old not getting around to doing what Clinty referred to as her duty. The legendary gangster's father was a farmer and, research reveals, a fine person.

However, Dillinger was without doubt the most cool, calculating desperado of the era. Had he expended his intelligence and energy toward the legitimate acquisition of wealth, he possibly could have been one of the few entrepreneurs to rise to the ranks of millionaire during the depression years.

His first appreciable known crime was the robbing of a grocer in Moorsville, Indiana. He continued his informal education in crime while in prison. When paroled, he and a Harry Pierpoint, a fellow prisoner, went on a bank-robbing binge that would have paled the great post-Civil War escapades of Jesse and Frank James.

Dillinger was captured, and Pierpoint engineered a successful raid on the prison, liberating Dillinger. Soon they were raiding police stations for guns and robbing banks in Indiana, Wisconsin, Illinois, and Ohio—shooting their way out of encirclements.

Apprehended in Arizona, Dillinger was returned to Chicago. Then, using a wooden gun, he bluffed his way out of jail, taking with him some of the jail's guns and a fellow prisoner. He and one of his henchmen once cleverly posed as east coast detectives, checking out how towns were dealing with plans to catch Dillinger. An unsuspecting policeman unwittingly revealed his town's plan. Dillinger, of course, used a different route and managed to escape after robbing a bank. Later, convincing a banker he was a burglar alarm salesman, he gained access to the vault, then came back to relieve the bank of its money—smooth, one would have to admit.

John Dillinger wanted poster—$15,000 was a heap of money in those days.

FBI poster, courtesy of Gertrude Horan

Meanwhile back in Happyland Police Chief Kidder hadn't appeared too concerned when the post office bulletin board became so crowded with criminal photos they needed a new board. But, when his desk started to overflow with most-wanted bulletins, something had to be done—gotta have space to write reports to the council ya know! Then things really got serious when the news flashed that Dillinger's gang was raiding police stations for guns.

Then came a report that Dillinger's gang had robbed the hardware store and grain elevator at Williams—just 14 miles from Happyland! Speculation was the gang had hit the hardware store to get ammunition for their weapons. Rumor had it they had used too much explosive to blow open the elevator safe door—blew the damn thing through the wall—still unopened! Clinty's response: "Not professional enough for Dillinger—besides the only way he'd pull a job like that would be if they had a flat tire and needed something to do while they were changing it!"

But the police chief didn't take the Dillinger report lightly—to be forewarned is to be forearmed. Now even a novice knows if your going to prepare for an emergency, you've got to have a meeting—yep, they had one. The Chief pulled in the entire force—all three of them and even the cop assigned to night duty.

First things first: each cop had to ensure his assigned weapon was in top operating condition. Jack Ziegler had nothing to worry about his marksmanship; he was a one-time cowboy and was known to hit thrown bottles and cans in midair. Not too long back Jack had twice ordered a fleeing burglar to halt. He wouldn't stop and Jack, while the man was on the dead run, halted him with a shot to the leg. The incident touched Jack deeply when he discovered it was a married man of his acquaintance, badly in need of money.

Ralph Tucker, the watch repairman, enjoyed telling how Jack used to hone his marksmanship during long boring nights sitting on the park bench in front of city hall. Jack would take out his trusty revolver and pick off sparrows across the street on the parapet atop Steve Dermand's Cafe. Steve finally closed the shooting gallery; he allowed Jack was scaring hell out of his tenants on the top floor.

The police didn't have a weapons firing range but, with the gangster scare, Chief Kidder sent Jack to the city dump with the other two cops for a little shooting iron practice. There Jack's proteges scared the daylights out of the rats for a few days and gave them an exciting story or two to pass on to their offspring.

With sidearms tested and a couple of new shotguns in their arsenal, the Happyland police were about as ready as possible to face the forces of evil. And well they were for not long afterward on March 13, 1934 Dillinger's gang struck again. They held up the First National Bank in Mason City, just 63 miles away. The gang had leaped from their car spraying submachine gun bullets up and down State Street just to let those in the area know they meant business. There was excitement aplenty when the news reached Happyland.

Mr. R. L. James, who was secretary of the Mason City school board, was entering the bank and received a quick education in crime. One of the bandits opened fire on him, then somewhat apologetically told him he thought he was a cop—small solace, for he had taken two slugs in his leg. James' son, Tom, came to his father's aid; the bandits fired but missed him and hit a car.

Then a short distance away one of the bandits shot Clarence McGowan in both of his knees. Some of the people across the street in the Kelroy Fuel and Furnace Company building thought someone was filming a movie. No way would John Kelroy buy the movie theory after Curtis Yelland said he saw one of the gangsters laugh. Kelroy knew they wouldn't do that—he'd seen too many gangster movies to be taken in by such a performance.

But, it appears there was someone in town that day with a movie camera. H. C. Kunkleman, a guy with a flair for the unusual, was shooting a newsreel and decided to film a little of the action. A gunman drove up and shouted, "Hey you, if there's any shooting to be done we'll do it; put that damn thing away." Kunkleman's handywork was shown at the Cecil Theater the following day—good show!

The bandits kept spraying bullets into cars—even made one driver back up because he was parked too close (not to a fire hydrant—the bank!) Inside the bank, president Willis G. C. Bagley had been really surprised to see someone enter the bank, brandishing a gun—customers just didn't do that—this wasn't the old west. Yes-siree—at this point he knew things were getting a mite serious.

Bagley headed for his office to phone the police—with one of the gunmen hot on his trail. Hurrying through the door, he slammed it but it bound. Glancing down he could see the barrel of the bandit's gun in between the door and door jam. When the bandit tried to pull his gun free it discharged, sending a bullet whizzing by Bagley's vest. Old-timers sometimes wore bullets for watch fobs, but it was for sure he hadn't ordered one c.o.d. On a second firing attempt the gun clicked but didn't fire—the gunman departed. Bagley tried to phone the police, but the switchboard operator's parents hadn't raised any stupid children—by then she was on the floor—smart girl!

Using a submachine gun, the bandits sprayed the bulletproof glass cage, occupied by Tom Waters, the guard, but the bullets didn't pierce the glass. Tom couldn't shoot for fear of hitting innocent people, but he quickly gathered his wits and released a tear gas bomb. If nothing else, the tears probably made the bandits appear a little remorseful for the dastardly things they were doing.

About that time city policeman James Buchanan and Deputy Sheriff John P. Walare, from cover behind the G.A.R. monument in nearby Central Park, exchanged fire with the gunman on guard at the bank door. The gunman was a good shot and chipped rock away from the side of the monument. Richard Stoyles still believes Buchanan and Walare were the first persons in Iowa to adopt a pet rock.

By that time the robbers had bank employees, their eyes bubbling over with tear gas, pretty well under control. They forced assistant cashier Harry Fisher to the safe and made him hand out packets of currency, mostly five-dollar bills. Meanwhile, others in the gang were rounding up cash from teller tills like award winning charity solicitors. When they finished, they had collected $52,000.

Judge John C. Shipley, whose office was directly above the bank door, decided to deal out a little courtroom justice from his office, so he raised the window and opened fire. The gunman returned fire, but Shipley had to stop for the gang was now bringing hostages out to the get-away car.

The bandits took with them Emmett Ryan, Ralph E. Wiley, Lydia Crosby, all bank employees, and happenstance hostages Francis Stephens, Mrs. Howard Krieger, Fred Avery, Carrol D. Mulahy, Bob Lee Wright, Bill Schmidt, Mrs. William Clark, and Mrs. Frank Graham.

Using the hostages as shields, the gunmen herded them to the getaway car. There was no room for the hostages in the car, but that was all the better. They made the eleven hostages stand on the running boards and hang onto the outside the best they could—what a shield! Clinty allowed that Mason City streets must have been better maintained than those in Happyland or all the hostages would have been bounced off the car in the first two blocks. But, they must not have been that good as the bandits drove through the streets at twenty-five miles per hour. Some of the hostages said they even avoided bumps until they got on the smoother open road when they sped up to over forty—very thoughtful.

The police followed but could not fire for fear of hitting the hostages hanging onto the car. The bandits fired once, hitting the police car. Fearing the hostages might be harmed if they continued the pursuit, some four miles out of town the police turned back. The bandits crossed over the highway near Hanford and released all but Mrs. William Clark and Mrs. Frank Graham. A short distance later

Mason City's famous pet rock—lower right corner of photo
Photo courtesy of Mason City Public Library Historical Collection

First National Bank, Mason City, Iowa—tall building on left
Photo courtesy of Mason City Public Library Historical Collection

they were dropped off. The robbers stopped again, picked up another staked-out automobile and sped off.

Policeman James Buchanan felt he could identify the leader as John Dillinger. Mr. Walter, who walked within a few feet of a bandit, said he looked like Dillinger. Mrs. Clark said she was sure she could recognize one of the bandits, the one that winked at her! Sorta added a romantic twist to the sordid affair. With the eyewitnessed accounts, Sheriff Jack Robertson was convinced it was the infamous gangster who led the raid.

Dillinger eventually made a mistake; he befriended a woman in Chicago—one of slightly shady character herself. Newspaper headlines heralded the news that on July 22, 1934 police, acting on a tip, set a trap for Dillinger. When he came out of the Biograph Theater in Chicago, in the company of two women, he was killed by a hail of bullets. At least twenty deaths were attributed to the vicious Dillinger. Strangely enough he was never caught in the act of robbing a bank.

It was a certainty that John Dillinger had no Robin Hood characteristics, for he had no intentions of sharing his loot with the depression stricken poor any more than with the bankers. Still, most Americans remained staunchly convinced that with a little government ingenuity the depression could be overcome with perseverance and hard work. But wait—not everyone was indoctrinated with the American way of life—some could be swayed! It was inevitable that communism would rear its ugly head.

Communists successfully infiltrated some unions and colleges. Sadly a few union members and students became brainwashed with Marxist theories and joined the party—an act that would come back to haunt them in later years.

On the world scene another villain, Adolf Hitler, was emerging. He would drastically affect the lives of millions of depression era children and young people.

As background to events occurring in Germany, it is important to remember the Allied Armies had done a commendable job of winning World War I, but they were about to learn they had failed miserably in attaining a lasting peace.

At the end of World War I in 1918, the Germans had been forced to sign the Treaty of Versailles, with both sides knowing full well that the terms spelled economic disaster for Germany. Although the Deutschland leaders had established a democracy, the Allies had contributed little or nothing toward its survival.

U. S. President Calvin Coolidge, knowing a country with a sick economy is ripe for dictatorship, had warned World War I Allies of the foolhardiness of enforceing the full terms of the agreement.

The NAZI Party in Germany had grown in strides in the past few years. The proud, but militant, German people could not and would not forever live under such miserable, ill conceived restraints. Now Germany was also in the depths of a depression, receiving strong pressure from industrialists. Germany's President Paul von Hindenberg had been forced to make Adolf Hitler his Chancellor on June 30, 1933. Only two months later Hitler had pushed von Hindenburg aside and was given dictatorial powers. Hitler would become Roosevelt's biggest problem during his White House years.

Adolf Hitler with President von Hindenburg. Hitler pushed him aside.
National Archives photo courtesy of Gertrude Horan

With President von Hindenberg's death, Adolf Hitler exerted even more force and influence to attain his goals. Although von Hindenberg had little to say about the conduct of the government's affairs before his death, the famous old war hero still held the respect and admiration of the German people.

On July 25, 1934 Austrian Chancellor Engelbert Dollfuss was assassinated by the NAZIs. Dollfuss had strongly opposed Hitler's efforts to draw Austria into his fold.

Hitler hastily took over the title of president and named himself fuehrer. Taking no chances, he required each member of the German Forces to take loyalty oaths to him.

Heinz Ebel, a major in the German Army during World War II, told the author, "There was no one I knew who didn't take the oath;

maybe they felt they might not be around for the next roll call if they didn't!"

Capt. Ernest Roehm, a notorious vicious homosexual, engineered the forming of Hitler's dreaded Storm Troopers and headed that infamous organization. As villains go, Roehm had done a commendable job, in the saddest use of the word, of assembling some of Germany's toughest World War I veterans. Adding to that nucleus, he recruited the meanest cut-throats and thugs he could find in all of Germany.

Adolf Hitler and Capt. Ernest Roehm—Hitler's hit man.
National Archives photo courtesy of Gertrude Horan

Roehm's Storm Troopers had clashed with and prevailed over all dissidents that opposed Hitler. By 1934 Germany had a crack regular army of over 100,000 men—sharp, well trained and loyal to the cause. Though not numerous enough to be called an effective force, they would form a nucleus for a highly formidable army that would soon emerge. Now Hitler, basking in glory, felt he had truly begun to lead his country back to prosperity and on to the world prominence he had promised.

Soon the paunchy, raunchy Roehm, who thought he had curried and attained Hitler's favor, came into the fuehrer's disfavor. Hitler realized that Roehm and his hoodlums were getting just a mite too big for their boots, so to speak.

Hitler, who held no liking for Roehm in the first place, solved the problem simply by having him murdered. He then ordered the purging of the Storm Trooper ranks and turned their mission over to Heinrich Himmler and his vicious SS Gestapo, which would later become the terror of all Europe and parts of Scandinavia and North Africa.

Rudolf Hess had become Hitler's confidant and deputy. Hermann Goering, a World War I flying ace, second only to the fabulous Baron von Richtofen (the Red Baron), was his appointed Minister of Air—head of the German Luftwaffe.

General von Seect, who had trained the highly effective German Army (Wehrmacht), was now preparing to enlarge Hitler's ground forces. Joseph Goebbels, perhaps the most bloodthirsty human outside of Himmler and Hitler himself, had already begun his wave of terror on any Jews who might question his authority.

Left to right: Adolf Hitler, Hermann Goering, Joseph Goebbels, and Rudolf Hess—a ruthless quartet.

National Archives photo courtesy of Gertrude Horan

Germany, by treaty, had been extremely limited in weapons of war such as aircraft and tanks. Hitler first launched a program to train flyers with gliders; engines were added later and soon trained pilots emerged. Restricted on the manufacture of armor, the Germans overcame that problem by designing, testing and having tanks manufactured in Russia.

Not just the rank and file of Germans had been taken in by Hitler. He had promised prosperity and good things for his people and, amazingly to them, in some ways he was making good his promise. The great German autobahn highways were built, and they have yet to be equalled in durability in the United States. Tank movements in Germany during and after World War II didn't so much as crack the concrete and smaller aerial bombs had little effect on the road's near-impenetrable surface.

Germany's direct dial long distance telephone system, which was later to be re-invented with much fanfare in the United States, was improved by Hitler's order to afford quick direct communications among all military installations and governmental entities.

Before Hitler's rise to power, most Germans could not afford automobiles and depended on rail, bus or bicycles for transportation when distances were too great to walk. Yes, they had the fabulous Mercedes Benz automobiles even in those days, but they needed something less expensive—something like Henry Ford had brought to America.

Hitler ordered the development of the Volkswagen (folk car) which was built in government plants, and the sturdy, economical little car that swept the globe after World War II was born.

Although Hitler was defying the terms of the Versailles Treaty, he was putting German people back to work and restoring their dignity. They liked what was happening. Little did they know what their accepted leader had in store for them.

Hitler's hatred for the Jews was no deep dark secret. His book, "Mein Kampf" had brought out his feeling for them clearly. He and others held that the Jews in Germany were being given favor in the area of international trade, while those of German extraction were being held to the letter of the law on post-war agreements. Brutality toward Jews would soon rise to horrendous heights. To further stir the German people's wrath Hitler quoted France's Georges Clemenceau as saying, back in 1918, that there were twenty million Germans too many.

The key cast had been selected, props were being built and Hitler's Third Reich Productions were beginning to rehearse for their big play—while the rest of the world looked the opposite way hoping against hope that the opening presentation would somehow be a harmless rendition of "A Midsummer Night's Dream" rather than the nightmare Hitler was preparing for them.

As the tentacles of poverty tightened their viselike grip on the United States, more and more people felt the crunch. Maintaining good morale became nearly as important as the necessities of life. Costly entertainment was out of question for the average person. With more time spent together, families became closer knit and neighbors were extremely important—communities joined hands to create a tolerable lifestyle.

Social life took on a much broader spectrum than intended in Webster's dictionary. A good sense of humor was a priceless asset and the ability to create happiness under adverse conditions was rated high on everyone's list of accomplishments.

VIII
SOCIAL LIFE DEPRESSION STYLE

Being poor is not something described in romantic, poetic phrases by the great bards. Only one who has experienced the heart rending, humiliating effects of poverty can understand fully the hardships experienced by the unfortunate.

During the terrifying depression years, many a youngster, upon arriving home from school, sought out an unoccupied room to weep in solitude as a result of some spoiled brat's belittling him for his tattered, threadbare hand-me-down clothes.

When you were down to your last two pairs of socks, the removal of your clothing to dress for gym class was a devastating, soul shattering experience. It revealed socks with holes (or darn upon darn) and cardboard insoles in the shoes, necessary to keep the feet separated from the ice and snow. Hank had been a recipient of a few of these thoughtless comments.

As unemployment rolls increased throughout the nation, more and more of the students experienced the embarrassment of shoddy clothing, and cruel remarks about wearing apparel declined.

Whoever coined the saying, "misery loves company," came forth with a thought worthy of high merit. The only way a teenager could cope with his penniless predicament was to take solace in the fact others were in the same dire financial straits, and one never had to look far to find them.

Kittenball, a form of baseball, had been introduced during World War I as a form of recreation for servicemen. Catchers didn't need heavy protective equipment and players did not wear spiked shoes.

The kittenball was softer than a baseball, had high ridged seams and could be played without baseball gloves. Pitchers threw the ball underhanded and a much smaller official field was needed than that required for baseball.

A harder ball, called a softball, was introduced during the depression—the first baseman and catcher were then allowed, but not required, to wear a glove. Competition in the sport surged and soon businesses, organizations and churches were fielding teams. Normally there was no admission charge for these games and the sport provided a cheap form of recreation for both player and fan.

Pitchers soon learned to throw the ball like a bullet, all players were allowed to use gloves and fast pitch softball was born. Stan Nelson of Fort Dodge could throw a softball at near blinding speed. Spelled occasionally by brother Pete, he pitched and played his way to winning the national championship for Olson Jewelry in 1930—the team was unbeaten for three years. Stan later, while pitching for Boone in the national playoffs, struck out thirty-eight batters in nineteen innings of play. The great Stan was inducted into softball's National Hall of Fame.

Baseball had been the favorite summertime sport in Happyland prior to the depression. Even small towns fielded semi-pro baseball teams. Weldon Swedlund, a staff writer for the Stratford Courier, apprised the author of some interesting facts about early baseball in Stratford. It is just possible Stratford was the only town of its size in Iowa (or the United States for that matter) to spawn two major league players from the ranks of its semi-pro teams.

When people gathered at the Pioneer Cafe or Neil & Pat Sturtz's for coffee or bellied up to the bar at Deek's Tavern (now "The Bar None"), the oldtimers often talked about the semi-pro team Rue Corbin captained a decade or so after the turn of the century.

No doubt the oldtimers had just cause to do a bit of bragging. While playing with the Straford team Ray Blades accrued a mind-boggling .458 batting average. He went on to play with the St. Louis Cardinals from 1922 to 1928 - and again in 1930 and 1932. When he hung up his glove he had a lifetime batting average of .303. No, he never left baseball. After he quit playing - he managed the St. Louis Cardinals (the famous "Gas House Gang") during the 1939-1940 seasons!

Earl Marriott, the other Stratford semi-pro great, went to the "Windy City" and played for the Chicago Cubs from 1917 through 1921. He then played for the Boston Braves in 1924. Earl ended his career in 1927 playing for the Brooklyn Dodgers.

Weldon Swedlund beams with pride when he talks about the old-time semi-pro teams—for his grandfather, Gust Erickson, was a catcher for some of those great baseball nines. There were no minor league—farm teams back in those days and most major league players were selected directly from the semi-pro ranks.

Times became so hard after the stock market crash that a kid couldn't bring his baseball out of its hiding place for fear some other kid would eat the leather cover. Even though Hank played softball, his first love was baseball.

Although baseballs were scarce, the boys who played together always managed somehow to pick up a few at the games held annually in conjunction with the county fair. On game days, after sneaking into the fairgrounds, a couple of kids backed up the catcher on the spectator side of the backstop and a few augmented the left fielder along the third base line.

Foul ball hitters, rather than those who could pole the ball out of the park, became their heroes. When someone hit a foul ball liner or a pop fly, all that was necessary was for one of the kids to snatch it, outrun the players to the opposite end of the fairgrounds and disappear into the "free acts" crowd.

The biggest problem, by far, was sneaking into the fairgrounds since most of the time the younger ones of meager means didn't have the price of admission.

That particular year the fair board hired an unusual number of men to walk guard along the fence. This made it more difficult to sneak into the place than it was to get out of the county jail (and the jail was being broken out of with regularity.) One could see the reasoning behind it since the citizenry had to vote on a new jail and all the fair board members had to do was to hire their relatives and friends to patrol the fence.

For almost two hours on one occasion Hank and his pal Vernon "Bud" Brandt circled the fair ground perimeter like buzzards. The crowd had assembled at the ball park, and the desperate duo was getting a mite anxious to get in and snatch the foul balls. The situation finally became so critical they were no longer hunting for an opening between guards—instead they were looking for a guard they were certain they could outrun.

At last they spotted a member of the security force who had developed faster in the mid-section than he had on both ends. He was guarding the area near the stock and poultry exhibits. After finding the peerless perimeter protector of their choice, they went into a subversive session just west of Doctor Buxton's house to develop a plan.

In final resolution Bud was to engage the one who was working the stockyard district in conversation while Hank shinnied through a not-too-well patched hole in the fence. After getting through the fence, Hank was to rattle it just enough for the securer of the sow section to hear him. When the guard hot-footed off in pursuit of Hank, the plan called for Bud to slip through the hole and rendezvous with Hank in the pullet section of the poultry barn, or some such place.

When Hank's fence bustin' compatriot approached the guard, he had more than a little difficulty striking up a conversation with him. He appeared to have as much pride pulling guard duty on the building with the boars in it as the British do in protecting Buckingham Palace. Relaxing at last, the wary one finally turned his back and Hank made for the poorly patched fence and, with a few twists of wire, was able to squeeze through the hole. Once on the inner side, Hank gave the fence a dainty rattle.

With the first squeak of the wire, the guard sucked in his food storage system, and for fifty yards Hank thought he could feel the guard's chin whiskers chafe the calves of his legs. For an old-timer that man could sure rattle the ragweed and trample the tall grass. It was now evident to Hank that his portly pursuer soon was going to ring down the curtain on his afternoon's performance if he didn't take emergency evasive action.

Craftily, Hank circled the penny pitch with a burst of speed and, thinking he had outwitted his pursuer, he doubled back through the poultry building where he got the surprise of his life. While Hank had circled the game of chance, the guard had taken no chances and stood still. When Hank loomed into sight, the guard was soon hot on his heels and damn nigh cornered him somewhere between the Rhode Island Reds and the Plymouth Rocks.

Dashing out the door, Hank dodged around a man leading a cow, then ran between two refreshment tents in one final attempt to evade capture. As he sped between the tents, he hooked an ankle in a tent rope and a steel tent stake and for the next ten feet rotated head over toe, ending up a few feet from the stock area where the prize calves were being sold.

Up until this time, Hank had been exceedingly proud of his performance, but at this very moment he was madder than hell. The guard must have been attracted to the area when Hank almost knocked down the tent. When the guard rounded the corner, Hank was sitting down rubbing his, by now, swelling ankle.

Being a bit irritated at the irony of it all, Hank cut loose with a few choice words and asked the guard if he got a bonus for broken bones. The guard didn't answer and Hank assumed the guy was too mad to talk, but when he looked up at him, he found this not to be the case. The man was panting so hard he was giving off sounds like a centrifugal pump in a mud hole. For a brief moment Hank thought he saw cigar smoke coming from his pursuer's ears as he wheezed and gasped for oxygen.

His eminence, a track star of days gone by, finally collapsed against the side of the tent and sat down—whereupon he and Hank had a little tit-a-tat about the merits of moving too fast through the moo cow section.

Hank found out the guard wasn't all bad, for now he was sympathizing with him about his injured ankle. Hank in turn apologized because he hadn't run faster and, don't you know they got so friendly for a minute or so that Hank thought the guard was going to invite him to his house for Sunday dinner!

Hank allowed as how his day was ruined. That generated so much pity in the guard's heart that he contacted Mr. Scott Wagoner, who was delivering ice cream on the inside of the tent where Hank was recuperating, and asked him if he would give Hank a ride home.

Mr. Wagoner and the guard helped Hank hobble over to the ice-cream truck and Hank rode home in deep pain. When he arrived, Cousin Clinty and Mother Lucy were sitting on the front porch enjoying the evening air. The calliope-style music from the merry-go-round at the fairgrounds could be heard in the distance, and they looked so comfortable Hank wished he had been sitting on the porch all day.

As he hobbled from the milk truck to the house, Hank could see that Mother Lucy was terribly worried and he hastened to assure her he would be all right. Of course she asked the inevitable question about how he injured his ankle, and Hank explained the entire episode. Cousin Clinty looked at Hank with utter disgust, and his Mother appeared extremely upset at his behavior.

Cousin Clinty asked Mother Lucy to heat some water and epsom salts. Hearing these instructions, Hank became just a little more than belligerent. Hank advised Clinty that he didn't have constipation of the ankle and that if he thought he was going to feed him hot water and epsom salts, he'd best get warmed up for a chase.

Cousin Clinty laughed and told Hank he was in no condition to jump to conclusions, much less participate in foot races, and explained he only wanted Hank to soak his ankle in the epsom salts solution.

After getting out Mother Lucy's home remedy book as proof, Clinty finally managed to convince Hank of the merits of a laxative for his ankle and Hank soaked it for a couple of hours before hobbling upstairs to bed. Amazingly enough, the treatment did help.

The balls donated to their team by the county fair board usually lasted through the next baseball season and although the balls were not given to them willingly, they were greatly appreciated.

The long winter passed at last—spring had arrived. Happyland High School hadn't fielded a baseball team in a long, long time—then a notice appeared on the bulletin board that baseball was being introduced to the school's sports activities. Hank hurried home to tell everyone in the family the good news.

Mother Lucy shared Hank's enthusiasm, but Cousin Clinty's first comment was, "Whose going to furnish the balls? I hope you haven't volunteered to acquire them from the fair board for the school board under your disastrous catch-run and hide plan!"

Hank didn't have baseball shoes, but he did have tennis shoes. He did however have his brother Bill's old glove. The padding was beaten down; it was floppy and the leather in the pocket was worn thin from years and years of use. He knew no one in the family could afford to buy new baseball shoes or a glove for him and would have been ashamed to ask.

Hank signed in as a candidate for the pitcher or third base positions. However, his aspirations tumbled when Coach C. P. Lenz advised that he wouldn't have a strong enough arm to play either position. He was dejected of course, but with encouragement from older boys Warren Maxon, Will Ostlund, Maynard Olson, and Meyel "Bud" Haack, who had seen him pitch sandlot ball, his morale was boosted. Hank gave the tryouts all the effort he could muster. He survived the cuts and was issued a uniform.

A few nights later the relief pitcher Kenneth Richardson couldn't attend practice. Bud Haack and Leonard Olson, a fan, had a little talk with Coach Lenz. Hank was sent in to pitch against the first team in a scrimmage. Bud Haack was switched from the first team to catch him.

Hank surprised himself and the coach by striking out an impressive number of the first team members. He had been ribbed by a boy from one of the more well-to-do families for not having spiked baseball shoes. Hank's feelings were hurt deeply and it was with much pleasure that he set the thoughtless one down on three successive strikes. Coach Lenz came over after the practice and gave him a pat on the back—then somewhat apologetically said, "Hank, that long skinny arm of yours is sure stronger than it looks!"

As the season progressed, Hank saw quite a bit of action at second base—his hitting became an asset to the team and when the team was well ahead he had been allowed to pitch several innings. However, the coach hadn't developed total confidence for he always kept Don Shelton, the starting pitcher, in the game at another position—ready to take over. Clinty cheered more for Hank's only double than a Yankee fan would for a home run. When the season ended, Hank was more determined than ever to make baseball a career.

There really was always much work that needed to be done. However, if you were a teenager looking for a job where people paid you promptly for your work, it was a rough go. Most jobs available to a teenager were sort of a fifty-fifty proposition; fifty percent of the time was spent working and the other fifty percent trying to collect your pay.

To be socially prominent in Happyland, one had to be in business. If a person should be so much as manufacturing or selling outhouses for louses, he was automatically endowed with the power and wisdom to manipulate elections, engineer streets and bridges and speak in an authoritative manner on any subject. This was Cousin Clinty's considered opinion, and Hank was prone to believe him.

Cousin Clinty said some guy named Kendall Young had solved the financial solvency problem right here in Happyland. He had accumulated such wealth that after his death, with the concurrence of his widow Jane, he gave money to the city to build a new library in 1905 to help educate all the people in town.

With summer everything had become green except the papers Hank carried in his billfold. Ever hopeful, he launched himself to the Kendall Young Library to conduct an extensive study of the principals of business and economics.

A couple of the books told about stocks and bonds. The bonds interested Hank, but he sure as hell couldn't get too enthusiastic about stock since his job taking care of Fred Hahne's Aberdeen Angus cattle had left him fuming in more ways than one.

One book's author was on some kind of a kick about people having to make up their minds about whether the country wanted guns or butter. That sounded ridiculous as all hell when Forresters had a good creamery and there were plenty of guns in Power's Hardware Store.

Powers Hardware, Francis Powers in rear. Note gun racks on right.
Photo courtesy of William Powers

Earl Forrester tests cream in early days.
Photo courtesy of Lori Forrester Wilkie

Forrester's Creamery had plenty of butter.
Photo courtesy Helen Forrester Mertz

Harry Forrester, Jr. delivers milk.
Photo courtesy Helen Forrester Mertz

After evading the issue for several chapters, the book finally got down to brass tacks and told how banks loaned money to people to go into business—and the whole money-making scheme unfolded right then and there in front of Hank's eyes. He figured there really was something to this education thing and wondered why more people in Happyland hadn't been taking advantage of the wonderful library.

Hank reasoned the local businessmen had kept things kinda' hush hush about the books with all the secrets about tapping the teller at the bank for all that money. Also, it dawned on Hank the books he had found on business and economics were stored off in a corner, kinda secretive like.

After scanning the second book, Hank figured he had all the money making methods down pat and all he had to do now was figure out what business he wanted to enter. He finally asked the librarians, Jessie McMurray and Charlotte Crosley, what sort of business Mr. Young had been in to make so much money he could afford to give the town a library.

The two librarians clued Hank in on the fact that Mr. Young had operated a merchandise store, had been president of the First National Bank and owned several farms. As he strolled from the building, he thought of his Father's misfortune in farming and figured he didn't want any part of that business.

With all this money-making knowledge, Hank hurried home to get Cousin Clinty's advice on what venture he should choose for a starter. His knowledgeable cousin said he thought it would be a good idea for Hank to start with something small—like a candy and soda pop business and perhaps sell the items at the sale barn, if Val Wehrheim would give him permission.

Clinty advised Hank to give himself at least a year to get established. That, he went on to say, would allow him enough time to learn how to handle his checking account and adjust to his new social status.

Consulting with Shorty Sinn, who had garnered some success in the candy and pop stand business, he found out twenty-five dollars would give him a fine start. Hank headed for the bank with stars in his eyes and ready to reach for his pie in the sky.

After several strolls back and forth past the Farmers National Bank window, Hank finally worked up enough courage to go inside. The tellers, the guys who were supposed to tell people "Hell yes" or "Hell no" when they asked for money, sat on stools behind steel bars.

It was easy to see why they kept the tellers kinda caged up; from the looks on their faces, Hank had a hunch it was going to be about as tough to get a fist full of fives from them as it had been for Doctor Van Diest to extract one of his deep-seated molars.

Waiting until no one was around, he approached a cage determined to give the teller a pitch without a hitch—one that would inspire the man to vault to the vault for his cash. The teller asked him if he wanted to open an account, and Hank told him he would right after he loaned him twenty-five dollars.

Hank thought he detected a somewhat humorous twinkle in the teller feller's eyes, as he summoned up what must have been his most serious profile, arose from his stool, drew himself up to his well over six-foot-four-inch height and peered down at the little loan seeker over his low-set spectacles.

It was at that precise moment that Hank knew what an earthworm must feel like when about to be devoured by a bird. Hank thought the teller was grinding his teeth a bit as he told him to come back in a few years and talk about the loan.

By then, it became obvious to Hank that either he had read the books wrong or the teller feller hadn't been to the library, for the man just didn't want to do things the way the book said.

Hank decided that robbing the bank would probably be a helluva lot easier than borrowing from it. He told the guy behind him that he'd better get in another line as he sure as hell wouldn't get any money from that teller. With that, Hank beat a hasty retreat.

When Hank reached home, he told Cousin Clinty about trying all the methods of getting money the books had to offer. He had ignored the guns and butter part though he told Clinty he was just about ready to try the guns.

From his odd jobs Hank had been able to purchase some clothing and still had a dollar or two to spare. It was while he and Vernon K. "Bud" Brandt sat in Twin Parks that Hank decided there must be something good to be said about the boy-girl combination old Adam and Eve worked out during their little get-together in the garden.

Most of the female types Hank knew didn't appreciate hunting, fishing and sports, but they did seem to like attending talking pictures. However, his finances weren't usually good enough to consider an expensive outing. After all, hamburgers were now up to ten cents, and ice cream sundaes a staggering fifteen cents. With a few simple deductions, it became readily apparent that, if one took a girl to the movie and she had a surge of thirst and a sweet tooth to boot, one could blow a whole dollar in the course of a short afternoon.

Nevertheless Hank, feeling his education in courting had been sadly neglected, decided he owed it to himself to rectify the situation. After eyeballing one of the classroom cuties (we'll call her Hipsabella Herkmeyer) for a week or so, he finally summoned up the courage to ask her if she would attend a movie with him. Getting a grip on himself, he sensed Hipsabella might suspect he didn't have the price of admission plus popcorn or candy, so he nonchalantly flipped a silver dollar in the air to set her abash with his cash.

Hipsabella hesitated a little too long to suit him, and he began to wonder if she thought he was displaying his purchasing power because the pockets were worn out in his trousers. With this he casually pulled out his prestige billfold, (stuffed with paper for the occasion) and cached the cash in the coin compartment.

The sweet young thing stood first on one leg and then the other with her dainty forefinger on her dimpled chin. Then she looked at Hank in bewilderment, as if he had just asked her to help him shovel all the snow off hospital hill. But after Hipsabella pondered over the silver dollar and the thickness of his billfold, the deal was sealed. Hank hurried home to brush up on helping her in and out of doors and sat for awhile on the davenport holding hands with his dog just for practice.

That Sunday afternoon when Hank called for the little lady at her home, he received the close scrutiny of her mother, father, brother, and their dog. After discussing the past three baseball seasons, foreign affairs (all affairs were foreign to him) and the potholes in Bank Street, her parents agreed to let Hipsabella accompany him to the picture show. The dog, however, seemed to be insisting Hank leave part of his fanny for security.

Walking down to the town proper, Hank assumed somewhat of an air of dignity, befitting one who had attained a certain social prominence in Happyland. Just taking a date to the theater was sort of a status symbol and served veiled proof that the person was capable of a capital investment of at least one dollar.

As they passed the candy display in the window of James Orsi's Main Candy Kitchen, he offered Hipsabella a stick of chewing gum in a timely attempt to take her mind off her stomach. His strategy took on the outward appearance of being successful, for she gave only token attention to the caramel apples in the window as they strolled past.

Up to that moment, they hadn't discussed which of the two shows they would attend. They looked at the photos out front at each theater and when she carried on about how she detested cowboy shows, Hank knew he was out at least ten cents more since the face-licking feature was being shown at the Granada Theater.

While Hank dealt for the tickets, his date eased on into the lobby to wait for him. Hank urged Lois Forrester, the box office gal, on to fast action in returning his change and hurried on into the theater hoping to hustle his date past the bonbon bar. Alas, he was too late

Granada Theater

Photo courtesy of Willis Knight

as she had already suffered a sweet tooth seizure before he could reach her.

Looking over everything in the display case except the cough drops, she finally settled for a chocolate bar, and Hank threw conservation of cash to the wind and purchased one for himself. Feeling fortunate she hadn't popped the popcorn or pop question, he slipped her into the cinema before she could throw a thirst tantrum.

They had watched the news, the previews, the Mickey Mouse cat capers and were almost through a Laurel and Hardy one-reeler when one of those pie slinging scenes hit the screen. Within seconds Hipsabella's taste buds started acting up and she suggested Hank propel out to the lobby for popcorn.

Hank didn't get in a helluva lot of hand holding during the first half hour. In fact he was pretty well convinced holding paws with his pooch was just about as much fun and, by now he had learned, one helluva lot cheaper.

Just as the feature started Art Downard, the usher (later to become the owner), seated two people directly in front of them and Hank glanced up with everyone to see who else in town had the price of two admissions plus the treat trimmings. Hank noted it was one of the town's most eligible bachelors.

Hank couldn't figure out why the top casanova north of the Crooked Creek Railroad Depot was being so attentive to the woman seated with him since she definitely was not one of his girl friends. But Hank had enough problems of his own and decided to focus his attention on his hand holding and the screen to take his mind off his rapidly emptying billfold.

The movie wasn't advertised as a double feature, but the next few minutes convinced Hank that even Percy Long, the theater owner, couldn't schedule everything perfectly. Hearing a commotion to the front, he looked up to see the north side seducer receive a left jab - right cross combination which virtually created a sideburn out of his mustache. Whereupon the lady beside old lover boy asked, "Just who in the hell do you think I am?" It was readily apparent there was some misunderstanding as he half whispered, half shouted, he thought she was his girl friend.

By now it was quite obvious the local conquistador had experienced a problem adjusting his eyes to the darkness in the theater and had ended up being seated next to the wrong girl. Now that his eyes had adjusted he could see that the one with the strong right arm was still angry as hell, and the star of the best second attraction ever to be seen at the old Granada Theater beat a hasty retreat to the door.

Everything the feature movie had to offer from that point on was anti-climatic, but Hank was sure no one departed the theater feeling he hadn't received his money's worth, except perhaps the one who liked to spark in the dark.

The movie over, Hank and his date stopped for a snack. After she had eaten her way through a chocolate sundae, a grilled cheese sandwich and damn near half a napkin caught up in the rush, he finally succeeded in getting her out the door.

By this time Hank was a nervous wreck and his romantic inclinations, he now knew, must be laid aside until he could obtain some loaded dice and organize a floating crap game. However, as always, when he arrived home, he did seek out his Cousin Clinty to get his advice on proper procedures for dealing with dating problems.

When Hank completed explaining his financial and other embarrassments incurred during his first movie outing with a real girl friend, Clinty apprised him of the fact that as a youth he had been exposed to several similar situations. He then allowed as how Hank needed "Cousin Clinty's Crash Course in Girl Courting."

He averred that Hank's most crucial mistake was not submitting the girl to a "Sweet Tooth Sensitivity Test" before asking for a date. Clinty went on to say the sensitivity test was really quite simple and could be administered by walking past a girl at a distance no less than ten feet, whilst eating a five-cent sack of chocolates.

In severe cases, Clinty continued, one proficient at administering said sweet test could detect a slight quiver of an afflicted one's nostrils, even at great distances. With a humorous twinkle in his eyes, Clinty pursed his lips a bit, abruptly arose from his seat on the sofa and turned on the radio.

During the depression social activities for the younger set in Happyland were centered around several places: Jim Orsi's "Main Candy Kitchen," Miller's, Fastenow's and Joselyn's drugstores and Charley Alexander's, Lee Groves' or "Pop" Love's pool halls. The title "Main" Candy Kitchen was redundant as this was the only candy kitchen in town.

The drugstores provided a little more dignified environment for those who, due to their disposition and composition, needed to be near a ready source of purgatives. The pool halls, although frowned on by some, provided free entertainment and were professed by others to be a little more educational, as one could always practice adding in his head while keeping score at the snooker table.

Everyone, but everyone, went downtown on Saturday nights and they dressed up in the best clothing they possessed. Some walked over to the railroad station to watch people come in from far away places, such as Des Moines, Sioux City, Dubuque or Council Bluffs.

Those who had automobiles, and were fortunate enough to arrive early on Saturday night and pre-park them in good spots on main street, sat and watched the people walk up and down the sidewalk—over and over again. Sound like fun? Read on!

Even those who frequented the pool parlors dressed up in their Sunday best, did the same things they did at night all week long—sat and watched or played pool.

The city had installed its first traffic signals, called "stop" and "go" lights in those days—and, strangely enough, some people still call them that today. Interestingly, the signals were installed in square metal posts in the center of intersections with the signal inside the hollow post rotating from stop to go, causing many to wonder if progress would ever cease.

For the first couple of months some of the town's inhabitants spent a good deal of time on Saturday nights watching the signals change. Then, too, some thrills were provided by the confusion of drivers making left turns since they didn't know whether they should turn in front or behind the signal post. There were many last minute decisions and all one could do was watch the two vehicles collide and listen for the tinkle of glass.

After car crashes, it was interesting to listen to the arguments about who had the right-of-way. At least one of the signal posts was knocked down nearly every Saturday night. For people who would

Main Street—note post-like traffic signals

Photo courtesy of Daily Freeman Journal

have had nothing better to do than watch the second hand jump on the clock in Zolnosky's Jewelry Store window, this was a lot of excitement.

When it was all boiled down, most people would have to conclude the favorite and cheapest form of entertainment was undoubtedly the "Saturday Night Fights." The tickets to the fights were dirt cheap, except perhaps for the contestants, who usually paid through the nose.

If the localites spoke of going downtown to watch the Saturday Night Fights, you could rest assured they were not referring to the equivalent of the television fight shows of today. They referred to the nude knuckle, nose nudgin' contests conducted on a weekly basis in the alley between Second Street (main street) and First Street.

The matches were usually staged between eleven o'clock at night and one o'clock in the morning since, with the movies completed at the Isis and Granada theaters, attendance was naturally better.

For a short period the fights were starting at ten o'clock, but the early hour drew violent complaints from the farmers, especially during harvest seasons. They couldn't get their chores and town trading completed without missing some of the preliminaries.

A variety of fighting was available for the viewing public and, within a three-block area, there were fights to satisfy the pugilistic palates of all spectators. Of course, if one had a date in those days, some consideration had to be given to the language of the cheering section.

The preliminaries most frequently started in back of the Main Candy Kitchen, where the younger and relatively inexperienced brain bashers battled spontaneously over a stool at the soda fountain, a girl in a booth, a booth for the girl, or both. The fans from the sweet tooth shanty never turned out very well after ten o'clock because by that hour most of them were broke and dared not leave their seats for fear of losing them.

One had to be alert and on his toes to catch the main attractions that emanated from the back door of the pool parlors. No particular scheduling was established and the fights jumped from place to place on the card.

Just when the jelly bean jolters at the Candy Kitchen Fight Club were getting well underway with their preliminaries, only a few hundred feet up the alley in back of the pool parlor a "main go" would take place over someone shooting some eight ball in the corner pocket. No one was ever seriously wounded by these shots since they usually hit the person where he didn't bleed but was hurt the most—right in his billfold.

When the streets and alleys were icy, the fans had to settle down in one place and resign themselves to the fact that they couldn't dash back and forth to take in only the best attractions. This meant a look-in on the early fights behind the Candy Kitchen and about midnight, half sliding, half walking down the alley, either a block west or east, catching the fights behind the taverns.

One thing about the taverns: you could pretty well count on the schedule being fairly tight and the fighters too. The events were always best from the top of the clock until one o'clock in the morning. An added attraction was Dad Chase's popcorn wagon, located on the corner of Des Moines and main streets, and those who still had a nickel could buy a bag of popcorn or peanuts enroute from one pulverizing performance to the next.

The city jail had only a couple of cells and since the hold-me-tight rooms were usually filled by 9 p.m., there was no space in the place for other creators of turbulence in the town's tranquility. After the cells were full, the police were somewhat at a loss for something to do and, for lack of something better, the poor souls just wandered aimlessly from battle to battle acting as sorta unpaid, unofficial referees.

When the police appeared on the scene, a round was automatically called, and the fighters retired to the corner of a building, where they sat down on garbage cans and rested. After the police departed, the match was promptly resumed.

Cousin Clinty said there was some talk going around that the best fighters (like Lyle "Casey" Jones, George Van Winkle, Dick Woodard, and Arnold Liligard) were considering giving up the game if the council didn't add a few more police to the force. Clinty claimed the fighters' main complaint was centered around the fact that the police were hard pressed to cover all the fights and the pugilists were getting a mite tired of the long rounds they were forced to battle during the rush hours. Clinty expressed fear that if something wasn't done soon, the poorer people would drift back to gossiping and shooting rats at the city dump as a free source of entertainment.

Hank didn't suffer too much for lack of excitement, for he spent every spare moment practicing his baseball pitching. There was no opportunity to watch major or minor league pitchers, for the teams were to be found only in the larger cities. Occasionally a top flight pitcher was shown on the theater newsreels. However, he seized every opportunity possible to watch the semi-pros.

In 1934 Hank attended an interesting game played at Riverside Field in conjunction with a celebration at Nokomis Park. The localites were playing a strong Fort Dodge area nine.

With Duncombe's hard-hitting Barnes brothers and long ball hitters like Orville "Joltie" Eckstein, his brother John, and Keith Van Winkle, neither pitcher could perform at his best. However, Hank watched every move the pitchers made and did pick up a few good pointers.

Joltie miraculously resembled the great Yankee star, Lou Gehrig, in looks, build and long ball hitting ability. Amazingly, Hank and other Happyland fans saw Joltie perform one feat that day that even the great Ruth or Gehrig never accomplished—he made a hole in one in baseball.

The feat came about while the hotly contested game was in progress. Joltie stood at homeplate waiting for the pitch with three men on base. Grinning broadly at the opposing pitcher, handsome Joltie didn't take his bat off his shoulder for the first three pitches—two balls, one strike.

Joltie stepped out of the batter's box, knelt and retied a mythically loose shoelace. The pitcher knew he was facing a devastating batter and was, by now, all but chewing his gloved hand fingernails.

Joltie stepped back up to the plate, still grinning. The pitcher was determined to blow a fast ball by Joltie, but the ball came right smack down the middle. With a well-dug-in strong swing and twist of his powerful wrists, Joltie met the ball squarely and it virtually sizzled as it split the air to left field—deeper—deeper and deeper.

Everyone's eyes were glued on the ball when it descended, well over the left field fence, still moving rapidly toward an outhouse in far-away Nokomis Park where the celebration was in progress. Then a roar went up from the crowd—the ball had gone through the half moon cutout in the outhouse.

Joltie's ball could be heard ricocheting off the inside walls of the outhouse like a bullet and soon a man shot out the door like a jack-in-the-box, clutching the top of his unbuttoned trousers. Those near-by swear they will never forget the panicked look on the outhouse patron's face. As Pat Steinbauer later quipped, "If the guy was constipated, old Joltie's hole in one surely solved his problem!"

About this time Sheriff James O'Malley was beating the drums trying to convince the citizens to raise their taxes to build a new jail. Occasionally some prisoner would develop an aversion to staying overnight in the little building which came to be known as O'Malley's Hotel. Hardly a week went by that an out-of-town inmate didn't kick out the bricks in the south wall and escape. From research it appears the jail was constructed in 1876. Most of the inmates wouldn't have attempted an escape had they been given their own private keys. After all, they had committed minor crimes to draw ninety day sentences just to get in out of the cold winter weather and receive three meals a day.

The county residents always voted against the new jail bond issue. Cousin Clinty said nothing would ever be done to build a new jail until a local inmate contracted pneumonia from the draft created by some stranger kicking holes in the wall on his way to freedom.

"O'Malley's Hotel" had a facelift in 1937 (a concrete shell). There had been 11 holes poked through its old bricks since 1933.

Photo courtesy of Daily Freeman Journal

Actually, had an expense ledger been maintained, the money spent patching walls conceivably could have paid for a new structure.

Details of one of the interesting stories surrounding the jail breaks never were recorded fully. George Aden, the former county attorney, told the author that one of the regular seasonal guests at O'Malley's Hotel complained of having his sleep interrupted by the clinking in the "clink" and catching cold from undesirable guests poking bricks from the "pokey."

The jailbird, by choice, had complained to Sheriff O'Malley about the problem and, of course, all the High Sheriff of Hamilton County could do was to suggest he spend part of his spring, summer and fall vacation from the place selling the citizens on the fact they needed a new jail.

Fed up with escape-induced insomnia and discouraged with previous bond failures for a new "slammer," the distraught winter resident decided to take matters into his own hands. He didn't have to wait long, for the following morning he heard an out-of-county bonafide prisoner make the announcement he would escape that night. The break-a-way man invited others to accompany him, but no one accepted or rejected the invitation. Being a boastful one, the in-transient inmate even went so far as to name the escape hour!

When Deputy Sheriff Eugene E. Meller brought food in that morning to the one with the runny nose, the irate prisoner slipped him a note that the big break was on at midnight. The deputy contacted the young county attorney, George Aden, and asked him to assist in planning a little reception for the remover of masonary matter.

Now, most lawmen would have made a less eventful occasion out of the event by merely meeting the prisoner at the punched-out hole, but young Aden was always known to be quick thinking and was famous for his sense of humor. Not too long after midnight, so Aden relates, Meller and he arrived on the scene. Deputy Meller was armed and, as planned, they waited in back of the bushes to capture the guy. Some thirty minutes elapsed, Aden relates, before the escapee could be heard kicking out the final layer of bricks.

Soon the prisoner's head emerged from the hole and he looked around, kinda like the groundhog checking his legendary shadow, Aden says. Seeing no one around, he slithered through the hole dragging his legs behind him. On his hands and knees the man had barely started to rise to his feet when Aden shone his flashlight straight in the man's eyes. Deputy Meller fired his shotgun in the air, while the tall attorney, with excellent timing, threw a handful of sand in the escaping man's face.

Surprisingly, George goes on to say, the prisoner dropped like a steer that had been hit in the head with a sledge hammer. The county attorney and the deputy approached the man and found he had fainted. When he came to, he seemed real surprised he was still alive. Thus ended one of the most humorous events which ever occurred in the history of O'Malley's Hotel.

Anecdotes surrounding the old county jail could fill a book. Affable George Drake, who worked in the county engineer's office for many years prior to becoming a deputy sheriff, remembers the old county jail with a fondness normally reserved for an old friend.

Although a crime wave continued to sweep the country, Cousin Clinty predicted that none of the big-time gangsters would ever descend on Happyland. He maintained that one ride through the town's streets would have convinced even the most vicious gangster it would be inhuman to reduce the residents' standard of living any further.

Of course, the police department had not gotten wind of Clinty's prediction. Mason City wasn't all that far away and Dillinger had struck that town. Then too, road conditions could cause the gangsters to detour through Happyland—heaven forbid! At any rate, there was speculation by the police department and a few prominent townspeople that the Happyland bank could become a target.

The Police Force in Happyland consisted of Chief Kidder, Jack Ziegler, and two stately middle-aged paragons of crime prevention. The townspeople had but to stroll past the police station and see them sitting on the benches out front to realize that a bastion against crime did in fact exist. One developed a confidence that nothing serious could happen in Happyland if Ziegler was on duty and the damn bench just didn't fall down.

Even though some of the major gangsters, who had been terrorizing the midwest rural areas, had been disposed of, City Manager James A. Dunkel still seemed to think the police might be in peril and ill equipped. Many people thought he meant a new bench was needed to replace the old one in front of the police station.

Shortly after his appointment, Dunkel proceeded to order a bullet proof police car from Kayser Motor Company without the consent of the city council. Now, if any grade school kid thinks going to the bathroom without permission gets him into major trouble, he needs to know it is nothing, absolutely nothing, compared to the flak descending on a city manager who orders a police car without approval of the "city fathers."

Cousin Clinty and Hank were fortunate enough to get a glance at the land-going battlewagon as they walked downtown the day the little fortress arrived. The entire police force stood around it, kicking the tires and checking it over in general. One thing did appear obvious; at least the police force would be safe if bank robbers came to town. Cousin Clinty said it might have taken a little doing, but with it being a four door and all, the three councilmen might just be able to squeeze in too.

The townspeople were raising much hell about the expenditure for the car, and that prompted the mayor to announce it would also be good for speed chases in pursuit of bank robbers. One of the local lumpheads immediately retorted they didn't need a new police car as the police chief drove the present one all of the time in low gear, and second and high gear were as good as new.

Say what they might, they had to admit that Chief Kidder did look menacing sitting behind the wheel of the sleek armored car. He was quite short and squatty and all one could see through the bullet proof glass windshield were his hat, his glasses and the top of his nose as he stretched his neck to see above the steering wheel. But, really it was an impressive looking hat and a robber would have had no way of knowing that it wasn't Elliott Ness, of Federal Bureau of Investigation fame, beneath it.

The Happyland citizenry remained displeased with the hefty expenditure for the bullet proof car. They had pretty well forgotten the "Great Court House Robbery" of 1932. Bootlegging had kinda dropped off since prohibition had been repealed, but a few of the poor souls were still eking out a living by drastically cutting prices—sort of a price war, but no guns were involved. Oh yes, there had been a robbery involving guns July 24, 1934 at a farmhouse near Stanhope. A couple of gunmen, one armed with a sub-machine gun, broke into the house and relieved poker players of $900 of their gambling money. But, this was a county problem—let the sheriff convince the county to buy him a bullet proof car!

The council chambers were packed with howling residents, and a few even put up an impromptu scaffold to peek through the outside windows. Mayor Fred Hahne and councilmen Arthur Frank and Fred Schroeder were to set a record for long meetings that stood as long as the old city hall.

The political ferment that ensued resulted in the city council adopting a resolution disaffirming the purchase and not accepting the car from the dealer. Although many expressed fear Happyland would become a target, the gangsters never did descend on the town.

The local citzens never dwelt too long on one subject because they constantly had a ready supply of things about which to argue and feud. Talk was a cheap form of entertainment and with a subject like the bullet proof car, a lot of people had hastened to take advantage of the bargain.

Interest in Happyland government soared to a new high. In fact many residents decided attending the meetings provided great entertainment—better yet, admission was free.

As if the city council didn't have enough problems dealing with armored cars, gangsters and city managers, the local fun-loving E. W. "Pat" Steinbauer decided to rattle their cage a bit more.

Pat had worked the previous night on the railroad control tower and had walked up Broadway Street toward his home. As he walked along, he saw city workers trimming a tree on the parkway.

Moving along the sidewalk, he was continuing past the tree when a small branch fell, bumping his hat and head. The rim of his sailor straw hat held, but his head pushed out one side of the top of his hat.

As Pat told the story, his head wasn't bumped all that hard, but his sailor straw hat was ruined. But wait, the hat was kinda Pat's trademark and the tree had rendered it worthless. The thought of his favorite work hat being ruined sorta griped him. It wasn't so much the hat as the principle of the thing, you know! Pat figured the tree was being cut by city workers and was on city property, and he'd just present a little claim—stir the council up a bit.

At the next council meeting Pat was at last recognized by the chair. Arising, he looked around the council chamber like a prosecuting attorney delivering his opening or final argument. Pat opened his suitcoat, hooked his thumbs in the armholes on either side of his vest, threw back his shoulders and pointed his finger occasionally at a councilman as a prosecutor would point at an accused while making a salient point.

Pat was an eloquent speaker, in addition to being clever and witty. One would have thought the councilmen were up for murder when he presented his claim and described the assault of the tree on his hat.

He had the council thoroughly baffled, and the members were figuring out a clever way to handle the claim when the local clothier and councilman, Arthur Frank, managed to stop laughing long enough to tell Pat that if he would come into his store the next morning, he'd give him a replacement for his three dollar hat. As he rested his case, Pat laughed and averred, "By the way, don't jail the tree; it wasn't its fault!"

But not everyone in Happyland was content just attending the Saturday night fights, council meetings and partaking of such mild entertainment as watching pigeons fly in and out of the city hall clock tower through broken windows. The arrest of Sonny McIntyre and a few of the localites for gambling had done little to curb the appetities of people for sociable low stakes poker or crap games.

How in the world could anyone expect a gambler to be happy in Happyland without gambling? However, there are always stalwart citizens who expect everyone in town, except themselves, to conform in all instances with the true letter of the law—such a person was Cyrus Sleuther (good name for him; we'll use it.)

It was another one of those days when driving a nail in the floor would have created excitement. Cy was appalled, or something like that, when he heard Tip O'Flaskagin in the pool parlor talking to Pat O'Kettlebelly about a crap game to be held that evening at the abandoned Crooked Creek Railroad depot.

Cy had enrolled in one of those investigation correspondence courses he had seen advertised in a detective magazine. He was about halfway through the "ten easy lessons" and had learned a little—damn little, he was to find out—about citizen arrests.

Cy had convinced his cousin, Sam Sleuther, to take the course and he was soon asking Sam to accompany him on his first citizen arrest. Sam allowed as how he wasn't that far in the book yet, but Cy finally convinced him he'd be ahead in the game if he'd help him on his practical application.

Cy told Sam that all detectives do their best work at night and the two students of crime departed shortly after dark for the railroad depot. After circling the building a couple of times, they spotted a light shining through a hole in a blanket covering the baggage room window.

Crooked Creek Railroad Depot
Photo courtesy of Daily Freeman Journal

Sam hoisted Cy up on his shoulders. Peering through the window, Cy reported seeing a lantern on a box and six men hovering over a blanket and a galopin' domino game in progress.

With adrenaline flowing in the crafty pair, down to and including their shoelaces, they pried open a window on the far end of the building. Crawling through the opening, they tiptoed to the baggage room door. Willie Sipmore had the dice and was giving them some verbose encouragement when Cy slammed the door open, leaped through and shouted, as the book prescribed, "This is a citizen's arrest; come with me!"

The gamblers looked up at Cy and Sam. Recognizing the youths, Willie resumed shooting as he quipped, "You two had best be getting home before your folks find out you're out after dark!" Cy, undaunted and surmising he hadn't been convincing enough, took a deep breath and nearly blew the blankets off the windows when he again shouted, "Citizens arrest; come with me!"

By now Willie was getting more than a little provoked for good reason: one of the game participants had lurched when Cy let out his blast and knocked over his freshly opened bottle of homebrew. Willie yelled, "Time out," and with that, all the gamblers leaped to their feet. The gamblers soon had the would-be investigators subdued, their hands tied behind them with belts and their eyes blindfolded with handkerchiefs.

After a little private conference, the gamblers quickly ushered the two frightened correspondence course cops out of the building and herded them down the Illinois Central Railroad tracks to the Boone River railroad bridge, threatening to separate them from their toenails if they uttered a sound.

Arriving, they carried the two men out onto the bridge where one of the gamblers announced, "Let's do away with these two meddlin' SOBs!" With that, Tip O'Flaskagin and Pat O'Kettlebelly threw a part of an old railroad tie they had found along the right-of-way into the river. In the quiet night it made a terrible splash. Since both were blindfolded, Sam couldn't see Cy and Cy couldn't see Sam. Sam thought Cy had been thrown into the river and Cy thought Sam had been thrown in. Each thought the other was a "goner."

Finally the gamblers untied the two frightened youths, removed the blindfolds, and warned them that if they bothered them again, they'd throw them in the river for sure. "No doubt," George Drake, a former deputy sheriff, averred after finishing the story, "they both went home and ashcanned their correspondence books as neither one ever became an investigator!"

Lest the readers form the opinion that no one was ever happy in Happyland during those long depression years, perhaps some clarification is in order. There were sources of happiness during those trying times that are not readily available to most people during periods of plenty.

For example, during the do-without-thirties you were happy: when you had enough food to eat; warm clothing to shield you from the wintry blasts; heat in your house and money with which to pay the utility bills!

You were happy to have doctors who were sworn to the hippocratic oath, and didn't have their fingers crossed when it was administered to them. They subscribed to its content! They treated people even when the patient had no means of paying the bill. Often, when possible, they recommended effective home remedies if the patient could not afford to have a prescription filled.

There was no government medicare or medicaid program. Even people employed were not given access to hospitalization and medical insurance. Workmen's compensation insurance was unheard of and if you were injured on the job, tough luck—you and your family just suffered. Oh yes, one could sue, but few people could afford a lawyer.

Many doctors, if they knew the patient could spare same, took chickens, canned pork, beef, rabbits, vegetables, or anything of value for services rendered. Unlike today few people were known to be refused treatment because they were destitute.

Across the nation in rural areas there were many doctors, like Doctors Wyatt, McCauliff, Hall, Lewis, Galloway, and Crumpton, who merited a degree of sainthood for their unselfish service to mankind—they even made housecalls for the seriously ill.

Under the Roosevelt administration basic food and condiments were handed out, but no frills were included. Food stamps could not be used to buy steaks, ice cream and nice-to-have items, as they can at this writing. Now proposed legislation requiring people to work for assistance rendered is met with strong opposition from many of those who think labor is for the stupid.

Across the nation, during that era, people were happy to work to help themselves and each other. In rural areas land was set aside for gardening. Knowledgeable gardeners were provided as advisers and people who had never so much as planted a potato hand spaded gardens, pulled weeds and canned produce for hungry mouths.

Sewing rooms were set up; materials were provided by the government or were donated. Women of all walks of life combined their efforts making new or altering second-hand clothing for the needy. Flour sacks became shirts, blouses and dresses. From early morning until late at night sewing machines hummed. Only items that could not be used by someone ended up in the city dump.

Of course, there was no name brand clothing doled out, but people then were happy to have something to wear. At this writing children are known to commit suicide due to some knuckleheaded, ill-mannered kid berating them for not wearing name brand apparel. Some are more impressed with the label than the garment itself!

Most entertainment was, we might say, hometown spun. People played a lot of cards, checkers and low cost games, like darts and croquet. They read and exchanged books and magazines, worked jigsaw puzzles,and traded them to tackle new challenges. People gathered in parlors to sing along to records, mouth organs, and in the homes of the more affluent, pianos and organs.

During summer months there were band concerts each Thursday night in the park. Occasionally a medicine show came to town. This meant free entertainment—singing, a comedian and, oft times, a clever magician.

Of course, medicine show attendees were given a chance by the barker to purchase a special patent elixir—guaranteed to cure corns on the feet, dandruff on the scalp and all anatomy problems in between. Most of the elixirs contained just enough alcohol to provide temporary relief from most ailments. Needless to say, Mother Lucy wouldn't allow them in the house.

Occasionally Chase-Lister or Tilton and Guthrie brought their tent shows (vaudeville) to town. Pretty Laura Bashford, sister to one of Hank's best friends, Eugene Bashford, was a star actress with Tilton and Guthrie. She occasionnally gave Eugene, his brothers Frances and LuVern, and Hank free passes.

The Tilton-Guthrie Tent Show

Photo courtesy of Darlene Guthrie Denger

Most organized recreation in small towns was centered around church or school activities. For little money—plays, operettas and potluck dinners could be attended. In Happyland the focal point of recreation and entertainment was sports. People would gather to listen to sports events on radio. Popcorn was usually quite cheap and popular. Then, too, many people raised it or had a friend on a farm that did. What a treat!

The town's residents, where sports were concerned, were true fanatics. Even the hard pressed tried to set aside enough change to attend games. Like money, good losers were scarce in Happyland. However, at the games their problems were put aside—all that mattered was that the home team be victorious.

IX
DO OR DIE FOR HAPPYLAND HIGH

To the poor and destitute, Roosevelt's smiling face and encouraging words constituted a survival message. How could a man, robbed of the strength in his legs, be so powerful a figure? Like many in the United States struggling to overcome poverty, he struggled on near-lifeless limbs to offer them encouragement. He battled with seemingly endless energy to bring prosperity back to the nation and food, shelter and clothing to the masses.

The United States was, at the time, the only industrial nation in the world without national old age and unemployment insurance. Roosevelt was deeply concerned with the plight of the elderly for, without financial resources, they had to depend on their children or public or private charity. Now he was even more firmly convinced something must be done. In 1934 he had directed Frances Perkins, the first woman Secretary of Labor, to come up with a bill.

From the book "FDR," by Nathan Miller, his instructions were as follows: "You want to make it simple—very simple, so simple that everyone will understand it. And what's more, there is no reason why everybody in the United States should not be covered. I see no reason why every child, from the day he is born, shouldn't be a member of the social security system . . .

"This system ought to be operated through the post offices. Just simple and natural—nothing elaborate or alarming about it . . . And there is no reason why just industrial workers should get the benefit of this. Everybody ought to be in on it—the farmer and his wife and family . . . I don't see why not. Cradle to the grave—from the cradle to the grave they ought to be in a social insurance system."

It was with determination that Roosevelt sent his new Social Security Act to legislators in January 1935, knowing full well it would draw a lot of complaints from big business leaders. With the submission of his tax message to Congress in 1935, he damn nigh blew the lid off the teapot of tranquilty. His tax levy was designed to pull more cash from the wealthy through increased taxes—inheritance and gift taxes and corporate taxes commensurate with the income of corporations.

To add fuel to the fire, Roosevelt directed his attention toward the Public Utilities Holding Act and the New Deal legislation that controlled public utilities. His cousin Theodore had launched a similar campaign during his presidency from 1901 to 1907. The Standard Oil Trust, established in 1882, quickly claimed over 90 percent of oil refining in the United States. In 1890 the Sherman Anti-Trust Act had been passed to break up monopoly, but very little had been done to enforce its provisions.

The Supreme Court in 1895 had pretty well discouraged any anti-trust prosecutions when it ruled the Sugar Trust, which controlled 98 percent of the nation's sugar refining, was not in violation of the law. By 1904 some 318 trusts controlled 40 percent of the total manufacturing.

President Theodore Roosevelt's efforts eventually resulted in dissolving the huge Northern Securities Trust. Later the Supreme Court finally dissolved the Standard Oil Trust and American Tobacco Trust, but in so doing they paved the way for big business to divest holdings under huge conglomerates.

In 1914 Congress passed the Clayton Anti-Trust Act with plenty of loopholes in its text, and big business conglomerates continued to bud and bloom. Now came President Franklin Delano Roosevelt attempting to shorten the horns of the big business bulls.Would Roosevelt succeed in his endeavors? While he battled big businesses, they in turn sent lobbyists, with millions of dollars to spend, to swarm on legislators like locusts.

The legislators, of course, made the laws and if it so deigned, the Supreme Court could rule them invalid. With the presidents appointing the justices, Roosevelt felt that over the past decade the Court had become stacked with justices who held little favor for New Deal programs. The nation was stunned on May 27, 1935 when the Supreme Court ruled the National Recovery Act (NRA) and many of the New Deal programs unconstitutional.

As for the New Deal, the Court ruled that, "It is not the providence of the Court to consider the economic advantage of a centralized government. It is sufficient to say that the Federal Constitution does not provide for it."

In the area of employee remuneration, the Court ruled, "We are of the opinion that the attempt to fix hours and wages of employers of defendants, in their intrastate business, was not a valid exercise of federal power."

John L. Lewis, leader of the United Mine Workers, and William Green of the American Federation of Labor were staunch and tough in their demands for labor and were not to be bluffed. They held ground gained and no one, not even the Supreme Court, could budge them.

The Supreme Court action threw the entire nation into an uproar. People had just got a fleeting glimpse of the light at the end of the depression tunnel. Now, many felt, the Supreme Court was trying to fill the peek hole with concrete. The question was: What the hell could anyone do now to curtail the Court's miserable ruling? After all, they were lifetime appointees.

Conditions were bound to deteriorate even further if something wasn't done soon—but the Constitution forbade anyone, including the President, doing anything about the actions of the Supreme Court. This meant that the Wagner Act, the only protection the common man had against labor exploitation, was invalid. Also, many of the work relief and welfare programs adopted by government had to be held in abeyance.

When one reviews the massive government programs and controls implemented during the latter half of the 1900s, the Supreme Court rulings of 1935 become even more ludicrous and apparently politically motivated.

Roosevelt would battle to break the back of the Supreme Court, often referred to as the nine old men, who didn't wish to entertain modern means of overcoming age-old problems. Roosevelt stated, "The ruling is the most important since the Dred Scott Case which helped bring on the Civil War. The justices have turned the Constitution back to the horse and buggy days."

Strange how times change—Roosevelt's governmental influence would have paled before the bureaucratic domination of the last quarter of the 20th century. The federal government now tells people whom to hire, whom they must promote, and where their children must go to school.

States can no longer countermand federal decree in matters of schooling, highway construction, public works, etc. without threat of withdrawal of federal revenue sharing, highway funding and other such federal government supporting funds. Were Roosevelt's National Recovery Act laws giving too much control to the federal government? By today's standard, most people would agree, they were miniscule.

The Supreme Court's shooting down the New Deal program wasn't the only unhappiness to strike at the hearts of the country's people. America awakened to receive the news August 15, 1935 that one of its most beloved actors, Will Rogers, and the famous airplane pilot, Wiley Post, had died in a plane crash off Point Barrow, Alaska. Will Rogers, with his down-home humor and acting ability, had earned the love of all Americans and especially those of the state of Iowa, for it was he who had played the lead role in the movie "State Fair," based on the annual fair held in Des Moines. The one-time Oklahoma cowboy had even been placed in nomination for Democratic presidential candidate.

As the reader recalls, Wiley Post had won the Bendix Speedway trophy and had, along with his navigator, Harold Gatty, set a new record circling the globe in 1930. In 1933 he became the first aviator to fly solo around the globe. He was a legend in early aviation.

It might surprise many readers to learn that Fay Gillis, the daring aviatrix, not Will Rogers, had originally been scheduled to accompany Post on that fatal flight. After her sister Beth's wedding, Fay had returned to the United States from Moscow the fall of 1934. Still intensely interested in aviation, she soon came in contact with her old friend. Wiley was planning what he called a flight to Moscow via Alaska and asked Fay if she would go along, and she hastily accepted.

Many of Post's friends felt that when he and Rogers crashed they were initiating another globe circling flight—this time traveling west. Fay Gillis still subscribes to that theory and told the author, "I'm still confident the trip would have been around the world, for it would have been just as close to fly on across the Atlantic from Moscow as to return via the Pacific."

But again fate had interceded for Fay. In Russia she met Linton Wells, renouned correspondent and author of his autobiography, "Blood on the Moon" (the story of his adventures as a foreign correspondent covering the world.) While correspondent Wells was stationed in Moscow, Fay's romance with him blossomed and bloomed.

Wells, between assignments, was also back in the states the spring of 1935 that same summer, intent on marrying Fay. But Fay had already agreed to go on the flight with Wiley. After Wells agreed Fay should keep her commitment to Wiley, they eloped on his birthday, April 1, 1935, taking sister Beth with them because they needed to borrow her wedding ring, and Clyde Pangborn left a QB meeting to join the party. Enroute to California in June to meet Wiley, Fay got a telephone call from Wells saying the "New York Herald Tribune" wanted him to cover the Italo-Ethiopian war from the Abyssinian side and did she still want to go with Wiley or honeymoon with him in Addis Ababa?

Fay went on to tell the author that she did a lot of thinking. Then, with that marvelous twinkle in her still beautiful blue eyes, she stated, "I finally decided it would be easier for Wiley to get a substitute for the flight than it would be for me to obtain one for my honeymoon—Wiley agreed!"

Fay's eyes still grow misty when she recalls the death of her dear friend and Will Rogers. As Fay recounts, thinking back, those old planes were much more hazardous to fly on long hops than the current models. One was always riding the borderline between life and death.

Thrills were not lacking in Ethiopia for Fay and her husband Linton Wells. They were caught in the middle of an Italian bombing raid and ground action. Linton was wounded in the arm, though not seriously. Fay plays down her exciting life, but from research it is readily discernible that she was, in fact, a legend in aviation and is still in demand for speaking engagements at high level aviation functions around the globe. Transportation Secretary Elizabeth Dole presented Fay an award for pioneer aviation achievements.

Fay had other interests and with her, adventuresome spirit, they would be a little on the wild-thrilling side. She had two pet cheetahs, one in Ethiopia and another, six years later, in Angola. Wells gave her a leopard cub for Christmas, 1935 in Addis Ababa, and for the next three years the Queen of Sheba, "Snooks" for short, travelled everywhere with them. Snooks was an instant star in Hollywood. A remarkable lady—yes. The author apologizes for not writing an entire book about Fay's adventures.

With war clouds again threatening Europe and with Washington in political ferment, the spirit of the average American was dulled in most activities except, perhaps, sports. Athletics provided an outlet for mental anguish, and pent up frustrations were released in and at athletic events.

There is something about autumn in the freeze belt of America that stirs the soul. Wooded hills in a blaze of leaves changing color, winding streams and fields of golden grain foretell the coming of winter. Baseballs, except for the world series, are stored away and as a chill sweeps in on the early morning air, football season arrives and basketball season is not far away.

Of course everyone, who could spare the time and had access to a radio, listened to the World Series. However, the 1935 season ended on a sad note as the nation mourned Babe Ruth's retirement as if it were a death. He had been traded by the New York Yankees to the Boston Braves and had played out his final season in his hometown. On May 25, 1935 the mighty Babe hit his last home run for the Boston Braves against the Pittsburgh Pirates.

Baseball fans throughout the nation could hardly believe the legendary Ruth was leaving the game, for his name had become a household word. Ruth was the highest paid athlete of the era, receiving an $80,000 salary in 1930-31. His salary would be considered insignificant compared to the pay top athletes receive in the 1990s. But let's not forget this was during the depression and he was paid in good dollars—not the funny money that has existed since the 1980s, and his pay was possibly the equivalent of $10,000,000 or more at this writing.

The great Babe, "The Sultan of Swat" as he was called, had hit 60 home runs in the 154-game season. Roger Maris of the Yankees was to hit 61 home runs in 1961, but that was in a 162-game season.

In a fifteen-year period Ruth had led the Yankees to seven pennants and the winning of four World Series championships. He accomplished the awesome feat with a much less lively ball than those in use today and with much inferior equipage. Small wonder he still, to most, remains the most famous player of all time. It was the great Babe who vaulted baseball to prominence in American sports.

Like many of his friends, Hank liked football. He had played junior high school ball and, although he was 130 pounds of muscle, bones and intestines, he was quite lanky and not really built for the game. Nevertheless he thought he'd give high school football a whirl for all his close friends were trying out for the team.

He was a little late getting in line and the student manager, George Wheeler, managed to issue Hank a uniform so large both he and Big Brother could have got into it at the same time. The helmet would have fit him nicely around the elbows had his shoulders not been broad enough to hold it up and the shoulder pads draped halfway to his wrists. Although not afflicted with claustrophobia, Hank was constantly searching for a way out of the damn thing.

The boys were allowed to take their uniforms home the first night to make minor adjustments. Coach Robert Lamson never said anything to Hank about how he should adjust a uniform that was too large for husky lineman Sam Heffner. It dawned on Hank the coach could have thought he was the student manager—just carrying a stack of unissued uniforms back to the equipment room.

When Hank got home, he immediately donned his uniform to let Clinty have a look-see. Clinty expressed his doubts that the coach would even recognize Hank, even though he only lived a block or so away and Hank had been mowing his lawn all that summer.

Hank's capricious cousin encouraged him to grin and stay within his uniform as he felt reasonably certain the coach would want to know if a school board member's son was inside before cutting him off the squad. Clinty did offer a word of caution after giving the helmet problem a little thought. He advised Hank to stay away from the river bank, which paralleled the north side of the playing field, until he could get to the library to check on when the turtle mating season commenced and ended.

Someone must have started the rumor that Hank had been seen in the dressing room and, with rumors being what they are in a small town, the word soon got to the coach. At any rate, he apparently recognized Hank's Adam's apple or the tip of his nose that afternoon at practice and told the doler of duds to issue Hank a different uniform.

Football prowess was definitely on the rise in Happyland. Two speedsters, quarterback Warren Maxon and halfback Ralph Frank, were a threat each time they carried the ball, and Don Mertz could block with the best of them. Walter Willson, Jr. was a powerhouse at fullback. Mertz was to be injured and replaced by Will Ostlund, an extremely versatile athlete.

John Stepp anchored the line at center with Merlin "Jumbo" Crouse and Armor Miller at the guard positions. Strong, hefty Sam Heffner and George "Fritz" Warneke were the tackles, while on the flank ends were the dynamic Ralph Burton and Luverne Whitson. Don Shelton, Arleigh Newland, Oliver Meyers, and John Chambers saw a lot of action.

When the season wound down, the team had lost only to powerful Boone, whose Mike Enich would become legendary as part of the Iron Men team of the University of Iowa (a teammate of Enich on that powerful Boone team, Norman Erbe, would go on to become Iowa's governor). Happyland fell to Clarion which fielded one of the toughest teams in that school's history. In all, Happyland had an impressive season—winning five, tieing one and losing two, while racking up 118 points to the opposition's 33. Yes, prospects for another fine team at Happyland High were good, for nine of the aforementioned would return for the following season.

On the academic side, history classes had begun to take on a different flavor; the teachers became more serious. As if the Japanese moving into Manchuria wasn't enough, Italy's dictator Benito Mussolini now had his chest out so far he was nearly popping the buttons off his tunic. He and German Dictator Adolf Hitler had become buddy-buddy, and he wanted to impress the German leader and the Italian people. Now he had decided the time was ripe to show everyone that a newly cloned Julius Caesar had returned to lead the Italian people back to world prominence!

On October 3, 1935 Mussolini's armed forces attacked the hapless North African country of Ethiopia. Ethiopia had been free of foreign domination for nearly 3,000 years. Emperor Haile Selassie, who came to power in 1930, had set up a parliament and a constitution and had made many improvements in the tiny impoverished country.

The war was no contest, for the Ethiopians were armed with spears and old muskets—with but a sprinkling of more modern weapons. Ethiopia's rag tag soldiers did fight gallantly but were slaughtered by the Italian Army's more advanced weaponry.

Newsreels of the time showed excerpts of the action. What a sad spectacle that was—with proud Italians strutting back to Italy and Mussolini bragging as if his forces had defeated a formidable foe. Hell, they even brought back a few elephants and camels as prizes of war. During World War II in Tunisia, North Africa, their smiles would turn to gloomy frowns.

Of course everyone, except Germany and Japan, condemned Italy's invasion of Ethiopia, but no one came to Ethiopia's aid. The United States was still snuggled in a neutralist cocoon. In Happyland there were only two immediate concerns: when the depression would end and who would win the next ball game.

On any given Saturday morning when you walked into either Jensen's or Fastenow's drugstores, you had best duck your head as the air was full of basketballs, footballs or baseballs.

When the townspeople realized Happyland had not only enjoyed an excellent football season, but now had the best basketball team to scurry around the court since 1926, they nearly went beserk. Interest reached a fevered pitch and the gym was full and overflowing. People who could afford it, and some who couldn't, paid their admission to stand in the outer hallway, depending on someone inside to relay the score to them.

Most games were played on Fridays, and the following morning one could see the unpaid, unsolicited assistant coaches beating a trail to the drugstores in a mad dash to get a seat at the soda fountain. However, they did take time to sidestep a light pole properly, stiff arm a fire hydrant, or soar high in the air to touch a low hanging sign, as if scoring a last minute basket.

Happyland, like most small towns, always had a bountiful supply of men over thirty who considered themselves better coaches than the man hired to do the job. Call them drugstore coaches, Saturday morning quarterbacks, whatever—they felt themselves a driving force to be reckoned with. If the game had been won the day or night before, each took due credit for having shouted vital instructions to the players from the sidelines or slipping the coach some timely strategy before the game.

A lost game was another matter and the group's conversation took on a somewhat different tone. Someone usually brought up the fact that the officials might just as well have been wearing the uniform of the opposing team, or that the school board should be voted out of office for hiring a couple of valedictorians from the Vinton School for the Blind to do the officiating.

Breezy McBagpipe (a very appropriate alias) was probably one of the best drugstore quarterbacks ever to straddle a Happyland soda fountain stool. He was shifty, and could streak around a waiting line at the soda fountain faster than anyone in town. And could he pass; he could pass the ketchup bottle with lightning-like accuracy. Then, too, one might say Breezy was a triple threat man, for he also kicked hell out of other people's ankles in his haste to crowd onto a vacant stool.

Breezy had his ups and downs as a drugstore coach, but he damn nigh lost his coaching privileges at Jensen's Drugstore one Saturday morning. He was notorious for demonstrating how it was done back in his heyday. One demonstration is worth a thousand words, that's what Breezy always said! Yes, siree! Funny how he always gave people the thousand words, even though he'd given them the demonstration.

Anxious to draw the crowd's attention one Saturday morning, old Breezy McBagpipe leaped off his stool while driving home a salient point. Assuming a defensive tackle's stance, he fended off two mythical blockers, bolted forward, slipped on the slightly wet highly waxed floor and with a bit of razzle dazzle, managed to careen off a gondola counter stacked with sampler chocolates. Somehow he managed to stay on his feet and come to a wobbly-legged halt by the cash register counter.

Always a quick thinker, Harry Jensen, the proprietor, had just finished collecting from a customer. Harry nonchalantly poked the "no sale" button on the cash register, reached over and said, "Breezy, here's your quarter back; now go take a damn shower!"

Hank was proud to have made the basketball squad. Clinty said he was downright happy as he had said many times that, with Hank's teenage clumsiness, he would probably be the only boy in Happyland ever to cut his fanny with a paring knife while peeling potatoes.

Hank had asked Marion Hughes, a former Happyland High athlete and operator of the neighborhood grocery store, for a job. Marion hired him to stock shelves, keep things neat and clean and pack baskets for delivery to customers.

Late the night of December 20, 1935 the fire siren pierced the bitter cold night air. Soon fire truck sirens were coming, and they appeared to stop nearby.

Everyone leaped from bed, donned clothing and went outside to see where the fire was. Bright flames could be seen shooting up from business buildings in the next block.

Firemen, in sub zero weather, fought valiantly but to no avail; the flames continued to spread. Seeing the fireman with icicles forming on their nostrils was too much for Eunice "Ma" Spencer, who ran a boarding house and sold a little liquor on the side. She went home, got some whisky, came back and gave badly-chilled firemen a stomach warming drink.

Seeing Ma Spencer give the firemen a drink, local police immediatley placed her under arrest. Spectators booed loudly, but the police took her away and booked her.

Ma was an extremely kind and generous person. Hank had packed many baskets of food at the grocery store to be delivered to unfortunate familes. Ma never allowed anyone to tell the family who sent the groceries. Undoubtedly Ma was one of the kindest, sweetest persons in all Iowa. She always kept the dining room table in her boarding house laden with food. Hank played ball with Ma Spencer's grandsons, Bob, Jack and Ned Patterson. Many hungry people, to include hobos, were seen going in to Ma's place, but no hungry people ever came out.

Of course, there was no money exchanged in the liquor transaction, so they couldn't charge her with bootlegging. But they did charge her with dispensing liquor without a license on a public street. The police were a long time living down that arrest.

When the flames were snuffed out, Harry Brin's furniture warehouse was gutted (he was to have several more bad fires over the years.) Thorpes Auto Parts and Burnett's Hatchery and Produce lay in ruins and Marion Hughes' store received heavy damage, forcing him to close for repairs.

Hank did not go back to sleep that night. With his source of income smoldering a block away, he wondered how he possibly could remain in school. Marion, a kindly man, would often throw in a half-pound of meat or other food for an unfortunate family.

Christmas of 1935 was not the happy occasion it could have been. Those in rural areas were extremely apprehensive, for they feared the Supreme Court would hold the Agriculture Adjustment Act invalid. Stock growers were wary of markets and began to tighten up. James Arthur was not finding hay baling jobs plentiful and hay sales dropped off.

During the entire holiday season Mother Lucy could be seen frequently walking off to the corner of the room, dabbing at her eyes with her apron. This wonderful woman was a direct descendant of General Israel Putnam of Revolutionary War fame and her father, Seymour Lester, had virtually fought through the entire Civil War as an infantry company first sergeant. Obviously, she was not crying for want for herself, but for her family. Hank made several trips to look out the window while suppressing the tears that kept welling in his eyes.

Hank sat at the dining room table that Christmas day and, as the blessing was being said, he was truly thankful they had any food on the table at all. He wanted at least a high school education, but he knew at that precise moment he couldn't accept more money from his Mother and Father.

The next day he and Clifford "Tip" Van Doren were discussing Hank's financial problems when Tip's father overheard the conversation. Mr. Van Doren, a kindly man who then was operating a dairy, suggested Hank work for him cutting wood from their timber for sale as fuel. The job would last for the rest of the holiday season.

For the next several days Hank more than pulled his share of a mature man's work in the woods. When the school bells again chimed, Hank asked Mr. Van Doren if he could continue for another week to earn money for warmer clothing. Mr. Van Doren consented, but did so with obvious sorrow for he wanted Hank to continue his schooling.

Hank's sister was reduced to tears when she learned her youngest brother was considering giving up formal schooling. She, as always, offered to help him, but it was readily evident to Hank that, with her salary, she could not afford very much.

Several days into the next semester Hank had accumulated some twenty dollars from his job (his pay consisted of meals and a dollar for each 10-hour day). As he sat one noon at the table, Mr. and Mrs. Van Doren continued to encourage him to complete his schooling.

That afternoon about five o'clock they finished felling a tree and, while resting, Hank looked down from the hill across Brewer Creek and toward the road leading to the schoolhouse. Thinking of how he would like to join his friends at basketball practice, he decided to take the twenty dollars and, with some help from his sister, attempt at least to finish out the year.

While felling trees Mr. Van Doren decided to cut one for Hank's family—said it looked like an exceptionally cold winter settling in. James Arthur was happy to get the additional fuel and the wood was quickly hauled with an automobile trailer and stacked in the basement.

As the thermometer plunged to record lows for far longer periods than normally experienced, coal supplies dwindled throughout the midwest. Even the fuel supplies at schools were dropping to a dangerously low level. At last the school board announced on February 17, 1936 that schools would be closed due to the coal shortage.

Parents had been keeping their homes at very low temperatures during the daytime to conserve fuel while children were in school; now the children must stay home.

Dressed in their warm clothing people huddled around space-heating stoves or warm air registers. Burnables were gathered from every source possible. People could be seen at the city dump gathering cardboard, discarded wooden boxes or crates—anything that would burn. Many could be seen dragging dead limbs and cut branches from along the river bank and from parks; still others tore down and burned wooden out-buildings.

James Arthur's family was fortunate indeed, for the tree given to them by Mr. Van Doren carried them through the coal shortage. At

Elmer Reisner—a self-educated electrical genius. His power plant carried Happyland Municipal Services through the Great Depression.

Photo courtesy of Ann Reisner Smith

last coal supplies caught up with demand and there was a break in the cold weather. School classes resumed February 24. But not all the misery was alleviated. Some people had used electric heaters to survive through the cold spell—now they couldn't pay the larger electric bills.

Elmer Reisner, utilities superintendent, said the saddest thing his electrical department had to do was to obey oders to cut off the electrical services of those unfortunates who couldn't pay their bills.

Many things, other than record-breaking cold weather, originated in Happyland, but the world as a whole was never fully apprised of the fact. For example, it can be reasonably substantiated that brainwashing was a psychological expedient invented by English literature teacher, Bertha Teal—devised to take over the thinking tissues of those members of her class who had contracted athlete's brain.

She was slender of build, sharp of wit, but as desperate as a Girl Scout leader selling birdbaths in Nome, Alaska to fund a February day camp. There were times when she must have been convinced it would have been far easier to teach some of her less cooperative students to communicate with drums in lieu of the written word.

Actually the "Literary Lady" lost complete control of her brain bonnet on only one occasion to everyone's recollection. And, if one is to be considerate and allow for all she was forced to endure, it can be said this was highly commendable.

The time she almost tossed chalk, the class grade book and one of the smaller kids in the front row out the window came about while she was doing her best to stimulate her students in an analysis of one of the world's great literary works. She had explained to her students how they must throw themselves into the story to appreciate fully the works of great writers and absorb the true feelings behind the words.

To emphasize her point, she dramatically read a bit of prose involving a hermit who lived in a shack by a small stream. Her reading was superb and her pantomimes were priceless; one could easily sense she was throwing her Sunday punch in a last-ditch effort to instill appreciation of the literary word in some of her less inspired students.

Completing her theatrical-like performance, she searched the room with piercing eyes for one who might serve as a living example of her inspirational reading. Her roving eyes at last focused on Armor Miller, who was sitting in the front row beside Hank. In her most appealing voice, she said, "Armor, when you hear the poem read with emphasis and feeling, can't you just hear the water trickling over the little stones in that beautiful winding brook?"

Now Armor was a star tackle on the football team—tough, hard, and far from stupid. But literature was a long way from being an oasis in his desert of interests; the question kinda baffled him. His initial reaction indicated he might well be convinced of the merits of prose. Miss Teal's eyes reflected great pleasure.

After pondering for awhile, the recently-consulted classroom critic leaned back, clasped his hands behind his head and looked up at the ceiling, as if giving the subject deep thought. After a brief repose, he lowered his nose, looked straight in the eyes of the purveyor of verbs and adverbs and in a voice clear, distinct, and positive said, "Hell no!"

The answer reached "Literary Lil" (who had weathered the likes of the mischievous Pulitzer Prize winning author, MacKinlay Kantor) and her reaction was spontaneous. Her mouth flew open, her glasses slid to the tip of her nose, the book fell to the floor and, in the confusion that followed, no one heard the bell sounding the end of the period.

At the closing of the class Miss Teal normally returned to her desk and sat calmly while the class filed out. But this time she dashed out the door and with the thrust of a roadrunner, bolted into the office of Principal C. E. Miller for one of those closed-door-type conferences.

Armor wasn't expelled, but he did have a lengthy session with the principal who, our gridiron great was the first to admit, wore the pants in the public school. In fact Armor later confessed that what the principal had to say to him was, "Non-fiction—but very inspiring!"

As March winds began to blow and become blustery, so became Germany's Adolf Hitler. The Germans still harbored much bitterness about land that had been taken from them and could not forget some of the disasterous terms that had been forced upon them at the end of World War I.

Germany's economy was shattered after World War I. In 1923 France, angered by Germany's being unable to make reparations agreed upon at Versailles, had occupied the Ruhr, Germany's principal base of industrial might and the key to that country's economic recovery.

The author sat visiting with Betty Ritterbecks of Bamberg, Germany and her sister Conny Sousette, now of Hope Valley, North Carolina. Betty was in the University of Florida Hospital in Tampa recovering from a fractured hip, suffered while visiting her two daughters in the United States.

Betty is the widow of former German army Major Bert Ritterbecks, whom the author had known while Bert was a chief of police during the author's tenure in the U.S. Army of Occupation.

A discussion evolved around the French occupation of the German Ruhr industrial complex during 1923. Betty and her sister agreed that the French occupation of the Ruhr was the biggest single contributor to the rise of Adolf Hitler to dictatorship and his ultimately leading that country into World War II. Within six months after the occupation, the sisters recall, millions of Germans, even the middle-class barely eking out a living at the time, were thrown into unemployment and hard core poverty.

In the end it was American loans that eventually lent some hope to Germans for their country's future. Although the Allies lifted some of the sanctions in 1925, the German people had never forgiven the Western European Allies one hundred percent for the extremely strong measures they had taken to ensure Germany would never again become a world power.

Hitler was determined to gain back some of the territories seized from Germany and taking revenge against France was a high priority for him and his people.

His armed forces had developed far faster than most people could have visualized. On March 7, 1936, when he marched 4,000 cavalrymen and infantrymen into the Rhineland, which had been established as a demilitarized zone after the war, he was relying somewhat on his bluffing expertise. His feelings were that Britain was not ready for armed confrontation and that France, which had suffered some ten million casualties during World War I, had ingested a belly-full of shooting wars and was not ready to fight over the relatively tiny strip of land.

Hitler's assumptions were correct; there were strong protests but no armed intercession. Many historians still feel that had Hitler's move into the Rhineland been met with armed confrontation, the brutally long World War II possibly might have been averted—or would have been a much shorter struggle.

On the lighter side at the college level, basketball had undergone almost the same revolution football had when Knute Rockne unbridled heavy use of the forward pass at Notre Dame. Stanford University had unveiled a sophomore, Hank Luisetti, who consistently used one-hand push shots; his accuracy was phenomenal.

During Luisetti's first year Stanford was trailing Southern California by 15 points. As the ball was fed to Luisetti, the young deadeye poured in 14 straight points—an outstanding game accomplishment for the stars of that era. Luisetti would go on to score a mind-boggling 50 points the following year, a feat found difficult for professionals, even at this writing.

Basketball underwent an additional dramatic change. In previous years, after each basket, the ball was taken back to the center of the court; the referee threw the ball up between the two centers and the best jumper tapped it to his team. Most plays originated from the jump center. Now in 1935 the ball would be taken out of bounds by the team scored against and play initiated from that end of the court. The game was speeded up tremendously, and no longer did the team with the tallest center have so great an advantage.

Back in Happyland the 1935-1936 high school basketball team had enjoyed a tremendous season, bowing in the state finals only to Mason City, whose coach, Judge Grimsley, always fielded strong teams with such players as Stoecker, Fletcher, Hirt, Lane, and Wallace setting a torrid pace.

Don Shelton, a tall, strong lad with a remarkable one-hander, Will Ostlund, Warren Maxon, Ralph Frank and Meyel "Bud" Haack or Ralph Burton made up Happyland's key players. Shelton would be selected on the second all-state team, bowing only to Mason City's Howard Stoecker.

During spring vacation Hank was again blessed (damn little) with another opportunity to earn money with which to become socially prominent. Would the wonders of Roosevelt's New Deal ever stop! Mother Lucy had received a call from Albacrombe Alheart, we'll call him that, who lived down the block. He wanted Hank to haul a few ashes out of his basement.

This call to use arms prompted Hank to reason there could be quite a demand for this type of work and enroute he contemplated starting a new service agency headed up by himself under the trade name of "Kid Klinker!"

Mr. Alheart hustled Hank off to the basement, where he discovered if he started a new business he would have to incorporate, for he would surely need help. The furnace room was so full of ashes that it was no longer possible to close the door; in fact one couldn't get near enough to the window to shovel them out.

The only way to get the ashes out was to carry them in a bushel basket from one end of the basement to the other, up a flight of stairs, through two doors, out of the house and another seventy five feet to a spot Mr. Alheart had chosen back of the garage.

Hank was convinced the railroad should have been bidding on the ash hauling job but, still young and gullible, he visualized the joy of getting into Alheart's back trouser pocket and basking in his billfold a bit. Hank did, however, notice that each time he mentioned money, Alheart ignored him as if work was the only subject matter of concern.

The task review completed, Hank was shown the shovel and the wooden bushel fruit baskets in which he was to carry the ashes. Hank asked Alheart if he had a wheelbarrow and was told that it was out at his farm and made no offer to make it available.

Mother Lucy was very proud of Hank for having cornered the contract for conveying the coal remains and excited about the possibilities of his getting ahead with Alheart, who was reasonably wealthy. Cousin Clinty allowed as how Hank should eat oatmeal three times a day and whinney when he wanted to be fed as he felt Hank was doing the work of a horse.

Hank arose half bright and early the next morning and started the job. He then discovered he must learn the route to the back door like the palm of his hand for he had to work in semi-darkness; Mr. Alheart didn't approve of wasting electricity. If a busy boy is a happy boy, Hank was hilarious as hell all day.

By six o'clock that evening Hank was cursing the guys who designed the house, invented the furnace and mined the coal. He envied every truck driver who drove by that day and vowed someday to pulverize personally the pea brain who perfected the portable basket. As he departed the house for home, Willie Sipmore went by leaning into a non-existent strong west wind like a weather vein and muttering something to himself about the city building the sidewalks too narrow.

When Hank arrived home, Cousin Clinty took one look at him and said, "Boy, you're suffering from lack of exercise. Why don't you run upstairs to my room and fetch me a bag of Duke's Mixture tobacco to kinda limber up your legs?"

The next morning Hank dragged himself from his bed beset with a backache. When he arrived on the job, he found a couple more bushels of coal residue had been added to the pile. That entire week was like a nightmare full of fire and ashes. Cousin Clinty told Mother Lucy Hank's job in many ways was as beneficial to him as going to church and that she could rest assured Hank wasn't going to hell; with all his experience, he would be fearful of getting assigned to the ash hauling department.

When Hank carried out the last basketful of soot separations, he was convinced that a boy with his work all done is a helluva lot happier than a working boy, and he quickly informed Mrs. Alheart of his happy status.

Old arrogant Alheart soon arrived on the scene and Hank allowed that the time was ripe for reaping the rewards for his services. Alheart was no man for bickering about bullion and came precisely to the point, indicating he would pay Hank three dollars, if Hank sportingly would spade his garden that spring as part of the deal.

Now Hank had been willing to put in a week's work anticipating reasonable reward, but he was in no mood for jokes. He asked Mr. Alheart if he could be serious. He allowed as how he was, and it quickly sank through Hank's reasoning rafters that arbitrating with Alheart was a hopeless cause.

There were a few words back and forth until Hank warmed up real good—he then told Alheart where he could shove his spade, and it wasn't into his garden. After this brief dissertation, Hank departed the premises. Alheart's son later apologized to Hank and several weeks later Mrs. Alheart, bless her heart, managed to pay Hank what amounted to five cents per hour for his work.

Notice was placed on the school bulletin board that 1936 baseball team tryouts were scheduled. Hank was determined to make the first team that year.

Clinty asked Hank if the school furnished baseball shoes for the first team since Hank had none the previous year. Hank hadn't thought of that and a gloomy expression must have come over his face. Clinty said he had a couple of dollars he wasn't using and Big Sister said she would help. Hank knew they couldn't spare the money and replied, "I'll just use my tennis shoes and if I make the first team, I'll worry about shoes then."

Hank reported for practice the next night, and the feel of the ball and bat in his hand was like a homecoming to him. He had made the Happyland High baseball squad his first year of high school and had seen action in several games at second base, but had only been allowed to pitch when the team was well out ahead of the opposition. Hank had done a lot of sandlot ball pitching; now he was anxious to land a first team slot and more pitching time. However, his confidence faded rapidly when he noticed the large number of juniors and seniors out for the team.

A few days into the tryouts, Hank was busily catching ground balls being hit for infield practice when he noticed Coach Oscar Johnson standing behind him. When the next ball was directed to him, his heart was pounding like a trip hammer and he felt like he was trying to catch rattlesnakes by hand instead of baseballs.

The ball was a sizzling grounder and it certainly didn't have handles on it, but Hank went after it as if it was a large stick of peppermint candy. When the ball had bounded to a point some three feet to his front, it hit a stone or lump of dirt and veered sharply to his right. Hank fielded the ball partially with his glove but mostly with his bare hand. The pain in his hand couldn't have been worse if someone had handed him a red hot stove poker, hot end first. Having no intention of losing his big chance, he gritted his teeth, pivoted, came up throwing and successfully delivered the ball to the first baseman.

After the next ball, the coach called a scrimmage and Hank was sent to the second base position for the first team. He was overcome with joy, but his hopes faded fast when the coach looked down and remarked that he needed baseball shoes if he was to move about fast enough to field the ball in the infield.

Hank couldn't bear to raise his head and tell the coach he couldn't afford shoes. This, he felt, was the end of the season for him. Glancing at Hank's old glove the coach said, "You'll also need a glove."

At last Hank was able to muster enough control and replied, "No way could I put together that much money—guess I'll just have to sit out this season. Maybe I can get some by next year." Walking from the field, the coach commented that even Hank's tennis shoes looked too small.

While gathering up equipment, Coach Johnson insisted Hank take off one of his tennis shoes—said he wanted to look at it. After the coach looked the shoe over carefully, he said, "Hank, are you sure these shoes don't hurt your feet? It's bad to wear shoes that don't fit." Hank assured him the shoes fit just fine.

While walking home Hank tried to figure out a way to tell the family he wouldn't be playing baseball that spring. When he arrived, Clinty asked him how practice went. Hank responded, "Great—just great!" After supper, Hank wanted to be alone. He arose and told Mother Lucy he was going over to the park.

Somehow Hank's dog Jack must have sensed he was very depressed. Jack was beginning to get up in years and had not been well of late. The wonderful dog spent a lot of time just lying on a rug in the corner of the dining room. However, this time when Hank left the house Jack arose on stiff legs and went with him.

Hank didn't quite make it across the street before tears were streaming down his cheeks. He sat on a park bench by the old fountain for about an hour trying to convince himself that the end of his world had not arrived.

Jack's soft brown eyes had never shown pain for himself, but they did for his master. The dog sat patiently by Hank's knee occasionally licking one of his hands while being petted with the other.

At last Hank came to grips with the reality of life and remembered what Clinty had told him, "There are some things in life that are just not meant to be—you do the best you can with the cards life deals you." When he stood up and strolled back home he resolved he would still become a professional baseball player even if he had to wait another year to prove his potential.

The following day after classes Coach Johnson called Hank into the athletic office and presented him with a new baseball glove and shoes. Hank was dumbfounded. He then realized why the coach had looked over his tennis shoe so closely—he was getting the size.

He thanked the coach over and over for his generosity and told him he would work hard to show his appreciation. Hank knew full well the coach must have deprived himself of something to give him these items, because teachers didn't receive much salary during those years. Hank's tears of sorrow had turned to tears of joy. His determination to justify his mentor's kindness knew no bounds and hustle became his middle name. With the coach's encouragement he could have sold peanuts and popcorn in the stand and played a regular position at the same time.

The season was one game old when Hank was called in from second base to pitch. Unlike previous times, the game was nip and tuck all the way. Now he must prove his worth as a pitcher. Hank tried to convince himself high school ball was not too much different from sandlot ball—except there were no ground squirrel holes to trip in and, unlike some of the cow pastures he had played in near Woolstock, when you slid into second base, you could pretty well be sure that a cow hadn't manufactured it.

Meyel "Bud" Haack, the catcher, was probably the nearest thing to a pro most people around Happyland had ever seen. He clued Hank in on the next batter's weaknesses, patted him on the shoulder, then returned to his position behind the plate. For some reason all Hank could think of was getting the ball manually past the batter—no particular place, just past him, near him, or for that matter through him!

Hank wound up like a gandy dancer with the gout and reared back so far that Maynard Olson, the first baseman, later said, "I thought Hank was going to knock the second baseman's cap off." When Hank came forward to release the ball in the direction of homeplate, he looked like a runaway eggbeater.

The throw was so wild he felt certain that if the third baseman had been just a little longer of arm and quicker of foot or had been equipped with a butterfuly net, he might well have received Hank's first pitch. Hank thought that day he was the originator of the first audience-participation baseball game, as more spectators were fielding his pitches than players.

Bud Haack talked to Hank. The coach said a few kind words of encouragement, and the next pitch actually came close enough to the catcher to allow him to lay a glove on it. Bud looked the ball over real good and rubbed it fondly as if he might not see one again for awhile. After walking the first man, Hank's pitching settled down to the point that the next batter, at least, had the opportunity to swing at a couple.

Bud talked with him again; the coach gave him a little calm-down conversation and Hank even did a little talking to himself. At last the tension-breaking point came when the coach's laugh could be heard from the bench as he yelled, "Hank, if you're going to hit the batters, hit them in the head so they won't limp!"

All at once calm descended over Hank. He shook his arm loosely at his side, pulled the bill of his cap low over his forehead, and the coolness he had enjoyed as a sandlot pitcher returned. His wind-up was slow and calculated and his delivery was graceful and easy; the ball followed a true course to the catcher's target and the umpire happily called a strike. The crowd roared; Bud Haack shook his head in relief, and the bat boy came out from his hiding place behind a tree in neighboring Nokomis Park. The batters even seemed to relax a little. Up until that moment, they didn't know on which side of the plate they should stand or, for that matter, what part of town.

The next several balls Hank offered up curved in and out and dipped to their target and, much to his surprise (as well as the batters), the side was retired with no runs allowed. For the balance of the season, Hank was to play second base and relief pitch in several games.

With baseball attracting so many athletes—it fell on the shoulders of five men to carry the Happyland colors in track and field events. Two great stars, Lloyd "Red Rocket" Rinehimer and "Jumpin' Jack" Phillips provided the backbone of the squad.

"Red Rocket" specialized in the 100 and 200 yard high and low hurdles. "Jumpin' Jack" ran the 100 yard dash, low hurdles and participated in the broad jump. While Rinehimer and Phillips were resting they filled in vacant slots in the 220 and 440 yard relay teams with Will Ostlund, Milo Segar and Gene Wehrheim.

Amazingly the five-man team took first place in the conference meets with Rinehimer amassing twenty points—Phillips followed closely with 19-1/2 points. Phillips took first place in the broad jump and second in low hurdles in the tough Iowa City indoor meet. The team placed high in the Drake Relays. Phillips took first place in the broad jump during the state high school track meet. Later on, while at Iowa State College, Jack would shatter Iowa college records with a broad jump leap of 21 feet, 8 inches.

Summer arrived and Louis Nichols was looking for something new to promote. He had watched in utter disbelief the growing interest in fisticuffs by Happyland's sporting crowd. They had become wrestling fanatics of sorts a few years back when one of the native sons, Howard Cantonwine, had risen to the top ranks of worldwide wrestling.

According to his mother, Lou had been a promoter extraordinary since birth. She always said that,as a small boy, he could hardly wait until Saturdays to con his younger brothers Kenneth and Howard

"Fuzz" out of their money to invest in some surefire venture that was a cinch to make them all rich.

Probably a dynamic example of Lou's ability to convince people came about in 1927. After he graduated from high school, he decided he needed a little time to physically mature before playing college athletics. Forewith Lou, with younger brother Kenneth's report card, proceeded to Sarasota, Florida, where he convinced school administrators he was Kenneth and enrolled in high school.

Lou quickly became the school's first-string quarterback and was soon burning up the turfs with long touchdown runs. Newspapers carried accounts of his prowess. After he sped to four touchdowns against a strong Winter Haven team—sportswriters dubbed him, "The Gallopin' Blue Devil." Sarasota proclaimed, "We have the state's best quarterback!"

Everything was going great for Lou until someone from up north, who knew both Lou and Kenneth, came for a visit to Sarasota. A proud host took his guest to see the fabulous Kenneth Nichols in action. The astonished visitor announced, "That's not Kenneth Nichols—that's Louis Nichols, but your right about one thing—you've got the best quarterback in Florida. But he has already graduated from high school once!"

Of course, the word was soon out that Lou had outfoxed the school administrators and then the "Gallopin' Blue Devil" was forced to

Cadet Louis Nichols—he later flew for U.S. Army.

Photo courtesy of Carmalita Nichols

Louis Nichols—in flight for Lombard (Knox) College.

Photo courtesy of Carmalita Nichols

gallup out of the school. Later Lou sadly recalled that the school had to forfeit all the games won in what could have become the best season Sarasota High School had ever enjoyed.

In retrospect, it appears almost a shame Lou didn't live during the era of P. T. Barnum, the great circus man, as they would have made an awesome combination—although Barnum would have had to exercise due care or Lou soon would have owned the entire circus.

Lou had been a dynamic athlete, a triple sport star at Happyland High School and at Lombard (later Knox College, Galesburg, Illinois), back in the twenties. He could project the image of the ultimate businessman—articulate, knowledgeable, intelligent, and convincing. Hell, Lou could convince even the most skeptical that he had the ability to make the Boone River flow backwards, even over dams.

Lou promoted carnivals, bingo, celebrations, and races, but he was most successful in promoting dances. Now Lou was convinced his calling was the promotion of boxing matches.

It was around the spring of 1936 when Lou had his brothers Kenny and Fuzz, along with Hank and anyone he could convince to help him, clear debris from the basement remains of the Second Street old shoe factory that had burned back in 1927. With a ticket box and bleachers installed, the ring built and the high perimeter fence up, Lou brought professional boxing to Happyland.

But Lou was cagey. He didn't hold his fights on Saturday nights; that was his dance night and, besides, he knew it would be hopeless to try to compete with the free fights. However, he hadn't counted on one thing—some of the Fort Dodge local pros he had on his cards were always in need of new sparring partners, and they started showing up on Saturday nights to look over the crop.

Bob Ruhl and the Habhab brothers, from Fort Dodge, sometimes would drift in later on in the evening in search of partners for Bob's stable of boxers. After some prodding, the Fort Dodge pros occasionally would put on an exhibition bout or two. Of course, with their status and all, they wouldn't fight in ordinary places like behind the pool halls and taverns; they preferred the area behind the Elks Club, a little more dignified—little more class!

Actually these exhibitions were quite educational for any local boys who had aspirations of attending dental college, since Ruhl and the Habhabs always displayed their most up-to-date techniques for extracting teeth from those willing to participate.

But, there was one night the pro's demonstration turned into a main event. Jake Beltum, we'll call him that, a huge young man from Kamrar, was in town and after quite a bit of pushing and shoving, he finally held a front row spectator position. Jake was one helluva fighter, but his mother's sister-in-law's brother's cousin, or somebody, had convinced his mother fighting was undignified. As Cousin Clinty said, "Hell, he wasn't even allowed to switch from one-piece BVDs to boxer shorts until he was twenty one years old."

At the peak of the exhibition contest, the alley light bulb burned out just as Nazzey Habhab was cutting loose with one of his famous left jabs. Habhab's opponent ducked and it being dark and all Jake, in the front row, didn't see the punch coming, and "blam" he got it right in the "snot locker."

Now Jake was normally a quiet and unobtrusive person, but he was a powerhouse. He did know how to fight, and it was a well known fact he didn't know his own strength. When the blow creased his nose, he cut loose a flurry of punches and by the time he stopped swinging, half the spectators were on their backs.

Jake apologized to the unfortunate ones afterward, said he just kinda got caught up in the excitement of it all—that he wasn't really angry. But, as Maynard "Babe" Olson, a fine boxer in his own right, said, "There were a helluva lot of people there who wouldn't have taken a chance after that night. In fact most would have hotfooted it out of town if they even heard old Jake was slightly displeased."

After Jake Beltum waylaid half the spectators at the exhibition battle behind the Elks Club, some of those who caught a punch or two must have raised hell with the mayor and council. At any rate, it became quite noticeable that burned out bulbs in the alleys of that area were replaced far quicker than those in other parts of town.

Although Hank's financial posture had improved somewhat, the year brought him terrible sadness. Throughout all Hank's trials and tribulations, his dog Jack had been at his side, a constant companion. He would trot alongside Hank on his paper route, fishing and hunting jaunts—often even accompanying him to work or to play ball. Jack had been injured when a truck struck him shortly after the family moved from the farm but he had recovered with no ill effects. It was obvious old age had caught up with Jack for he had continued to spend most of his time in the house sleeping.

One Saturday as Hank sat by the radio listening to a baseball game, Jack came over to him. In slow painful movements he let Hank know he wanted to go outdoors. Hank opened the door but, concerned, went out with his wonderful dog. Once in the yard, Jack lay down. Hank then knew his dog must be terribly ill.

Alarmed now, Hank knelt on the ground beside Jack; the dog was breathing hard and choking. Reaching down, he lifted Jack's still beautiful head and cradled it in his arms. Jack looked up with his brown somber eyes, almost suggesting more concern for Hank than he did for himself. Hank held Jack closely, speaking to him in a low comforting voice. Between gasps Jack continued to lick his master's hand.

Then Jack's eyes closed, and he let forth a long sigh and stiffened. Hank knew then his wonderful dog was gone. He was quite certain his dog's heart had somehow been weakened and failed.

Tears streamed down Hank's cheeks, as he rocked his beloved dog's head back and forth. At last he arose and went back to the house, passed the news to his Mother and went up to his room. There would be a void in his heart for that almost human animal that would be there until his dying day.

LAMENT TO A CANINE FRIEND

Dad brought Jack home—a wiggly pup,
With anxious arms Hank picked him up.
Jack snuggled close—then nuzzled his ear,
Hank felt his warmth and held him near.

From that day forward Jack was his trust,
At work and play his presence a must.
They walked thru pastures, fields and flowers,
Jack was his companion throughout all hours.

Rain or shine—whether early or late,
Jack always met him at the gate.
Exhausted from a blizzard, Hank fell to the ground,
Had it not been for Jack, too late he'd been found.

Jack brought him joy in times of strife,
To please Hank was his goal in life.
Jack helped him through his childhood years,
Comforted him—licked away his tears.

The years rolled by, Jack's gait grew slow,
His heart grew weak—blood hardly flowed.
Cradled in Hank's arms, while his life did ebb,
He licked Hank's hand 'til he was dead.

by H. R. Ankrum

Life has its sorrows—life has its tears, but the loss of a child's dog, like the loss of a family member and close friends, can be devastating. Only one who has experienced giving, as well as accepting love of one of those wonderful animals, can appreciate their loss. As Cousin Clinty always said, "There are no bad dogs—only bad masters who have taught them to be mean!"

Time heals heart wounds brought on by the loss of a canine friend. And so it is that happy memories come drifting back over time. You remember the unabated joy and the vigorous wagging of tail when your pet greets you. Those soul-searching eyes when you pet him. Yes, and those little licks on the hand when he is telling you that of all the billions of people on earth, you are the most important!

What? You still don't like dogs? Then, my friend, you have never fully lived!

Yes, life went on for Hank—he busied himself finding and working at odd jobs. At every opportune moment he poured himself into baseball. But, he was beginning to give some token thought to the military if his dream of a career in baseball failed to materialize.

X
GENERAL PERSHING'S REPLACEMENT?

The sun was just creeping up over the treetops in Twin Parks, and Robert Simpson, his brother Hio, and Hank had just returned from some early morning fishing. It was the beginning of another extremely hot summer day, and no relief was predicted.

There was a slight breeze; the birds in the trees surrounding the old bandstand were conducting a concert of melodic splendor (unlike today when pesticides and herbicides have reduced their numbers drastically).

Hank proceeded to the porch rocker to do some heavy thinking that strangely enough involved guns. He had been giving some serious thoughts to joining the local National Guard company. He knew he must obtain a year round part-time job if he was going to continue his schooling. He had been pitching fast pitch softball and the local Guard Company had a strong team. Lieutenant Lou Nichols, a promoter fantastic, and Sterling Bonner had been encouraging Hank to enlist and take over the pitching chores. Hank knew he could use the two-dollar enlistment bonus, the one dollar a week for the two-hour weekly drills and the fourteen dollars he would receive for the two week annual encampment. Why not, he thought? I'll do it!

Hank started for the armory that warm, balmy June 6th night to enlist. For some reason he felt his chest measurement came into play; therefore he expanded his chest as much as possible and stretched himself to his full height. Although he was but fifteen years old, he aged a few years each block he walked and damn near felt like he needed a shave by the time he passed Dermand's Cafe and turned west on Second Street. By the time he reached the old Willson Hotel,

Hank was beginning to think he could be General Pershing's replacement and was wondering when he'd be issued a horse like the general rode during World War I.

Arriving at the armory, Hank found First Sergeant Otis Lacey sitting at his desk, and he walked in stretching his neck skyward and keeping his chest properly expanded. When asked his age, Hank lost much of his confidence and part of his chest as he answered. He was then asked his birthday, which he gave as July 10, 1918. Luck was with him as Sgt. Lacey merely reminded him that he must have been born in 1917 since, with his birthday in July, he wouldn't be eighteen yet. Hank grinned like a hound dog with hemorrhoids and complimented the sergeant on being such a fine mathematician. Lacey completed the papers and Hank hastily signed them. He then took the oath to defend the United States, its territories and a small portion of the sergeant's backyard for good measure.

The first sergeant instructed Hank to go upstairs to the supply room where he would be fitted with a uniform. Before the fitting session was over, Hank was not sure the past tense of fight wasn't fit as it was one helluva battle to get one that fit him. The uniforms in stock didn't allow for persons with twenty-six inch waists as everything was for more mature men. The only thing that fit was the pup tent and wrap leggings and the latter took him nearly a half hour to put on.

After deciding which Hank looked the best in, the pup tent or the uniform, the supply sergeant Boyd Bonner told him to report to the drill sergeant Henry Mahoney for a little drill instruction. The drill sergeant, who was a bit portly, sat on a chair and put the recruits through their paces. One of the principal recruit functions was to ensure that the drill sergeant had tailor-made cigarettes for the ten minute break periods.

Sgt. Mahoney did get a few points across and although Hank didn't look too much like a soldier, the drill sergeant did, in disgust, address him as such on a couple of occasions.

Hank was relieved when he had learned the marching commands and their execution to the satisfaction of the drill sergeant. Virgil Gage, Merlin "Jumbo" Crouse and he were allowed to join the company on the main armory floor for participation in regular drills. Several of Hank's friends and a few enemies belonged to the company, so it wasn't long before he felt right at home.

As summer progressed, so did the hostile feelings toward Germany. Newspapers and newsreels were filled with pictures and articles that encouraged further antagonism feelings toward Hitler's Nazi Germany. Even sporting events were permeated with a desire to win over Hitler's proclaimed super race.

Joseph Louis Barrow (his fighting name shortened to Joe Louis), a Negro born of a poor family in Alabama and raised in the slums of Detroit, was rising quickly in boxing circles. Joe had continued to pulverize his boxing opponents through 1934 and 1935.

Speculation was that Joe would fight current champion James Braddock in 1936. Somehow something went amiss, for he was booked to fight Germany's champion Max Schmeling, also a strong contender for the world title.

Louis was felt by most Americans to be an odds-on favorite to win the bout. Never had a pugilist received more encouragement from fans. A victory for Joe, everyone felt, was a victory against Hitler and Nazi Germany. Joe, himself, had a thing to prove too—that the Negro race was not inferior to Hitler's supermen.

On July 18, 1936 people gathered around their radios hoping for a Louis victory. How could Joe lose? One of his six-inch punches could virtually fell an ox! But, Schmeling was a cunning fighter and detected flaws in Joe's defenses. Stunned in earlier rounds, in the tenth round Schmeling won by a knockout. Was Schmeling truly of a master race? Wait, Joe would get another chance in 1938.

Less than two months had elapsed since Hank's enlistment in the Guard when word came July 17, 1936 that civil war had erupted in Spain. The prevailing reaction in the United States was, "What's to worry, the United States won't be involved! Let's tend to our own knitting and deal with the depression!"

Trouble had been brewing for some time in Spain. In 1931 a democracy had been established in that country and many reforms had been initiated. These reforms were not looked upon with glee by those who supported the aristocracy or by the leaders of the Catholic Church, who had reigned supreme under the quasi-feudal system that had existed for centuries.

When civil war broke out, the vast majority of Spain's military forces joined ranks with the insurgents against those loyal to the democratic government. General Francisco Franco, who was governor of the Canary Islands at the time and a fascist at heart, seized the opportunity and led Moroccan troops in an attack on loyalist forces.

Both Germany's Adolf Hitler and Italy's Mussolini sent arms and supplies to the rebels. Mussolini, anxious to impress not only his own people, but Hitler as well, committed troops and aircraft to the rebel cause. He would show the world, not unlike Caesar, that his forces would bring Italy back to world prominence.

Hitler in no way wanted to see a democracy in Spain, but he also had other motives. The civil war in Spain provided him with a means of testing his newest aircraft and armaments in actual combat.

The World Olympics, to be held in August in Germany, was getting a lot of play in the media. Almost as on the field of battle, the athletes, especially those from the World War I Allied countries, had but one thing in mind: beat the Germans.

Unfortunately the Olympics was developing into a vindictive spectacle in which sportsmanship would all but be cast aside. The verbose Adolf Hitler had now convinced the Germans that they were a super race, and his bold claims had all but taken away the individual and team sportsmanship associated with the event.

Hitler held little regard for athletes, other than those of pure Aryan extraction, and it was obvious he had only contempt for those of the Negroid race, considering them a step below inferior. Now, the United States was sending a black man, whose speed bordered on that of lightning, to compete in track and field events.

Jesse Owens, son of a not-well-off Cleveland, Ohio family, was working his way through Ohio State University. Just that May he had shattered three world records in a Big Ten track meet, winning the 100 yard dash in a run of 9.4 seconds, a broad jump of 26' 8-1/2" and the low hurdles in 22.6 seconds.

Not since the 1912 Olympics in Stockholm, Sweden had the United States fielded such a strong field and track contender as Jesse Owens. Jim Thorpe, the fabulous Sauk-Fox Indian born in Oklahoma, had competed in the decathlon and pentathlon and won and placed in so many events King Gustav of Sweden proclaimed him the world's greatest athlete. Thorpe also became a professional football and baseball player.

Now Jesse Owens had captured the heart of all Americans and he would set Hitler's super race illusions into a tailspin. He shattered the 100 meter record with a 10.3 second run. Next, came the long jump and the world record fell when Owens cleared over 26 feet. Not satisfied yet, he established a new world record for the 200 meter dash, posting 20.7 seconds.

Capping off his performance Owens contributed heavily to the United States 400 meter relay team, winning a gold medal. No one individual is likely ever to best his amazing performances that day.

With Germany flagrantly disregarding the Versailles Treaty March 7, 1936 and moving into the Rhineland, and Mussolini's troops overrunning Ethiopia, the world situation became of greater concern. Then when Germany and Italy sent troops and equipment to overthrow the loyalists in Spain, military training began to take on more serious overtones. These were the conditions that existed August 9, 1936 when the local National Guard Company departed for its annual encampment at Camp Dodge, Iowa.

The camp was a World War I facility, partially torn down with the balance retained for National Guard training. Camp Dodge nestles in a beautiful rolling valley just north of Des Moines. Neat old residential-type officers' quarters dot the fresh green hillsides and rows of orderly brick buildings lie along the main road. The troop tent areas

Camp Dodge, Iowa

Photo courtesy of Gold Star Museum

Company mess halls, Camp Dodge, Iowa

U.S. Army Engineer photo courtesy of Charles E. Poch, Iowa National Guard photographer

were located west of the street, behind brick buildings containing space for company headquarters and mess halls.

Hank wondered as they marched from the railhead to the regimental area that day just how many young men had marched that route during the Spanish American War and World War I and later had given their lives for their country. This camp had also been the place where 10,000 soldiers were hospitalized and 700 died during the great flu epidemic of 1918.

Erection of the tents completed, the men hurriedly changed uniforms and cleaned their weapons in preparation for retreat. Thirty minutes later they fell into ranks all spit and polish, and Hank felt really proud when the command "squads right" was given and in column they marched out to the street that passed the front of all the buildings housing the company headquarters and mess halls, virtually extending from one end of the camp to the other.

Back in the retreat formation Hank and the others were all facing east and standing at attention. The flagpole was across the street and on the lush green hillside in front of them the setting sun was playing upon the stars and stripes of the United States flag, as it furled and unfurled lazily in the slow breeze.

On command each unit reported to the regimental commander and the command "parade rest" was given. They were then called to "attention" and the command was repeated by battalion commanders down the line of troops until it disappeared like an echo in the beautiful hillside.

Then the command "present arms" was given; rifle slings popped as each soldier brought his rifle to the proper position in salute to the colors. Simultaneously with this command a big bass drum boomed and the regimental band, under the command of Warrant Officer William Laurier, struck up the "Star Spangled Banner."

In all Hank's previous and future life he had never seen and was never to see so beautiful a setting, nor feel more proud. The flag waved majestically on its pole in the fading sunlight and, as the drums rolled, it was drawn down the lanyard closer to earth. A sort of chill crept down Hank's spine, a lump came into his throat and a slight tear welled in his eyes. That flag he then knew was more than cloth to him. It represented a great country, a way of life and a pride in being that words cannot explain. Francis Scott Key wrote the anthem's words in a time of duress for his country and a more inspiring song will never be written.

The training was well conducted; instructions were excellent. Hank and the others were highly impressed with the weapons issued to them. World War I U.S. Army doughboys had prevailed over

German army units with this equipment—what more assurance did they need?

The principle armament in infantry rifle companies, such as, Co. "E" which Hank was in, was the 30 caliber 1903 Springfield bolt-action rifle with clips holding five cartridges each. Officers and platoon sergeants, and others not issued a rifle, carried 45 caliber automatic pistols—when fired they sounded like a hand-held cannon. Each rifle squad (8 men) had a gunner, who was issued a 30 caliber Browning automatic rifle (BAR) capable of 40 to 60 well aimed shots per minute.

In addition to their individual weapons, heavy weapons companies were issued Browning 30 caliber, water-cooled heavy machine guns. The Browning was fired from a tripod or hand pulled cart. When hand carried, components were a sizable load in rough terrain.

Regimental howitzer companies were equipped with 37mm anti-tank guns to defend against armor, along with Stokes mortars to lob short range, high angle fire shells onto enemy machine gun and mortar emplacements.

Backing up the four infantry regiments was an artillery regiment, whose batteries were equipped with truck-towed 75mm and 155mm howitzers (cannons as they were sometimes referred to in those days, or big boom sticks in the infantry vernacular.) These weapons provided overhead fire in support of both attack and defensive actions.

To the Guardsmen all of the weapons issued appeared devastating, but they were antiques compared to the weaponry then being issued to German troops and appearing on the drawing boards of German armament experts.

No one gave too much thought to world events. The United States had plodded along with ill-equipped military forces since World War I. Why should there be concern? Weren't the Atlantic and Pacific Oceans wide and deep? Who would launch an attack against the United States? Isolationists, of which there were millions in the country, were strongly opposed to American forces becoming involved in another overseas war.

Although events shaping up in Europe normally would have stirred up considerable interest, the general feeling in the United States was one of apathy. Nothing seemed to move the government or the people to increased preparedness.

With several days of fine training concluded in marksmanship and squad and platoon tactics, the battalion, under the command of Major Robert Heath, Fort Dodge, moved out of the camp for a three-day maneuver. The heat was fierce as the troops marched along the gravel roads and across the hills, for the summer of 1936 was to become the hottest year on record. With temperatures rising to 109 degrees, newspapers carried photos of people frying eggs on sidewalks. Those not in excellent physical condition suffered until they adjusted to being out in the sweltering heat all day and to the strenuous exercise inherent in infantry training.

There was some time for relaxation. A few men went to Des Moines on week nights when passes were available and on weekends after the Saturday morning inspection if they were not assigned duties on post.

PFC Sylvester Spooner, we'll call him that, was the great lover of the outfit. He was tall, handsome and wore a neatly trimmed mustache, not unlike Douglas Fairbanks, Jr., the swashbuckling movie star of that era. Actually Spooner bore a striking resemblance to the actor.

When Spooner strolled the downtown area of a city, he not only used the sidewalks but, as far as most women were concerned, he owned them. He wore his uniform as proudly as a peacock wears its feathers. Yes, he was a striking soldier, even in the likes of a World War I vintage uniform. Despite all this, Clinty always said, he did have a bit of a coon dog swagger, kinda walked sideways with one shoulder slightly out.

His uniform was always clean, neat and, its creases were razor-sharp. His shoes shone like brown encased mirrors. Suave and debonair, he looked more like an officer than most officers.

Strangely enough, his looking like an officer led him to problems of great magnitude which came back to haunt him the day Hank was detailed to pull guard duty with the great emancipator of female passions.

The guard mount had been conducted, troops had been inspected and guard posts assigned. It was 4p.m. when the corporal of the guard, Ralph Olmstead, completed posting his relief. PFC Spooner had been posted at the main gate, where he could and would impress all seeking entry to the camp.

On the other hand, Hank had been assigned the duty of guarding the camp's swimming pool. His first thoughts were, "Why in the hell would they need a guard on a swimming pool? Who's going to steal the water?" He posed the question to Corporal Olmstead. The corporal, perplexed, rubbed his chin, then said, "Hank, I'm going to level with you; I don't know." This shook Hank no end as, at the time, he thought corporals were all knowing.

Hank wasn't at all familiar with the decisiveness with which a military order is issued and that privates don't question the why for of anything; they just do what they are told. So it was that Hank irritated his corporal a bit when he continued, "There's just got to be a reason why I'm to guard the damn thing." Right then and there the

Camp Dodge swimming pool (Hank's guard post). Note—no water missing!
U.S. Army Engineer photo courtesy of Charles E. Poch, Iowa National Guard photographer

corporal, all two hundred twenty-five pounds of him, gave Hank the best reason in the world when he barked, "Start walking that post or I'm going to ruin all the photographs in your billfold." Sounded like a helluva good reason for Hank to walk his post and he had no further questions.

Hank had just settled nicely into his duties of taking charge of his post and all government property in view, as the general orders provide, when he saw Sgt. Rollie Holkan driving up to the main gate. Dismounting from his car Holkan walked over to Spooner. One could see the sergeant had brought some very important news to Spooner, for the suave one was shaking his head and waving his arms like he was trying to stop a fast freight train. To say the least, he didn't appear to be overcome with joy.

While the sergeant remained at the gate, Spooner dashed down the hill to Hank. Arriving, he blurted out, "Hank, you've just got to change posts with me; it's a matter of grave importance, possibly my grave."

Although by now leery of asking even a PFC (private first class) the why for of something, Hank chanced it and asked Spooner, "Why?" Spooner hastily said, "A girl friend I met is coming out from Des Moines, and she thinks I am a lieutenant." He went on to say that "if she ever sees me, or the company commander finds out about my wearing a second lieutenant's bar, I can be court-martialed for impersonating an officer."

As Hank headed for the gate, Spooner was still yelling, "Hank, you gotta keep her from getting to the company headquarters." Hank had only been on the gate a few minutes when a gal drove up a new red

Ford V-8 convertible. Leaning over the door with the afternoon sun glistening off her beautiful blond tresses, she popped Hank one of those toothpaste ad smiles and said, "I'm here to see Lieutenant Spooner. How do I get to Company E?" Wonderful, Hank reasoned, she didn't say what regiment and there is a Co. "E" in all regiments.

By that time Hank was so impressed he was ready to abandon his post and go with her, but his sanity prevailed and he directed her to the 168th Infantry Regiment area, instead of the 133rd, telling her as she drove off, "You can't miss it." Stock answer and, as everyone knows, when one receives this advice he's in for trouble.

Troop area tents, Camp Dodge, Iowa
U.S. Army Engineer photo courtesy of Charles E. Poch, Iowa National Guard photographer

All of the tents and mess halls looked alike and if one didn't know to look at the unit-designating guideons posted out front, finding a particular unit could be a very difficult task.

An hour elapsed before the attractive young lady again drove up to the main gate. "How'd you make out?" Hank asked. "Not so good," the fair maiden responded, "That was the 168th Infantry. I'm sorry I didn't tell you, I'm looking for the 133rd Infantry."

Hank then directed her past the supply depot, a round about way to the regiment, hoping she would get disgusted and abandon the search. Gotta save old Spooner, even from himself.

It was nearing six o'clock when the damsel in distress, with her convertible and matching red dress, again appeared at the main gate. At first glance she appeared to be unhappy and the second glance proved unnecessary. Hank asked her if he had found the lieutenant. There was no flashing smile when she responded, "Hell, no, and he isn't a lieutenant and I wouldn't go through that again, even if he were General Pershing." With that, she put her pretty little convertible in gear and tightened the street bricks six inches as she careened around the corner heading back to Des Moines.

Hank hurried down the hill to change guard posts with Spooner before the corporal of the guard returned to relieve them from duty.

Spooner was sweating from everything but his ear lobes, dreading going back to the company. Spooner was sure that, by now, word surely had got back to the company commander about his pretending to be an officer.

After retreat the following day the first sergeant asked if any of the men could type. A couple of rookies held up their hands, hoping to land an office job. Instead, First Sergeant Lacey picked out a man and advised him "You're just the type I'm looking for; report for duty tomorrow morning as latrine orderly."

Company commander, Capt. Eugene E. Meller, announced he wanted to see Spooner in his officer's tent immediately following the formation. Spooner later related the "old man," as company commanders were dubbed, had taken more skin off of his fanny than was there when the chewing started. Spooner was one helluva soldier and had already made corporal once and had been reduced—but he was an expert marksman and an excellent, well-rounded soldier.

When Spooner returned, he had a little private ceremony, at which he officially resigned his unofficial commission, burned the gold braid and tassle he had switched for the blue one on his campaign hat the night of his big date with the red convertible gal, and trashed his officer's crossed rifles and second lieutenant bars.

Training proved interesting during the two week period. Time was devoted to squad, platoon and company tactics, along with some highly effective rifle and pistol markmanship training.

Most National Guard rifle and heavy weapons companies of that era maintained a strength of around seventy men, far less than half the strength of a wartime company. Military funding precluded units being recruited to full strength. They were a nucleus but, before combat, employment filler personnel from the draft or other sources would be necessary.

Training was excellent within time and scope authorized. However, Minnesota, North and South Dakota units, comprising the balance of the division, trained at encampments held in their respective home states. There was no combined arms training, which is imperative to the effective employment of an infantry division in battle.

Leadership in most Iowa National Guard units was provided by World War I veterans and fortunate that was, for the veterans had been exposed to working with artillery, tanks, and yes, horse cavalry. The United States Army still maintained a goodly number of cavalry units at a time when Adolf Hitler was gearing his German army for tank warfare.

The Iowa National Guard also fielded the 113th Cavalry Regiment, 57th Cavalry Brigade, 24th Cavalry Division. The 24th consisted of units from Iowa, Kansas, Wyoming, Idaho, Colorado, and Washington and was the only complete National Guard Cavalry Division in the United States.

It was the dedication and diligence of the World War I veteran leadership that held the Guard together. They provided instruction or, when possible, observed instruction being given in every class. Rifle marksmanship was heavily stressed and first aid was given due attention, for many of the officer veterans wore wound stripes on their sleeves.

Commanders brought it across forcefully that a chain is only as strong as its weakest link and that, in a company, a squad is that link. Squad training, of course, was given top emphasis. But, lack of full strength companies hampered training in company tactics. Actually, battalion tactics at guard strength was the equivalent of deploying a war strength company—this while Hitler and Mussolini were feverisly gearing up for full scale war.

Despite the busy training schedule, most evenings provided time for relaxation and relief from boredom through devious pranks.

One of the young men, a new recruit, had never so much as been away from home overnight and was constantly stating he wished he was back on the farm. We'll call him "Lonesome Louie."

Everyone in the tent was engaged in telling humorous stories, laughing and carrying on when Private Virgil Gage, an expert prankster, happened to look over at Lonesome Louie, by now blissfully sleeping in his bunk. Gage nonchalantly spoke up saying, "I wonder if old Louie would be happier if he woke up tomorrow morning back on a farm."

On the day of arrival, the guardsmen had been allowed to stuff their mattress covers with straw from a stack not far away, located on a farm directly behind the U.S. Property and Disbursing Office's supply warehouses. Soon the mischievous fellows were discussing how they could get Louie the six blocks or so and behind the stack.

Now Louie was a good sleeper, no doubt, for he had slept through laughter, crap and poker games and people jostling around in the tent, but would he awaken if they picked up his bunk, him in it, and carried it down behind the strawstack? Everyone decided the effort was worth a try. Why not, it couldn't hurt him! Besides Corporal Olmstead was already deep in sleep and an exploding artillery shell wouldn't have awakened him—he was a calm man.

Merlin "Jumbo" Crouse, Robert "Bob" Harris, Hank, and Virgil Gage cleared out all obstacles and each took a corner of the lonesome one's bunk. Carefully they lifted him up, litter style, and proceeded out the tent door. Louie didn't so much as squirm.

The gate to the farm was locked, but the fence was standard farm barbed wire, not too high. Carrying the bunk up to the fence, everyone started laughing and suppressing the laughter became impossible. They set Louie down and moved back a few feet or so until they could control themselves. Louie still didn't squirm.

At last composed, or so they thought, they returned to their mean scene to lift the still snoozing Louie over the fence. With the cot over the top, they had to set one end on the wire while two shinnied over to hoist up the other side. When the cot was set on the wire, it squeaked quite loudly. Louie wretched a bit, rolled over on his other side—but didn't completely awaken. Soon they had him over the fence, sleeping comfortably behind the stack.

The next morning everyone bounded from their bunks and, much to their surprise, Louie wasn't back in the tent. Near panic reigned. It was too late to go get him; reveille was only minutes away. This they had not anticipated for they felt surely he would have awakened during the night and come storming back into the tent.

As they stood in ranks, they cast worrisome eyes in the direction of the stack. At last, just as roll call began, Lonesome Louie could be seen coming across the field in his shorts. Each step he took was with care, for the oats stubbles were gouging his feet.

Approaching the formation, Louie yelled, "Here!" First Sergeant Lacey then asked him, "Louie, what in the hell are you doing out strolling barefoot in your shorts?" Louie waved his arms violently, with a wild look in his eyes and pointed toward the supply depot and said, "Hell, Sarge, I don't know; I woke up out there in my bunk behind a haystack. I don't know how I got there."

Sergeant Lacey turned his head, walked over and looked in a tent like he was checking on something, still half biting his tongue to keep from laughing. He finally blurted out: "Who in the hell put him out there? Speak up!" The four guilty parties stepped forward, figuring with the sergeant cracking up over the incident, they wouldn't get court-martialed. Their assumption proved correct, but Hank and Crouse were assigned kitchen police duty and Harris and Gage to the camp's garbage detail.

During Hank's tour in the mess hall he became better acquainted with Patty O'Kettlebelly, the first cook, and Tippy O'Flaskagin, who had been assigned temporary duty as a cook's helper. It was obvious to everyone they had missed their calling, for with their verbal exchanges they could have become fine stage comedians. They were without a doubt tremendous morale boosters for the men in the unit.

The two Irishmen were exceptionally good workers, and their lighthearted, humorous bantering kept everyone laughing. Although peeling bushels of potatoes, washing heaps of pots and pans and scrubbing floors was not what one could call enjoyable work, listening to the bantering Irishmen was, and time went by rapidly.

The highlight of the summer training was the Governor's Day Parade. Two extremely fine military bands played the troops onto the field—the 168th Infantry Band, Council Bluffs, under its director Warrant Officer Keith P. Latey and the 133rd Infantry Band, Fairfield, under the direction of Warrant Officer William Laurier. Both bands were fabulous and, with their stirring march music, keeping step was no problem. Once you got into the swing of it, the cadence held you as if on a treadmill.

On the review stand were Governor Nelson G. Kraschel, Commander in Chief of the Iowa National Guard, and Major General Mathew A. Tinley, Command General, 34th Infantry Division, accompanied by Brigadier General Charles H. Grahl, the State Adjutant General, and Brigadier General Loyd D. Ross, 67th Infantry Brigade Commander.

With bass drums booming and cymbals crashing, the 168th Infantry Regiment band moved out smartly, followed by the regimental commander, Colonel George F. Everest, a World War I veteran, and the troops of his regiment. Next the 133rd Infantry Regiment, under the command of Colonel Gordon C. Hollar, another World War I veteran, followed the 133rd Infantry Band along the review route. Next to pass the review stand were the division's special troops.

The two week summer encampment had honed the marching precision of even the newest recruits, and the parade was highly impressive for the civilians who had assembled at the parade field.

Those who haven't participated in or observed first hand a well conducted military parade have missed a thrilling spectacle. The color guards, bearing old Glory and division or regimental colors, the latter adorned with battle streamers, marching proudly to the front of well drilled troops offer a sight that will long be remembered.

Hank was happy to be back in Happyland with the fourteen bright, shiny new silver dollars he had received in pay for attending the summer camp. But he was hoping to earn a few more dollars with which to purchase clothing to replace some he had outgrown and second hand football shoes.

Many youths in rural areas worked summers on farms during the depression years. Working hours were from daylight to dark with room and board provided. Fortune smiled on Hank when Father James Arthur came home and advised he had got him a job helping a farmer with his haying. He was extremely proud when told the wage would be one dollar per day.

James Arthur drove Hank to the job the next morning and introduced him to the farmer, hereafter referred to as Roy Rumblegut. Roy was a big burly, friendly type individual who told Hank between burps that he was glad to have his help, and they headed to the barn to finish the chores.

As they walked to the house after the morning's work was completed, old Roy Rumblegut told how he had written into one of those romance clubs advertised in love magazines and had started corresponding with Harriet Heartthrob, we'll call her that.

In the months following the arrangements had been concluded and Roy had traveled down to the Ozark Mountains, where the wedding rites were consummated. As they strolled along, he told Hank she was a "looker," and after they entered the house Hank knew for damn sure no one could contest that statement, for she looked like Mr. Rumblegut had dragged her all the way from her home to Iowa behind his car.

She was sitting in a chair reading a paperback love magazine, not unlike the one in which she had found the matchmaking advertisement. Looking up at them as if they had got into the wrong house, Harriet exerted half the effort she intended to expend that day by raising her cute little arm and pointing to the table, her bubble gum catching in her teeth as she announced, "It's ready and waitin'." Mr. Rumblegut went to the kitchen cabinet and devoured a couple of tablespoons of baking soda in a glass of water.

It was obvious the food was ready and had been for some time. The only prepared food on the table was a fly laden three-layer cake with green frosting, probably brought by a neighbor as a welcoming gesture on the day of her arrival. Roy burped and cooed over his cute little puddle of intestines for a few minutes, and she finally leaned forward with a strained effort and gave him a slight kiss on the cheek, exercising due care that she didn't spoil her bubble gum.

Mr. Rumblegut ate like he was never going to see food again. Hank surmised the meals had probably been getting progressively worse and he wasn't going to take any chance on what the next day would bring. Hank was glad Rumblegut was eating well and not paying too much attention to him, for he ate very sparingly of sandwich meat and bread.

Before the evening meal, while milking the cows, Hank drank several tin cups of milk and at dinner sneaked a couple of slices of bread out of the loaf wrapper, told his boss he didn't feel too well, excused himself and went to bed. Rumblegut didn't contest Hank's retiring early, as he no doubt wanted to take some more baking soda and stay awake long enough to see if he was really going to live.

The next morning Hank was awakened on the before side of five o'clock. With chores completed, Mr. Rumblegut and Hank returned to the house for breakfast. It was then Hank noticed the eggs and toast on the table, obviously prepared the night before, cold and waiting for them. Hank did convince Roy to reheat the coffee and that with a slice of cold toast constituted his entire breakfast. Roy finished eating, lowered the baking soda box another half inch, and they headed for the field.

The morning was about half completed when Hank felt like Mount Vesuvius had been transplanted into his body. He would pitch a few forks of hay and then run like mad, holding his breath, for the woods which bordered the field. Each trip was a challenge and a race against time. By the third trip Hank wondered why they didn't let that woman do the cooking for the Olympic teams as he figured her food would sure as hell cut four seconds off anyone's time running the hundred yard dash.

Before the afternoon had ended, Hank was a mere shadow of his former self. His trips to the woods became leisurely strolls as, by this time, he knew his bowels were only bluffing. Hank walked home that night and every night thereafter—and when he returned, he carried a sack lunch for his noon meal.

Cousin Clinty said he would wager old Rumblegut's wife was in actuality the daughter of a home remedy laxative manufacturer for their part of the hills, and she had just naturally slipped back into the family's old trade.

No one who had eaten Harriet's cooking could ever understand how that parcel post partnership could endure. Perhaps with the modern aids for indigestion there was hope, but at that time old Roy's stomach undoubtedly went through worse tremors than the San Francisco earthquake.

XI
THE MIDDLE-AGED TEENAGER

Two middle-aged teenagers, too old for light thinking and too young for heavy thinking, Hank and his side-kick, Bud Brandt, sat on the porch looking across the street at Twin Parks where the Happyland Municipal Band was starting to tune up instruments for the final concert of the season. The night was extremely warm for late August and undoubtedly the birds thought the musicians a bit demented as they observed from trees filled with prematurely golden leaves.

Older people were sitting on park benches and chairs, brought along for the occasion, while others sat on grass which, due to the long hot summer, had already turned the color of threshed oat straw.

Youths strolled around the park, some eating popcorn and peanuts from the nearby popcorn wagon, while little children dashed around playing, seemingly oblivious to the still sweltering heat.

Everyone loved a band concert for it was an activity that lifted spirits in a troublesome world and, as everyone knows, music can establish moods for any occasion. Culture and the arts had enjoyed a strong upsurge west of the Mississippi since the turn of the century. Talent had always been present, but clearing land, planting, harvesting and preparing for the long cold winters had consumed most of the settlers' waking hours.

Throughout the nation many small towns, like Happyland, boasted an opera house. The name "opera house" was used to please the affluent for rarely, if ever, were the works of the great masters presented. However, during better times the Gordonaire Stock Company and Edison Company had occasionally provided stage productions in the building.

Mason City was, and still is, considered by many to be the cultural center of Iowa. While other rural towns and cities were enjoying the likes of tent shows, Mason City people were being entertained by some of the nation's finest.

Early settlers in Mason City, H. G. Parker and A. T. Parker, had built the Parker Opera House before the turn of the century. In 1902 a new theater was built, but it was destroyed by fire. Determined Mason City people soon had a new Cecil Theater.

Mason City had drawn from a great reservoir of local talent to present many wonderful plays and musicals. But throughout the years they also attracted many of the nation's notables—among them Sarah Bernhardt, May Robson, Lillian Russell, Wallace Beery, Edgar Bergen, and Walter Winchell. Even Douglas Fairbanks, Sr. put in a guest appearance. Foreign notables included the likes of the great Scottish singer Sir Harry Lauder.

With the coming of larger trucks, pianos and organs were no longer prestige items found only in the homes of the very wealthy. They could now be found more frequently in family parlors. Elders, such as Bessie Cook Lemke, who had studied music at the New York Conservatory of Music and had been a concert pianist in Chicago, began to give lessons to those who could afford them. Urban growth brought more demand for entertainment and music, and the literary arts continued to gain popularity, despite the depression.

When anyone discusses music, Mason City and that town's Meredith Willson are almost certain to be included in the conversation. Small wonder for both names are synonymous with the word "music."

If one met a person from Mason City, he was just automatically assumed to be a musician, for Mason City elementary schools had bands when most high schools were struggling to field one. Mason City bands began to gain national prominence in 1929 when they placed eighth in national competition at Flint, Michigan. Then vest buttons really began to pop in 1930 when their band advanced to third place in national competition in Tulsa, Oklahoma.

It was small wonder the 1920s found Meredith Willson playing with the all time favorite marching band of John Philip Sousa, the New York Philharmonic and the New York Chamber Music Society. Willson would later bring national fame to his hometown when he published his famous musical, "The Music Man," which became a legendary state of the art and perennial favorite. If Mason City youths were not good musicians they were most probably good athletes, of which the town always seemed to have a goodly supply.

Back in Twin Parks in Happyland the band to the delight of the young people, had just completed playing a few selections of popular music, such as, "Blue Moon," "The Music Goes Round and Around," etc. The bandmaster, Wesley Schaub, turned to face the audience, then invited Karl King, another noted Iowa band director and composer from Fort Dodge, to come forward. Presenting him the baton, Schaub asked King to direct the band in a medley of marches King himself had composed.

Of course, the band had rehearsed the numbers and when the great King raised his baton high above his head, the band strove mightily to outdo King's own Fort Dodge Band in its rendition of "Barnum and Bailey's Favorite" and "The Purple Pageant March." The march portion of the concert concluded with the all-time favorites, the "Washington Post March," and the soul-stirring "Stars and Stripes Forever."

Somehow when the band played the "Star Spangled Banner" that night, more tears than usual were visible. Perhaps the elders had a premonition that the isolationists could not possibly succeed in keeping the United States out of War.

The concert over, Bud and Hank decided to sleep out of doors that night, so they grabbed blankets and proceeded to the park. They lay on the ground discussing the uneasy world situation and both concluded the United States eventually would become involved in another shooting war.

Pre-dawn brought cooler weather than the youths expected and they arose early and headed back to the porch, where they sat as the sun came up in another blaze of glory. From all appearances it would be another hot, miserable day.

There were signs of life in Happyland, even during the early morning hours. Willie Sipmore was trudging up the street carrying his tiling spade musket style, appearing not to have enjoyed a good night's sleep.

Sam Sampson, the jovial round-faced railroad maintenance section boss, had gone by at a deliberate pace chewing on his never-lit long cigar. Sam's steps, from work habit, were the same length as the distance between railroad ties.

Shakey Plenty, we'll call him that, was moving up fast on Sam from the outside with an extra motivated thrust. Bud and Hank surmised he had again caught hell from his wife for not emptying the pot he kept under the bed and was getting away from the house. Shakey, who was afflicted with a nerve disorder, was never able to convince the little lady that, with his vibrations and all, he just couldn't handle the chore.

Meanwhile Hank sat in a rocking chair, massaging his still swollen knee, which had been dislocated when he collided with the opposing team's second baseman during their last baseball game.

Not wanting to spend the money he had saved for football shoes, he had refused a doctor. After some persuasion, he had been able to convince Bud and Bludge Patterson to hold his shoulders while Maynard "Babe" Olson exerted a powerful leg jerk, which successfully snapped his knee back into place. They had brought him home from the fairgrounds in a wheelbarrow that had been loaned to them by Charlie Grandgeorge, who lived nearby.

Hank reported to football practice early that year, fearing he would get the same oversized uniform he had received the year before. Although his performance was not up to par, he managed to get through the first week's practice.

More problems beset Hank for, in addition to knee problems, his feet began to feel like they were on fire and the skin between the toes began to crack. He knew at once he had contracted athlete's foot, a condition for which no surefire quick cure had been discovered at that time.

After trying several patent medications without success, Hank proceeded to Coach Robert Lamson. The coach advised Hank to find some freshly deposited cow manure, stand barefoot in it, wiggle his toes until they were thoroughly covered and remain with his feet immersed until the manure cooled. Continuing, Lamson advised Hank he should then step out of the manure, wait until it thoroughly dried, wash his feet and resume normal activities.

Hank was dubious about his coach's advice, for he was known to be an excellent practical joker, but Coach Lamson had held a straight face, and neither his eyes nor facial expressions belied the seriousness of his statement. Knowing he didn't have anything to lose except the athlete's foot, Hank proceeded to Van Doren's dairy farm and patiently waited for a cow to make a fresh deposit.

When one tries such a remedy, there is always the possibility of someone questioning his sanity. At last a cow made a nice deposit near the cow shed out of sight of the house. Hank hastened over and was soon standing in the cow pie feeling stupid and wiggling his toes. All the cows stood in a circle watching him play twinkle toes in the cow pie, except one heifer, who disdainfully shook her head and walked away. Smart cow, Hank reasoned, "Probably smarter than me!"

At last the manure dried and some ten minutes later he washed his feet with a bucket of water from the stock watering tank, donned his shoes and hurried home. Sounded crazy, but his feet healed. Hank, in later years, wondered why he didn't bottle the cow manure when he was helping Fred Hahne at his cattle sale. He'd have made a fortune on the patent.

When Hank told Cousin Clinty and Mother Lucy about the marvels of manure, they could hardly believe their ears. But they both knew of many strange home remedies, holdovers from the pioneer days when medical doctors were not to be found in most small rural communities.

From Ruby Greiner Nail's book, "Home Remedies From Hamilton County, Iowa," it is learned that some people thought skin cancer could be healed by placing a toad in a sealed can, setting the can in the sun and, after a few days, applying the oil from the squeezed toad onto the cancer. (The book didn't provide instructions on how to squeeze the toad, but it is doubted anyone used their bare fingers!)

Bleeding, it was said, could be stopped by the application of spider webs. To stop a nosebleed one tied a string around a little finger and placed dried hog manure in the nostrils.

Cold cure remedies included the application of either skunk or goose grease. Some claimed a better cold cure could be obtained by wrapping a rag soaked with kerosene and lard around one's neck. To relieve coughing one could take cough syrup made from cocklebur brew. Cramps in the limbs, it was said, could be cured by wearing eel skin garters.

Probably one of the most popular cure-alls of those early days involved Watkin's liniment, bought from the "Watkins man," who came around with his horse and wagon in earlier days and now by car. This liniment was purported to cure backaches, cholera, morbis, diarrhea, earaches, flux, dyspepsia, headaches, cramps, pains and strains (but not worth a damn in fudge which the author's wife tried when she mistook it for vanilla extract in her childhood days!)

Clinty was happy the cow manure worked but said, "In a way, Hank, you should be a little proud because now at least you can say you have had an athlete's disease."

That year Happyland High School fielded the most powerful football team it had produced to date, perhaps for all time. Hank was pleased he made the second eleven and saw action in a few games. The opponents only had to withstand the crunching attacks of the line and crashing headon drives into the line by fullback Walter Willson, Jr. one game during the season, but the reserves had to suffer it out in every practice.

Walter Willson, Jr., a direct descendant of one of the town's founding fathers, was a movie-star-handsome 185-pound human battering ram. Teamed with halfbacks Donald "Red" McCammon and Don Shelton, quarterback Ralph Frank, and two great ends, Ralph Burton and Virgil Gage, they were a difficult scoring combination to beat.

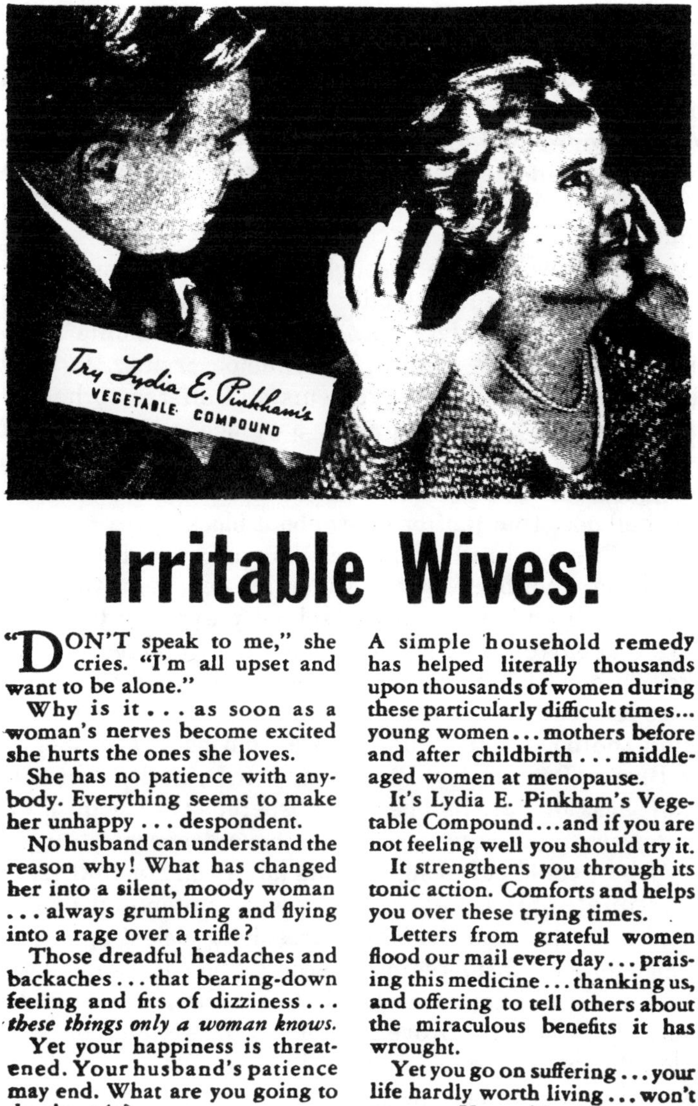

Lydia Pinkham vegetable compound advertisement
Photo courtesy of Ruby Greiner Nail's Collection

Anchoring the center of the line was Sam Heffner, a bruising 200-pounder. Oliver Meyers, a husky farm lad was a guard, and Merlin "Jumbo" Crouse, 145 pounds of dynamite, was the other guard and two muscular well-built tackles, Armor Miller and Arleigh Newland, halted virtually anything that came their way.

Tackling and blocking practice was a grueling experience at Happyland High. Coach Lamson believed strongly in intense body contact. Additionally, he favored the one on one use of live dummies, (the second eleven) as opposed to dead weight tackling dummies and skid-mounted blocking racks. Concluding the practice one night, Lamson had raised hell and put props under it when Jack Marvel, a tough promising lineman, failed to perform up to his expectations. He made it abundantly clear to Jack that he must improve his blocking technique.

In duress, the worried Jack sought out Armor Miller in the dressing room and asked him to lend a hand in improving his blocking. Squared off with Miller, Jack was receiving a few pointers when the janitor, A. K. Westervelt, strolled in. While observing, Mr. Westervelt quickly noted some of Jack's problems and offered to help. He set down his mop and pail and quickly assumed a lineman's blocking stance. Observing from some distance away, the team's star quarterback, Ralph Frank, (out of earshot) skeptically exclaimed, "Now, what the hell does that janitor know about blocking?"

Much to Frank's (and everyone's) surprise, A. K. soon showed them. Had there not been a wall, Miller, his demonstration opponent, could have well ended up on the school playground. When A. K. Westervelt departed, Miller, one of the best tackles in the state, remarked, "I don't know where that old boy learned to block, but he could sure teach all of us a thing or two."

Though the boys didn't know it, the "old boy", a former football star at Brown University, Providence, R.I., had made some all-American selections. He had been a prosperous banker until his bank failed along with so many others. In those desperate times a man took any job he could get to support his family and, actually, A.K. was fairly fortunate, for failed bankers were not much in demand. Bernard, his brother and the bank's president, picked up a spade and dug ditches for local farmers until he could find something better.

All had not been happiness that year, for shortly after mid-season in a game against Eagle Grove Donald "Red" McCammon suffered a nasty double compound fracture of his leg. "Red," Coach Lamson said, "was destined to become the greatest athlete Happyland ever produced and had the makings of another 'Red' Grange." John McCollough, a husky sophomore, did his best to fill in for "Red."

Sadly enough, schools were not required to have insurance on their athletes in those days, and "Red's" father could not afford a specialist so, consequently, "Red" would lie in the hospital a long time and be crippled for the balance of his life. The family, heartbroken, moved from Happyland that year. It was a sad ending to a fabulous athlete's career. Hank visited his friend in the hospital several times.

"Red" never complained, but Hank was terribly depressed each time he departed.

As the last game of the season approached, the team was undefeated, untied and unscored upon. Interest was at a fevered pitch as the last of the students hurried out the door that afternoon to attend the game. Freddie Siders dashed out, caught some late departers and said, "Principal C. E. Miller was unable to get a message out in time, but he asked me to pass it on. There will be no school Monday if the team remains undefeated, untied and unscored upon in the final game against Iowa Falls."

The word spread like wildfire and when the team closed the season with 261 points to their opponents' nothing, the following Monday only a smattering of students attended school.

Principal Miller finally discovered that Freddie had started the rumor about the impromptu school holiday. He did have every intention of reprimanding Freddie for his prank, but each time he looked at him he said he couldn't stop laughing. Thus, for years to come, Freddie became a legend in his own time! From that day forward, "Freddie says" would replace "Simon says," a game that is popular with young children, even today.

Coach Lamson introduced razzle dazzle to high school football. Passes filled the air to balance off a tremendous ground game. With his speedy ball handling backfield, triple lateral passes were not uncommon. Ralph Burton captured the end position on the first all-state team. Ralph Frank was selected for the second all-state quarterback position.

Basketball soon got underway and there was renewed hope. With three returning first line players, Don Shelton, Ralph Frank and Ralph Burton, teamed with two fine players, Robert Ostlund and Richard Fleischer, everyone was convinced another thrilling season was at hand, and it was!

Whereas the situation in Happyland was quite tranquil and routine, on the national scene the political palavering continued. The Republicans had nominated Governor Alfred M. Landon of Kansas as their presidential candidate. He had endorsed some of Roosevelt's "New Deal" measures and his popularity had allowed him to survive the Democratic landslide in 1933.

Roosevelt and John Nance Garner, vice president, had been selected to carry the Democratic banners. The election didn't appear to be shaping up to be much of a battle, for Roosevelt had endeared himself to most American working people and in one of his speeches he even appealed to a few of the isolationists.

Roosevelt spoke of his experiences as Secretary of the Navy—of seeing blood running from the wounded, of seeing men who had been gassed coughing out their gassed lungs and of seeing 200 survivors of a 1,000-man regiment limping exhausted out of the lines, etc., and concluded his speech with the words, "I hate war!"

The election results in November were no surprise to most people; it was a landslide victory for Roosevelt and his Democratic Party. The final tally showed Roosevelt had won 523 electoral votes (to Landon's eight) and along with him he took a significant number of Democratic Congressmen into office, giving a Democratic majority of 333 to the Republican's 103, and a whopping 75 Democrats into the Senate.

There were also no surprises on the local scene, for Hamilton County voters again voted down the construction of a new county jail. Quoting the great booze bard, Willie Sipmore, "The prisoners in these hard times will just have to make do with what they have. We've all had to tighten our belts a bit!"

Like a day that becomes joyful when the sun is bright, life takes on a certain glow when people are friendly. However, having the means to subsist does give substantial comfort to the human animal. So it was that life started to become a little more tolerable on the Happyland scene as 1936 drew to a close.

Shoppers were much more prevalent in the stores buying Christmas presents, though they were not purchasing lavish items. Shop owners had stocked more goods but, having learned their lesson in 1929, they were cautious.

Everyone in Hank's family was working, and the hay business and baling had been better for James Arthur. Fire damage to the building housing Marion Hughes' neighborhood grocery store had been repaired, and Hank was again working in his spare time. Hope sprang eternal—could the worst of the depression be over?

With a little more money available, more durable goods and much-needed clothing was being sold and some worn-out appliances were being replaced. Local investors had pooled what money they could raise and purchased the old Monarch building. They formed a new company, Beam Manufacturing, and electric wringer washing machines were now rolling off an assembly line in ever increasing numbers.

William "Bill" Naden, the Happyland High basketball coach who had patented a new electric scoreboard, had started a factory and was now employing several workers. Farmers were beginning to make some profit but, as a whole, rural America had not seen the appreciable gains found in metropolitan areas. For most people engaged in agriculture, making a modest profit meant cutting every cost saving corner possible; it took a heap of perseverance, hard work and ingenuity.

Robert Burton and the author sat in LeRoy Matteson's car-body shop, which by now had come to be one of the best places for a few of the old-timers to gather and swap yarns. LeRoy was usually busy and only on occasion got into the conversation.

LeRoy was straightening out a fender on a fine one-ton truck owned by one of the local farmers. The conversation soon centered

Richard Stark, Sr. (left) with early day cornpicker combine
Photo courtesy of Richard Stark

Richard Stark, Sr. with modern combine
Photo courtesy of Richard Stark

around all the wonderful farm equipment of the 90s, like that owned by farmers Wilfred and Richard Groves, Richard "Dick" Stark, Sr., Warren Snell, and Bruce Yungclas, some of the midwest's most successful. The equipment includes huge tractors pulling 6-7 bottom plows, 27-30 foot discs, 12-16 row cultivators, and 12 to 16 row planters and huge combines for picking corn, reaping soybeans, oats and wheat. The aforementioned farmers hadn't always had it so good for they could remember the days on their father's farms when they used horse drawn equipment.

Of course, the conversation drifted back to the depression when very few could afford to own a pickup or hire one, and most of the farmers never even so much as owned an automobile towed trailer. A discussion ensued on the ingenuity of various farmers in getting along with what they had. Burton grinned, shifted his lanky 6'-7" frame in the chair, then said, "Let me tell you how old Furman 'Buck' Hensel solved the grain problems during hard times." LeRoy stopped pounding on the pickup fender, looked up and said, "Hell, yes, Burton, that's a knee slapper for sure!"

Buck, at that time, was supplementing his earnings by raising a sizable flock of chickens. When the need arose for chicken feed, old Buck just drove his weather beaten four door Model A Ford into the Farmer's Elevator, grinning from ear to ear and yelled, "Fill 'er up," much as a motorist did at a gas station. The two grain attendants always laughed and asked if he needed his oil checked, windshield washed, etc.

Pulling down the long chute, the attendants placed it through the back window and filled the back seat level with the windows and the top of the back seat with oats. This routine had gone on for years and one day the attendants decided to surprise old Buck and really fill 'er up, as he had said. They didn't cut off the chute but kept the grain flowing into the front seat until it sloped down to only inches below the dashboard.

No, old Buck didn't panic and jump out of the car; he just let them keep filling though he certainly registered surprise. The attendants had a hearty laugh and, much to their amazement, Buck was now laughing along with them. Buck knew exactly the amount of grain the back seat held, having measured it in a bushel basket as he emptied it the first time. He had the correct amount of change for his order in his hand.

Congenial Buck had the last laugh. Under the oats he found the starter, clutch and gear shift, dropped the pay for the grain out the window on the elevator floor and drove off up to his armpits with the extra grain. Buck never paid for the bonus bushels—no, the elevator attendants never billed him!

Except for many of those engaged in agriculture,people nationwide ushered in the year 1937 with a little more hope than they had in the previous year. Although the midwest was still lagging terribly, factories were starting to hum in the large metropolitan areas, bread lines were not as prevalent and jobs for some of the unemployed created a certain amount of optimism. Even across the plains states people had a little more money to spend.

Greed is a state of mind that knows no boundaries. A good number of factories and commercial businesses were beginning to experience sizable profits. However, knowing the Wagner Act had been invalidated by the Supreme Court and collective bargaining outlawed, most were neglecting to pass on some of their increased earnings to employees in the form of better earnings. Additionally, many employers commenced working their employees ten to twelve hours a day, as well as all day Saturdays, with straight hourly rates.

When people see their employers raking in huge profits while paying them low scale wages, they become disgruntled. Sensing this, unions took full advantage of their susceptibility to promises of higher wages, standard work hours, better working conditions, and time and one half for overtime.

Police battle strikers in Minneapolis, Minnesota.

National Archives photo, courtesy of Mrs. Gertrude Horan

Labor unions, thoroughly disgusted with the Supreme Court's rulings against union representation and collective bargaining, became ever more rancorous in their demands and during 1937 strikes spread from coast to coast.

Automobile sales had shown a dramatic increase and workers in automobile plants were demanding some of the fruits of their labor. General Motors, riding on the strength of the Wagner Act repeal, refused to negotiate. The end result: employees at the Flint, Michigan plant initiated something new—a sit-down strike! They stayed in the plant and refused to budge.

Michigan's recently elected governor, Frank Murphy, exerted all persuasion possible to get General Motors' executives to negotiate with the newly established United Auto Workers Union, but to no avail. A bitter stalemate developed.

Factory police surged on the Flint plant but were driven back by determined workers hurling anything throwable they could find. A court injunction was obtained to have workers evicted from the plant. Governor Murphy was forced to call up the National Guard. John L. Lewis, Iowa born president of the CIO Union who had gone to work in the mines at fifteen years of age, defied the governor and Murphy, not wanting a blood letting, refused to send the guardsmen into the plant.

Roosevelt adamantly refused to use force against the workers. He was disgusted with the union but was equally disgusted with General Motors and encouraged the company to sit down and talk. Strikes spread quickly to other automotive plants in Detroit, Michigan, Cleveland, Ohio and South Bend, Indiana.

While the violent strikes were raging, cold wind and rain whipped at Franklin D. Roosevelt's body January 20, 1937, as a huge throng of people, struggling to keep their umbrellas from inverting in the brisk wind, watched Roosevelt being inaugurated for his second term as president.

Roosevelt, with the huge plurality of votes he had garnered, was now ready to take off the kid gloves and do battle with the Supreme Court over their shelving of his economic recovery programs. On February 5, 1937 he came out of his corner fighting when he submitted a Judicial Reform Act to Congress.

Under the Act, if a member of the federal judiciary did not retire within six months of his seventieth birthday, the president would be empowered to appoint an additional judge. Six members of the Supreme Court were over seventy. Court members nearly panicked when the bill reached Congress, for it was obvious some of their power structure could be dissipated.

Probably because there were some signs of economic recovery, a hue and cry went up that federal assistance was no longer needed and strong feelings prevailed that American business and industry could fill the void if fewer governmental supports were provided.

President Roosevelt was fully aware of the inherent danger of giving people money and felt those who could work for their livelihood should be required to do so. There was much palavering about balancing the budget. Roosevelt also believed in a balanced budget, although he felt this was not the time to slack off on federal depression-fighting expenditures. So it was that Roosevelt, under heavy presure, conceded that perhaps he should go along with those clamoring for a reduction in federal programs.

The budget deficit for the fiscal year 1936 had been $4.3 billion,in 1937 the deficit was $2.7 billion and projections were that, in 1939, the budget would be balanced with revenues. When compared to budgets under Presidents Ronald Reagan and George Bush during the period 1980 to 1992, the budget deficit during the depression era seems infinitesimal. Of course, a little money went a long way in those days and was not to be compared to the funny money of the last quarter century.

The Federal Reserve Board raised its bank reserve requirements for member banks to fifty percent, and the Works Projects Administration funds, needed to keep people working, were drastically reduced.

Meanwhile back in Happyland the basketball season was drawing to a close, and the high school had enjoyed a winning one. When the uniforms were stored away, the team had won 15 and lost 7 games. The last loss was a hotly fought contest with Marshalltown in the finals of the district tournament. Marshalltown in the closing minutes had won by a single point and went on to be runners up in the state finals.

Hank had got into more games that year, but probably his most dynamic performance came after, and not during, a game. Happyland had played at the neighboring town of Fort Dodge. After the game he had stopped to talk with a friend, James R. "Bob" Otto, who would later play with the famous University of Iowa Ironmen football team of 1939—and then coach at Buena Vista College and Mankato State University.

Bob and Hank stood in the hallway and conversed much longer than intended. Everyone except Willie Wilkinson, the assistant student manager, had departed from the dressing room when Hank strolled in. As Hank headed for the showers, Willie hurriedly grabbed his uniform.

Meanwhile the top student manager, Don Fleischer, returned, relieved Willie of his duties, finished picking up the last box of uniforms, locked the room where Hank's street clothes hung on a hook and departed the building, unaware that Hank was still in the shower.

His bathing completed, Hank returned to the dressing room where he soon discovered the cage was securely locked, the uniforms gone and the dressing room completely deserted. Terror descended upon him when he realized the manager had also taken his towel from the bench, where he had placed it for ready accessibility.

The situation was becoming just a mite precarious as Hank was not only stranded, but stranded naked. He tried to envision what Cousin Clinty would do in a situation like this, but when the answer came to him, he knew drinking water wouldn't do the trick.

Blocking the door open with a bench, Hank slinked out into the hall. The thought of finding a telephone and calling for help crossed his mind, and he checked several office doors only to find them locked. Panic-stricken, he pussy-footed down the hall close to the wall and worked his way back toward the locker room door.

As Hank neared a stairway, he heard the sharp click click of heels and, knowing he couldn't explain to a female type teacher why he was out strolling without clothing, he streaked down the corridor, rounded the corner and dashed into the dressing room before she could reach the bottom step.

By this time, Hank was beginning to wonder if he'd be forced to spend the weekend in the building. The idea didn't appeal to him too much and, after a few minutes had elapsed, he decided to launch another bare fanny attempt, and again he dainty-footed down the hallway toward the outside door. Reaching the stairway, he was a little more cautious but, much to his surprise, he made it all the way without incident.

Looking out the glass door panel, he could see he hadn't been deserted. He had ridden in a car with the assistant coach, Leonard Skoglund, who was now standing on the sidewalk talking to the other boys in his group. After several crude, nude gyrations and much hand waving Hank finally attracted their attention and seeing his plight in the light, they hurried to his rescue.

Hank's problems still weren't over as the manager had departed in another car, and a janitor could not be found. One of the athletes had a finger length coat which was definitely made for a short fingered man but, since he also wore a heavy sweater, he loaned the coat to Hank for the ride home. It was a cold night, but who could be choosey in a situation like this? Coach Skoglund turned on the automobile heater, Hank donned the garb and made a dash for the car.

Arriving back in Happyland, he still faced the problem of getting out of the car in the middle of the business district and up to his brother-in-law and sister's apartment, where he was now living. Fortunately the traffic thinned down and, when only men were in sight, Hank gathered his exposure composure and all hookered over like a girl trying to wear a garterbelt with her bobby sox, ran like hell for the stairway enclosure. Hank's sister laughed when he came racing through the door and asked just what kind of stakes he was betting on the game that caused him to lose his pants.

On the national scene the long bitter strike at Flint, Michigan (spread to sixty plants in fourteen states) had finally been settled. Roosevelt appealed personally by telephone to William Knutson, president of General Motors. Shortly after that, General Motors went to the bargaining table with the union and later recognized the United Auto Workers (UAW) as bargaining agent.

Chrysler and smaller auto manufacturers soon followed the General Motors lead. However, Ford Motor Co. held out and would not negotiate with the union, although, it might be added, their workers were soon given the same benefits.

With the coming of spring, the nation soon realized that the federal budget reduction and curtailment of federal economic programs had indeed been premature. The unemployment figures started to rise, and the stock market began to decline.

Roosevelt's battle to shake up the Supreme Court continued, but he couldn't, as yet, muster enough votes to pass his Judiciary Reform Act. He had fought and would continue to fight the good fight. With unemployment on the increase, strikes were now beginning to become even more bitter. Time after time social economic programs had been proposed, only to be struck down by what Cousin Clinty called, "The Supreme Beings."

It was obvious the Supreme Court didn't enjoy having the President and the American public hacking at their fannies, and they were beginning to realize it was time to mend fences with the people. In a surprise move they upheld a state's minimum wage law, the Railway Labor Act; then on April 12, 1937 they reversed their previous decision and upheld the Wagner Act and the Social Security Act. Roosevelt was jubilant—would wonders ever cease!

Along about this time Hank was again getting interested in girls and wanted to take up dancing. Of course, he couldn't dance and, as usual, he went to Cousin Clinty with his problem. Clinty was a terrific tap dancer but said he had become a bit rusty on his ballroom dancing, though he agreed to help Hank with his problem. Hank was determined to become a smoothie with the girls, like Don Coulter, Wilfred "Bill" Groves, Willis Foster and Richard Maxson.

Big Sister was called upon to be Hank's partner. She hadn't learned many steps yet, and Hank only knew one and that was dancing on one foot—not his own but his sister's. Big Sister held up pretty well on the waltzes, but when the faster dancing lessons started, Hank began stepping on both her feet. That is when she drew the line, so to speak, saying she had to be able to walk to work and, with that, she dissolved the dancing partnership.

Hank finally saw an ad in a magazine, one that pictured the footprints and all, showing how each step was to be done. After a few days' heckling, Clinty finally agreed to act as Hank's partner. Hank complained to Clinty that he, Clinty, didn't look like a girl and he couldn't get inspired. After a few foot stompings and bunion bumpings, Clinty said he'd had enough and fetched Hank the dust mop, which he averred, held upside down, somewhat resembled a girl with a fuzzed top hairdo.

Jitterbugging was getting popular and Clinty said he'd have no part of that and, making the comparison, he told Hank he should have paid a little more attention when Cousin Willobee did his "Hot Sole Shuffle." But, Hank was bound and determined to learn dancing and, after dancing with twenty five or so gals at dances (none the second time), Zelma Hyatt finally polished him off, and it wasn't long before he must have had the dancing bit down pretty well, as girls were accepting him for a second dance!

It is said that in the spring a young man's fancy often turns to thoughts of love. Hank, at that age, liked girls but he loved baseball. He had memorized the immortal "Casey at the Bat" and could almost recite it backwards.

Don Shelton, a big strong right-hander, who would later pitch for a Pittsburgh Pirates farm team, was now a senior. Hank would not be the starting pitcher, but would be called in from the first base position to relief-pitch in several games.

Coach Johnson and assistant coach Leonard Skoglund would continue to devote much time to helping Hank with his pitching and hitting, and he was improving rapidly. The team enjoyed a winning season and Hank continued to work hard to bring himself to full potential.

Memorial Day in those days was always a big occasion in Happyland, as in other small towns. There were many speeches honoring deceased veterans and those who had given their lives in defense of their country, and, of course, there was the paying of respects to family members and friends buried in the cemetery.

Civil War veterans had all but disappeared from parades in the United States. Happyland had only one surviving member of the Grand Army of the Republic, E. N. Lee, but a few Spanish American war veterans still participated with World War I veterans, marching with members of the local American Legion Post.

Hank was proud to march with the local Guardsmen in the parade, although keeping in step behind a high school band became a bit of challenge since its cadence was much different from the military—requiring almost a half step. The company provided the bugler and firing squad for the concluding ceremony, conducted at a stately rock bandstand in the cemetery. There were several highly effective speakers. With the program completed, the company marched to the graves of each former company member and fired salutes.

Col. George W. Crosley, assumed command of 3rd Iowa Inf. Regt. when ranking officers became casualties during the battle. He was given a battlefield promotion to Major—also led troops in the battle of Vicksburg.

Photo courtesy of Carlton Crosley

While the Guardsmen were firing blanks in ceremonies at the Happyland graves that year, police in Chicago were firing live ammunition at strikers and creating a need for new graves. United States Steel had refused to bargain with union representatives, and strikers got out of control. Police were called to the scene and opened fire; ten people were killed and hundreds were wounded or injured.

After what came to be known as the "Memorial Day Massacre," U.S. Steel recognized the union as its employees' bargaining agent, but what a tragic loss of life.

On the lighter side, there were a lot of St. Louis Cardinal fans in Happyland during the 1930s. Hank was one of them. Jerome "Dizzy" Dean and his brother, Paul "Daffy" Dean, a couple of admitted "ridge runners" from Missouri, were spelling each other, often every other game, pitching some fantastic baseball. The "Gashouse Gang," as they came to be known, was rounded out with some fabulous hitters, such as Stan "The Man" Musial and Enos "Country" Slaughter.

Old Diz always made for good press and his radio interviews were hilarious. He literally fractured the English language and kept everyone rib-sore with his down-in-the-hills witticisms. He captured the hearts of everyone except the English teachers with his statements, "Me and Paul can whup 'em - Me and Paul will wipe 'em out with our wrinkle balls—the second baseman caught him when he slud into base", etc.

No one who was listening will ever forget the time old Diz later was interviewed by Herman Hickman, the Yale coach. Hickman paid Diz some nice compliments. Diz shrugged it off saying, "Shucks, I get embarrassed cuz I say ain't and words like that." Hickman chuckled, then retorted, "Diz, I know a helluva lot of people who don't say ain't that ain't eatin'!"

Semi-pro baseball had been dropped for a couple of seasons, but with the "Gashouse Gang" at the peak of its popularity, there was much talk in Happyland about again fielding a team. Some was idle chatter, but enough was serious to cause a stir in the imagination of fans and players.

It seemed almost uncanny that while all the renewed interest in a town baseball team was reaching a fevered pitch, Charlie Catchum (we'll call him that) came to town.

Baseball caps were not a commonly worn head dress off the diamond until much later years when the seed corn companies started giving them away, but Charlie never took his off. It was a real honest-to-goodness St. Louis Cardinal cap.

It wasn't long before Charlie was mingling with the townfolks showing them newspaper clippings, telling about his awesome feats on the diamond when he was playing in the minor leagues in Texas. Of course, he was from Missouri and knew many of the St. Louis players and was on speaking terms with Diz and Daffy Dean and some of the others.

Hank was in Harold Farnum's Barbershop the day Charlie casually posed the question, "You have a semi-pro baseball team here?" There was a pause, then a chorus of answers, "No, we haven't had one since 1934, but we sure as hell need one!" "Got a good catcher?" Charlie asked. Earl "Baldy" Kiestner spoke up, "Got a new kid who moved here from Wellsburg by the name of Bud Haack, but he hasn't played semi-pro ball." Nothing was said for awhile; then Hank Moose spoke up, "Why do you ask?"

Charlie tugged at the bill of his cap as if shielding his eyes from the sun, twirled some keys on a ring he was holding and said, "I've done a lot of catching in my time—did a stint in the minors down in Texas. Had a little trouble with my shoulder, couldn't play two or three games a week, but I was hoping you'd have a semi-pro team here. Catching a game a week wouldn't bother me at all."

Now that Charlie had the attention of everyone in the barbershop, he casually mentioned that he had sold his sporting goods store in

Missouri and was thinking about opening one in Iowa, possibly Happyland, then hastily added, "People tell me you have excellent schools and it's a good place to raise kids." Charlie went on to say he was sure the little woman would like it here. His statement had a homey touch—family man and all, everyone thought—stable, dependable—good thinker. Everyone in the barbershop immediately liked Charlie.

It wasn't long before a meeting of interested citizens was held, and the managership and catching job of the new team was virtually forced on poor Charlie. Yes-siree, Happyland was on its way to having a first-class baseball team.

Charlie appeared extremely flattered—said he would put up some money toward new uniforms and equipment. Pete Pillman, we'll call him that, a local businessman, had played second base at the University of Iowa and was extremely interested in getting a team started. Charlie threw in the first one hundred dollars to start a fund raising drive. Pete Pillman had a bank box; everything was perfect.

When asked to head up the fund raising drive, Charlie begged off—saying it should be one of the localites! However, after some coaxing by the group and some of the prominent local people volunteering to go with him to call on people, Charlie at last agreed—what a relief!

In the days ahead Charlie and his St. Louis Cardinal cap were a constant part of the main street scene. Hell, he even went into a catcher's stance while drinking a beer. Occasionally he'd demonstrate how he threw out Willie Whirlwind, or some such person, who was touted to become another Ty Cobb. His form was good; no one doubted his word.

As Charlie made the rounds collecting contributions with one of the local baseball enthusiasts one day, he carried with him his old catcher's mitt and sought advice as to who in town could best sew up a seam that had broken. Everyone recommended Bill Bittner's shoe repair shop.

Bill Bittner had the only shoe repair shop in town. When Charlie got around to asking Bill for his contribution, he naturally had the mitt repaired there. Of course, Bill never charged him!

Little more than one week later, enough money had been donated by Happylanders to purchase new uniforms for twelve players and catching equipment, bats, balls, bases, chalk machine, the whole kit n' kaboodle. Charlie said it wouldn't be necessary to purchase catcher's equipment as he had his own. "Great guy—damn nice of him," were the remarks most heard!

With a few balls and bats, practice sessions were called. Charlie turned out to be a pretty good catcher. The top players were chosen, and Charlie announced he could schedule a guy to come up from Des Moines to measure the players for the new uniforms, which, by the way, were to look a lot like those the St. louis Cardinals wore. What a thrill, everyone agreed.

The uniform salesman arrived on the scene the next day. Charlie had him show everyone the sample. He then got out his order blanks and proceeded to measure everyone. He seemed extra careful, repeating some measurements twice—said he wanted good fits, it was good advertisement and all! When he finished he said, "I hope Charlie told you; I only deal in cash; got stung a few weeks ago—team ordered a set and I got stuck with them!" Charlie assured him there would be no problem—that the money was in the bank.

Finished with the measurements, the uniform salesman said, "Wait just a minute." He then checked the measurements against some figures in a notebook he had taken from his sales kit. Grinning, he announced, "You're in luck. I have enough uniforms the other team didn't take to fit all but two of your players, and I can have those for you in a week. I'll give you a break; you can have them for five dollars less and I'll pay for changing the letters." "What a deal," everyone thought, "old Charlie really knows how to operate."

The funds raised had been secured in a bank box and the bank was closed. The salesman said, "That's O.K.—you might as well bring the cash down to Des Moines tomorrow and pick up the uniforms at the same time." With that the salesman departed to catch the bus. Someone suggested Charlie and Mr. Pillman go to the bank the next morning, then take the cash to Des Moines. Charlie asked, "Pete, is that okay with you?" Pete said, "I can't get away from the store tomorrow but, Charlie, you could go alone." Charlie reluctantly consented.

Charlie then said he might as well pick up some new bats, balls and bases, and save making another trip. Sounded sensible, everyone agreed.

The next morning Pete and Charlie proceeded to the bank. Charlie allowed they'd best leave a hundred dollars of the $600 collected as it might be needed to hold them over until ticket revenues started rolling in. "Great idea," Pete said. "Charlie thinks of everything."

Pete and Charlie discussed bat brands awhile, then Charlie mounted his vehicle, waved and headed for Des Moines. Poor old Charlie must have taken the wrong road and become lost as that was the last anyone ever saw him. Had he met with foul play? Hell no; Charlie no doubt joined up with the uniform salesman and then headed out for another state, another small town to work the scam all over again. All members of the committee were too embarrassed to tell anyone how they had been taken in by the amicable Charlie Catchum.

While the Happyland baseball committee was traumatized at having its finances wiped out by the con-man Charlie Catchum, Blairsburg, a small but avid baseball town led by of Cecil Mullins, successfully raised enough money to field a town team.

The Blairsburg team needed three players to round out a potentially strong nine, and Bud Haack, Ralph Burton and Hank were asked to fill the slots. Hank was extremely proud to play with the likes of Raymond Ades, George and Keith Van Winkle, Jimmy Gleason, Zeke Walruth, and the great Orville "Joltie" Eckstein, possibly the best player Happyland (and the entire state for that matter) had ever produced.

"Joltie," normally a third baseman, could throw a ball like a bullet, often turning Keith Van Winkle, the first baseman, halfway around, while containing a throw. Cecil Mullins, the coach, decided to try a new combination and had Joltie start a game as pitcher. Of course, Eckstein could pitch; could ducks swim? Hell, Joltie could play any position in any popular sport. Joltie fired fast balls for five innings until his arm began to tire. It was then that Cecil Mullins, the manager, implemented the second phase of his plan and called Hank in from second base to pitch.

Now Hank had pretty fair speed, but nothing like Eckstein's blistering fast ball. Hank threw a wider variety of curve balls and Earl Forrester had taught him how to throw a good knuckle ball floater that dropped, but looked like a balloon to a batter who had been swinging at fast balls. The combination of the pitching duo was hilarious as the batters nearly broke their backs swinging while adjusting to the pitching.

With a strong leadoff hitter like George Van Winkle and powerful long ball hitters like Keith Van Winkle, Bud Haack, Eckstein, and Ralph Burton, opposing pitchers were dealt nightmares.

Both Eckstein and Haack could bat from either side of the plate and while playing a strong William-Dows team, they both sent home runs into opposite fields. A few weeks later at Clarion Bud did it all. The game was played in a new athletic stadium—first time it had been used. Haack commissioned it by belting an unbelievable four home runs out of the park, two left-handed and two right. Both Eckstein and Haack were major league quality players and could have played with any team today, but neither pursued a career in baseball. In those days minor league players rode buses from town to town—Haack said he didn't want any part of that! Hank—he would have walked from town to town between games.

Meyel "Bud" Haack. He started catching at a young age!

Photo courtesy of Miner Haack

Bud Haack poles home run for Butler University.

Photo courtesy of Meyel "Bud" Haack

Across the United States on June 22, 1937 most of the populace gathered around radios to listen to the James J. Braddock - Joe Louis fight. Louis had been given an opportunity to win the heavyweight boxing title from Braddock. Many were surprised that Max Schmeling, the German champ, was not given first chance at the title since he had defeated Louis. But, since Americans were doing the fight promotion and the Germans were being held in less than friendly regard, Louis was given the nod.

Louis had now aged a bit and was rapidly becoming a seasoned boxer, adding a string of knockouts to his credit. Braddock absorbed heavy punishment from Louis, and a lesser opponent would have thrown in the towel. However, in the eighth round, badly battered and bleeding profusely from wounds, Braddock was knocked out.

Sports fans were happy when Joe Louis issued his challenge to Max Schmeling, but that happiness soon faded when, on July 2, 1937, the news was broadcast that Amelia Earhart and her co-pilot

Fred Noonan, an experienced navigator and former Pan Am pilot, had vanished in the Pacific Ocean on a flight from New Guinea to Howland Island during a globe-circumventing flight.

The pretty young flyer had captured the hearts of all Americans when she became the first woman to fly the Atlantic, the first to fly from Hawaii to the mainland, first to fly solo from Los Angeles to Mexico City, first to fly solo from Mexico City to Newark, N.J., and the first woman to fly at 14,000 feet.

On the world scene war and saber-rattling went on unabated—increasing in tempo daily. The League of Nations (equivalent to today's United Nations) had stood by doing nothing when Italy had attacked Ethiopia.

However, National Guard training became a very serious matter. At the local armory there was no horsing around, so to speak, during drill periods. Capt. Meller and Lt. House, both war veterans, observed classes carefully and urged everyone on to peak performance. Their standard remark, "Pay attention—you may need this training sooner than you think!"

XII
THE BIG MILITARY PICNIC

Since the days of the founding fathers, America has been known as the land of opportunity. Through use of a goodly amount of energy, determination, resourcefulness, perseverance and education, a citizen, or even an immigrant, could expect to reach his cherished goal of acquiring a home and, sometimes, land or a business.

Those who immigrated to the United States after 1886 sailed into New York Harbor pent up with emotion, for they would never forget the beckoning sight of the raised arm of the Statue of Liberty seemingly pulling them to the bosom of America, God's golden land of freedom and opportunity.

So it was that by the summer of 1937, eight years after the bubble burst on Wall Street, millions of birthright Americans and adopted sons from foreign soils continued to feel the pangs of depression. Despite the purported improvement in the economy, their principal goal remained that of keeping a roof over the heads of their families and food on the table.

Ma and Pa restaurants, groceries, haberdasheries, and mercantile shops were beginning to close, succeeded in many instances by chain stores. Proprietors of these small stores had cared about the plight of their fellow townspeople, often extending credit until they themselves were no longer solvent. Not a pleasant thought, but it happened. Many were the people who began to wonder if the opportunity to achieve their American dream would ever return.

People were extremely proud and hated to admit they needed help. Just the thought of going to the "poor farm," as the county home was called in those days, struck terror in the elderly poor; many would rather have starved to death.

Now thousands of once-skilled laborers and professional men had been reduced to performing menial tasks if they were fortunate enough to find work at all. Many people, as a last resort, entered government subsidized programs and, yes, some turned their backs from friends not wishing to be seen as they stood in public welfare lines.

Although the economy was picking up a bit, there was little news that gave cause for joy. If the news media weren't hawking tragedy and hard times, they were painting a grim picture of militarism on the world scene—oh the joy of it all!

On the world scene a Japanese division stationed in North China, seeking to gain the release of one of its soldiers, was refused entry into the city of Wamping. Enraged, the Japanese Army leveled the town with bombs and artillery bombardment, then brutally bayoneted and burned civilian inhabitants and raped many of the city's women.

Full scale, although still undeclared, war was then launched by the Japanese with deeper troop penetrations into China. Chinese Communists, who heretofore had been battling Chiang Kai-shek's nationalist troops, now were joining forces with those of their avowed enemy to fight the Japanese.

In Europe, surprisingly enough, the Loyalists were still putting up a strong battle againt General Franco's Rebel forces. Some 20,000 idealists and soldiers of fortune from around the globe, including some from the United States, had joined the Loyalist cause. However, by the end of 1937 Germany would have 9,000 technicians in Spain, and Italy would have committed 65,000 troops to help the Rebels. Germany claimed none of their technicians were directly involved in the fighting, but later this was disproved when their "condor squadron" literally demolished a small Spanish village.

While the Germans were testing new, advanced weapons in Spain with still more coming off the drawing boards, the World War I Allies, for the most part, were still plodding along with weaponry used in World War I. Only in the area of aircraft and naval vessels had any appreciable advancement been made—although it would later be discovered that United States aviation had lagged far behind.

In 1925 General William "Billy" Mitchell of the U.S. Army Air Corps had become a little too verbose in his insistence that the United States Army Air Corps upgrade its air war capabilities. He had been a brigadier general during World War I, then assistant chief of the Army Air Service from 1919 to 1925 and was thoroughly convinced strategic and tactical aerial bombardment would become the ultimate offensive weapon in future wars.

The great Mitchell, weary of his attempts to prove that aircraft could sink heavily armored ships, directed an unauthorized test: the bombing of several obsolete battleships. His superiors were unwilling to yield even after proven success. Mitchell accused them of incompetency, negligence and almost treasonable administration of the Navy and War Departments.

Mitchell was court-martialed in 1925 for insubordination and suspended from the Army. This drove him to make the suspension permanent by resigning in 1926. He died in 1936, some say of a broken heart. Mitchell's theories proved overwhelmingly correct during World War II. However, it would be 1945 before the court-martial was stricken from his records and he was awarded the Medal of Honor posthumously

When would the United States and its Allies awaken? Contrary to the provisions of the Treaty of Versailles, Germany was already producing vastly improved weaponry, rapid fire machine pistols, more effective machine guns, improved mortars, and versatile hard-hitting combination anti-tank anti-aircraft guns.

Determined to avenge the Treaty of Versailles, Germany had already combined its technology with Russia's to manufacture new and improved tanks. Germany was now producing better bombers and the Stuka, a new fighter plane with tremendous dive bombing capabilities.

Meanwhile, back in the United States, the Army struggled along below strength and with obsolete equipment. The regulars were never too pleased with the reserves and were unwilling to share any appreciable amount of meager defense budget allocations. This bickering had gone on since George Washington's time and still exists today.

On paper the National Guard divisions appeared to form a formidable force, but when one considers such divisions were maintained at well below fifty percent strength, it is apparent that their effectiveness in combat would have been severely handicapped. Line rifle companies fared even worse; most were less than one-third of full strength and not fully equipped, even with obsolete equipment. There was little cause for joy in Mudville, so to speak!

Mussolini called the U.S. National Guard a paper tiger, whose members went on picnics and ate ice cream. The paper tiger part the guardsmen would later grow to understand, but they sure as hell weren't going on picnics. They were conscientious troops that trained hard with what equipage they were provided. Mussolini would later be forced to eat his words!

To help the reader (and any of Mussolini's descendants that might be around) gain insight on the type of training the pre World War II guard received, the author takes you on one of those encampments. Let the reader be the judge as to whether it was a picnic.

Saturday night August 10, 1937 Happyland guardsmen assembled at the local armory to pack and load military impedimenta onto cars in preparation for rail movement to Camp Ripley, Minnesota. It appeared someone in Washington, D.C. was at last giving some thought to national defense—since this would be the first time the entire 34th Infantry Division had been assembled since World War I. For many it would be not only their first train trip, but their first time out of state.

It was three o'clock in the morning when preparations were completed and the last of the equipment loaded on railroad cars. A few of the men opted to catch a catnap on the armory floor.

After a pre-dawn breakfast, the company, in full packs, marched to the Northwestern rail siding at 4:30 A.M. Capt. Meller gave orders to entrain and 1st Lt. Mathias J. House, 2nd Lt. Louis Nichols and sixty-two enlisted men boarded the passenger trains.

The railroad cars appeared to be before turn-of-the-century vintage equipment that had been converted to troop carriers for World War I. Sgt. Donald Andrew quipped that he thought he saw a couple of arrowhead dents in the baggage car door.

Dawn was breaking as the old rail cars shook, rattled and rolled over the railroad bridge at the north bend of the Boone River while the engine slowly chugged toward Minnesota.

It wasn't long before Forest Pringle, Eugene Gordon, Larkin Woodie, and Joe Luppes had a penny-ante poker game going. Soon Robert "Speed" Gilman and Carl McCollough had the cash exchange cubes clicking and a low-wager (damn low) crap game was in progress.

Of course, there was no air conditioning in those days, nor was there a good ventilating system in the old cars. The heat was stifling. With no small amount of effort the well-rusted train windows were pried open but, to everyone's disgust, each time the firemen fired the huge locomotive boiler, soot from the mighty steam engine poured through the cars.

By mid-morning the train had switched lines and was now rumbling through Mankato, Minnesota. Lt. House, the company executive officer, reminded Hank and fellow guardsmen that New Ulm, just twenty miles away, had been the site of a vicious Indian attack. "Soon," House said, "we will be going through St. Peters and LeSueur. Those towns sent militia (forerunners of the Minnesota National Guard) to help New Ulm people defend against the attack." As Hank looked out of the train window at the beautifully cleared rolling land, it was difficult to imagine that less than seventy-five years ago much of what he was seeing had been virgin forest.

History pretty well authenticates House's version of the attack. The Civil War was raging and many of Minnesota's young men had answered the call. The Sioux Indians decided time was ripe to strike a blow against ever encroaching settlers. New Ulm (900 settlers) was the largest settlement near the Indian reservation. The first evidence of an uprising was the Dakota Sioux warriors ambushing a group of Civil War recruiters near New Ulm August 18, 1862. Of the sixteen

The Sioux were ferocious warriors—dueled to death.
Photo courtesy of Amon-Carter Museum—from painting of "Duel to the Death" by Charles M. Russell

recruiters, twelve were killed, but four escaped to alert residents of New Ulm.

A militia, consisting of forty men with guns, was assembled. Women and children were crowded into the Decotah Hotel and nearby sturdy structures. While barricades and other defenses were being hastily established, riders alerted farmers in the vicinity, and most of them were soon hastening into town. A scouting rescue party, returning from along the Cottonwood River, was ambushed—this time eleven were killed and again four escaped.

Other riders spread the request for help—militia units commenced their march from St. Peter, Traverse de Sioux, and Nicollet County. However, before reinforcements arrived, the New Ulm Militia, with the aid of a squad from Swan Lake and Nicollet, had already repulsed a one-hundred warrior attack. The defenders suffered casualties of six people killed and at least five wounded.

That night Charles Flandrau arrived with a militia from St. Peter and LeSueur. He brought with him four doctors to help New Ulm's only doctor, Carl Wescke. One of the four was Dr. Charles H. Mayo, whose sons William and Charles would later found the now famous Rochester Mayo Clinic. Others to-become-famous personages on the scene were future Minnesota governors Henry A. Swift and Horace Austin.

Charles Flandrau had been a member of Minnesota's constitutional convention and sat on the state's supreme court. He was soon elected commander of the militia and given locally the rank of colonel. When all outside militia had arrived, Flandrau's forces numbered some 300 guns.

Then word came that Winnebago Indians were threatening settlers in Blue Earth County. A company of South Bend Militia departed to protect their own home area. To add to the problem, lookouts spotted a huge fire which appeared to be Fort Ridgely (located just north across the Minnesota River). Col. Flandrau dispatched Lt. William Huey with a company of seventy-five men. The Indians quickly cut off the company. It was later discovered the fire had been started by the Indians as a tactical ploy. Fortunately Huey and his men managed to escape entrapment and returned to New Ulm the next day.

Fort Ridgely had been attacked. Chief Little Crow of the Sioux was reportedly wounded in that battle. Among the chieftains leading some 650 braves in the New Ulm assault were Mankato, Wabasha and Blue Eagle. (Nothing is mentioned of Inkapadutah, who led the Spirit Lake attack.)

The defenses had been prepared as well as possible, given manpower and resources available. Guns were loaded and ready—those

Chief Little Crow in later years
Photo courtesy of Brown County Historical Society, New Ulm, Minnesota

The rugged Sioux Indians preferred teepees—they could move them on the hunt.
Photo courtesy of Bernice Sealine Lund

without firearms were armed with pitchforks, axes, sledge hammers, knives, and any other object capable of killing or maiming.

Kenneth Carley in his writing, "The Sioux Uprising of 1862," does a fantastic job of describing the scene. "At about 9:30 a.m. the Indians streamed out of the woods onto the prairie west of New Ulm and formed a long, curved line on the upper terrace. Flandrau directed (Capt. William B.) Dodd to meet the Indians well outside the barricades."

Carley quotes Flandrau's description of the Indian attack, "Their advance upon the sloping prairie in the bright sunlight was a very fine spectacle, and to such inexperienced soldiers as we all were, intensely exciting. When within about one mile and a half of us, the mass began to expand like a fan. The advance increased in the velocity of its approach, and continued until within about double rifle-shot, when it had covered our entire front. Then the savages uttered a terrific yell and came down upon us like the wind."

Fight as the settlers did, the Indians surrounded the town—burning buildings to produce smoke to cover their advance. Settlers burned more buildings to deny the Indians cover and concealment. In all, 190 structures were burned. At the height of the attack coura-

Sioux Indians attack New Ulm, Minnesota settlement.
From oil painting by Alexander Schwendinger, courtesy of Brown County Historical Society, New Ulm, Minnesota

geous militiamen counterattacked, whooping their own battle cry. Col. Flandrau felt the countercharge was the turning point in the battle.

The Indians made an appearance the next morning, fired a few rounds, but opted not to resume the attack. It was then decided New Ulm settlers should be evacuated to Mankato. Two thousand settlers from the area left in wagon trains and on foot, under the protection of Capt. E. St. Julien Cox and 150 men, recently arrived from Nicollet and Sibley counties. The defenders of New Ulm had lost thirty-four dead and sixty wounded. Fort Ridgely, like New Ulm, had withstood two attacks. (Some earlier accounts of the battle ranged casualties up to 1,100 dead.)

Back on the train headed for Camp Ripley, the locomotive engineer must have been accustomed to picking up eggs and cream, for he stopped for everything but ants on the track. But notwithstanding, by noon the train was moving through Minneapolis. By that time the men's faces were so speckled with soot a doctor could have diagnosed them as having black measles. The poker players called time out when Corporal Larkin Woodie complained the cards were getting so smudged he couldn't tell the kings from the queens, even when he peeked.

Eating the noon meal proved to be a memorable experience. A chow line was formed in the bouncing, swaying cars and as the men filed through the kitchen car with their mess kits, some of the food ended up on Corporal Spooner's shirt. Patty O'Kettlebelly, a cook, paid Spooner a compliment saying, "Spooner, you look good in everything you eat!" Surprisingly the food was exceptionally good despite the fact First Cook Frank Meller and Specialist Pat O'Kettlebelly and helper PFC Tip O'Flaskagin had prepared it in an old kitchen car equipped with a coal fired cook stove.

The south half of Minnesota, with its near flat sections of fertile land, was much like Iowa, but as the train moved northward, the terrain and topographical features changed dramatically. This, one could readily discern, was the land of the fabled Paul Bunyon and Babe, his big blue ox.

Much of the countryside was still virgin soil, still uncleared and the rolling hills were covered with huge old pine and oak trees interspersed with color-contrasting white birch. Yes, northern Minnesota, with its clear unpolluted lakes and streams, was a nature wonderland.

Homesteads were few in number and far apart. The land had been settled primarily by Swedes, Norwegians and Germans and the houses, a few constructed with logs and although not elaborate in any sense, exhibited pride of ownership.

George Whaley family Minnesota cabin near Sioux Reservation

Photo courtesy of Delevan Whaley

Northern Minnesota, although now more heavily populated, is still one of the few areas in the United States that has retained a goodly portion of its natural beauty. The settlers who first viewed this land, unravaged by the white man, must surely have died with a pictorial memory that can never again be duplicated.

Shortly after 4 P.M. the train slowed even more, then moved onto a siding. There before the guardsmen's eyes was sprawling Camp Ripley, a huge reservation covering some 53,000 acres.

Troops detrain at Camp Ripley—note open windows on cars!
Photo courtesy of Minnesota Military Museum

Orders were given to detrain, and soon troops led by guides were marching toward pyramid-type tents stretching virtually as far as the eye could see. Each tent was sixteen feet square and provided quarters for six men. The guardsmen were extremely surprised to find tents had already been pitched. Canvas cots were soon issued, packs unrolled and blankets from their individual packs in place.

Kitchens consisted of a canvas fly (cover only) and a single ridge pole, with wire mesh installed around the bottom. They appeared to have been designed to keep out the rodents or keep in those unhappy men assigned to kitchen police (KP) duty.

There were no ice boxes; instead, holes were dug and lined with boards. Ice was placed in the bottom of the pit. Perishables were stored above the ice on board racks with more boards and canvas placed over the top of the hole. Surprisingly enough, the crude ice box served its purpose and kept food from spoiling.

Dusk was settling in when the men lined up for supper. As the soldiers started to move forward in the chow line, a low monotone hum could be heard and Minnesota mosquitos, often referred to as the "Minnesota state bird," came diving out of the sky. Cunning, these mosquitos knew the men couldn't lay down their mess gear to fight them off. All the guardsmen could do was battle the miserable pests for their share of the food. That night everyone slept with their heads under the blankets.

On Sunday, time off was allowed for all guardsmen, who desired to do so, to attend church. The balance of the day was spent in preparing for the forthcoming field exercise.

The following morning, somewhere around the first croak of the frog, the men stood reveille in the dark. Of course the mosquitos had nearly finished their meal before the men had started through the serving line. There were reports that one had landed at the airstrip and the ground crew would have filled him with gas—if the damn thing hadn't had hemmorhoids.

Along with the breakfast, each guardsmen was issued a sack lunch consisting of three sandwiches—one ham, one jam, the other cheese. Oh, yes, and an apple, which they wouldn't learn was green until sun-up.

Falling in with forty-or-so-pound packs and weapons, the guardsmen were soon marchng down dirt trail-like roads, in single file on both sides, heading into the deep forest. This was the day the three battalions in each of the four infantry regiments would begin performance tests in all phases of combat operations.

Troops march to maneuver area—Camp Ripley, 1937.
Photo courtesy of Minnesota Military Museum

The initial test involved battalions taking up pursuit of a withdrawing enemy force. The advance guard company took up the pursuit with a point (scouts) well out front. Flank guards were dispatched to both flanks to detect enemy presence or warn of an enemy flanking attack. Also, the flank guards served as a connecting link to adjacent units. The advance guard company followed, held in reserve to clear out any small pockets of enemy resistance set up by the enemy's delaying forces.

Moving along to the rear was the main body, the balance of the battalion, consisting of the battalion headquarters, the two remaining rifle companies and a heavy weapons (machine gun) company. The main body (battalion) would be committed only if strong enemy resistance was encountered.

Temperatures continued to crowd or break the 100 degree mark and sweat poured down the backs of guardsmen dressed in woolen shirts, khaki jodhpurs and heavy woolen wrap leggings. Only the broad brimmed campaign hat was appropriate attire for the prevailing weather.

Going was tough enough for the men marching down the road, but for the flank guards it was sheer hell thrashing through thick underbrush, jumping small streams, wading through marsh lands and circling lakes while attempting to keep up with the main body of troops.

It seemed like each bush contained a thousand mosquitos and deerflies. Liking perspiration, they stung the men at will. What the mosquitos and deerflies couldn't accomplish, the chiggers did and those on scouting duty were soon referring to the pesky vermin as crotch crickets. There was no problem keeping the adrenaline flowing in the point scouts and flank guards as the brush timber undergrowth had a plentiful supply of timber rattlers.

Umpires had initiated several enemy delaying action problems and as the afternoon wore on, the mythical enemy main defense line outposts were reached. Major Henry "Bob" R. Heath, Fort Dodge, Iowa, battalion commander of the 2nd Bn., 133rd Inf., was a World War I veteran and a good tactician. He quickly moved the battalion into assault positions, called for artillery and mortar barrages and launched his attack. Bayonets were fixed—blank ammunition was fired during the assault, creating a bit of realism. Companies were soon on their objective after action reports were submitted, and the test ended.

Never at a loss for wit, PFC Richard "Dick" Lee reported the umpires were wrong about the enemy being driven from the hill. He allowed as how the hill was still occupied by a half million mosquitos, thousands of grasshoppers and a few hundred snakes.

After occupying and outposting the objective, digging individual defense positions (foxholes), the men were given time to eat their sandwiches. Some of the men became nauseous, not from the green apple but from the heat and from drinking too much water.

To remedy the situation strict water discipline was implemented—one canteen per day was allocated with no replenishment allowed from lakes, streams or farm houses.

Corporal Quench, (we'll give him that moniker) a powerful man, was accustomed to drinking heavily of water while working out of doors during the summer. He drank conservatively from his own canteen, borrowing a drink, as he called it, here and there from others, quipping, "I'll pay you back when we get back to camp!" Everyone was hot, dusty, thirsty, miserable and more than a little disgusted with Corporal Quench for his water-mooching ways.

Now back on the march, deeper into the forest to a bivouac area, the company at last halted for a rest break. PFC Tip O'Flaskagin, the devilish-minded little Irishman, could soon be seen watching a tiny frog hopping around on the bank of a nearby stream.

Suddenly O'Flaskagin dropped to his knees, reached out and snatched the little critter. He then pulled his canteen from the carrier, looked at the frog, then his canteen. Seeing this, PFC Virgil Gage turned to Hank and said, "Now I wonder just what in hell old O'Flaskagin is up to."

Soon the little Irishman was back at the roadside where the men were sitting. Corporal Quench sat a short distance away, his back turned, oblivious to O'Flaskagin's activities while he was on safari at the streamside.

O'Flaskagin, standing not far behind Corporal Quench, raised his finger to his lips imploring silence. He then carefully crawled to where the thirsty one's pack lay on the ground behind him. Quietly he loosened the cap of Quench's canteen, inserted the little croaker, then loosely replaced the cap to allow for oxygen inside.

Back on the road marching, Quench was soon asking other men for a drink from their canteens. No one responded. When the column next halted, the parched-lip one decided they were now near enough to the bivouac area that he could safely drink some of his own water.

Everyone watched attentively as the huge corporal unscrewed the canteen lid. Quench didn't drink from a pop bottle with one side of the opening pressed against his upper lip, he just wrapped his lips around the neck and drained it. Now he was really thirsty and, in his usual eager way, started to gulp water from his canteen like he had just received word that the only remaining well in Minnesota had gone dry.

The expression in his eyes when the tiny croaker landed on his tongue was a sight to behold. The look was not easily described—but one could say his expressions were not of anxiety, fear or contentment—nor did he look like the cat that just ate the canary, but he did bear a very strong resemblance to a corporal that had just damn nigh swallowed a frog.

As Quench opened his mouth, the little croaker made a heroic leap for life and with record breaking bounds headed for the stream. Needless to say, Sir Quench, the oasis seeker, never asked anyone to share their canteen contents again and no one ever heard a croak out of him.

As they marched toward the bivouac area mother nature lost control of her elements and rain fell in torrents—caused everyone to contemplate the possibility that all of Minnesota's 10,000 lakes had become airborne and were being released from the clouds at the same time.

Shoes, not already filled with water, soon were. The short time allocated at break precluded removal of wrap leggings to empty water from shoes. Besides it would have taken the entire break period for some men to remove the sandburs and nettles from their leggings.

As they slogged down the muddy roads, they passed several barns and cattlesheds that could have provided shelter. It was the first time Hank ever longed for the life of a cow. But, maneuvers are designed to afford as much realism as possible and nothing can be more realistic than rainwater.

Army raincoats of that era were designed to keep sweat in and very little water out. A steady flow of sweat and water trickled down the men's backs all the way to their shoes. Pvt. George J. "Jazzy" Northrup was carrying an envelope of coffee in his rear pocket and said he could have heated a cup when he later emptied his shoes—that is, if he'd had a dry match.

Ten miles later the column reached the bivouac area. Packs were unrolled with drenched blankets and pup tents were pitched. A stand-up dinner of beefstew that tasted like alley cat alamode was served—liberally mixed with rainwater. The meal afforded the privates another opportunity to make a decision during the maneuver. They could either tip their campaign hats back and let the water drip down their backs or tip them forward and let the water drain into their mess kits—decisions - decisions!

There was no casual after-supper talking—everyone gulped the food and ran like hell for the tents. They bedded down in fanny sogged splendor to wrestle the chiggers and mosquitos to see who would sleep in the blankets. Would the joys of this Mussolini described picnic ever cease?

Early the next morning the battalion moved out of bivouac and dug World War I type trenches for defensive positions. By the time the trenches were dug using individual entrenching tools, everyone was muddy, in addition to being water soaked. Examining his billfold Corporal Spooner screamed, "Dammit, the water even took the curl out of my girlfriend's hair in her snapshot!"

Next they were tested in a "battalion in withdrawal action." While the main body moved to the rear, one company with attached machine guns performed rear guard duty, their mission being to delay the enemy until the battalion could withdraw and establish more advantageous defensive positions.

Much emphasis was placed on the withdrawal action, for this phase of battle has always been known to be the most difficult to coordinate. Control becomes a critical problem and contact with troops on either flank can be lost.

Hank was with the flank guard, and he knew contact with the adjacent unit was good when he heard a man from Fort Dodge's "G" Company shout, "Damn, that was close." He had leaped over a log and crushed a rattlesnake's head under his heavy soled shoe!

Umpires created several situations wherein the enemy caught up with the rear guard, and delaying actions had to be implemented to hamper their advance. It was then the umpires advised Major Heath the enemy was moving up rapidly, and the battalion must be prepared to dig in and organize defensive positions under simulated fire.

While one company of the battalion held the enemy at bay, the other two companies established defensive positions by digging individual trenches or foxholes as they were later called in World War II. Fields of fire were established for machine guns and when that was completed, the company out front established reserve positions to the rear. The enemy attack was repulsed and the test was concluded.

The cooks had brought a warm meal up, chicken chow mein. It was one of those meals—you know, the kind you can't wait to take the second bite of to see if it's as bad as the first! The troops had gone through the line at a tactical five-pace interval and were now seating themselves on logs on the ground.

One of the unit's prime troublemakers was old "Bully Boy", the kid Hank had problems with back in grade school. When he walked past he intentionally kicked sand in the mess kit of James Stamy. Stamy, a much smaller man, rose to challenge the guy. Hank decided he would attempt to whip the bully and stepped between them. The bully caught Hank by surprise and delivered a blow to the chin that sent him reeling back over a log.

Hank leaped to his feet and the fight was on. Finally Lt. House heard the commotion and came down and broke up the fight, saying he couldn't allow bare knuckle fighting; someone might get hurt. Hank couldn't help wonder what kept him so damn long; he was already hurt!

Back in camp, as was the army custom at the time, the chant went up for a grudge fight. The boxing gloves were brought out, and Hank and his avowed enemy were soon donning them. Actually the padding had shifted so much in the old pre-depression gloves that they might as well have used bare knuckles. The bully was still quite a bit bigger than Hank, but Hank had done a little boxing since they had last done battle. Still in all, the guy was tough and Hank had no illusion about winning a decisive victory, for this was the third time he had fought him.

Tired Co. E, 135th Inf. Regt. troops return from maneuvers, Camp Ripley, Minnesota.

Photo courtesy of Gen. William Kreger

Hank moved cautiously from his corner, knowing he could in no way win a slug fest, for the man was much stronger. Dancing and weaving, Hank kept his left glove in the guy's face so much the fellow must have thought he was in a leather factory.

At last "Bully Boy" came at Hank with a flurry of wild punches. Hank ducked his head, but one grazed his hair and the next caught him on his already sore jaw. Hank skidded on the ground and came to rest among the spectators. A couple of the boys stood him on his feet. The odds seemed better now for Hank was seeing three of his opponent, and he knew he ought to be able to hit at least one of them.

Oh, yes, rounds were called, but only when the fighters appeared too exhausted to continue. Hank must have looked mighty tired, for they finally called a round. Sgt. Donald Moon and Floyd "Cocky" Espinosa, both from Mason City's Co. "F," came to Hank's corner. Actually there was no corner and no ring; it was an open field.

Cocky had seen quite a bit of ring action. His advice to Hank was, "When the guy comes at you throwing wild roundhouse punches, fade back, give him a couple of lefts. Then when he is fully extended, step back quickly and come over the top of his arm with your right hand like you throw a baseball." Hank, a pitcher, understood his instructions real well.

Someone hit the claxton that hung by a tent, normally only used to sound a fire alarm or signal a gas attack. Hank was getting a lot of encouragement from the crowd, and he was determined to stretch the guy's neck so far it would split the seams in the crotch of his underwear.

He didn't have to wait long, for "Bully Boy" came at him swinging roundhouse haymakers with both hands. Hank, as per instructions, moved back with the punches, then after his adversary had made a strong rush, Hank took a quick hop step backward, braced his feet and came over the top of his opponent's arms with a punch he started somewhere behind the camp watertower. He then followed through with all the strength he could muster.

The punch caught old bully boy smack dab on the end of his nose. He looked up at Hank in amazement. His nose started bleeding and now Hank could tell by the vengeful look in his eyes that he was angry and in addition to that, madder than hell. Time after time he rushed at Hank flailing both fists, and each time he met Hank's right fist on his lower nose and mouth. Hank was throwing strikes every time.

Determined, he finally nailed Hank with a strong right hand—Hank moved back to allow the cobwebs to clear from his brain. A few minutes later the referee, who was cleaning his fingernails or something less important, finally called the fight and gave it to Hank on points. It was a good thing he did, for Hank was nearly out on his feet and felt like he had fought a buzz saw and lost every round.

Hank awoke the next morning, stiff, battered, skinned up, and bruised with both eyes badly blackened and puffed. His jaw felt like it was dislocated and he could hardly eat his breakfast. Was this Mussolini's idea of a picnic? It sure as hell wasn't Hank's. Unlike the picnics he had attended before, no one even passed him the fried chicken or potato salad. But he did appreciate it when Specialist O'Kettlebelly, the cook, passed him some raw beef to put on his blackened eyes.

The morning had been set aside for care and cleaning of equipment. Hank sat on the edge of his cot cleaning his weapon. Two of his tent mates, Virgil Gage and Merlin Crouse, encouraged Hank to go challenge the bully again, saying he'd no doubt continue to make life miserable for him if he didn't. Hank wasn't too fond of the idea, but it did have some merit. Hank thought, "I'll do it!"

When he arrived at the old bully boy's tent, he found him sitting on his cot holding his head in his hands. It was with one helluva lot of reluctance that Hank finally summoned up the courage to ask the guy if he wanted to finish the fight.

It was when the ruffian looked up and refused to accept the challenge that Hank knew he had not completely lost the battle. The guy's broken nose was taped and a front tooth was missing. Hank turned and walked back to his tent. From that day forward, the man never bullied him again. In a way the experience was very beneficial to Hank for he now knew for damn sure he didn't want to be a professional boxer.

That Saturday morning, August 16, 1937, the entire division marched to the camp's one mile by one-half mile airfield to participate in a division parade. The heat was again over 100 degrees and the full packs and equipment bore heavily into sweating backs as they marched at quick cadence into position.

Camp Ripley airport
Photo courtesy of Minnesota Military Museum

This was the first time most midwesterners had seen an entire division on a parade field. Even at a reduced strength of some 8,000 men it was a stirring sight. Thousands of civilian spectators from Minnesota, North and South Dakota and Iowa lined the parade ground.Moving on line were:

67th (Iowa) Infantry Brigade - consisting of the 133rd and 168th Infantry Regiments.

68th Infantry Brigade - consisting of the 135th (Minnesota) Infantry Regiment (1st Bn. from North Dakota) and the 164th (North Dakota) Infantry Regiment.

59th (Minnesota) Field Artillery Regiment - consisting of the 151st and 125th; each with two direct support artillery battalions equipped with towed 75mm Howitzers.

185th (Iowa) Field Artillery Regiment - consisting of two general support battalions equipped with towed 155mm Howitzers.

Special troops included South Dakota's 109th Engineer Regiment, Iowa's 136th Medical Regiment, the 109th Quartermaster Regiments from Iowa, Minnesota and South Dakota. Minnesota provided the 109th Ordnance Co. and South Dakota a Signal Company. Rounding out the force was the 34th Division Military Police from Minnesota.

Now the entire divisision—plus special unassigned units, such as anti-aircraft artillery—were assembled on the field. Their American flags, unit colors and guideons were an impressive sight in the morning sun.

Orders were given to display equipment. Packs were unrolled, pup tents pitched and all equipment displayed to include two heavy wool blankets, socks, underwear, towels, soap, shaving kits, etc.

Men stood at parade rest, a rigid position in those days, and were called to attention while the corps commander, division commander, four governors and designated staff members trooped the line in vehicles.

With the field inspection concluded, tents were struck, packs again were rolled and shouldered and troops fell into position in a company front. General Tinley, the division commander, then gave the order to pass in review.

At the rigid position of attention, the heat (hovering around 110 degrees) was becoming unbearable as each of the four infantry regiments, artillery and special troops, in columns led by the respective bands, marched around the perimeter to pass before the review stand.

Some of the men, who were not accustomed to being out in the hot sun for so long a period, began keeling over like dominoes. With fixed bayonets by their right shoulders, it was amazing some didn't impale themselves.

The 113th Cavalry Color Guard leads the way.
Photo courtesy of Meyel Haack

Co. E, 135th Inf. Regt. passes in review at Camp Ripley, Minnesota.
Photo courtesy of William Kreger, Brig. General Ret.

With the 133rd Inf. Regt. band out front, led by drum major, Glen "Joe" Little, the regiment was soon on the march. Now out of their rigid in ranks position the men began to feel better. As they approached the review stand, the command, "Eyes Right" was given, and with the commanders saluting and all eyes right other than those in the extreme right column, near perfect alignment was achieved.

Maj. General Stanley H. Ford, Seventh Corps area; Maj. Gen. Matthew A. Tinley, 34th Division Commander; and Governors Nelson Kraschel of Iowa, William Langer of North Dakota, Les Jensen of South Dakota, and Elmer Benson of Minnesota received the honors. As the last troops passed the review stand, National Guard aircraft swooped low in a final salute.

With much relief, the men marched off the field. Adrenaline was no longer flowing and dozens of men could be seen staggering from the column, then falling to the ground. Did it provide pride of unit? Yes! Did it teach discipline? One would have to admit it did, but many men suffered heat stroke and had queazy stomachs for days.

Passes were issued to those who were not assigned detail or guard duty. Corporal Eugene Gordon had been allowed to drive his car to Camp Ripley and invited Hank to ride into town. He announced he would be leaving shortly after dinner. By the time Hank and Gage had showered, the company chow line had formed. The situation looked desperate—if Hank had to wait at the end of the line he was afraid he'd miss his ride.

At last one of Hank's better ideas came to him. He hadn't strained his brain for pranks since Cousin Willobee left the farm. He bounced the idea off Gage and Crouse and they readily agreed it could solve the long line problem.

Mess kits in hand, they strolled leisurely past the long line formed at the edge of the gravel street across from the kitchen tent. Hank walked casually up to the top cook, Frank Meller, and asked when chow would be served. Meller responded, "Oh, in about five minutes." The tentmates strolled back past the chow line and Hank griped loudly, "Hell, I'm not about to wait in this line another half hour—I'm going back to my tent!"

Those in the chow line overheard and said a few choice words; the line broke up. Hank and his two tentmates walked into their tents, crawled under the back tent flaps and hastened back to the kitchen tent and were first in line. They were through the line and eating when first cook Meller began wondering where all the men were—finally he had the bugler blow chow call again and the troops came flying out of their tents. Fortunately the men had a good sense of humor and nearly everyone took the prank in good spirits.

Hank had solved his worries about being on time for his ride and when dinner was over he, Corporal Spooner, Specialists O'Kettlebelly and O'Flaskagin were soon traveling down the road with Corporal Gordon to Little Falls.

Spooner was one of those rare individuals who could have worn his army blanket and still have looked debonair. Just alighting from the automobile, he reeked of aristocracy. His walking gait was steady and controlled—head high with nose tilted slightly upward. For some reason he didn't trip on cracks in the sidewalk like Hank did when he tried to emulate him.

Of late Spooner had started to let his mustache grow out just a tad with a slight twirl on the edges. Even women across the street stopped to stare at him. As they walked past a grocery store, a pretty young teenager nearly fell over an apple basket display out front while attempting to sneak one last glance. Hank was beginning to wish he had brought a notebook with him.

But Hank's observations would be delayed a bit. Everyone wanted to see the house where Charles A. Lindbergh, the great trans-Atlantic flyer, had grown to manhood. Lindbergh no longer lived in the United States. Still grieving over the loss of his son through kidnapping and murder, he had moved his family to England. He desperately wanted out of the limelight and feared for the safety of his family. England was chosen because that country's murder and burglary rate was less than ten percent of that in the United States.

It was a thrill to see Lindbergh's home and walk the same streets he had. The entire nation had been sad at the great man's departure, but he had at least accomplished something: Congress passed more stringent kidnapping laws.

After strolling the streets for awhile, they went to a cafe for a snack. Of course, Spooner, O'Flaskagin and O'Kettlebelly wanted to have a few drinks. Corporal Gordon, a married man, decided he'd like to take in a movie and Hank chose to go with the worldly trio. Hank was too young to imbibe, but the proprietor said nothing about his entry into his establishment—perhaps because he was in uniform.

Seated in a booth they were soon enjoying the atmosphere and the music of a four-piece band playing, what else, Scandinavian music (the town was crawling with Swedes.) Now O'Kettlebelly always considered himself a fantastic dancer, but in actuality his repertoire of fancy footwork was pretty well limited to waltzes. But, old twinkle-toes was convinced his only appreciable competition in banging brogans against the floor was Fred Astaire, the famous dancer of the era.

Deciding there wouldn't be any slower music, O'Kettlebelly asked a girl in the next booth to dance. She consented and he threw a smug glance at his buddies while escorting her onto the floor. The next dance was a polka and old twinkle-toes waded in with feet flailing and elbows flying while the gal held on for dear life. About the second time around the floor he caught sight of some of the local boys doing the stomping bit and quickly worked that into his routine.

By now the floor was quite crowded. There was a lot of knee-knocking, body-blocking and pushing for space to dance. O'Kettlebelly hadn't as yet stomped on his dancing partner's feet, for by now she was holding him at arm's length. But the proprietor came over and asked him to slow it up a bit—said a man had complained about him stomping on his toes, even though the guy was still seated in a booth. While the proprietor talked to O'Kettlebelly, the gal took off for the powder room—one could almost see the splinters fly as she raced across the floor.

At last the band played some slow romantic music. Corporal Spooner arose, adjusted his meticulously pressed trousers, straightened his tie and gave his mustache a slight twirl. Then the suave one asked a gorgeous blond to dance. She literally flew out of the booth and into his arms.

Spooner was soon dancing with her so closely O'Flaskagin said he couldn't tell which one was wearing the brassiere. Skillfully he glided with her around the floor until they were in a remote corner—there old lover-boy just up and gave her one of his Spooner specials—Wow! The kiss, old Spooner professes (with no hint of exaggeration), is designed to make a gal's slip roll up and down like a window shade.

Unfortunately while Spooner was giving the gal the thrill of her life, her boyfriend walked through the door. The irate suitor dashed up to Spooner with fire in his eyes. There was no talking it over; he just cut loose with a haymaker swing. No, he didn't catch Spooner off-guard—the great one side-stepped the blow and the jealous one's punch nearly tore off a booth hat rack post.

While the guy circled the dance floor weaving, bobbing and howling with pain, the four guardsmen slipped unnoticed out the side door before half the Swedes in Little Falls could descend on them. Thus ended Hank's first opportunity to watch the great Spooner in action. Yes, he concluded, he could learn a lot from the mighty master of female mind manipulation. But, that would have to wait for another time.

Early the following Monday, under cover of darkness, the division took to the field for regimental and division tactical tests. They would oppose the regular army's 7th Infantry Division, which had been encamped some thirty miles away.

Each man carried with him the inevitable ham, jam, and cheese sandwiches and the never-to-be-forgotten green apple. It was August

18th and everyone wondered just where in the hell they managed to find all the green apples.

Since the food was purchased locally, Specialist O'Kettlebelly speculated that the Minnesota Guard's procurement officer, or some high-up officer or politician, had a relative with an orchard full of unripened apples.

On the other hand, the miserable sack lunches afforded the privates an opportunity to make on-the-spot decisions during the exercise. They could decide which sandwich to eat for an appetizer, main course and dessert and into which brush pile they would throw the green apple. Another decision to make—what was a private to do!

Hank was by now a private first class and his pay had gone up from $1.00 per day to $1.35. He was assigned maneuver duties as a runner to carry messages between the 1st Battalion and his own assigned 2nd Battalion. This would prove a most interesting job as it meant a lot of fast dashs through the timber, for radios had not been issued to guard companies.

Major Leonard Greenfield of Fairfield was the 1st Battalion Commander. Greenfield was a hulking and powerful, but jovial, man. He was extremely intelligent and, as Hank was to learn, a very capable and experienced tactician, having commanded a machine gun company during World War I.

Hank was allowed to observe as Major Greenfield briefed his commanders and staff at the operations map. The major's situation briefing and the operation orders he issued were clear and concise.

Everyone was further impressed with the major's insistence that all the non-commissioned officers and men be kept abreast of the situation and aware of the role they were playing. For some reason, Major Greenfield took a liking to Hank and, when he was not busy, he explained some of the rudiments of tactics to him.

Greenfield left an everlasting impression on everyone, including the umpires. He was convincing proof that, with adequate funding, manpower and updated equipment, he and commanders like him would have provided a highly viable military force of guardsmen.

Of course, most regular Army officers did not hold the guard in high esteem, feeling their officers were people of political influence. On the other hand, many West Point cadets were the recipients of political appointments. Then, too, in time of war the guard officers held rank they felt should be reserved for those of the regular establishment.

In the pre World War II National Guard, those commanders at the battalion and lower levels of command seemed to be predominently World War I veterans and well qualified, although some appointments at the higher level were no doubt politically motivated.

The maneuvers proved to be quite successful, and much was learned by those who never before had been in the field with a large force. However, the maneuver ended with sadness. Two young soldiers picked up an artillery dud, probably thinking of a souvenir. The shell exploded, killing both of them.

The balance of the week was spent in training and firing individual weapons on the rifle range. When the week ended, they headed back to Happyland. For years all field maneuvers were compared to Ripley in '37. Even when going was rough during World War II, someone would quip, "If you think this is tough, you should have been at Ripley in '37!"

Although Hank and the others had seen many weapons of war for the first time, nothing new to the army's arsenal had been introduced to the guardsmen. There were many heated discussions involving armaments already issued. Three men were usually the center of the verbal action: James Stamy, John Richardson and Richard Lee, all exceptionally intelligent men. Hank marveled at their inquisitive minds, inventive thinking and theories, all of which were far above those of the average person. Their conjectures on futuristic armaments were unique for that time. Hank hoped some day they would be allowed to use some of their creative thinking.

Hank's hopes were to be fulfilled. James Stamy finished his last semester at Iowa State College after World War II. He became right hand man to German rocket scientist, Werhner von Braun, and helped put up the first U.S. guided missiles, then contributed much to the development of the rocket that put the first U.S. satellite into orbit. As a part of the NASA team, he helped put the first man in space and later, the first man on the moon. As a side note, he was chief engineer on the project that developed offshore buoys for sophisticated weather reporting—what a contribution to technology!

John Richardson was graduated from and received his PhD at the University of Iowa. During World War II at Massachusetts Institute of Technology, John helped develop radar for military use. Then at a naval ordnance test station and at Hughes Aircraft he contributed to the development of computerized sight systems for air-to-air missiles. Next, his inventive mind led him to Rockwell International, where he helped develop electro optic systems for laser applications—a great man indeed.

Surprisingly their hometown has never honored James Stamy and John Richardson, although in later years a newspaper article about Stamy appeared in the "Daily Freeman Journal". Much acclaim has been given an Iowa astronaut, but none to this great man who contributed heavily to man's first trip to the moon! Richardson is yet to receive any acknowledgement locally for his strong contributions to national defense.

Then let's not forget Richard "Dick" Lee. Dick went on to become a commissioned officer in the U.S. Air Force, retiring as a colonel. His alert, keen mind resulted in his becoming an expert logistics officer. From the early 1950s until his retirement in 1967 he was heavily involved in developing better logistics systems for the Air Force. As a special projects officer, he was a part of a highly qualified team of intelligent men that developed a standard automated logistics system which was installed in U.S. Air Force bases worldwide. It contributed heavily to the successful supply of forces in Vietnam—a great benefit to the country.

It is hoped by the author that these writings have dispelled any thoughts that a National Guard summer encampment was like a picnic or that its ranks were devoid of competent personnel.

In Happyland the baseball season was capped off by the Blairsburg nine playing a strong Ellsworth-Radcliffe team for the fair championship. Ellsworth's Carrol and Maynard Kuhfus, now joined by their brother Glen, played fabulous baseball. Hank remembered Carrol and Maynard well, for they were among the long ball hitters when Hank and Bud Brandt were hawking the sidelines to snitch up fowl balls for their kids' team.

Both teams played their hearts out and the game remained tied inning after inning. At last the sun descended, but the play continued as long as the players could see the ball. At fourteen innings the game was at last called—still tied. Both teams were declared winners.

Sadly, those days will never be duplicated, for baseball no longer draws the crowds in small towns and but few have semi-pro teams. The betting, although not for high stakes, was active. Many was the time someone, who had made a rare substantial wager, shouted, "Strike him out" or, "Out of the park and it's worth five dollars." My, how those old-timers loved baseball.

Maurice Stark, retired Fort Dodge attorney and long-time friend of the author, can substantiate the old-timers' love of baseball. Stark recalls a favorite story told to him by Walter B. Stevens, Editor of the "Fort Dodge Messenger." It seems Ronald Reagan, the future President of the United States, then a sportscaster for radio station WHO-Des Moines, had agreed to umpire a baseball game at Gowrie. Reagan made what the hometown fans felt was a poor call and was all but run out of town!

XIII
FLICKERING HOPE, THEN WAR CLOUDS

Cool crisp mornings had begun to work magic on the landscape. The beautiful, colorful wild flowers in the city dump had started to wilt; baby birds were now on the wing; this year's crop of rabbits had left their mothers; fields of golden corn had commenced to mature. Willie Sipmore was laying in his winter supply of homebrew and everyone was certain an early fall was on the way.

Willie had a pretty good handle on what stock he needed to lay in for the winter. However, on the national scene, unsold inventories were beginning to build up in some big businesses and industries.

The harsh reality was beginning to settle upon the nation that, as Roosevelt feared, business and industry could not provide enough jobs to offset the New Deal programs which had been dropped or drastically reduced in the 1937 budget.

Many of Roosevelt's outspoken critics, and a few advisers, made jokes of Roosevelt's budget statement that the nation was on the way out of the depression. Now, again, the purchasing power was down, breadlines were growing longer in cities, and the stock market had declined severely.

Funds were not budgeted and readily available to take action immediatly to restore programs. Where were the people who staunchly insisted the budget be cut and the national debt reduced? They, as is often the case in politics, were busy blaming everyone but themselves for their shortsightedness.

Of course, Roosevelt had been concerned about national indebtedness and he knew increasing the money available meant devaluation of the dollar. The United States dollar was fully backed by federal gold reserves and could be redeemed for gold.

Congress in 1934 had authorized the reduction of dollar-backed gold to be held in reserve. Roosevelt had caused gold to be revalued from $20.67 to $35 per ounce, thus allowing more money to be circulated. Gold was no longer to be held by individuals as legal tender.

But wait, was the lowering of dollar gold reserves critical at that time? Roosevelt and the legislators thought so. Today they would be appalled, shocked and, in addition to that, damn angry, for at this writing the gold reserve as a monetary standard has literally been blown off the charts.

During the period 1980 to 1992, Presidents Ronald Reagan's and George Bush's administrations compiled a mammoth national indebtedness—used primarily to stimulate big business. A drop in value of the dollar enabled the collection of more taxes, but the increased revenue could in no way keep pace with the rising interest and principal on the massive debt. Government reports indicated little increase in the wholesale price index. Although the rise in the cost of living index was reported as minimal, prices continued to soar in retail outlets. Gold standard—there was no gold standard. The government just borrowed more money from domestic and foreign investors, revved up the presses and printed more money!

But first things first; let's get back to Happyland. Students were beginning to gather around the beautiful old campanile that stood, surrounded by lofty elm trees, between the Happyland junior and senior high schools. The pebble dash structure bore no small resemblance to the corner guard tower of a medieval castle.

The campanile's bell had rung out in celebration of Happyland athletic victories before the turn of the century. However, now its clear, sweet melodic tones were tolling students to their classrooms for the beginning of the 1937-1938 school year.

Soon clean, neat, but not overdressed, students were pouring in school doors. Most girls wore skirts, blouses or sweaters, bobbie socks and white saddle shoes. The boys, except for a very few, were unpretentiously attired in corduroy trousers, white tee shirts or sweat shirts and sweaters—preferably a letter sweater.

Oh yes, there were cliques, for that will always be so as people share different interests, and friendships cannot be dictated. However, as the depression wore on, few students belittled others' clothing, for if they did, their popularity dwindled rapidly. Would that the same attitudes prevailed at this writing!

Cousin Clinty, many of Hank's older friends and Oscar Johnson, his former baseball coach, now principal, had advised Hank he'd best forget football as he could be injured badly and spoil his opportunity for a career in baseball—but in the end he was determined to play football.

Reporting to practice, he was already in fine condition, for he had spent the summer stacking eighty-pound hay bales, unloading truck loads of boxed canned goods, sugar and flour, etc. at H. A. Selby's new grocery warehouse. To rest up from this work, he pitched a couple of softball games each week and baseball nearly every Sunday.

Hank had gained a little weight and no longer had to run fast in a rainstorm to get wet. He had been issued a uniform that almost fit. Then too, he no longer had to put cotton in the toes of his last year's brand new secondhand football shoes; he was as ready as he would ever be.

Ralph Burton, Armor Miller, Virgil Gage, and Merlin "Jumbo" Crouse were among those still around from the 1936 championship team. Clark Mollenhoff, a big lad who played center, had transferred in from Algona. Ralph Burton, an all-state end, had been moved to quarterback; John McCollough would occupy the fullback position; and Hank, a reserve end the past year, had been switched to a halfback slot. John Boeye or Joe Segar would occupy the other halfback position. Gage would be back at one end and Wayne Maudlin at the other. The balance of the line would be manned by John Rutlege, Jack Marvel, Don Bradshaw, Keith Draper, Melvin Greenley, and Bill North.

Unfortunately, Hank would only last until they met a strong, big, fast Sac City team. The Sac City backfield was getting through the front line and into the secondary with plenty of blocking interference still out ahead.

During that fateful game Coach Robert "Bob" Lamson devised a little strategy that involved Hank—damn little, as Hank only weighed 140 pounds, not counting his lucky penny.

He had taken Hank out of the game and whispered sweet do-somethings in his ear and let him in on all the destruction he was to unleash on the opposition. The imaginative mentor then wound Hank up tighter than his Aunt Minnie's purse strings, stood back and watched him spring with false confidence back into the ferocious fray.

Somehow the opposing team hadn't got the word on what a devastating dogooder Hank was charged up to be—and really wasn't ready to concede defeat when he unveiled the coach's trickery. The cozy conversation between the coach and Hank had involved his dashing in like Dauntless Dolliver from his defensive line backing position and bowling over the opposing blockers like ten pins with a crushing below-the-knees cross body block.

Everything proceeded as planned and when the ball was snapped, Hank was off and running like the bangtails at Churchill Downs. The opposing blockers started through the side of the line with their number one star, Fleetfoot Flanigan, or some such person, tagging safely along behind.

Hank's rib-rocking (his ribs) cross body block was successful, and the leaders of the protective procession piled up on him. The scatback was knocked on his backside; the crowd roared and a minute later Hank crawled out from under a half ton of humanity and, to his surprise as well as the coach's, was uninjured.

Hank glanced at the bench to see the coach grinning as if the school board had just doubled his salary, along with giving him exclusive fishing rights in the school fountain. Coach Lamson had held up his hand to Hank and shook his head up and down, indicating Hank had handled the situation to his satisfaction.

Hank's head finally stopped whirling as he walked back to his defensive position and, by the time the next play started, he could hardly wait for the opportunity to upend the opposition again.

The play developed as had the previous one and Hank was ready to launch himself at the blockers with literally pain's taking precision. But something told him, as the blockers hesitated, that all was not right on the right side of the defense line. Because of the slight delay of the men running interference, his baffling block was premature. On that play he might have failed to turn the pumpkin into a coach, but he sure as hell turned the coach into a pumpkin.

The worthy opponents raised their knees high like harness ponies and pranced over Hank's prostrate position on the playing field. He had neglected to protect his forearms and one of their prime movers stomped his hand full of shoe cleats, just as a passing gesture.

Back on his feet, Hank could see that his left hand looked like it had been imprisoned for six months in a waffle iron. His knuckles were unsocketed and his forefinger was pointing so far straight up in the air that he couldn't have pointed at the culprit who clobbered him unless they stood the guy on the town watertower.

Walking over to the sideline, Hank conversed with the coach, who allowed as how there was something wrong with his hand. The coach grasped his fingers one by one, giving them each a tug. When the knuckles snapped back in place, it sounded like someone pulling the corks out of three champagne bottles. A few tongue depressors, some sponge rubber and half a roll of tape later, the coach said he was as good as new and put him back in the ball game.

Hank's hand throbbed and pained all through practice the next week, but somehow he got by tackling with a semi-cross body block and right hand tackle. However, his enthusiasm for playing was dropping as rapidly as the pain was increasing.

The following game he was still in the starting lineup. A few plays into the game he tackled the opposing fullback. There was no one-armed tackling of the big guy, for he was moving like a runaway locomotive. Hank had to use his left hand. Excruciating pain shot up his arm, and it felt like a bone in his hand was pulling apart. Hank, dejected and thoroughly disgusted, walked head down to the sidelines.

The next day Dr. Crumpton took x-rays, which divulged one broken bone and two badly cracked ones. He was thankful it was not his right hand, for at least his baseball pitching days were not over. Although the team was not championship caliber, it did go on to a winning season. Hank was happy to have at least won his letter.

By the time basketball season rolled around, Hank's hand had mended though his knuckle joints were still weak and sore in spite of the fact that he had squeezed a small rubber ball for a month. Hank and Max Doolittle handled the guard positions. John Boeye and Joe Segar were at forward and the fabulous Ralph Burton was at center. Clark Mollenhoff, the team's only above-six-footer, was just coming into his own as a basketball player and, as the first reserve off the bench, he turned in some fine performances.

Although not expected to be strong, Happyland's team was soon racking up victories against many of the state's most powerful quintets. Before the season ended the team was dubbed, "The Golden Hurricane."

The school's Christmas break had begun and the Happyland basketball team was on an overnight trip to Des Moines. They had just defeated Dowling High and team members were in a joyous mood. This was Hank's first trip to a larger city and he was thrilled no end to be staying in the tallest building in Iowa, the Roosevelt Hotel.

Hank was still nursing a sore shoulder from the previous night's game. He was stiffer and sorer than he'd ever been since his ash-hauling experience with Albacrombe Alheart, but at least this time his pain had provided a few laughs and a little joy.

His injury came about when, shortly after the contest was underway, he intercepted a ball from the opposing team and, happy as a water salesman in a drought area, headed for the basket.

From the corner of his eye Hank could see one of the host hoopsters, who appeared to have a yen to head him off at the bend, moving with diarrhea-like dispatch to halt his progress. Hank was hovering over the hardwood traveling full speed when the guy grazed his legs and, for a few yards, Hank weaved like Willie Sipmore coming home from a New Year's Eve party.

Players are supposed to have natural instincts and such being the case, Hank must have qualified. He could either keep the ball in bounds for further play, or protect it from being ruined when he smashed into the wall. He opted to keep the ball in bounds and threw it back over his shoulder as he sailed out of bounds to the far right of the basket.

After releasing the ball, Hank gained sufficient control to see what was ahead of him and, from what he saw, he could have well used a travel agency to plan the trip since to his front was an open door.

Bolting through the doorway, he somehow negotiated his way down some steps and crashed shoulder first into the center of a wall locker. After causing a helluva boom in the locker room, he stood for a second or two, then slid to the floor and relaxed for a spell, cleared his brain and contemplated participating in something less dangerous, such as being shot out of a cannon.

Several people came into the room to see if taxes would have to be raised to buy new wall lockers. The coach checked Hank for damages or missing parts and, after a doctor had thoroughly examined the wall locker door and decided its future only hinged on new hinges, everyone proceeded back to the playing court.

Hank was astonished when the coach remarked about the beautiful basket he had made just prior to his lope through the locker room. It was all an accident, but who was Hank to dispute the coach, the fans and the scorekeeper? He humbly accepted the congratulations.

Shortly after breakfast the next day Bill Powers, who then lived in Des Moines, came to the Roosevelt Hotel to visit his Happyland childhood friends. It was a joyful reunion, after which Bill offered to take his old junior high teammates on a tour of the business district.

As they mingled into the milling crowds that sunny Saturday morning, Hank found it an overwhelming experience. He couldn't help wondering how all these people could fit into the pattern of big city life. How could they all find places to earn a living and adjust to the social structure of a large city? How could they find friends?

Although Des Moines was small in comparison to cities like Chicago, Hank reasoned there had to be more opportunities than existed in Happyland. There were still two hundred unemployed in sparsely populated Hamilton County, mostly excellent workers and heads of families. But Happyland had only four noteworthy employers: a threshing machine sieve factory, a small washing machine factory, a hog feeder factory, and a poultry processing plant—mighty slim pickings, he thought.

Hank was surprised to see so many well dressed people browsing through the more expensive stores. In the next block there were dozens of people in shoddy clothing with sad grim expressions on their faces, pouring through stacks of items on sale counters, obviously searching for something they could afford to give as Christmas gifts.

As they approached Younkers and Ginsbergs, the large department stores, more men and women in ragged clothing could be seen holding out their hands or tin cups. One elderly woman appeared to have adjusted to poverty, for the expression on her face never changed when people ignored her and walked on by.

Suddenly all the team members and Bill halted. They looked at each other, then simultaneously began reaching in their pockets for change and gave her a dime or so each.

Although the old woman's face was gaunt and pale, she still bore evidence of one-time beauty. Sadly she smiled her appreciation through kindly eyes, and they could see two front teeth were missing. In a weak, but pleasant, voice she wished them a Merry Christmas. As they walked away, it was apparent it would not be a Merry Christmas for that poor old soul.

Yes, there were still those attempting to peddle pencils and apples, now some nine years after the stock market crash. Some were clean and neatly attired in holdovers from the days when they enjoyed good paying jobs. But their once-expensive suits, shirts and ties were now threadbare and their shoes were badly worn.

One could sense some remaining pride in these once-prominent people, but their eyes reflected a lack of the confidence they obviously had once possessed. It was readily discernible that they were polished, intelligent individuals, whose loss of gainful occupations had badly tarnished their once self-confident images.

Hank's trip to the city left a lasting inpression on him. How could a nation so blessed with natural resources be so callous as to desert old people in their time of need? Here was a true example of inhabitants of a state that boasted twenty-five percent of the nation's grade "A" tillable soil being forced to beg for money to eat. Couldn't something be done? He was truly perplexed!

Back in Happyland Hank was to learn quickly that the poor and destitute were not completely forgotten or ignored, for, to everyone's surprise, a family was living in the old Hamilton County jail. George Drake, at that time the deputy sheriff, related the story to the author.

It seems Sheriff Rap Lear, a tall handsome, but rugged, individual with a very compassionate heart, had received an eviction notice to be served on a family living in an old farmhouse. They were unable to pay the rent, and the eviction had to be carried out.

Christmas was not far away, and the sheriff experienced several sleepless nights thinking about putting the fine, but penniless, family and their belongings out in the snowy ditches.

The eviction deadline was rapidly approaching. Rap sat dejected in his office repeating over and over, "I can't do it, I can't do it, I just can't put those people out in the snow!" George recalls he half seriously said, "Hell, Rap, we only have one prisoner in the lockup. If you could get rid of him, they could move into the jail until we can find them another place to live."

Sheriff Lear's eyes lit up and he leaped forward in his chair, then blurted out, "Sure, why not!" The man in jail was a Fort Dodge resident and Lear soon had Webster County Sheriff Robert Waldburger on the phone. "Say, Bob," Lear said, "I have one of your Webster County men in jail over here. Can you take him off my hands? I need a place to put a destitute family for a week or so, and I'd like to let them stay in the jail." When given the man's name, Sheriff Waldburger laughed heartily and retorted, "Hell, yes, the guy's a habitual. If he wasn't in your jail he'd probably be in mine. Bring him on over."

Hastily Sheriff Lear met with the county supervisors. As George recalls, the supervisors looked at Rap like he had sprung his lid and almost in unison said, "You can't be serious!" Rap allowed as how he was and after much head shaking, the supervisors finally went along with the idea.

Word soon spread through the town that a family was living in the jail and people started bringing food and clothing. For a few weeks the old jail rocked with children's laughter. People brought toys to be given to the children at Christmas time. On Christmas Eve a group of young people went to the jail to sing carols. The spirit of giving prevailed and many citizens, even though of meager means, gave something.

A thoughtful Sheriff Rap Lear, not like the innkeeper of biblical notoriety, will always be remembered for his kindness. When George's story was concluded he quipped, "Be it ever so humble, there was no old place like the Hamilton County jail."

People were a little more upbeat in Happyland during the 1937 holiday season. Snows had come early that year and the trees were decked out in their holiday finery. As they walked the downtown streets, people exchanged greetings with a little more lilt to their voices than during the past seven years, Hank noticed. He had received his National Guard drill check and was able to purchase a few nicer-than-usual presents.

Merchants had added some new decorations to their stores and it was obvious a few had purchased new record players and speakers, for Christmas carols sounded better as people browsed through stores and walked the snow crusted streets. Strange, even today, no one really notices the cold when the holiday season is bright and cheery.

The family would all be home for Christmas dinner with James Arthur and Mother Lucy. Cousin Clinty, having saved his World War I veteran's bonus and some of the money he had earned, had moved back to Perry. Everyone had begged him to stay, but he wanted to be nearer his brothers, Worth and Ernest. This was Hank's first Christmas without Clinty since 1924, and he missed him terribly.

On the world scene, the Japanese had been moving a large force deeper into China from Manchuria. Word had come December 12, 1937 that the city of Nanking had fallen to the Japanese invaders. Anger mounted as the news leaked to the outside world that again civilians had been shot, bayoneted, burned and raped. Broadcasts would soon tell of the fall of Shanghai, Peking, Canton, and other major cities. The Japanese had now gained control of most of China's eastern coastline.

After the fall of Nanking, Japanese planes bombed the U.S. Gunboat Panay and several Standard Oil tankers on China's Yangtze River. Spanish American War and World War I veterans couldn't understand why the United States did not retaliate.

The older veterans remembered the sinking of the battleship Maine by Spain and the instant armed response. In this instance, the United States merely issued a strong protest. The Japanese, evidently not anxious to draw the United States into the war with China at this time, made reparations to the United States in the amount of two million dollars.

Several important discoveries had been made in 1937. German engineer Wernher von Braun developed a jet rocket. About that time Frank Whittle of the Royal Air Force developed a jet engine. However advanced Whittle might have been with his jet engine, it was the Germans who would employ jet rockets and aircraft during World War II. Some readers will recall that von Braun helped the United States develop its first jet rockets that eventually put a man on the moon.

Another great invention that year was nylon, a tremendous synthetic advance—a material to use in lieu of silk. Nylon would revolutionize the clothing industry and provide materials of great durability for such items as parachutes. The material was developed by a Dupont team headed up by Dr. Wallace Carothers.

On the federal government level, the war against the depression continued. After the Supreme Court had found the Agriculture Adjustment Act unconstitutional, Henry Wallace, Secretary of Agriculture, produced a Soil Conservation and Domestic Allotment Act as a replacement funded within Supreme Court guidelines. The bill established a reservoir of surplus in good years to be used in bad ones and also provided a small crop parity. The bill was helpful but, by no means, did it fulfill all agricultural aid requirements.

Although reduced in funds, the Works Project Administration continued to provide jobs to millions working on thousands of projects. Monthly checks were not excessive, but most were taking home over fifty dollars per month working forty hours a week in a broad gauntlet of endeavors.

In the larger cities some WPA workers wanted more pay. The Workers Alliance, a Communist-infested organization, constantly was trying to rabble-rouse workers. Then, would you believe, the WPA workers in some larger cities, emulating the automotive union, went on sit-down strikes. Riots broke out, and order had to be restored by police in some cities. This drew comments, such as, "A lot of the WPA workers are already sitting down on the job; why in the hell do they need to strike to do that?"

On the national sports scene, the New York Yankees defeated the New York Giants and again won the World Series. Joe DiMaggio, in his second year with the Yankees, was fast proving a viable replacement for the immortal Babe Ruth, as he hit 347. Of course, the great Lou Gehrig, who was in his 12th year with the Yanks, was still wielding his magic bat.

Donald Budge, a fabulous tennis player, had been named the athlete of the year. The lanky speedster had taken the Davis Cup and racked up three titles at the Wimbleton matches.

Meanwhile, back to the war on the depression in Washington D.C., the politicians were again at their sport of arguing with each other. Shortly after the year 1938 got underway, President Roosevelt sent a 3.75 billion dollar budget to Congress. It was approved quickly for congressmen could see what was commonly called, "the writing on the wall." Heaven forbid, some of those, who had come out against the President's programs, were now agreeing that government spending was the only cure for the stagnant economy.

Roosevelt kept abreast of the turmoil in Europe and Asia, and he was shifting more emphasis rapidly to foreign matters as the smell of gunpowder was beginning progressively to pollute the globe. The President asked Congress for 1.04 billion dollars for defense spending, the largest since World War I. Most of the increase would go for naval buildup because the Japanese were now arming their battleships with 18-inch guns, while the United States had continued with 16-inch guns.

Nearly one-third of the budget was earmarked for the Works Projects Administration (WPA), the National Youths Administration (NYA), the Civilian Conservation Corps (CCC), the Public Works

Administration (PWA), and a new Agriculture Adjustment Act. There were still nine million unemployed and no one really expected the budget to solve everyone's problems.

Roosevelt further rattled Congress' cage when he asked for an investigation into the concentration of economic power. Investigators launched investigations of violations of anti-trust and monopoly laws.

Through further aggressive action, the Fair Labor Standards Act was passed. The law provided for a maximum work week of 44 hours with an initial minimum wage of 25 cents per hour. This would gradually be changed to a maximum 40-hour work week with a minimum wage of 40 cents per hour, with time and one half for overtime. Most Happyland workers would not benefit immediately from the act as it applied only to employers engaged in interstate commerce—but nearly 2.25 million American people did.

There was no cause for joy March 12, 1938 when the news media carried the announcement that Hitler had moved his troops into Austria. Hitler's Nazi Troops had murdered Austria's Chancellor Englebert Dolfus in 1934 and had continued with determination to bring Austria into the Third Reich fold.

The Western Allies of World War I had stood by and watched Germany take over the Rhineland, and Hitler had learned that threats could get him most of what he wanted, and he had acted accordingly.

History reveals that Austria's Chancellor Kurt von Schushnigg had usurped dictatorial powers and didn't care to share them with or turn them over to Hitler. In fact, he was so determined not to be undermined by the German fuehrer that he promised to let his people hold an election to decide if they wanted to be under him or Hitler. He was not popular with his people, but he knew, under those circumstances, that he would win the vote, for the NAZI Party was not yet that strong in Austria.

England protested intervention in Austria's affairs, but Hitler scoffed at England's attempt at exerting pressure. He moved his troops in, claiming he had liberated the Austrian people from the dictator, Chancellor von Schushnigg, and saved them from revolution. Hitler was accorded a hero's welcome from the large number of NAZI party members in Austria. His troops hardly had to fire a shot.

There were photos in the newspapers and newsreels of German forces' and Hitler's grand entrance into Austria. Their tanks, armored vehicles and other equipment looked far superior to those issued to the guard and even the regulars, as observed during the past year's encampment at Camp Ripley.

On the local scene, at last one of Iowa's colder winters appeared to be breaking, and basketball tournament time had arrived. With the local team still knocking off some of the state's championship contenders, Happyland fans and some of the drugstore hoopsters were clamoring again for a state finals team. Fans were back at feinting out mythical opponents and shooting scrunched paper balls into wastepaper baskets; tournament fever had again set in and the only locally-known antidote was Win, Win, Win!

The team showed considerable improvement during the season, largely due to the plays and techniques introduced by Leonard Skoglund, a tremendous athlete from what is now Northern Illinois University. Skoglund was later inducted into the Illinois Hall of Fame. He could not only coach; he could demonstrate.

Mason City, Happyland's arch tournament stumbling block, was, as usual, racking up wins in all sports. During the regular season, they again sent Happyland players home having conversations with themselves after beating them by a twelve-point margin. Happyland advanced through the sectional tournament and now was scheduled to meet another of J. A. Judge Grimsley's powerful Mason City teams in district tournament play.

Coach Lamson was the motivator magnificent. He had some of the characteristics of the great Notre Dame coach, Knute Rockne, a bit of the slyness associated with Sherlock Holmes and some of the mischievous mannerisms of Hank's Cousin Clinty. Lamson could convince a player he could jump up and snatch flies off the gymnasium ceiling.

Arriving well before the game, coaches Lamson and Skoglund quickly assembled the team and seated them on benches. Lamson pointed out that Mason City had a tremendous height advantage, were strong rebounders on the offensive and defensive boards and had reserves with almost as much talent as their starting five. Continuing, he emphasized, no one could doubt any of Judge Grimsley teams' scoring abilities.

Then, with a sad look on his face, Lamson continued, "You are fine athletes. You have played your hearts out all season. No one in Happyland expected you to come this far when the season started." Hank, as he sat on the bench, couldn't help wondering why the coach was consoling them and bracing them for an inevitable loss!

Then it came. Lamson's voice became stern; his eyebrows narrowed as he stared alternately at each player. Going on, he said, "Coach Skoglund and I have come to the conclusion that you boys can beat Mason City. They are fast, plenty fast, but you boys are faster—but you can only win by combining that speed with desire, determination, and sheer endurance. Boys, you'll literally have to run them off their feet. Now get out there and give it all you have and a helluva lot more!"

The Mason City squad with key players Wallace, McKenzy, Major, Hepner, Gorman, and Wood were already warming up when the Happylanders reached the floor. Judge Grimsley must have been confident in his team reaching the state finals, for they were already decked out in new uniforms. Hank eyeballed them; they looked taller than when they played them a couple of months back.

As the teams moved to the center of the floor to initiate the jump ball to start the game, Hank looked up at Jack Wallace, the guy he was paired against. Just the right height, Hank mused, to elbow hell out of my nose on rebounds. Somehow he wished Cousin Clinty could have come up with a body-stretching course.

With the game underway, Happyland players moved with all the speed and dexterity they could muster, fought hard for every rebound, loose ball, and shooting opportunity. Although Judge Grimsley substituted quite freely, Mason City still continued to hold the lead at half time. Clark Mollenhoff came off the bench and alternately spelled a couple of players and did a commendable job at either center or forward.

Clark was the youngest lad in the senior class. He had shot up rapidly to his 6'-5" height and, although still a bit awkward, he was rapidly reaching the potential that would make him a fine college player at Drake University.

At halftime coaches Lamson and Skoglund hastily pointed out a few flaws in the Happyland players' game, then told the team to lie down on the benches and rest—adding, "You'll need it!"

When the third quarter started, the team continued its fast pace with the talented Ralph Burton hitting a very high percentage of shots. However, by the time the third quarter ended, young legs were beginning to tire rapidly. However, no one on the Happyland team showed signs of slowing the pace—but now the score had narrowed.

At the end of the third quarter, instead of talking to the players, Lamson motioned them to lie on the floor for rest. Play resumed and, while in position for the jump ball initiating the fourth quarter, Hank's assigned opponent turned to him and said, "How long can you crazy fools keep up this pace?" Hank replied, "We go like this every night in practice." The boy grinned skeptically at Hank, then said, "Like hell you do!"

Back at the grueling game, the Happyland five was now closing in on Mason City's lead. Coach Lamson took advantage of every time out allowed; players rested in place. By now their leg muscles were aching, and tendons burned as if being stretched on a medieval torture rack—but when the horn sounded, they bounded to their feet with seemingly more determination than ever.

Minutes later the score was tied. Then playing on adrenaline alone, the team began to pull ahead. Hank, fouled and knocked out of bounds while moving in for a layup, was sent to the free throw line.

As he made his first free throw, he felt light-headed. His other shot he didn't remember, for his next recollection was sitting on the bench beside the coach, his head and face wrapped in a wet towel.

Pulling off the towel, he asked the coach why he had pulled him out of the game. Lamson explained—Hank told him he was fine now and begged to be put back into the game. Coach Lamson shook his head but honored his request.

During the remaining minutes, Happyland pulled steadily ahead and when the buzzer sounded, they held a twelve-point lead—a perfect and exact reversal of their previous loss to Mason City that season. Ralph Burton had scored eight field goals—a highly commendable performance in those days.

Happyland fans in the crowd went wild; pandemonium reigned. For the first time since 1926-27, the school had scored a victory over Mason City. The seemingly impossible task had been accomplished. Sleep was difficult that night—part of it was due to being keyed up over the game, and part was caused by knots in muscles brought on by over exertion.

The team, although extremely tired, was taxed further in winning the next game, but win they did, and they went on to the state finals, where they lost to a team most felt they should have beaten easily.

The team had played a heavier than normal high school season—a total of twenty eight games. Many people and sports writers felt that the Mason City game, after so grueling a season, had taken too much out of the players, resulting in burnout. Perhaps, but they had lost. No one fretted, not even the drugstore coaches—it had been a wonderful season. They had demonstrated their right to be among the sixteen best teams in the state.

Coached by Fred Deines, Stratford High School, fielded the best boy's team in that school's history. The team composed of Earl Nelson, Norman Daniels, Arnold Borg, Edward Spurling, Julius "Bud" Hook, Dale Kane, and Donald "Swede" Swanson won the District Class B Championship, then fell in the first round of the state finals.

As an interesting sidelight—it was during the depth of the depression in 1934 when Fred Deines, who had graduated from Luther College, Decorah, hitchhiked from his home in western Kansas to Stratford to make application for the coaching job. Receiving the appointment he went on to become one of the best coaches in Iowa.

Donald "Swede" Swanson had work to do after school!
Photo courtesy of Lois Berglund Swanson

Dale Kane ready for work with brother John.
Photo courtesy of Dale Kane

Being a farming community it was difficult for some of the young men to find time to practice—farm boys like Donald "Swede" Swanson and Dale Kane had a lot of work to do when they arrived home from school.

Baseball season came, and the Happyland High team enjoyed its best season to date. Hank was thrilled when he pitched his first no-hitter in the semi-finals of the district tournament. Coach Skoglund agreed to play off the finals the same day as he said he had to get back to Illinois.

According to high school rules, Hank was allowed to pitch only nine innings, and he had already pitched seven. This was disgusting, for only the past summer he had pitched a softball game in the morning and a baseball game in the afternoon, winning both.

Hank pitched two more flawless innings—then reverted to another position. Sadly, the team went on to defeat. He was deeply depressed for a state championship would have gone a long way to improve his chances for a baseball career. A New York Giant scout had sat in the stands and watched him pitch his no-hitter that spring. He was very impressed, but he said he wanted to take another look at Hank playing semi-pro ball.

At last graduation time rolled around. Hank had been able to buy a nice new suit and a few accessories, and he felt good that he would soon reach one of his goals. However, when he walked in the procession down the aisle May 27, 1938 with classmates, he didn't know what job or what future lay ahead for him.

He had determined there were a few occupations he didn't desire to pursue. Hank chuckled a little as the line moved slowly forward down the aisles, just thinking about some of the trials and tribulations he had gone through in his occupation endeavors.

Hank had long ago decided he didn't want to be a cowboy movie star or stunt man and, for sure, he didn't want to pick apples. It hadn't taken him too long to decide he didn't want to haul ashes out of basements for people like Albacrombe Alheart or tend to the toiletries of cows. He didn't have any illusions about getting more contusions from boxing, and it was damn certain he didn't want any part of helping the likes of Roy Rumblegut on the farm!

If he didn't succeed in being selected for a baseball career, Hank now hoped some day to become an army officer. He guessed the military might be in his blood. His direct lineage included three ancestors who fought in the Revolutionary War—the most famous being General Israel Putnam. From events in the newspapers, Hank reasoned the United States could become involved in a war in the near future and, in this event, his future could be decided for him for the duration of a war, at least.

Glancing up at the balcony as they marched down the aisle, Hank could see many proud parents. A high school education then, unlike today when college is all-important, was a considerable achievement. Many depression youths were forced to drop out of school for lack of money, and others needed to work to help their families keep food on the table.

At the podium the commencement keynote speaker spoke of all the country's vast natural resources and the opportunities that lay ahead, etc. etc. Hank, who still hadn't raised enough money to buy new shoes, looked down at the holes in his soles and almost got up to look out the gymnasium door to see if he was still in Happyland or heaven.

Hank remembered all the fine athletes and friends he had been fortunate enough to play with and know. His reminiscing continued, and his eyes fell upon a free throw line of the basketball court. His mind drifted back to a home game against Dowling High School of Des Moines. The clock was winding down rapidly. Ralph Burton had passed the ball to Hank shouting, "Shoot, shoot"

Hank received the ball, took one long step and let fly a two-handed shot from the foul line to the basket on the opposite end of the court. The ball nearly touched the ceiling, then began its descent. Now it was descending toward the basket in a perfect arch. Everyone watched in total silence. The ball dropped through the basket, then split the net—so dead center the net barely riffled. The crowd went wild, for Hank had made what many believed to be the longest shot to date in the state's history of high school ball. What a thrill! The game was won by a single basket.

His mind now back at the graduation: salutatorian Dorothy Isebrands gave a fine speech, and valedictorian Lester Welch was now winding down his address to the class. Ralph Burton, one of Hank's favorite friends, must have realized Hank had been reminiscing about bygone days, for he tapped Hank on the shoulder and brought his mind back to the gymnasium saying, "I think they are ready to award the diplomas. We better take them before they change their minds!"

Superintendent Burrus E. Beard presented the class and the graduates filed past Principal Oscar Johnson to receive their diplomas from school board President A. B. Halverson, then proceeded back to their seats. The young graduates congratulated each other, said goodnight and departed.

Although all the students were happy to graduate, it also was a sad occasion. Unlike today there were few, if any, graduation parties. When they departed the building, little did they realize it would be the last time they would see some of their friends. Of course, life would never be the same, for one cannot recapture high school days and all that zest for living.

Hopping from bed early the morning after graduation, Hank, like other graduates, hurried downtown to fill out more job applications and make the rounds of the business district to see if there were any "help wanted" signs posted. As he strolled west on the main street, the sun was just beginning to take the chill out of the early morning air.

Approaching the intersection of Highway 20 and Willson Avenue, he saw Dermand's huge boxer-mix dog "Sport" lying on the sidewalk on the northwest corner of the street. Hank spoke; Sport raised his head acknowledging him, then lay back on the warming sidewalk.

Front row, left to right: Ted Dermand, "Sport," George Patrou, John Patrou. Back row, left to right: Chris Dermand, Gus Dermand.

Photo courtesy of Gus Dermand

Sport enjoyed the sun and would always move across the street from Nick Dermand's hat shop on the far corner to catch the sun's first unobstructed rays. Hank mused on how closely one becomes acquainted with the people, and even the dogs, in a small town. As he came to the Freeman Journal building, he glanced at the encased-in-glass publication of the day before. It painted more gloomy news about the world situation.

Merlyn Best, a World War I veteran, was washing his drugstore windows, and Hank stopped for awhile to converse with him. Merlyn asked, "Hank, have you heard about Armor Miller?" Hank looked perplexed and Merlyn said, "He was killed last night in an automobile accident." Hank was dumbfounded. It was the first death of one of his close friends, and it struck him deeply.

Later Hank was to learn that Miller, the great football tackle with much college playing potential, had been out driving on an unfamiliar road with his girl friend. Although traveling at a reasonable speed, he didn't see the approaching dead-end of the road until it was too late.

Armor's courage was with him to the last. Barbara Kirschner, his girl friend, later said, "When he saw the crash coming, he threw his shoulders and upper body in front of me, taking the full impact himself." No, liquor or dope was not involved, as it frequently is now on graduation night—only two young people out on a wonderful ride on a beautiful night.

Merlyn consoled Hank in his grief. Then he said, "Hank, if this world situation doesn't improve, you will lose many more of your friends. Life can be cruel; you just have to learn to grin and bear it!"

Hank walked slowly across the street to the old sports' hangout—Jensen Drug. Sports fans sat around the soda fountain, stunned at Armor Miller's death. It was difficult for them to comprehend that even an automobile could kill the tough, hard-hitting tackle.

People remembered that twice during the 1936 season Miller had met the speedy Claude Santee of Iowa Falls at mid-field on kickoffs. Both times Santee had been carried off the field after Miller's powerhouse head-on tackles.

But try as they might, no one could remember how many times Miller's knee had been dislocated during plays. Each time the knee had been snapped back in place by Dr. Crumpton and Coach Lamson. Taped up, knee brace again in place—the tenacious Miller had finished every game.

Hank, still devastated, continued checking out the businesses and factories to the west for help wanted signs.

On his return walk, he stopped in front of Fastenow's Drugstore, where he noticed "Sport" had again moved closer to his home along with the sun and was now some six feet out into the eastbound lane of traffic. A truck driver, obviously aware of Sport's routine, patiently pulled out and around the prostrate animal, not even bothering to honk his horn. Sport did kinda raise his head and appear to half grin as the trucker drove past.

A few minutes later Sport arose and made his round of the nearby taverns where he received a tiny amount of beer in a saucer from each of two proprietors. After that he watched Ted (later to become an all-stater) shoot basketballs at his hoop for an hour or two. As Ted and Gus Dermand relate it, Sport never deviated from routine, except on Sundays, when somehow Sport knew the taverns were closed.

Stopping in Steve Dermand's Cafe, Hank saw Rex Swanson, a local contractor, approaching him with a smile on his face. Rex patted him on the shoulder and said, "Cheer up. Would you like to work with me this summer? The pay is thirty-five cents an hour." Grinning from ear to ear, Hank asked him, "When do I start?" Rex responded, "Now!" Hank never bothered to go home to change into work clothing. He proceeded straight to the job.

Swanson Construction had the contract to make some badly needed depression-delayed repairs to the Bank Street bridge. The abutments needed to be shored up; the decking was worn and rotted, with wide gaps between the sidewalk planks. Hank's spirits were high at the end of the day, and he ignored the blisters on his ungloved hands, for at last he had found some work!

Hank had worked for the city water department during spring vacation, spade-digging out water mains for repair. His boss then, Ray Wilcox, and Pete Racobs, a friend of Hank's, had approached Fire Chief Milt Wensel, a strong sports fan, about Hank becoming one of the volunteers who stayed at the fire station nights. Chief Wensel agreed, but told them Hank would need a release statement from his parents since he was not yet eighteen years of age.

After obtaining the release statements Hank moved into the bunk room. For each drill or fire call volunteers received one dollar, a little less than a day's wages for unskilled labor. Pete Racobs, Tom Bowman, Don and Wayne Passwaters, and Del Whaley, all long-time members of the department, gave Hank an assist in training.

Two fire department drills had been held before the first fire call came in. When the loud bunkroom squawker sounded Hank was taking a shower. He streaked for his bunk without drying, soap still on his feet. He took a few long strides and skidded like a skier into the swinging door to the bunkroom.

A fellow fireman, Richard Beermann, had just started to open the door from the opposite side when Hank came crashing through shoulder first. Fortunate for Hank, Dick was off balance and reeled back with the impact, Hank moved on like a perishable fruit freight train toward his fire boots and trousers.

Bunk rooms were on the second floor. The chief had cautioned Hank to always grasp the brass sliding pole between his crooked arm. In his haste he leaped through the opening—grabbing the pole with his hands. Painful as it was, he held on rather than risk crashing through the floor to the basement.

As the sound of the siren pierced the air, the trucks sailed through the open door. The fire was in an apartment above a downtown store. When they arrived, smoke was coming through the door. The door was locked, but it was easy to open with an old fashioned master key. Once inside, they discovered the old-timer, who lived there, had gone down the hall to visit with a neighbor and forgotten he had been cooking beans on the stove. It was just a matter of pulling the pan off the stove and holding it under a faucet—an easy dollar. Hank was beginning to believe he could earn enough to go to the local junior college.

Meanwhile back on the Bank Street bridge job, Willie Sipmore, Lavere Thompson, "Carp" Hutchinson, and Hank were hand-spading a ditch in which to pour a replacement concrete bridge abutment. Hank couldn't help but marvel at the spading ability of Willie—he was the equivalent of a thousand gophers in his chosen field of endeavor. The crew had been working almost a week and excavation of soil to a depth of nearly twelve feet had been achieved. Proper safety measures had been taken—track jacks with bracing boards had been installed to prevent a collapse.

It was mid-morning—the boss man, Rex Swanson, had called a coffee break. There had been a slight earth slide on one side of the ditch and Hank had been shoveling out the loose dirt. He had decided to finish the job before taking his break. Completing the task, Hank proceeded to the far end of the ditch to ascend the ladder.

Mounting the ladder, he had climbed but a few rungs when he heard a noise like a clap of thunder; several boards behind the track jacks had snapped. With haste Hank climbed upwards—he was near the top of the ladder when tons of excavated dirt came smashing into the open ditch. Soon he felt the dirt crushing against the ladder beneath him, it swayed toward the side of the ditch—he heard the ladder crack and for a fleeting moment he thought he was a goner.

Then the most powerful hand he had ever felt grabbed him around his upper arm below the armpit; suddenly he found himself being pulled from the dirt and sailing through the air to the ground beside the ditch. Looking up, Hank saw the kind blue eyes of Willie

Sipmore. Willie's quick action undoubtedly saved him from death or, at a minimum, serious injury.

Hank thanked Willie for saving his life and the boss man assured Willie there would be an extra ten dollars in his pay envelope that week in appreciation for his quick action. Willie grinned and denied he was a hero, but he did admit he could sure use the money.

Shoveling out the loose dirt was not as difficult as the original spading and when work began the dirt flew, though much still needed to be done at days end. Before departing for home, Hank looked at the huge amount of dirt still in the ditch—he was thankful he had not become the second person from his class to die shortly after graduation.

That night rain fell in torrents. Reporting to work the next day, the men found the ditch full of water. Rex Swanson advised them he would have the ditch pumped out, but work would have to be suspended for a few days. Hank decided it would be a good time to hitchhike to Perry and visit his Cousin Clinty. Mr. Swanson gave his approval. He hurriedly changed clothes and, with good fortune still with him, arrived in Perry before noon.

Clinty's brother Worth directed him to the house his amicable cousin had purchased with some of his bonus money. Hank walked up to the door of an old, but neat, little bungalow and gave it a few knocks. He was a bit impatient as he was anxious to see his wonderful cousin.

The door opened and a young woman said Clinty was living out back. Hank hurried around the corner. All he saw was what looked like a chicken house, but he knocked on the door. Clinty answered, and there was a flood of tears from both as they hugged each other.

Clinty, a fine carpenter, had done a commendable job of remodeling the small building into living quarters—it was neat and clean in every respect. Although modestly furnished, it was quite livable and comfortable. As they sat in chairs reliving old times, Hank asked why Clinty was living in the chicken house. Clinty looked at Hank through the kindest brown eyes he would ever see and explained that his friend's daughter had married a nice young man who, shortly after their marriage, had lost his job. They had no place to live. "Shucks," Clinty said, "I just fixed up this old building and let them use the house!"

This good gesture was so like his wonderful Cousin Clinty—Hank supposed he'd never change. They mostly just sat around for a couple of days reminiscing and listening to the radio, and on June 22, 1938 the big rematch fight between now-champion Joe Louis and Max Schmeling was broadcast. While waiting for the fight to begin, Hank and Clinty laughed about the time he had taken Cousin Clinty's clobbering course.

The media had given the fight such an anti-NAZI buildup that one would have thought Schmeling was a vicious Hitler henchman. Hank was to learn later in Germany from Heinz Ebel (who, as champion of the Berlin police department, had once fought Schmeling) that Schmeling was a good person and a fine boxer who was only attempting to win the world crown.

Louis lost no time; he had improved tremendously and made none of his previous mistakes. Hank, Clinty and his two nephews, Dewey and Dwight, had hardly been seated comfortably by the radio before the referee was administering Schmeling the count of three. The roar of the crowd nearly shook the radio. After a flurry of punches, Louis landed a hard right, said to be near the kidney, which sent Schmeling screaming to the floor. But the tough German rose again only to be knocked to the floor unconscious.

There are still Germans today who claim Louis indeed hit Schmeling in the kidney as he purportedly suffered for a long time from the blow. He did later serve in the German Army Paratroopers and jumped in Crete. But even without the kidney punch, Louis would have no doubt won an easy victory.

The following day Hank hitchhiked back to Happyland and reported to work and a few nights later pitched a softball game. The local guardsmen softball team was now fielding a championship team. Hank was surprised to see a one-legged man with a crutch enter the batter's box for the opposing team. It was Sidney Kallem, a handsome young man from Ellsworth.

Hank had played against a one-armed player, Wayne Coffman, from Ellsworth's neighboring town, Radcliffe. Wayne, an outfielder, could field the ball with his gloved hand, flip the glove under his partial arm, remove the ball and have it on the way to the infield faster than most two-armed players.

Mike Kuhfus of Ellsworth speaks proudly of the baseball playing Kuhfus family. His uncle, Glen Kuhfus, had pitched Radcliffe High School to a state tournament runner-up win over Van Meter. This was highly noteworthy at that time since Van Meter's star was the legendary pitcher, Robert "Bob" Feller. Feller later would become an all-time baseball great while pitching for the Cleveland Indians. He would be inducted into Baseball's Hall of Fame. Wayne Coffman was a strong contributor to Radcliffe's winning of the state championship. He was also strong with the bat, hitting a one-arm home run against North Des Moines in the semifinals of a state tournament.

Back at the softball game in progress, Sid detected Hank's astonishment at seeing a one-legged batter and gave him a broad grin. The game was a good one for Hank with very few batters reaching first base. He delivered his pitch fast and across the plate. Sid swung his bat hard, meeting the ball firmly. The crowd gasped in amazement and so did Hank, as the ball sailed well out between the right and center fielders.

With the crack of the bat, Sid threw his crutch aside and down the baseline he sped, hopping like a kangeroo. Surprisingly, he made it to first base as fast as some two-legged runners.

Research reveals that in 1923 Sid had contracted diptheria at the tender age of eleven. Gangrene had set in the young man's leg. Quarantined, his parents, Randolph and Anna Kallem, called for a doctor. Their family doctor, a Dr. Buddy of Jewell, responded and made the determination that Sid's leg must be amputated if his life was to be saved.

His sister, now Mrs. Gladys Kallem Hare of Waterloo, seems to recall that Dr. W. W. Wyatt and two nurses from Happyland were called in to do the surgery, while Dr. Buddy and Dr. E. E. Slater of Jewell assisted.

1935 Radcliffe team that beat Bob Feller and was runner-up in the State Tournament. Back row, left to right: Clifford Thompson, Ralph Skartvedt, John Taylor, Clifford Skeie, Everett Eike, Russel Krause, Gene Coffman, Coach R. J. (Hoovey) Halverson. Middle row: Alfred Lee, Donald Larson, Glen Coffman, Ralph Mason, Keith Berve, Laverne Buland. Front: Manager Donald Erbes, Dale Orton, Wayne Coffman, Glen Kuhfus, Lloyd Larson, Arnold Thompson.

Photo courtesy of Michael Kuhfus

Preparations were made to accomplish the operation on the dining room table. There was no possibility of full anesthesia, but available drugs were administered. Sid remained semi-conscious throughout the terrible ordeal. Gladys said, "Mother, dad and my sister Mavis were told to go down by the barn, but we could hear Sid scream—I guess the good Lord was with him."

Sid's sister Gladys and brother Curtis were staying in an upstairs bedroom during the quarantine and were told to remain in their room. The pain of the surgery was excrutiating and they recall hearing the screaming. Sid's cousin, Marjorie Peterson of Ellsworth, remembers that her father, Theodore "T" Kallem, knowing of their deep concern, climbed up a ladder and onto the porch roof to relay information to Gladys and Curtis on the progress of the operation.

At last it was over, and all they could do now was wait and pray. Miraculously, Sid survived the deadly diptheria and the operation as well. Over the years he had become phenomenal in the use of his one leg.

Sid's interests were wide and diverse, but he loved sports best of all. No, his participation was not limited to baseball; he would play high school basketball and football as well, all four years!

The Ellsworth newspaper carried the basketball story that "Ellsworth, remaining undefeated to (the date of the article), will play Britt in the semi-finals of a tournament, Ellsworth featuring the play of Sid Kallem, the one-legged star!"

Ellsworth High School football team. Front row, left to right: A. Olson, K. Severson, G. Gabrielson, H. Danielson, W. Pitz, W. Bergeson, L. Swenson. Back row: H. Mailand, A. Swenson, K. Voga, M. Golden, V. Peterson, A. Ahrens, F. Holt, Sidney Kallem.

Photo courtesy of Walter Bergeson

A football writeup told how Coach Otto Freese inserted Sid Kallem into the Ellsworth lineup as guard. The article goes on to say, "But, one-legged or two-legged, Sid played and did well. In the first play, he took his man out clean as a whistle and, on the second play, he got his man and two others—not so bad for a hopping person!"

Sid had a lot of things going for him: courage, tenacity, intelligence and a wonderful personality. In school he also participated in school plays and operettas, and he was an accomplished musician. He later organized and led a small dance band.

Was Sid's one leg strong? You could bet on it and he did too! On one occasion he bet a man a dollar he could jump over a pool table. Naturally the man said, "You're on!" Several people hastily offered wagers that Sid could perform the feat and, of course, there were takers. With some of the bettors shouting encouragement to Sid, they offered him a share of the winnings.

Those who bet against Sid stood by in amazement. There were a few tense moments; Sid assumed a semi-squatting position; then, like one shot from a catapult, he leaped to the other side of the table. Grinning broadly, Sid collected the bet and the encouragement money, grabbed his crutch and laughingly hopped all the way out the door.

Hank and everyone who came to know Sid admired his determination. Like Ed Snow, the superintendent of county schools who had lost both arms, Sid never complained. Sid said about his handicap, "It does gripe me when I have to pay for two shoes and only use one!"

Hank continued to pitch semi-pro baseball each weekend and there was always plenty of excitement. Since many of the games were played at celebrations of one type or another, each weekend brought a new experience.

One of the small towns had a constable who was an avid baseball fan, but he rarely was among the observing when the final inning was played. The localites liked a little more freedom with their gambling and drinking and better girlie shows than the law allowed and, with the keeper of the peace still on his feet, the festivities of the day were a bit too mild for their liking.

While the pitchers were throwing low balls, the rural rowdies were behind the bleachers throwing highballs into the law-man, and it wasn't long before the imbiber and the innings were neck and neck, both well into their fifth. When the fans were ready to take their seventh inning stretch, the old boy was already taking his under a shade tree in back of the bleachers.

With the constable temporarily expired and all sides retired, the celebration took on a new flavor. The taverns began serving liquor by the drink. There was poker in the pool parlors, fighting in the streets and the girlies at the girlie shows threw away their fans.

With a two-week leave of absence from his job, Hank along with other members of the Guard, departed for Camp Dodge. They expected a more rigorous training session as the world situation had again worsened. However, Camp Dodge was small and lacked maneuver space, and training was confined to small drill fields and parade grounds. When off post, the units were pretty well confined to roads.

Training was intensified within the scope afforded. Every class was dead serious. But, regardless of the miserable two weeks they had spent at Camp Ripley, they all wished they were back there for the area afforded more realistic training and maneuver space. However, ample funding was no doubt unavailable.

The two-week encampment ended on a not-so-happy note and the guardsmen returned to their hometowns, still dubious about what the future held in store for the military and wondering how long it would be before their country's military capabilities would be upgraded.

When Hank returned to his daytime job, weather was favorable, and the job on the bridge was winding down rapidly. Work was in progress on a new sewage disposal plant. Rex Swanson suggested Hank go to the site and approach his old friend, Roy Mills, for a job.

Zitterell-Mills Construction Company had the contract and was now pouring concrete, constructing huge cylindrical digesters. It was one of the first sewage disposal plants of its type. Happyland, like most small towns, previously had been dumping sewage through tiles into the river.

As Hank approached the gate shed, he could see two long rows of job seekers seated on benches, hoping to go to work. If a man did not prove to be a good worker, he was immediately pulled, paid off promptly at the gate shed, and a replacement was hired.

Roy Mills, standing fifty or so feet away, happened to glance Hank's way. He beckoned Hank to come over to him. The top flight engineer and the company's construction boss then said, "I understand you're trying to earn some money to go to college. Rex tells me you're a good worker!" Hank responded in the affirmative.

Roy, still busy watching workers, quipped, "Go over there and grab a wheelbarrow. We'll see how good you are!" Hank felt sorry for those sitting on the benches, but who was he to argue? He made for a wheelbarrow like he was propelling to second base in a ball game.

When depression-era youths spoke of working their way through college, few had plush jobs; most had to work hard for their money. The concrete mixers were powered machines, but the concrete and gravel was hand-shoveled into mixers. Concrete was flip-dumped into wheelbarrows and wheeled to the digesters, now under construction. This in itself was not bad but, as the digesters grew in height, plank ramps were elevated and when the man hit the lower ramp approach, he'd best be moving fast since he had to wheel the wheelbarrow to the top, then dump it.

There was no splitting of a concrete pour as a crack could exist and possibly cause leaks; the pour must be continued until finished. It was 7 p.m. before the pour was completed. The wheelbarrow with its load was not all that much lighter than Hank's weight, and he was now more determined than ever to go to college—for, much as he appreciated the job, he didn't want a lifetime of such work.

When college enrollment time rolled around, Roy gave Hank time to go to the school. He then told Hank that if he wanted to come down and work between classes, after school or on Saturdays, he could. Hank said he could and he would.

Dean William Wesselink, later dean at Buena Vista at Storm Lake, approved of Hank working between classes and also gave him permission to leave classrooms to answer fire calls. With that understood, Hank was promptly enrolled. Dean Wesselink was aware that Hank was a member of the local guard company, and they discussed the current world situation. Hitler's German propaganda expert, Joseph Goebbels, had launched a decisive and thorough news media campaign, complaining that neighboring countries were mistreating those of German descent, primarily in Czechoslovakia.

Hitler had caused expert dissenters of German extraction to stir up trouble in Czechoslovakia with demands for an independent socialist state within the now borders of that country. Konrad Henlein proved a very able exponent of Hitler's cause. Riots and confrontations among Czechosolvakian factions flared.

France and Russia involved themselves trying at least to preserve a Czechoslovakia. Britain's Prime Minister Neville Chamberlain exerted his influence on Czechoslovakia's Premier Eduard Benes to turn over all area in which more than fifty percent of the people were of German extraction.

The premier finally acceded to Chamberlain's pleadings, agreeing to give up Sudetenland where German population was heaviest. Chamberlain, thinking he had solved the problem, returned for his second meeting with Hitler. Hitler now wanted more. September 29, 1938 Prime Minister Chamberlain and France's Premier Edouard Deladier consented to Hitler's demands, but the Czechoslovakian people as a whole did not. Chamberlain returned to Britain hailed as a peacemaker.

In England a feeling existed that peace would prevail; however, there was still a goodly amount of speculation that Hitler's appetite for conquest would not be satisfied by appeasement. Rearmament of Germany was not being accomplished for nought; Hitler wanted to avenge World War I and literally to shove the Versailles Treaty down the throats of the British and French.

There had been so much speculation that Hitler would launch an attack on France that Hank and Meyel "Bud" Haack thought that day had arrived on October 9, 1938. Dean Wesselink called them from their classes and advised them that an alert call had been received from the local Guard Company ordering them to report to the armory at once.

Upon arrival at the armory they learned, with no small amount of relief, that the unit wasn't being mobilized for war, but had been called up by the governor to perform strike duty at the Sioux City Swift Meat Packing Plant.

When the guardsmen arrived at the Sioux City plant, it was obvious control of the strikers had been lost. A crowd of over one thousand strikers and sympathizers were milling around and were throwing bricks through building windows and at anyone trying to enter or leave the plant. It was very apparent guardsmen were not exactly a welcome sight to the strikers.

The packing house union had declared "bash your buddy week" and some of the members had started peeling hides on the outside of the plant when non-union workers continued peeling hides on the inside. Strikers held sort of a "block party" in which they blocked the entrance to the plant and provided a punch for every worker attempting to enter.

Radical union members were tipping over automobiles of those trying to enter the plant. Those attempting to cross the picket lines were being beaten and some had been critically injured. In some instances, guardsmen were told that strikers had been painting SCAB on the houses of some non-strikers and threatening their families.

Over the public address system Major Heath, the battalion commander, advised the strikers to leave the packing plant premises—they completely ignored the order. Several of the most radical leaders stood up on truckbeds making riot inciting speeches—stirring the emotions of strikers to a frenzy. One speaker went so far as to throw the American flag on the ground, curse and then stomp on it. Striking was one thing, but this act of disrespect for the United States flag infuriated the guardsmen.

Riot control teams were formed and the order was given to fix bayonets. In an inverted "V" wedge formation with men forming the wedge with rifles and fixed bayonets, the guardsmen moved slowly and deliberately forward through the crowd. Opening the wedge when they arrived at the one who had degraded the flag, they quickly engulfed him within the wedge. The radical soon felt the blow of a rifle butt to his head; he was placed on a stretcher and promptly removed from the premises.

Machine guns were set up on top of the buildings and along the docks. Major Heath repeated the order that all strikers were to leave the packing plant premises. He then read from a manual excerpts on military mob control procedures. Concluding, he called to the strikers' attention the fact that a mob is to be given adequate warning and reasonable time to disperse and, further, that military commanders were not to bluff. The major closed his speech, telling the strikers they had five minutes to clear the premises.

A minute or so later the group was still acting belligerent and not moving back. On Major Heath's signal Capt. Stuart N. Grummon, commanding officer of Co. "H," 2nd Bn., 133rd Inf., a powerfully built man from Mason City, gave the order to his machine gunners to load their weapons and a battalion of troops faced the rioters with fixed bayonets. Hank watched apprehensively—would the order to fire be given?

There were a few tense moments—then, faced with the glittering of the sun on belts of brass machine gun cartridges, the strikers decided to leave the plant property and occupy picket lines on city property out front. The guardsmen all breathed a sigh of relief, for in no way did they want to fire on their own people. But there was no doubt in the minds of the guardsmen and obviously none in the strikers that, had the order been given, they would have been compelled to do so.

The violence was calming down somewhat and while off guard duty the battalion's men were quartered in a field house, sleeping on cots set up on the floor. Sleeping space was adequate, but quite confining. Those not performing guard duty had little to do, for at first they were not allowed to visit the business district because of possible friction with strikers.

Walter Herd, a fine young man from Stanhope, then a director at the Sioux City YMCA, paid a visit to the company. Knowing Bud Haack and Hank would soon be playing basketball he invited them to come to the YMCA for workouts. With Capt. Meller's approval, they got in a few good sessions.

Applying the old army theory, "Keep the troops busy and they stay out of trouble," Major Heath ordered every square inch of the field house cleaned. Cleanup details had their work cut out for them, the most undesirable, of course, being latrine cleaning duty.

Hank's Big Brother had again joined the guard after returning from his stint in the Civilian Conservation Corps (CCC). Big Brother, now a corporal, was placed in charge of that undesirable detail, that of cleaning latrines. Assigned to perform the unpopular task were Haack, Gage, Crouse, and Hank.

Big Brother formed them up and marched them to the vicinity of a second floor balcony latrine. It was then Big Brother spotted another detail approaching. Walking up to the corporal in charge, he bellowed, "Where in the hell have you guys been? I was just about to report you to your first sergeant." Pointing to the cleaning supplies, he barked, "Now get to hell in there and start cleaning that latrine!" Big Brother's detail watched in amazement.

With the other detail hard at work, Big Brother moved his men smartly out to the side of the fieldhouse, where they basked in the sunlight until noon. As far as Hank was concerned, this was Big Brother's finest hour, and he was pleased his brother had picked up all that "know how" in the CCC.

Walking guard posts was not a pleasurable assignment during the strike, especially on the docks bordering the rail sidings where strikers hurled an occasional rock at guardsmen. However, unlike his guard post at the swimming pool at Camp Dodge, Hank understood full well why he was walking his post.

One rock hurler got the surprise of his life. Lt. Bruno G. "George" Marchi from Fort Dodge, (he would later command the battalion in combat) as officer of the day, was making the rounds checking guard posts. Just as he approached the dock, he spotted a striker throwing a rock at a guard from behind a boxcar.

Marchi, a former University of Iowa track star, quickly vaulted over the rail car connector and was soon in hot pursuit of the striker—in no time at all he had him collared, his arm twisted behind his back.

The striker was panic-stricken. After Marchi threatened him with everything short of hanging, he released him with a bit of advice, "If I see you around here again—it is jail for sure." Released, the striker sped off for home faster than he had run when Marchi was pursuing him!

Fortunately none of the guardsmen was seriously injured when strikers demonstrated resentment to their presence. However, the guardsmen did receive a lesson in human nature; for one thing they learned that Americans can be vicious. They also knew from firsthand experience what guardsmen had gone through when they were called out for duty at the terrible automobile plant strike in Flint, Michigan.

Radios continued to be the cheapest form of entertainment and fortunate it was that several guardsmen had brought them to Sioux City. By the end of the second week most of the men were flat broke. Without radios most would have been climbing trees with the squirrels, shaking down the nuts to alleviate boredom. Radio had made tremendous strides since Hank had listened to the Dempsey-Tunney fight on the old Atwater-Kent crystal set.

On October 30, 1938 guardsmen at Sioux City were convinced they would be called to active combat duty at once—aliens from outer space were invading the United States. It had to be true—news bulletins were being broadcast over the radio and who could deny the authenticity? Guardsmen gasped as they listened to the horror-filled reports. Later it would be learned the broadcast had been intended as a joke, though it was received as gospel by many. How could a radio program be so realistically?

To give the reader a better understanding of the changes that had evolved in radio broadcasting since the mid-1920s, the author visited Ray H. Kremer in his Mount Dora, Florida home. Few people in the United States today know more about the golden days of radio than Kremer. Ray, you see, rose from announcer in small Chicago stations to sound-effects man for NBC and CBS. Later he would direct and produce programs.

His sound-effects were heard on some 7,000 network shows. His work enhanced such famous shows as "Gang Busters," "Grand Central Station," (which he later directed) the "Fred Allen Show," the "Helen Hayes' Theater," "Thirteen by Corwin," the "Columbia Work Shop," "Let's Pretend," and numerous soap operas.

Still handsome, slim-trim and alert, Ray smiles as he sits down in his favorite chair. Rubbing the palms of his hands together, his eyes radiate happiness for he loves to reminisce his years in radio. His wife Eleanor draws up a chair, looks admiringly at Ray and then says, "I never tire of hearing him talk about his pioneer days in radio; those stories will be lost if not recorded." The author shares some of Ray's career with readers.

There was a lot of static and fading of stations with the early Atwater-Kent and RCA Victor radios. Naturally sports and political events drew the largest listening audiences. However, with technological advances in transmitting and receiver equipment, both tone and quality of reception showed vast improvement. Soon listening audiences waited anxiously to hear Kate Smith's clear beautiful voice open her program singing, "When the moon comes over the mountain." What a thrill! Rudy Vallee's "Variety Hour" offered an array of fine talent. Edgar Bergen, a ventriloquist, with his dummy Charlie McCarthy, offered a dialogue so realistic it was difficult to detect which was the dummy. Alice Faye and Frances Langford, among others, sprung to stardom from Vallee's program. Al Jolson and Eddie Cantor were popular, but Bing Crosby soon grabbed the spotlight.

Wayne Elkin and son, Eric listen to Grandpa Elkin's old 1930s model radio.
Photo courtesy of Wayne Elkin

Programs offered by national networks quickly became more diversified. Big bands grew to unprecedented popularity. People could now dance in their living rooms or just listen to such greats as Guy Lombardo, Glen Miller, Benny Goodman, The Blue Baron, etc. Lucky Strike's "Hit Parade" drew millions of listeners as their designated big bands played the week's top fifteen songs sung by such artists as Frank Sinatra, Dick Haymes, Ginny Sims, and Doris Day.

The midwest listening audience consisted of a lot of farm and small town people and many tuned in to the barn dance programs from WLS (Chicago) and WHO (Des Moines). But, as Ray Kremer says, "There were also many big city people in the audience enjoying Minnie Pearl and Grandpa Jones." Ray's friend, Bob Burns (the Indiana Hoosier), spun humorous yarns and played his bazooka. (A World War II anti-tank weapon would be named after the tube-like contraption!)

Ray had been quick to recognize that if comedy and drama were to command large audiences, more realistic sound-effects would be needed. Realizing he had talent in that area, Ray gave up announcing and was soon doing sound improvisions for NBC.

Amos and Andy, a black comedy program, had started out at WGN (Chicago) with Freeman Gosden and Charles Correl as Sam and Henry. When Gosden and Correl switched to NBC the program became Amos and Andy. As an interesting sidelight, the station was owned by the Chicago Tribune and WGN stood for World's Greatest Newspaper. WLS (Chicago) was owned by Sears and Roebuck; thus WLS represented World's Leading Store.

Other famous comedy programs quickly emerged in the 1930s and Ray found himself doing sound for the very popular "Fred Allen Show." For years Allen was to share the limelight with the notoriously great Jack Benny, George Burns and Gracie Allen, Fibber McGhee and Molly, Vic and Sade, and the all-time master funny-man, Red Skelton. Bob Hope joined the radio comedy scene in 1938.

Early on in the 1930s the soap companies sponsored programs quickly dubbed, "Soap Operas" and the women loved them. The "Goldbergs" and "One Man's Family" were among the first. Then "The Romance of Helen Trent" came along. Ray Kremer found himself providing sound-effects for one of the greatest radio soap operas of all time, "Ma Perkins." Tears flowed into the bread dough and mixed in soap suds with the dishes as women threw themselves into the drama of romantic adventures.

Time came when the cereal makers were hawking for a larger share of the childrens' breakfast food market—thus programs for youngsters emerged. Soon the "Lone Ranger" was galloping through living rooms, "Jack Armstrong" (the all-American boy) was scoring baskets, touchdowns and hitting home runs. "Little Orphan Annie" and the "Phantom" joined in to keep the kids busy while moms were cooking dinner. After supper, entire families listened to programs like "The Aldrich Family."

There was little need for parental monitoring of radio programs in those days. Comedians were good enough to evoke laughter without four-letter words and filthy language. Outstanding actors held the steadfast interest of entire families during adventure packed dramas. With a little imagination and good sound-effects the listener felt he was part of the action. Kids were prone to switch from Kellogg's corn flakes to Wheaties, Ralson—whatever, depending on their favorite program.

But as the 1930s wore on radio comedy programs and soap operas became secondary listening choices. Workers, students and other family members no longer passed their time at lunch hour with idle chitchat. As the military situation in Europe worsened, people gathered around radios listening to the latest reports by such notable newscasters as Edward R. Murrow, H. V. Kaltenborn and Lowell Thomas.

Most Iowa people tuned in to WHO to listen to two great newscasters—Jack Shelley and H. R. Gross. The personable Jack will be long remembered for his exceptionally clear voice, perfect diction and rapid fire delivery. H. R. Gross offered a lower tone voice, slower and more deliberate presentation of the news. Both were superb announcers. Gross went on to become a United States Senator.

Jack Shelley, WHO announcer
Photo courtesy of WHO Radio

WHO announcer, H. R. Gross—he later became a U.S. Senator.
Photo courtesy of WHO Radio

As a sidenote, Jack put aside his microphone to become a WHO war correspondent in Europe during World War II. Later he was transferred to cover the war in the Pacific. There he became the first correspondent to interview the bomber crews who dropped the world's first atomic bombs on Hiroshima and Nagasaki, Japan. To cap off his war time reporting—Jack was among the correspondents present on the battleship Missouri when General MacArthur accepted the Japanese surrender.

Radio audiences were beginning to receive and expect more and more on-the-spot reporting of major events. When the huge German dirigible "Hindenberg" arrived at Elmhurst, New Jersey May 6, 1937 Herb Morrison, WLS (Chicago), was on the scene. As the huge craft descended toward a mooring station it burst into flames. Morrison's vivid description of the burning and dying not only reduced him to tears, but the audience as well.

CBS Radio audiences had become somewhat accustomed to hearing about newsworthy events on-the-scene as they happened. The great newscaster Edward R. Murrow had been in Europe reporting direct on Hitler's activities. Programs were frequently halted with the announcement, "We interrupt this program for a special report from Edward R. Murrow in London (Paris or wherever.)" So it was that hearing on-the-scene reporting became a common occurrence.

Ray recalls that with all the sabor-rattling in Europe, CBS was beginning to be known for its on-the-spot reporting. This, the dirigible event and "Buck Rogers," a popular cartoon featuring outer space adventure, he feels, contributed much toward setting the stage for one of the most dramatic radio programs of all time. Ray, who had developed some fabulous sound-effects, was to play a large role in creating the realism that made the CBS presentation of Howard

Koch's adaptation of H. G. Welles' book, "The War of Worlds," the most famous broadcast of all time.

The drama was presented October 30, 1938 by Mercury Theater with a cast of that theater's players headed by Orson Welles and John Housman. As Ray recalls, "The program was actually presented as a halloween spoof, but it backfired and caused panic in New Jersey and the metropolitan New York area!"

Replete with news bulletins and on-the-spot reporting, the action centered around Grovers Mill, New Jersey, where Martians were reported to have landed in spaceships from outer space. (Ray clued the author that Grovers Mill was chosen because it was NOT a town, but a famous landmark.)

Those who were not tuned in when the broadcast began were spellbound at the authentic sounding news bulletins and reports when the fictitious invasion was aired. Much attention to detail had been given to the creation of sound effects and, with superb acting, the presentation was extremely convincing.

Eyewitness on-the-spot newscasts described tentacled creatures firing heat ray guns burning people to a crisp; terrifying screams of the fleeing and dying could be heard over the radio. Announcers pictorially described thousands of residents fleeing the area. The audience could hear railroad ties being ripped from beds, telephone poles crashing to earth, buildings tumbling, glass breaking, etc.

So fantastic were the sound effects and so dynamic was the cast's presentation that a later survey revealed one-fifth of the six million people in the listening audience thought the broadcast events were real and the end of the world at hand. People fled their homes by the thousands creating massive traffic jams. Still others grabbed their pistols, rifles or shotguns—then hastened to join militias to fight the invaders.

Hysterical callers swamped the telephone circuits to police stations, radio stations and newspapers. Some people were reported to have been seen jumping from windows. Ray shakes his head with sadness in his eyes when he states, "After the show we even received reports of suicides! Had we known this, the show (I am sure) would have been halted to announce it was only a play."

How could Ray Kremer and his crew create such realistic sound effects? It took a great deal of ingenuity. The rumbling and crumbling was created by a big piece of cowhide. The hide had been thoroughly water soaked—then stretched across a four-by-four oak frame and allowed to dry. When struck, it produced the rumble and thunder like effects needed for the main sound effects.

A microphone suspended by a long cord into an empty basement room served as an echo chamber. Ray points out that, with an echo

Ray Kremer (upper left) directs sound effects for CBS "Gangbusters" broadcast.
Photo used by permission of CBS Inc.

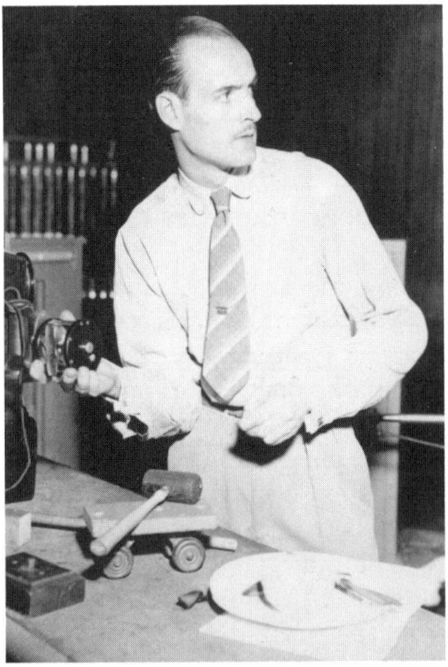

Ray Kremer, CBS sound director, with sound devices.
Photo used by permission of CBS Inc.

chamber, a man walking in a box of gravel sounded like boulders rolling around. A man on steps in the echo chamber created a sound like a rock slide. Wind was created by whirling blades in a special container. These and other ingenious devices proved to be excellent sound duplications—good enough to fool millions of people.

Ray says he will never cease to be amazed that "The War of the Worlds" created such havoc. But, he says a few good things resulted from the program: Orson Welles and John Housman were called to Hollywood where they enjoyed illustrious careers, and the Federal Communications Commission was formed and safeguards were installed in broadcasts to prevent any further recurrence of the panic resultant from "The War of the Worlds" program. Ray was happy the new rules were established, for the tragedies of that famous broadcast still live in his mind.

Meanwhile back in Happyland Dean Wesselink was getting a bit concerned about Bud Haack and Hank missing so many classes, he contacted their company commander and asked that they return to school. Besides basketball season was fast approaching and the dean wanted both of the students eligibile to participate.

Both Bud and Hank had taken their textbooks with them to Sioux City and had attempted to follow along with assignments. However, off-duty atmosphere and crowded conditions were certainly not conducive to concentration on book learning.

It took a heap of homework and the burning of a lot of midnight oil for Bud and Hank to catch up with their studies—but somehow they succeeded. Basketball season was soon underway. Meyel "Bud" Haack and Ralph Frank manned the guard positions. Clark Mollenhoff filled the center slot and Bill Powers and Hank teamed up as forwards. In the first game they handily upset a powerful Mason City quintet and a fine winning season was off to a good start.

XIV
BITTERSWEET REFLECTIONS

There was evidence even in Happyland that the depression was slacking off. More new cars were on the street, people were beginning to replace shingles on leaking roofs, broken windows and worn out clothing. A few new houses were being built and more trucks could be seen delivering coal to houses. Then, too, foolproof evidence existed: Tippy O'Flaskagin and Patty O'Kettlebelly were to be seen more

Chrysler Airflow (1937) out ahead in design.
Photo courtesy of Applegate & Applegate, Annville, PA

Lincoln (1937)—the sporty model
Photo courtesy of Applegate & Applegate, Annville, PA

Chrysler Imperial (1938)—a prestige auto
Photo courtesy of Applegate & Applegate, Annville, PA

Elvira and Ellen Hanson stand proudly by father's new 1938 Packard.
Photo courtesy of Ellen Hanson Ankrum

often in the state liquor store. The nation's economy was definitely on the rise.

On the national scene, politics continued as usual. Although Roosevelt and his programs remained popular with the majority of the people, Americans are known to want change, even if it's just their underwear. So it was that the Republicans scored many congressional victories. However, Roosevelt's Democrats remained firmly entrenched with a comfortable majority.

There was a vast difference in political parties in the 1930s. Oh, yes, there is some difference at this writing, but rarely is a campaign promise kept. Each party now complains vigorously about the other party's platform and program, but election of either party affiliate brings little change. Cousin Clinty always used the old cliche, "They keep all of their promises—right in their desk drawer—then bring them out for the next election."

Back in Happyland Hank was not searching for an enterprise in which he could make speculative investments. Eating at restaurants was stripping everything but the lining out of his billfold. James "Jim" Clave, an avid sports fan, gave him a job performing custodial services at the Production Credit Association. A week or so later Jim Orsi offered Hank a job working at his Candy Kitchen, which included some of his meals.

Two extra jobs improved Hank's finances and allowed him to be a little indiscreet with his money, though they did dictate he be fast on his feet. At five o'clock in the morning he leaped from his bed and headed for the Production Credit Association where he dusted desks, cleaned toilets, mopped floors and made a desperate effort to move dirt where it hadn't been the day before.

Between classes Hank dashed to the Candy Kitchen where he changed into a waiter's jacket and dished delicacies to hungry customers with one hand, whilst sliding a sandwich or two down his own culinary cavern with the other.

The noon hour over, he hurried back to the halls of hallucination, where the teachers imprinted a few more creases of creative thinking into his cranium. Four o'clock found him in the hoop hall for basketball practice. If the reader thinks Mohammed had a little trouble moving the mountain or if he has ever attempted assaulting Pike's Peak on a tricycle, then he has a slight idea of the financial problems Hank encountered while attending Junior College.

At the end of the day, his side jobs completed, Hank sauntered aimlessly back to the fire station to perform his night fireman duties and get in some studying. Small wonder he appeared calm and collected; he was so tired he would have welcomed being overrun by a truck just for the opportunity to lie down and rest.

The fire station was little more than a block from the school. When the call involved a fire south of the station, and there were not many firemen present, the chief always swung by the school and allowed Hank to mount the back of the truck on the run.

One particular fire call would never be forgotten. Hank was in class when the whistle blew; he bolted through the door, nearly running over Jeanette McCauliff, Marian Haack and Barbara Westervelt, who were just coming in. Dashing to the corner of Des Moines and Bank Streets, he caught the back of the number one truck.

The chief was alone and having a bit of a conversation with the spark plugs in his attempts to get more speed. While putting on his firecoat, Hank felt like he was riding to the fire on a pogo stick, as the truck bounced over the, by now famous, Bank Street potholes.

Smoke was boiling out of the basement when they arrived at the residence of Lacey Darnell. Lacey was a World War I veteran whose pride of service dictated that he participate in every patriotic holiday parade. There were those who maintained he stayed up all night dressed in his uniform for fear he might miss one of the events.

Hank felt like he was an entire fire company as the chief shouted, "Get the ax; get the hose; get down into the basement!" While Hank was complying with his order, the chief pried open the basement window.

With hose in hand, Hank catapulted through the open window and into the basement. Seeing a flame flickering through a wall of smoke, he opened the nozzle full force. Suddenly he heard someone emit an ear-splitting howl like a prize-winning coon dog on the trail. Moving forward, he spotted the venerable veteran in a well-drenched World War I shirt, with a look on his face like he had just knocked out six enemy machine guns in the Argonne Forest during a cloudburst.

Mr. Darnell croaked through the smoke, "Hank, you didn't need to pour the whole damn Boone River on me. I just about had the fire under control with a few buckets of water." Fortunately the old boy was suffering a bit from smoke inhalation and decided to put off dismembering Hank—leastwise until he solved his oxygen problem!

While Mr. Darnell held his head out the window trying to snuff up half the air in Hamilton County, Hank's hose aim improved and the flames were soon out. The fire was not widespread and had resulted from Mr. Darnell trying to thaw out a frozen burlap-wrapped pipe with a blowtorch.

Hank wet the area down a little more, not so much to alleviate any further burning, but in hopes the fire would die out in the old Hun hunter's eyes long enough for him to depart the premises safely. In addition to rage, Mr. Darnell was now suffering a severe case of ventilation vibrations while doing a stint in the open window.

At last Mr. Darnell withdrew his head, uttered some not so nice words and went back upstairs. Hank quickly shoved the fire hose out the window and crawled out behind it.

Hank could see Mr. Darnell standing in the window screaming and waving his arms like his uniform was shrinking and he wouldn't be able to wear it in the next parade. It was obvious he wanted to talk to the chief and couldn't come outside in the below zero temperature.

The chief finally went inside. Hank couldn't hear the conversation but when the chief returned he said, "Hank let me give you a little fatherly advice—if I were you I don't think I'd go back next summer and ask Darnell for a job watering his garden!"

On the world scene as the winter of 1939 wound down and the weather began warming, Hitler's thoughts again turned to conquests. March 15, 1939 Hitler moved a substantial number of troops into Czechoslovakia. In little more than a week that country was under German control. Then Hitler's troops smashed into Memel and Danzig, a territory which divided Germany proper from East Prussia. The Allies had turned that parcel of land over to Poland after World War I.

Meanwhile, in Spain, General Francisco Franco's Rebels had gained the upper hand in their battle to oust the Loyalists-Republic. On March 28, 1939 the Rebels seized Madrid and the long Civil War ended. Hitler had gained much in testing his latest armaments—now he was ready to put them to full use.

As March drew to a close, Poland and Great Britain were threatening Hitler with war if Germany attempted to take over Poland. Hitler didn't seem to be losing any sleep over their threats. Old "Joe" Stalin, the Russian leader, was now getting his dander up, for he knew full well Britain could not defend Poland without his cooperation and he evidently hadn't been consulted.

Down in spaghetti land, Benito "Bonehead" Mussolini, a bit disgusted, figured it was about time he did something to get out from under the shadow of Adolf Hitler, for he had been left out of the act. In fact Mussolini hadn't as much as been sent a copy of the script for approval. Even Hitler would have had to admit Mussolini was a far better actor than leader.

Somehow Mussolini knew he must get the attention of Hitler, the rest of the world and his own Italians. How could any self-respecting successor to Julius Caesar expect to gain notoriety if he didn't keep his troops committed to battle? After sweating it out for a few days, Mussolini came up with a foolproof attention getter that couldn't backfire. On April 7, 1939 he moved his troops into the Balkan state of Albania, which was already an Italian protectorate; great show—he drew cheers from his Italian people!

By now Hitler had decided it might be good thinking to get a little more cozy with Russia's Dictator Joe Stalin and perhaps get the Russian Bear to stay in its lair while his troops went on a little safari in Poland.

Hitler was a mite wrought up over England siding with Poland. He proceeded to cancel a British-German naval agreement (consumated in 1935) which, as far as Hitler was concerned, might just as well have been written in disappearing ink.

The German fuehrer, for some reason, must have thought he shouldn't attack Poland while Germany had a non-aggression pact with that country—so on April 28, 1939 he cancelled the agreement.

Time goes fast when you're having fun, and spring was soon on the way. Hank was beginning to settle into a somewhat normal routine; a great winning basketball season had ended. However, there were several baseball players in junior college and Dean Wesselink decided it would be nice to field a team.

The team needed very little coaching; all were in good condition and only a few practice sessions were needed. Hank was just beginning to rest up a bit when a group of junior high boys presented a petition asking that Hank be assigned to coach them in baseball. The school agreed to knock off part of Hank's tuition in payment. Now he had a full schedule again; everyone except Hank could relax.

There is nothing that stirs the human being in the freezebelt like the first warm refreshing days of spring. Only those who have forgotten to remove their winter underwear are irritable. Baseball season is just around the corner.

PLAY BALL!!

When spring has sprung and grass is green,
Then the umpires shout, "play ball,"
Kids from age one to one hundred,
By the millions will answer the call.

From the Atlantic shores to the Pacific,
'Cross the breadth and depth of our land,
They'll either be on the playing fields,
On the bleachers, or in the stands.

Then in crowded parks, both far and wide,
Lusty voices you'll hear harmonize,
Singing "Take me out to the ball game,
"Then for the National Anthem they'll rise.

Willie Whirlwind hits a long fly ball,
Like a streak down to first base he goes.
Then the pitcher throws a wild one,
Right past the batter's nose.

Willie Whirlwind dashes to second base,
Charlie Catchum can't throw him out.
Now as they say, "The ducks on the pond!"
And the crowd begins to shout.

While the aroma of peanuts and crackerjacks,
And popcorn floats through the stands.
All the home team fans rise to their feet,
Cheering and clapping their hands.

Louie Longball pulls his cap down tight,
As he steps up to the plate.
Now the fans are watching anxiously,
For he's been in a slump of late.

Whether Louie poles it out of the park,
Or, takes three strikes at the plate.
They'll keep rooting for the home team,
Long after they're out of the gate.

by H. R. Ankrum

At last on May 22, 1939 Germany got around to signing an agreement with Italy creating a pact between the two countries—it kinda made things legal-like and tickled Mussolini pink, for at last he had been included in Hitler's plans. Japan was invited to make the pact a threesome.

Independence Day July 4, 1939 was celebrated in the United States with a little more patriotic zest. In Happyland Hank and other guardsmen noticed a great deal more applause along the parade route to Graceland Cemetery. Patriotic speeches were delivered and received with far more enthusiasm.

That afternoon millions of Americans sat glued to their radios while a capacity crowd filed into Yankee Stadium for "Lou Gehrig Day." The nation was paying homage to a great personage and fabulous baseball player. That player was the great New York Yankee first baseman, "Lou" Gehrig. The baseball world had been shocked the past May when he benched himself. Later it was learned that the great man had been stricken with the terrible amyotrophic lateral sclerosis—a disease that would henceforth be known as "Lou Gehrig Disease."

Before taking himself out of the Yankee lineup Lou had earned the moniker "The Ironman" having played in a record 2,130 consecutive games. He had amassed a lifetime .341 batting average while poling 493 home runs. Lou had driven in 1,990 runs (170 in a single season)—second only to the great Babe Ruth.

The millions listening to radios, along with those in the stadium, would never forget that brave wonderful man's parting statement, "You have been reading about my tough breaks for weeks, but today I consider myself the luckiest man in the world." With that statement tears flowed across the breadth of America. (Lou would die in 1941, but his courageous spirit lives on in the annals of baseball history.)

It seemed like the summer of 1939 would bring nothing but bad news—the situation in Europe was growing more serious by the day. On July 24 Great Britain, France and Russia agreed to assist each other if one of the three came under attack. However, there were contingencies—the pact was not to go into effect until other military agreements were consummated. The accord must surely have baffled Hitler for it sounded like his adversaries had agreed to disagree if they didn't agree; this was high level diplomacy at its best!

There had been so many agreements and denunciations of agreements that by the end of July, it was difficult to decipher just what country would align with what country if an attack was to come from whatever country. It was beginning to appear the attitude of world powers was becoming, "What is one agreement more or less?"

But wait, there were more agreements to come. Germany and Russia on August 23, 1939 signed a non-agression pact. The world was then cognizant of the fact that Joe Stalin had something up his sleeve, for both Russia and Germany had always had designs on Poland. There was no more humor in the situation as would be learned in the days ahead.

The National Guard encampment had ended with training conducted as effectively as possible considering equipment issued. Although an increase of 1.7 billion dollars was made in military allocations, the National Guard saw little change. Oh, yes, they had been issued new cotton khaki summer uniforms—much more comfortable than the old khaki jodhpurs, woolen shirt and wrap leggings. But the National Guard evidently still couldn't afford to issue canvas lace leggings. Could this be progress? In Germany on August 27 of that year a jet aircraft, designed by Dr. Hans von Ohain, was taxied down a runway.

Returning to Happyland, Hank had enrolled for his second year of junior college, though he was doubtful he would complete the year, for surely the guard would soon be called up to bring them to better training posture.

Hank was even more convinced war with Germany was inevitable when radio programs were interrupted on September 1, 1939 at

German troops smash forward into Poland.
Photo courtesy of Mrs. Gertrude Horan

4:30 a.m. (German time). The German Army had rumbled across Poland's borders. The attack (estimated to be some fifty divisions strong) had been expected all summer and was now a reality. Hank slept little that night for he was certain this would affect his future.

German Stuka dive bombers created havoc in Poland.
Photo courtesy of Mrs. Gertrude Horan

So fast did the Germans advance, the Polish forces (though some three million strong) hardly knew what hit them. Never had the world witnessed such a strong, effective military force with employment of all its arms capabilities in a well coordinated attack.

German aircraft bombed strategic targets, while tanks cracked Poland's lines. Exploiting their breakthroughs, Hitler's forces slashed behind Poland's front line defense troops, denying reinforcement from reserves. Then, with Poland's forward and rear echelons isolated from each other, the German tank-infantry teams commenced their rout of the Polish reserve forces, destroying or capturing supply dumps.

Motorized infantry, mechanized artillery and assault guns moved in with precision to protect German flanks—then the entire scenario was replayed. The term, "blitzkreig," describing the action, was to become a new word in the English dictionary—and pincer movements, providing two-pronged attacks, were to become major factors in fast moving modern warfare.

Poland's terrain, for the most part, was ideal for employment of armor and, the Germans were far out in front of other countries in its use. Their armored tactics would reign supreme until near the end of World War II when most of their armor was destroyed, and sheer numbers outweighed their capability.

It was with amazement that the world would learn of the destruction wrought upon Polish troops, equipment, bridges, cities, and populace. German airpower had a demoralizing effect, both on the battlefield and among civilians.

A new art had been added to the use of airpower, for Germany had developed unbelievable air and ground forces coordination procedures. Their Stuka dive bomber pilots were directed by radio from liaison officers attached to commanders on the ground. Dive bombers performed a role, normally reserved for artillery, of bombing key defense positions out ahead of the fast-advancing German forces. This highly effective method of combined arms warfare proved terrifying to defenders.

If the rest of the world had any doubt about Russia's intentions, they were dispelled on September 17, 1939 when Russian forces came crashing across the border into Poland. Hitler had not counted totally upon this happening, even though it was later learned the two countries had agreed to split Poland between them.

The Russians launched their attack on Poland with a huge force; their intentions to get a share of Poland were quite clear. The Poles couldn't believe their eyes when the Russians started attacking them and taking Polish prisoners. Poles tried to retreat toward Rumania, allowing the Russians to come in, while fiercely resisting the German advance.

Russian troops struck deep into Polish territory. In the end only some 30,000 Poles escaped to Rumania. All Polish resistance had been virtually shattered by October 1, 1939 and the government in Warsaw had surrendered. A badly mauled Poland had been partitioned by Russia and Germany. Russians were no doubt wondering why it had allowed Germany, contrary to the Versailles Treaty, to develop some of its planes and tanks in their country. Charles Lindbergh, America's famous trans-Atlantic flyer, had warned the United States government of Hitler's mighty war machine, but he had been chastised and called a German sympathizer for his efforts to keep the United States out of a war with Germany.

When Germany began its blitz of Poland, threats were made and ultimatums issued to no avail. Three days after the invasion, an ill-prepared Britain and France declared war on Germany, though they made no efforts to launch an attack on their enemy.

Although everyone was deeply concerned about the war in Europe—most people continued to make a valiant attempt to carry on their efforts to shake off the effects of the depression. However, legislators favoring a United States isolation policy were beginning to dwindle in numbers—support for better military preparedness seemed to be gaining momentum. Young men of military service age became convinced a draft of manpower would soon be initiated. A few adventuresome youths, like Happyland's Robert Mitterling, would join the Canadian Air Force.

Meanwhile back at Happyland Junior College an array of fine talent had turned out for the basketball season. Three sharpshooting forwards, Bill Powers, Robert Titsworth and John Boeye were on hand to man the forward positions. Clark Mollenhoff and Melvin Keigan effectively handled the center position. Meyel "Bud" Haack had transferred to Butler University leaving Ralph Frank and Hank to handle the chores at guard.

When the end of November approached, Coach Leonard Skoglund was confident he had fielded the best team in Happyland Junior College history. But on November 30, 1939 the coach wondered how long it would be before his charges would be charging on a field of battle. The news media had announced that Russian troops had invaded Finland. The hearts of Americans bled for that tiny nation and admiration for the courageous Finns grew daily.

To put it mildly, the Finns put up one helluva fight, ambushing Russian armored and troop columns with their lightning-strike ski troops, sabotaging ammunition dumps and battling tooth and nail for land held. But, in the end, tiny Finland succumbed to the huge Russian forces.

Latvia and Estonia had been a part of Tzarist Russia until 1918, when they received their independence. They had absorbed a belly-full of Russian dominance and really wanted to be no part of Russia. However, Russia had pretty well reached an agreement with Germany that the two small Baltic countries would remain under Russian influence. They had no choice but to go along with Russia's desires.

Throughout the United States Christmas of 1939 would be remembered by many as a time when concern over the world situation began to outweigh problems created by the depression. Hank and many others had hoped that the 1940s would offer a better way of life. But from news media reports, it appeared more probable that youths of that era would be bartering with bullets instead of legal tender for their existence.

Strangely enough, progress had not been totally stifled during the tumultuous depression-ridden 1930s. Many advancements had been made in science and technology. Even Cousin Clinty had toyed with the idea of a new invention. No, not his combination corn-picking hook and pick, but a new cigarette lighter—a compass sensitive to phosphorus that pointed to the nearest man with a match in his pocket.

Commercial air travel, as predicted by Charles Lindbergh, had become a popular mode of travel for the affluent. Daily overseas flights were now being scheduled. As the reader recalls, several new flying records had been established in the 1930s. However, from all news reports, it appeared Hank's flight record of six feet (off a manure spreader wheel) remained unchallenged.

Throughout the 1930s movies had continued to be second only to radio as the most affordable depression years source of entertainment—some 80 million movie tickets were being sold weekly. With sound tracks greatly improved, musicals became all the rage. A host of singing and dancing stars quickly emerged. Among the notables were Bing Crosby, Dick Powell, Maurice Chevalier, Fred Astaire, Ginger Rogers, Ruby Keeler, and Eleanor Powell.

American audiences even developed a taste for finer music when the voices of Nelson Eddy, Jeanette MacDonald and Deanna Durbin were introduced to the screen. With all due respect to fantastic choreographers and outstanding dancers, none of them ever came up with a routine that could hold a candle to Cousin Willobee's "Hot Sole Shuffle."

Comedies were always surefire remedies for the depressed during those trying years. Laurel and Hardy, Hal Roach's "Little Rascals," Charlie Chaplin, Joe E. Brown, Bob Hope, Martha Raye, Zazu Pitts, and Joan Davis provided humor on screen. Yes, and even Jack Benny made a few side-splitter movies. But all humorous antics were anticlimatic when compared to James Arthur's sow-bustin' routine.

Cartoons had been introduced by Walt Disney in 1928 and had grown tremendously in popularity during the 1930s. Mickey and Minnie Mouse became the first rodents in the old Isis Theater that weren't eating popcorn under the seats.

With the crime figures of the prohibition and depression era providing an unlimited source of material, it wasn't surprising that gangster movies enjoyed success. Tough guy mimics like Edward G.

Robinson, James Cagney, George Raft, and Humphrey Bogart topped the posters of the public's most wanted-to-see in gangster movies.

Adventure films soared in popularity. Audiences were kept spellbound by Spencer Tracy, Henry Fonda, James Stewart, Robert Taylor, Cary Grant, Tyrone Power, etc. Leading ladies of that era included favorites such as Katherine Hepburn, Claudette Colbert, Jane Wyman, Carole Lombard, and Jean Harlow. Iowa audiences were partial to Don Ameche, who came from Dubuque, McDonald Carey, who hailed from Sioux City and John Wayne, who was born in Winterset. Of course Iowa had a bit of a claim on Gary Cooper—he attended Grinnell College.

But the greatest production of the depression era (perhaps of all time) was the filming in technicolor of Margaret Mitchell's book, "Gone With The Wind." Clark Gable and Vivian Leigh, with a superior supporting cast, helped make the 1939 Civil War movie an all-time classic.

Adding to adventure entertainment were growing numbers of investigative reporter films. For awhile these imaginative productions had some reporters thinking the news media had taken over law enforcement. One could readily discern when a good crime solving reporter film was being shown at the local theater—all the Happyland reporters walked around for weeks in trench coats and dark glasses with their hat brims set low on their foreheads.

Frankenstein movies hit the screen during the 1930s with Boris Karloff magnificently disguised as the monster. Actually he looked more like a pumpkin jack-o-lantern who had been caught up in a bolt throwing contest. Much interest was created in the drama when it was announced in the "Daily Freeman Journal" that the theater had hired a nurse to be on hand during the showing to offer immediate first aid to those who were prone to fainting.

Toward the end of the 1930s the careers of some of the great "B" western actors, who actually looked and played somewhat authentic cowboy roles, began to fade. With the introduction of the singing cowboys a resemblance to realism dwindled rapidly. After seeing his first singing cowboy western, Cousin Clinty confided to Mother Lucy that he would a helluva lot rather watch Hank perform his apple tree trick.

Oh yes, the more authentic well-filmed westerns still remained popular and continued to be surefire box office hits. A few of the old "B" movie stars switched to the more realistic westerns. John Wayne starred in John Ford's epic western, "Stage Coach." Randolph Scott did a fabulous job in "The Last of the Mohicans." Henry Fonda helped create a masterpiece in "Drums along the Mohawk." The great Gary Cooper would do a highly commendable job of acting in "Unconquered."

Admittedly the 1920s should always be called "the golden age of sports," for never have games and the athletes that played them shown such remarkable improvements. However, it would not be unjust to dub the 1930s "the gilded age of sports" for, as readers have learned, many of the stars of the 1920s continued their illustrious careers during that decade. It would have been a tossup as to whether Jack Dempsey or Gene Tunney could have bested Joe Louis. Jesse Owens proved the best of the decade's track and field stars. But no one seemed to equal the all-around athletic prowess of the great Indian, Jim Thorpe.

Bernie Beerman's remarkable "Big Ten" Golden Gophers of Minnesota became the terror of the plains during the 1930s. Many fantastic football players emerged: Bronco Negurski of Minnesota; Larry Kelly of Yale; Jay Berwanger, Chicago University; Dick Crayne of Iowa (Crayne kicked a football 103 yards!); Bobby Grayson and Bones Hamilton of Stanford; and a host of others. But, the performances of Red Grange, the "Gallopin' Ghost" from Illinois has yet to be equalled at this writing.

In 1938 Iowa State College (now Iowa State University) gained some national recognition when that school won the conference. Edward Bock, a tough Fort Dodge lineman, became that school's first all-American. Another Fort Dodger, Dale Brand, raised Iowa State to national notoriety in wrestling.

At last the University of Iowa, with its famous "Iron Man" team of 1939, rose to national prominence. Led by all-American Nile Kinnick, Iowa unleashed a furious air and ground attack. Mike Enich of Boone was a mainstay in the Iowa line. Hank was proud indeed that his good friend, James R. "Bob" Otto, of Fort Dodge was a part of that great assembly of football talent.

Following closely on Otto's heels, Art Johnson, an all-state back for Fort Dodge in 1939, took over the fullback chores at the University of Iowa. Starring in 1940-1941, Art took time out for World War II—then took over the Iowa fullback chores again in 1945.

Both Art Johnson and Bob Otto had carried on in the footsteps of two other great Dodger footballers - Don Geyer, who carried the ball for Northwestern University, and Mel Brokaw, a tough lineman for Iowa State.

It wasn't uncommon for a family to have several brothers competing in sports for several years running. Fort Dodge opponents were happy when all the Messerly brothers had graduated. Teams on Mason City's schedules were thrilled to see the last of the Hirt brothers fade from the athletic scene. And don't you know, there are those who thought Clarion would never run out of Sharp boys!

On the local scene (during the 1930s) Happyland High continued to turn out some fine athletes. Some chose not to attend college and others simply didn't have the financial resources. But, several did go on to college.

Basketball was probably the favorite sport in Happyland at that time and the high school produced some excellent players. Wayne Froning enrolled at the University of Iowa—then dropped out to play pro-ball for Universal Pictures. Lawrence Kayser and John McMurray played for Grinnell. Warren Maxon, a speedy forward, played at Iowa State. Sheldon Pringle, who was another Hank Lusetti in the making, played junior college basketball but opted not to continue the sport in a larger school. Don Shelton, a three-letter man, signed with the Pittsburgh Pirates.

Ralph Burton, Ralph Frank and Clark Mollenhoff would later play both football and basketball for Drake University. Melvin Greenley played college football at Coe. Keith Van Winkle played baseball with Iowa State Teachers College (now Northern Iowa University). Meyel "Bud" Haack (one of the greatest Happylanders to don baseball spikes) opted not to play big league baseball. Bud did play some outstanding ball for Butler University. Jumpin' Jack Phillips became a track star at Iowa State College.

To cap off local sports, three local swimmers brought home a host of blue ribbons in the state and regional meets during the latter half of the 1930s. Francis Hemingway walked off with the Australian crawl record and Iola Ingertson took top honors in the breast stroke. Both girls ranked high in other events. Lloyd "Red" Rinehimer, the track star, proved he was not only a rocket on land, but even swimming upside down he won the state title in the junior backstroke. Yes, Happyland produced some darn good athletes during the depression years.

Many small rural towns produced championship teams during the depression years. Older readers will recall the three "Ds"—Dike, Diagnol and Dunkerton for the names of those towns were synonymous with the word basketball.

Happyland residents were extremely proud of the nearby Kamrar High School girl's basketball team. Kamrar was so small that when one doorbell rang nearly half the town heard it and went to the door. Come game night the only people to be found at home were suspect of being bedridden. Until the game was over one could have fired a cannon loaded with ball bearings down main street without endangering a soul!

Kamrar's teams started their drive to the championship in 1937. Coached by Bill Templeton the Kamrar girls battled their way to runner-up in the state finals. Players that year were Marjorie Olthoff,

Beverly Olthoff, Leah Kennedy, Helen Welp, LaVonne Welp, Elizabeth Brinkema, Rowena Gilbert, Virginia Goodell, Charlotte Brill, and Lillian Arnold.

The team didn't quite make it to the state in 1938, but in 1939 they came roaring back to the finals. Carrying Kamrar's banners those years were Donna Kennedy, Leah Kennedy, Marjorie Olthoff, Beverly Olthoff, Edna Trampel, Helen Welp, Eunice Welp, Elizabeth Brinkema, Marjorie Arends, and Charlotte Clabaugh.

The following year (1940) Kamrar again made it to the state playoffs. Those giving their all for Kamrar High were Donna Kennedy, Beverly Olthoff, Edna Trampel, Helen Welp, Eunice Welp, Elizabeth Brinkema, Marjorie Arends, Charlotte Clabaugh, Wilma Ferguson, and Edna Ferguson.

During all these years another Hamilton County school, Stratford, was Kamrar's arch rival. The Stratford girls, coached by Fred Deines, finally overcame their Kamrar nemesis to advance to the state finals in 1943.

Kamrar's highly competitive girl's team wouldn't win the state championship until 1948 when coach Ken Bryant's battling basketball beauties finally brought home the coveted first-place trophy. The Texas State Champions (considered by many to be the best in the nation) challenged the Kamrar sextette. Kamrar accepted the challenge and in a hard fought game became the consensus national champions. In 1950 Kamrar, then coached by Richard Brauer, proved worthy of carrying the Kamrar banners and became runner-up in the state finals.

Of interest, are the number of sisters and cousins on the aforementioned Kamrar teams, as Fay Kennedy Buckles says, "If they weren't blood relatives they were most probably related by marriage—if not, they were close friends. Virtually all the girls in the school played basketball." Four Kennedy sisters played for Kamrar: Leah, Theda, Donna, and Fay. Yes, Kamrar fielded some beautiful and talented basketball players—a pleasure to observe both on and off the court.

The Happyland High School boy's basketball team would battle their way to the final game of the 1943 state basketball tournament - only to be defeated by their old nemesis Mason City.

Smaller schools also fielded some fine bands. Lake Mills (near Mason City) took top honors in the 1941 National Marching Band Contest held in St. Paul, Minnesota. Lake Mills won the Class C gold medal with 96 out of a possible 100 points.

Meanwhile back in Happyland Hank, in an effort to cheer up his family and friends, had spent more money than he could afford for presents that Christmas of 1939. To put it mildly he was down to his last five dollars. The superintendent of schools called him to his

Lake Mills, Iowa High School Band—National Marching Band Champs, 1941
Photo courtesy of Lake Mills Graphic

office. He advised Hank that the school board had directed that all tuition payments must be brought up to date. Hank had counted on coaching junior high baseball for his tuition, but the superintendant said that would cover only the last quarter.

Hank was reluctant to borrow money from anyone as he didn't know when or if he could ever pay it back. Irene Froning, the superintendent's secretary, intervened, hoping to convince her boss to allow Hank to remain in school, but it was to no avail. At last Hank arose and walked slowly from the room, picked up his books and proceeded back to the fire house.

For several hours Hank just sat on the edge of his bunk staring out the window contemplating his future—he had wanted that college education and wanted it bad. Across the alley atop the Hahne Printing Company building a few sparrows could be seen huddled around the base of a chimney attempting to find respite from the wintry blast.

The sparrows, Hank thought, looked even more miserable than he—probably hadn't eaten for days. In an effort to accrue enough money for tuition he had subsisted on the free lunch he received each day at the Candy Kitchen—plus bread, coupled with a box of chocolates Mr. Orsi had given him for Christmas. Now he could at least eat three meals each day!

Hell, yes, he thought, and why not give those miserable sparrows something to cheer them up a bit? He walked across the street to

Welch's grocery store, bought a sack of unpopped popcorn, popped open a window and put it on the window sill. A sparrow banquet was soon in progress. There was no guest speaker; all of them had something to chirp about. Watching the sparrows eat made Hank hungry and he decided to go down to Jim Phillip's cafe for a hamburger or two.

It had been somewhat of a nightmare attempting to keep up with his studies while trying to earn enough to stay in school—and remaining in school had been extremely tough at times. Hank consoled himself with the thought that if the guard wasn't called to active duty he could save enough money to finish junior college the next year. However, he was heartbroken when he wasn't along with the basketball team that spring when they advanced to the quarterfinals of the National Junior College Basketball Tournament. But, life must go on and one had to learn to take the bitter with the sweet during those years.

Wherever people gathered they discussed the latest events in Europe. On April 9, 1940, German troops marched into tiny Denmark and the helpless Danes, unable to mount a formidable defense, were forced to surrender. The Germans quickly moved troops into Norway, where they encountered bitter resistance. However, on May 3 of that same year, Norway surrendered.

Then the world was stunned. World War II was launched in earnest on May 10, 1940 when Hitler's Germany mounted a horrendous attack on Belgium, Holland and Luxembourg. No mercy was shown to the resisting military or to innocent civilians.

Newsreels divulged columns of refugees, with meager belongings, herded ahead of the German forces, whose aircraft were bombing and strafing them with machine gun fire to ensure they continued to clog the roadways.

France had rushed forces to Belgium, but with refugees clogging the roads, they were unable to get to the front to mount an effective defense. German armored and infantry columns moved forward unchecked. The aircraft of defender nations were no match for the strong German Luftwaffe and the three tiny nations were quickly overrun.

By May 28, 1940 the fighting, except for that of partisian guerrillas, was pretty well ended in the low countries. Now Hitler was ready to attend to his prime target: France and the British forces helping defend that country.

The French had busied themselves throughout the 1930s building the Maginot Line, which extended on the right flank from Switzerland to the thought-to-be impassable Ardennes Forest on the left. Much of World War I had been fought in miserable muddy trenches, and the Maginot Line provided far more creature comforts than one might expect in a ground defense installation.

While the Germans were developing new equipment, the French were building an elaborate network of underground troop tunnels, air conditioned troop quarters and a formidable array of strong gun emplacements with underground supply depots and railways.

One had to admit that, when viewed on newsreels, that the Maginot Line presented an impressive sight and appeared impregnable from enemy attack. Only one problem existed: no one had thoroughly convinced the Germans that they must go through the Maginot Line to get to France. But, unlike football, in warfare troops can go out of bounds to reach their goal!

On May 16, 1940 Hitler proved the Ardennes Forest to be worthless as a defense obstacle. He bypassed the Maginot Line beyond its northwest terminus, crossing the Meuse River in the Sidan sector. France's vaunted Maginot Line had proved to be an albatross around its neck. French and British Forces were now subject to a two-prong attack.

Now the powerful German army with its heavily mobile tank-infantry teams and quick-strike dive bombers drove hard across France pushing in pronged attacks toward channel ports.

The British, determined to run away to be able to fight again another day, pulled off an amazing evacuation of the majority of their troops from Dunkirk, France during the period May 26 through June 4, 1940. What an accomplishment! Every vessel available, from transports to commercial fishing boats down to pleasure craft, was assembled and pressed into action.

The courageous British Air Force and Navy fought like tigers, while a selected few troops out front of the withdrawal perimeter battled to their last round of ammunition and grenades. With fixed bayonets they held back the hordes of attacking Germans while nearly 350,000 of their buddies loaded on ship. However, had the Germans not halted to regroup for the final push, things could have been different. On June 5, 1940 Dunkirk fell to the Germans.

Mussolini had sat back about as long as he could waiting for Hitler to ask for Italy's help. Here Germany was about to take Paris, while Mussolini and his forces waited in the wings as Adolf was taking bows and curtain calls in Deuschland. At last, weary of waiting for Hitler to call him on stage, Mussolini on June 10, 1940 had his Italians declare war on France and England. Hitler didn't need his help as yet, but at least it was reason enough for Mussolini to make a few more speeches.

Paris fell without French opposition to the thunderbolt advance of the German forces on June 14, 1940 and one day later, with the German Army already at their rear, French troops on the stationary Maginot Line surrendered. Premier Paul Reynauld resigned and Marshal Henri Petain became Premier of France.

Newsreels revealed that Hitler nearly had outdone Cousin Willobee's "Hot Sole Shuffle," dancing with glee when, on June 17, 1940, he received the plea of France's Marshal Petain for peace.

Hitler wouldn't approve of the French surrender in France's former Marshal Foch's private rail car while it was parked in a building. Orders were issued to move the car to the exact spot in the Compiegne Forest, where it had sat at the time of the German surrender at the end of World War I.

The German fuehrer and other German representation sat at the same tables and in the chairs that had been occupied by the French officials that November 11, 1918 when the Armistice for the past World War was negotiated.

There was, however, a difference in the time required to consummate the agreement. Three days had been taken in 1918. Hitler allowed very little time for protest. The entire ceremony lasted less than one-half hour; on June 22, 1940 the Armistice was signed. To say the Germans were elated would be putting it mildly. The Treaty of Versailles had been avenged.

Meanwhile, back in the United States people were attempting to go about their lives as routinely as possible despite the war raging in Europe. The United States was in far worse military posture for war than either of its former World War I Allies. Most of the American people still talked isolationism, steadfastly resolving not to be caught up in another European war. But, was the ocean between the United States and Europe enough protection?

By now the United States Navy was getting a mite concerned; it needed a little upgrading of its present ships and a whole lot more of them. After France fell, the Navy asked for 4 billion dollars to create a two-ocean navy since now both Germany and Japan could pose threats.

Back in Happyland, U.S.A., and environs, baseball and softball games continued and, with each celebration and the economy improving, a carnival was a must. After the ball game, most players joined in the fun. Of course, in those days no carnival was complete without the "fight shows."

Each show had its own barker, who hawked tickets from a podium. Each barker also had his own little diddy worked up, usually with a little word tangling twist to it.

Lynn "Hook" Berryhill, Kamrar, was a powerfully built strong man. Hook had been a wrestling star at Iowa State College. The great Hook could have bodily picked up most "carney" wrestlers and thrown them through the ring tent, but he wasn't the vicious type and sorta toyed with them awhile, then slammed them to the floor and pinned them.

When Hook was at the carnival (and he didn't miss many), after he had defeated decisively all the wrestlers, the carney grapplers usually got a little canvas-shy and their eyes a bit tired from looking up at the huge light bulb illuminating the ring. It was then the barker switched his emphasis to boxing.

While in junior college, Clark Mollenhoff, one of Happyland's star athletes, had married the pretty Georgia Osmundson. Clark, a tall well built lad, was rock hard from working in Osmundson's spade factory. He enjoyed conning the con man at the fight shows.

For these occasions Clark wore a sailor straw hat, a big bow tie, and the gaudiest looking blazer he could find. When the carnie at the tent fights started beating on the claxton to draw a crowd out front for the brain bashing contest, Ralph Frank, Meyel "Bud" Haack, Jack Marvel, Vernon Brandt, Robert Ostlund, Maynard Miller, and others would push Clark out front and yell, "Our man can whip yours!"

Clark was about six feet five inches tall and broad-shouldered. He intentionally took on the appearance of a full-fledged yokel as he stood gawking up at the barker with his straw hat planted squarely on his head, his bow tie bobbing up and down on his Adam's apple. The "barker" would complain vigorously about Clark's standing too close, probably because the moisture from Clark's nostrils was tarnishing his zircon ring.

Sooner or later, if the barker was not successful in getting a more ferocious looking fighter to match muscles with one of his gladiators, he would center his barbs on Clark and offer to pay him three dollars if he could stay with one of his pugnacious predators for two rounds. Clark would then produce as stupid a grin as he could muster and ask if he would pay five dollars if he could last three rounds. The crowd would roar with laughter and the pitchman, figuring the match would sell tickets, then closed the deal and reached down to help Clark up on the platform.

Once up front, the amicable Clark would hold both hands clasped over his head in a victory stance and spar around awkwardly to the delight of the crowd. A tent full of ticket buyers was soon lined up to see the slaughter while the contestant was being taken to the makeshift dressing room in the rear of the tent to be outfitted for the fight.

When the fighters entered the ring, there was always laughter at the tent-sized trunks the challenger was wearing and, sometimes, at the fact he wore no shoes because the carnies had none to fit him. The barker normally doubled as a referee and continued belittling the battler in the baggy drawers until the opening bell. Clark always ignored the badgering and continued exercising at the ropes with ridiculous gyrations.

It was when Clark turned from his corner and started toward the center of the ring that the carnies and those in the crowd, who didn't know him, sensed all was not what it seemed with this youth in his teens. With the end of the instructions old "Clobbering Clark" would touch gloves with his opponent, step back and reveal a boxer's stance and the skill and footwork of a professional. Mollenhoff, a Burnside-born lad, had been mastering the art of boxing since he was five years old and could have been a topflight heavyweight contender had he chosen to make boxing a career.

When the two fighters came together, the one with the cauliflower ears who had drunk too many beers, saw more leather in his face than he had seen since his grade school class took a guided tour through a shoe factory. Moving with pugilistic precision from side to side, Clark would proceed to belt the daylights out of the big-mouthed brawler for the balance of the first round.

The second round was usually a prototype of the first, except that the punchy old carnival pro was now aware his opponent had boxed something other than apples and had swung on a whole lot more than a barn door. Before the fight was over, Clark usually had dusted every square inch of the canvas with his opponent's trunks and had him grabbing for ropes more times than a cowboy on a thousand-mile cattle drive. At the conclusion of the fight, if the ruffian was still in the ring, he had appealed twice through diplomatic channels to everyone but the League of Nations plus directly to Clark and the referee at least ten times to stop the fight.

Watching Clark perform when a tough guy challenged him at carnivals finally ended. It could have been he outgrew his blazer, but still others said his wife, Georgia, had put her little foot down as she felt fighting was a bit undignified. Clark would later become a Pulitzer Prize-winning journalist and spar verbally with President Nixon at one of his last press conferences.

Paul Swope, the local dry cleaning establishment owner, provided the uniforms for the town baseball team. Ollie Clave and Miner Haack took over the managing and coaching chores. Hank had made a fine showing pitching for Blairsburg against his hometown team the year before and was now asked to pitch for the Happyland nine.

Other Happyland ball players, who had played for Blairsburg, joined the localites.

That year the Happyland team played some of the top teams in the state. Hank was improving each day. Thousands of people jammed the fairground field bleachers and sidelines as Hank pitched some of his best ball against the Capital City Giants of the old Negro baseball leagues. His hopes of playing pro ball soared, but Hank, by now, also realized active military service could come first.

As guard camp drew near, many of the members hung out at the armory on Saturday afternoons. When ammunition was available, the men fired on the small bore rifle range in the basement, read manuals, discussed tactics and cabitzed on various subjects.

Frank Meller was the full-time caretaker and kept weapons and equipment up in shape. Frank, whose regular job in the company was first cook, normally wore a big broad smile on his face. He was quite difficult to stir from his usual good nature, but when badgered or aroused sufficiently he could vent more than a little temper.

National Guard pilots frequently flew the Iowa skies on weekends in preparation for the forthcoming training at Camp Ripley, Minnesota. They dropped paper bags filled with flour to simulate bombs. It seems one pilot became a little exhuberant and flew a mite too close to a farmhouse near Woolstock, then dropped a flour bag on a barn—nice hit—only he frightened the farmer's wife about out of her unmentionables.

With much haste, the farmer drove to Happyland and straight to the armory. When he entered, he wasn't smiling and he wasn't contributing a thing to Happyland's happy status. To put it mildly, he was madder than two people could normally get, even if they tried extra hard.

Charging into the armory, he approached Tippy O'Flaskagin and Hank, telling them all about the flour bag bombing and the pilot skimming the tree tops. He allowed as how he wanted to talk to the person responsible, right now! O'Flaskagin and Hank were getting quite a kick out of the old boy's display of temperament. O'Flaskagin grinned, then told the farmer that Frank Meller was the only one in the outfit who flew a plane and that he, the farmer, wasn't the first to complain about Meller's fancy flying. The farmer fumed out a few more words, then said, "Where in the hell is he? I want to talk to him." Hank motioned to the stairway.

The irate farmer with head down and hair bristling on the back of his neck, headed up the stairs. Meller was in the supply room, and O'Flaskagin and Hank listened from the bottom of the stairs.

The farmer told old Frank he had to stop flying so low over his farm dropping those damn flour bags on his barn; it was scaring hell out of his wife. He also alluded to the fact that if Frank didn't stop, he was going to shoot him down with his shotgun, etc. etc. Of course, Frank was totally baffled by the guy's outburst, tried to tell him he had nothing to do with it—but the farmer paid no attention.

Frank's voice, by now, was getting louder and louder, and anyone who knew Frank knew an explosion was about to come. Then it came—Frank, now red in the face with neck bowed, told the guy that if he didn't get out of there, he was going to wrap a rifle around his neck so far he'd think it was a necktie. Hearing that, the farmer departed in haste.

Hank and O'Flaskagin stood back in the office as the farmer sailed out the front door with Frank following him all the way with a rifle. Turning to Hank, Frank said, "Now what in the hell got into that old coot? He's got to be nuts. I couldn't fly a plane!" "Hell," he continued, "I don't even like to stand up in bed!"

Lately the attitude of the United States had begun to swing from isolationist to at least some preparedness. Large scale maneuvers were scheduled throughout the country. Participating would be 301,000 regular Army, National Guard and Reserve troops. The largest concentration would be in the east, with 91,000 officers and men taking to the field. Some 45,000 men from the U.S. Fourth Army area would maneuver in Minnesota.

Military preparedness had not been one of the United States' strong points. Let's review the history of the Armed Forces strengths since World War I. In 1936 it had been decided to increase the size of the Army and, by 1939, 225,000 men were allowed—an increase of 47,000 over the 1937 level, but still 55,000 men short of the authorization by the National Defense Act of 1920. It was not a significant increase when one considers the militaristic attitude of foreign countries during the decade.

Loading on a Chicago Northwestern Train August 2, 1940 at 3:10 a.m., the local guard company travelled to Camp Ripley, Minnesota, for not the usual two, but a three-week training period. The asemblage of troops was the largest since World War I.

Hank was now a corporal in charge of a rifle squad. Ranks of squad leaders were to change radically over the years. Before World War II would end a squad leader became a four-stripe staff sergeant. Those two little stripes meant a lot to Hank in those days. He was also happy to see Sergeants Kenneth O. Nichols and Donald Andrew had attained their commissions as second lieutenants through special study courses.

Infantry, armor, horse cavalry, artillery, and the then-Air Corps were all pressed into simulated combat. Field positions of all arms were pelted with flour sack bombs to simulate air attacks. Large firecrackers were used to simulate bombs-artillery and mortar fire and blanks were issued to inject more realism into small arms fire fights. Although equipment still hadn't improved, at least the soldier was being trained to utilize the poor armament he was issued.

As a result of the German luftwaffe's awesome display of air power during their drive across Europe, it was decided U. S. Army defenses against air attack should be beefed up. Two coastal artillery (AA) units were formed from Minnesota Guardsmen (infantrymen.) Before the maneuver began infantrymen were given a three week crash course in manning the 3 inch and 50 caliber water cooled anti-aircraft guns.

In their new coast artillery unit infantrymen learn to fire water cooled 50-caliber machine guns for anti-aircraft defense.
Photo courtesy of Minnesota Military Museum

Here Minnesota Guardsmen (infantrymen) are given three-week crash course in manning 3" anti-aircraft guns. They formed a coast artillery battery.
Photo courtesy of Minnesota Military Museum

During the second week of encampment news was released that the 34th Infantry Division was to be federalized for one year of active duty training. Hank's career for the immediate future and those of some 8,000 men, then with the division at Camp Ripley, had been decided for them.

Germany launched the battle for Britain in September 1940. The British Isles were under a bombardment, the likes of which the world had never seen. Nearly every day in Britain air raid sirens wailed while people dashed for bunkers or any sanctuary that offered even limited protection from the hail of bombs. Newsreels brought home the vivid impact of the suffering endured by even women and children for Hitler's Luftwaffe bombed, not only military, but the civilian populace as well.

Much adjustment in guardsmen's lives was needed upon their return from camp. There had been no date set for the call-up of the guardsmen, so those seeking interim employment found employers reluctant to hire them. Adding to the complexity was a newly-enacted law requiring that a citizen soldier be reinstated in his job upon his return from the service.

Hank was fortunate; Hop Ward gave him a job at his bowling alley cashiering and scheduling lane use. Mother Lucy had asked that he move back home and spend the time before departure with her. She had been failing in health rapidly and when she looked at him with sad blue eyes, he could do nothing but comply. He moved back home and helped with expenses.

Several guard divisions were mobilized in October, but Christmas found young men from Iowa, Minnesota, North Dakota, and South Dakota still biding their time. No one in Washington seemed to understand or be concerned about the undue stress and hardship being placed upon these men by the failure to project a call-up date—nor did anyone bother to explain that the delay was due to the fact that the camp they were scheduled to occupy had not been completed.

Oh well, at least the weather had been good. Temperatures during the fall months had been much warmer than normal. People had enjoyed the respite from early winter weather. It had been so warm that sap was still in the trees and, with no strong frost, some corn stood in the fields not fully matured.

Many people were out visiting or engaged in other fall-type activities that November 10, 1940. The duck season was open and hunters by the thousands were in blinds throughout the midwest when a powerful storm descended on the heartland.

Temperatures hovered around 55 degrees at 6:30 a.m. with moderate 15-mile per hour winds. Little more than a half hour later the temperature dropped to 30 degrees. Shortly after mid-morning it was well below freezing with snow falling, driven by a lashing wind with gusts up to 60 miles per hour in scattered areas. Considering modern chill factors, it was the equivalent of 50 degrees below zero.

In the blinding flurry visibility was cut to near zero, and duck hunter boats were capsizing from the strong winds. When the blizzard halted late on November 11, Armistice Day, many areas of the midwest had received upwards of eighteen inches of snow and some one hundred fifty people in the area had perished—drowned or dead from exposure. The terrible storm swept northeast and throughout the midwest November 12 through November 14. Temperatures became the coldest in recorded history.

Ducks, pheasants and other wildlife died by the hundreds of thousands. Unable to fly in the strong winds and poor visibility, they landed and succumbed to the cold. Some domestic animals and fowl fared no better. It was estimated nearly a quarter of a million turkeys died from the cold. Cattle were found huddled together against fences in pastures and sparsely wooded areas, some dead, but still standing. Foxes and wolves became brazen in their attempts to raid farmyards for food.

Farm losses were horrendous, not only in livestock and poultry, but in unpicked corn not yet mature, and the wonderful apple trees of which the midwest had an abundance at that time. Long-suffering farmers suffered still another blow—how much more could they stand?

There were a lot of bitter—but very few sweet—things that happened to people during the depression. However great the odds, there were some people who beat them. Hank had the pleasure of knowing at least two such people. It all came about when two middle-aged bachelor brothers, Amos and Chris Trosett, came into the bowling alley and struck up a conversation.

Hank asked the brothers, who farmed near Duncombe, how their crops and livestock fared during the storm. "Lost our corn crop," Amos said—yet there was a smile on his face. Hank was perplexed; he hadn't seen a smile on any farmer's face since the storm for losses had been catastrophic.

Hank had known the brothers several years. Amos had played trumpet in various dance bands in and around Happyland. Both were baseball fans. Chris, who spoke in somewhat broken English, held out his hand and said, "Hank, you're going away with the guard and we're going to Oklahoma—so we'll probably never see you again, but we do want to wish you a safe return!"

Shaking their hands, Hank thanked them—then out of curiosity he asked, "Why in the world would you go to Oklahoma? That state has had a terrible drought." At that, Chris pulled a somewhat crumpled telegram from his badly worn overalls pocket and handed it to Hank. The telegram read, "COME TO OKLAHOMA QUICK AS POSSIBLE—OIL ON YOUR PROPERTY—NEED CONTRACT TO START DRILLING."

Throughout the long depression con men had plied their trades throughout the United States, some selling real estate. Many were the investors who ended up with swampland in Florida or desert land in California and Arizona. Amos and Chris had pooled much of their savings and purchased a sizable tract in Oklahoma from a high pressure salesman. They were not worldly, but they had taken the deed to an attorney. The attorney had advised them against the venture, but told them that if they intended to go ahead with the deal, they should insist on mineral rights.

Although the salesman was a bit peeved, he did call and get the deed changed to include mineral rights. "What's the difference?" the owner probably thought. There was hardly a chance the worthless land had anything of value on it—besides they were getting their hands on some scarce money.

The years had gone by and Amos and Chris continued to pay the taxes on the land. Some day when times got better they planned on taking a little trip to Oklahoma to see if the land was worth anything. The telegram had answered their question. They were right; that was the last time Hank ever saw them. Of all the con men who came to Happyland during the depression, only the one who sold the Trosett brothers the Oklahoma land had left smiles on the faces of their intended victims!

During the last two weeks of January, 1941 telephone calls went out from the state adjutant general's offices of the respective states, ordering all guardsmen to report to home station for muster into the federal service. This was not the first time militiamen had answered the call to arms, for lineage of most of these units dated back to the 1800s when claxtons were sounded, church bells tolled or three shots fired—summoning the militia to arms to ward off Indian attacks.

As they answered roll call, their names echoed off cold armory walls. These echoes did not leave a mark, but the valiant deeds many of the men would perform would be etched forever in the annals of military history. Many new battle streamers would fly from their regimental colors before the conclusion of World War II.

Several of the men came from farms and neighboring towns, so at night folding cots were set up as sleeping accommodations in class and locker rooms. It became so congested a man couldn't tell in whose pocket he had his hand when reaching for a cigarette during break periods.

Infantry training in the field is rigorous even during warm weather, but during the depth of winter in the upper midwest the penetrating blasts of arctic air can literally shake one's grates. Field training was conducted at the local country club, and uniforms issued were far from adequate. Campaign hats provided no protection for ears, and overshoes were not issued; frostbite was not uncommon.

Home station for Co. "E," 133rd Inf. Regt. was an old cold building rebuilt after a 1920 fire, which had gutted the armory and a shoe factory next door. Rehabilitation expenses had been held to a minimum and when temperatures dropped to 15 degrees below zero, men would hover over the two gravity air registers in the drill floor to warm their bones during breaks.

A small kitchen, supply room, classroom, and locker room were located on the second floor. In the mostly dirt floor basement was a small bore rifle range. Oh yes, a slab of pavement had been set aside for showers! Water ran out on the dirt floor, offering those waiting in line the opportunity to knead mud pies with their toes while awaiting their turns to bathe.

In spite of the crowded conditions and the below zero temperatures, spirits ran high inside and outside of some of the men. After duty hours while the boxers were boxing, a few of the drinkers were drinking and a sort of holiday atmosphere prevailed. One Saturday night before departure, Specialist O'Kettlebelly and PFC O'Flaskagin decided to turn the bear loose. They put on a firewater gargling contest at Ralph Marlo's Steak House that couldn't be refereed, since the only man qualified to do so had damn nigh passed out from inhalation of cigarette and cigar fumes.

PFC Tippy O'Flaskagin and Specialist Patty O'Kettlebelly drank both socially and unsocially. As the hysterical evening grew older, they slumped lower in the booth and yet, in their own minds, grew larger in stature, each purporting to be a one-man wave of human destruction.

Everyone was enjoying their boisterous conversation, but somewhere along the line they began to believe their own exaggerated tales of terror. O'Kettlebelly announced he had stomped tougher men than O'Flaskagin to death while attempting to get to the scene of a real fight. O'Flaskagin then broke the news to O'Kettlebelly that he had never heard of a skin-head whipping a County Cork Irishman and, with that insult, the show was on. Both leaped from the booth on unsteady legs and squared off. Two banty roosters on a hot coal bed couldn't have put on a better show of agility.

O'Kettlebelly snorted and pranced around O'Flaskagin like a harness racing horse, striking out dramatically with wild swings, which served only to disturb the heavy cigarette smoke in the room. At times they appeared to be trying to blind each other with their dazzling footwork, weaving and bobbing from one side of the room to the other.

O'Flaskagin waltzed around the chrome-domed one and appeared to be looking for either an opening in the toilet line or the prancing one's defenses. One of the newly-enlisted cooks, we'll call him Specialist Spatula, put a nickel in the jukebox and played Wayne King's rendition of "The Waltz You Saved For Me," dedicating the number to dancer and prancer.

After the two combatants had shuffled all the dust on the floor from one side of the room to the other, Ralph Marlo, the tavern owner, became a little concerned and asked Sgt. Charles Meyers to help break up the fight. The proprietor said he was afraid one of the combatants, although fighting in the back of the room, would fall through the front window.

They concluded the ten minute ordeal with the only casualty being a fly, which O'Kettlebelly had almost swallowed during his snorting exhibition. Actually the two gladiators came closer together when they shook hands at the end of the fight than they had been during the entire evening.

They went through the usual routine—no hard feelings, etc., and everyone thought their animosity had truly subsided. They no doubt would have settled down in good shape, but for Sergeant Spooner's proclaiming that O'Flaskagin had won the fight. The sergeant was feeling no pain and, considering the air in the room was filled with smoke,"Lips" Tooterman, the understudy bugler, accused Spooner of judging the fight from sound alone.

The proclamation by Sergeant Spooner really hurt O'Kettlebelly where he lived, and the bald battler indicated he had been hampered in scoring a decisive victory by the lack of elbow space. There was a suggestion by Louis Lovelace and Gilbert Butler that the mean scene be shifted to Kendall Young Park, where the two could settle their differences.

Enroute to the park with the pair, Sergeant Frank Meller halted the car. O'Kettlebelly and O'Flaskagin were arguing vehemently, giving no thought whatsoever to their location. Sergeant Meller told the two adversaries to get out and settle their problems.

O'Kettlebelly, looking back over his shoulder shouting threats to his snarling opponent, stepped out of the car and abruptly disappeared from sight. A picture of power and confidence, O'Flaskagin followed and, like his predecessor, took one step, emitted a weird howl and faded into the darkness.

Shortly thereafter noises resembling a Sioux war chant split the cold night air. O'Flaskagin could be heard asking O'Kettlebelly if he knew just where in the hell they were. O'Kettlebelly bellowed, "How the hell would I know? I haven't been able to stand up and look around!"

Peering out, the spectators could see the two aggressive ones slipping and sliding on the ice-covered snow at the bottom of a deep ditch just to the west of the old White Fox Creek bridge. One minute their performance took on the tangle-footing grace of a kindergarten ballet, and the next they appeared to be playing "All Fall Down." O'Kettlebelly shouted, "I've never noticed a deep hole like this one in Kendall Young Park!" O'Flaskagin bellowed, "Why in the hell would the Civilian Conservation Corps dig an elephant trap in Kendall Young Park when we don't have a zoo?"

Sergeant Meller's intentions had been to disrupt their trend of thought by letting them out near the deep ditch, and he had succeeded admirably. Both pugilists had forgotten why in the hell they were out on a lonely deserted road in the first place. After being helped from the ditch, the two rode quietly back to town.

With February 10, 1941 set as the date for muster into federal service, standing in line became a way of life. Lines stretched up stairways to supply rooms for meals, physicals and from the drill floor past the latrine to the orderly room (office) for personnel records interviews. PFC Tooterman said in all deference to the system the last man in a line should have a card on his back stating his purpose since he had stood in the orderly room line until he damn near washed out the gold fillings from two teeth, waiting to get into the toilet.

The latrines had only two commode seats. One could deduce readily from the expression on a man's face when his toilet tolerance level had reached its peak. With a grim look of determination, the man would break from the line and dash across the street to Harold Hoffman's or Lloyd Smith's gas station to use their facilities. Smitty jokingly averred, "From the sound of things, I could have hooked a few of them up to the tire air hose and saved a lot of wear and tear on my air compressor!"

February 26, 1941 was one of those raw, cold dry days when the sun intermittently shines creating blue-tinged shadows on the snow. The command was given and Co. "E" marched down Main Street at a smart brisk cadence enroute to the railway depot to entrain for Camp Claiborne, La. As they rounded the corner on Des Moines Street, they could see pedestrians walking backwards for short distances to clear the cold north winds from their lungs. Shoes creaked as the unit marched down the snow-glazed brick streets, while sporadic gusts of wind pelted the men's faces with granules of snow.

A huge crowd was huddled in groups at the embarkation point waiting for the guardsmen to arrive. Steam from the coal-fired locomotive swirled flat, then dissipated into the somber sky—somewhat reflecting the mood of the men's wives, sweethearts, relatives and friends, who had gathered to see them off on their journey.

Hank's longtime friend, Bud Brandt, stood in the crowd bidding friends goodbye. He had tried to enlist in the guard, but allowable quotas had been reached. In many ways Hank was glad Bud wasn't going with them. Who knew what fate awaited the guardsmen in the years to come—and soldiering can't get any rougher than in a rifle company.

Hank's sister and her husband Sterling Bonner had brought his Mother Lucy, Father James Arthur, and Cousin Clinty, who had come from Perry to see Hank off. Sterling had failed the more thorough physical examination. The guardsmen bade farewell to those in the vicinity, then climbed aboard the train. Settling down in their seats,

Most people in Happyland turned out to see Co. E off to Camp Claiborne, Louisiana.
Photo courtesy of Daily Freeman Journal

they painfully looked out the window and managed to smile. Hank's sister, tears in her eyes, waved. Mother Lucy, a courageous, loving and compassionate person, waved and smiled, but Hank could see the mist forming in her kind blue eyes.

Father James Arthur, with a sad look on his face, managed to smile weakly, but Cousin Clinty could only wave and turn abruptly away. It was obvious from his actions he was aware of what these young men would go through before, if ever, they would return home.

The locomotive engineer engaged the throttle; a huge puff of dark smoke, laced with snowflakes, swirled outward then upward in the cloudy bright sky. Passenger car wheels creaked against the cold steel rails, and the train moved slowly away carrying the guardsmen on their journey to Camp Claiborne, where the youths who smiled through tears during the bittersweet years would become the "Dogfaces Who Smiled Through Tears" in World War II.

With the bombing of Hawaii's Pearl Harbor by the Japanese December 7, 1941 the United States would enter World War II. The Red Bull Division would be the first American Expeditionary Force in Europe, landing in Ireland. They would participate in the campaigns in Algeria, Tunisia, Naples-Fogia, Anzio, Rome-Arno, the Appenines, and Po Valley, fighting in such bloody battles as Kasserine Pass, Hill 609, Monte Pantano, Monte Morrone, Cassino, Anzio, Lanuvio, Villa Crocetta, Rome, Pisa, Cecina, Leghorn, Bologna, and the Po Valley.

They would accumulate more combat days than any division in the theater—517 days, with elements accumulating 611. In their route to glory the Red Bull Division, authorized at 14,253 men (but rarely attaining more than three-fourths of this strength) would suffer 21,362 battle casualties.

The quiet—shy Edwin Lemke, as previously mentioned, would perform harrowing, almost impossible feats. He would earn the nickname "Phantom" and be proclaimed a one-man army—the Sergeant York of World War II. Sadly many of Hank's friends would be killed or wounded in combat while men of the "Red Bull" Division etched their courageous combat performance into the annals of military history.

Yes, the spontaneous antics and humor of the two first cooks, O'Kettlebelly and Spatula, provided many amusing incidents. PFCs O'Flaskagin and "Lips" Tooterman kept everyone's morale up, even when the going was rough.

Sergeant Spooner, well, he became a terrific combat soldier—even took second place in the Mediterranean Theater International Rifle Marksmanship matches. Of course, he also became legendary emancipating the passions of females in several countries, including, some say, seven jills whom he chased up the seven hills of Rome!

Yes, the aforementioned were all real people; as the saying goes, only the names have been changed to protect the innocent—no matter how fragile that innocence might have been!

No, Hank didn't get his career in big league baseball. He had torn ligaments in his right leg severely while playing football with his regiment's team. Also, being gone all those years during the war dampened some of his desire to become a big-league pitcher. He had received a battlefield commission in Italy and had decided to pursue a military career—a career that had culminated in his requesting early retirement as a lieutenant colonel. Regrets? Yes, a few; he would still rather have played professional baseball.

Back in Happyland's Twin Parks an ambulance siren could be heard. Then across the street the back door to the Family Clinic, operated by two fine young doctors, Guy and Renald Bernard, flew open. Dr. Guy Bernard could be seen hurrying to his car. The old veteran was abruptly interrupted from his trip down memory lane.

The old-timer's dog had been sleeping comfortably in his lap until the siren sounded. Lifting his loving dog to the ground, Hank stretched a bit, rubbed his chin, and looked at the sun; it was nearing mid-afternoon.

Reaching down, he patted his little canine companion, then ambled out to the old fairgrounds, where he looked out across the site where he had spent many happy days playing baseball. The bleachers were gone, and the entire field was now overgrown with grass and weeds. Trees that were saplings then now stretched upwards to seventy-five feet.

As he stood there he reasoned that life, like the proverbial water over the dam, goes on but, unlike the water, it does have an ending. Many of his friends were among the departed. Someday he hoped he would be reunited with those friends and buddies he knew those long years ago during the Bittersweet Years.

But, as the great bard Willie Sipmore once quipped, "I don't want to go the same place as Patty O'Kettlebelly; I don't want to lose any more money to him playing poker." However, Hank did hope there would be baseball teams in his hereafter.

TWILIGHT THOUGHTS

We watch the flickering of the shadows
As they blend with the sun's last rays.
Watch the birds as they hurry to their nests,
Signaling the end of beautiful days.

We watch the sunbeams dance on a river,
Turning ripples to a golden glow.
Watch the water as it winds its way to the seas,
Ever changing—but a constant flow.

We think of the wonderful people we've known,
The good times—the bad times we've shared.
The laughter—the joy—and, yes, the tears,
While showing one another we cared.

Like the sunbeams that dance on the golden stream,
The waters that change as they flow.
Like the shadows that cloak the twilight,
We must fade in the afterglow.

But aren't we lucky we passed this way,
Bore the bitter and sweet—all with zest?
But we hope when we go to our maker,
We'll be credited with doing our best.

by H. R. Ankrum

EPILOGUE

I shall always cherish the memories of my Happyland (Webster City) High School classmates. I list your names with fond remembrances. If we do not meet again, then hopefullly some day - some time - some place, we can all join hands and again sing the praises of Happyland High.

Abbott, Ruth E.
Ambrose, Frances A.
Ankrum, Homer R.
Bates, Myrtle M.
Bernard, Stella M.
Black, Mildred M.
Blair, Ruth C.
Bohlen, Esther R.
Boston, Howard B.
Bradshaw, Donald L.
Brown, Ruth E.
Buettner, Margaret M.
Burns, Dorothy M.
Burton, Ralph L.
Calkins, Leslie
Chalfant, Roy L.
Chambers, Robert E.
Clabaugh, Clarine
Clave, Lucille N.
Cleveland, L. Rollin
Clifton, Edwin L.
Coulson, Margaret L.
Coulter, Don E.
Crouse, Merlin
Dally, Irvin
Deakman, Leona M.
Dickerson, Richard
Doolittle, Max
Doty, Marcelle
Draper, Keith
Eckstein, Richard
Elliott, Shirley
Elliott, Wendell I.
Ewing, Richard E.
Fear, Raymond C.
Foster, Gordon A.
Foster, Willis R.
Gage, Virgil
Greenley, Cecil F.
Groves, Wilfred, Jr.
Haack, Marian G.
Hall, Howard
Hall, Mary Margaret
Hansen, Betty Lou
Heins, Ruth E.
Hendrickson, Orpha
Hoover, Clyde E.
Huddleston, Eleanor
Hughes, Margaret W.
Hughes, Rees
Hunter, Bruce
Iles, Margaret A.
Isebrands, Dorothy
Janvrin, James A.
Jensen, Edith
Johnson, Bonita M.
Johnson, Roland
Jones, Margaret M.
Kitley, John W.
Koehler, Lucille M.
Koestner, Mildred C.
Koolhof, Albert H.
Lee, Phyllis I.
Lee, Richard
Leffler, Beryl I.
Lemke, Edwin
Lundell, Janet
Martin, June R.
Marvel, John W.
Maudlin, Hazel I.
Maxson, Richard
McCauliff, Jeanette H.
McConnell, E. Frances
McIntosh, Roger
McMurray, Barbara
Miller, Armor
Mollenhoff, Clark R.
Mourlam, Mildred M.
Myers, Alberta M.
Naber, Hattie A.
Nail, Wayne
Nelson, Arne
Nelson, Opal I.
Nickles, Doris E.
Nissen, Luciille
Noffke, Lenora C.
Norris, Phillip E.
Olson, John H.
Osmundson, Georgia G.
Packard, J. Merton
Page, Rena
Park, Richard
Park, Vivien E.
Petrow, John G.
Petty, Curtis
Pfaffenbach, Annabel L.
Pierce, E. Faye
Pringle, Katherine
Richardson, Irma L.
Riggs, Donald A.
Ross, Betty J.
Rothrock, Edna J.
Rutledge, John
Samuel, Elfriede
Schaa, Laura Mae
Segar, Verne C.
Shafer, Verla Jeanne
Sharkey, Truman D.
Shields, Francis E.
Short, Vesta
Simpson, Richard E.
Sinn, Lyle
Smith, Florence M.
Snell, Warren C.
Talcott, Joyce F.
Thierman, Betty
Thompson, Ruth E.
Underwood, Robert L.
Urich, Ethel L.
Vance, Billy F.
VanEngen, Phyllis
Vegors, Mason M.
Walker, Opal
Warneke, Marie M.
Welch, Lester L.
Wepel, Gladys
West, Leland
Westervelt, Barbara
Wheeler, Ardella M.
Widman, Kathryn M.
Wilkinson, Malcolm L.
Williams, Audrey
Williams, Marvin
Willson, Jane
Wood, Rollo
Youlden, Stanley G.
Zeiger, Maxine V.

INDEX

Note the unhappy back seat driver.
Photo courtesy of Bernice Sealine Lund

To Grandmother's house we go.
Photo courtesy of Bernice Sealine Lund

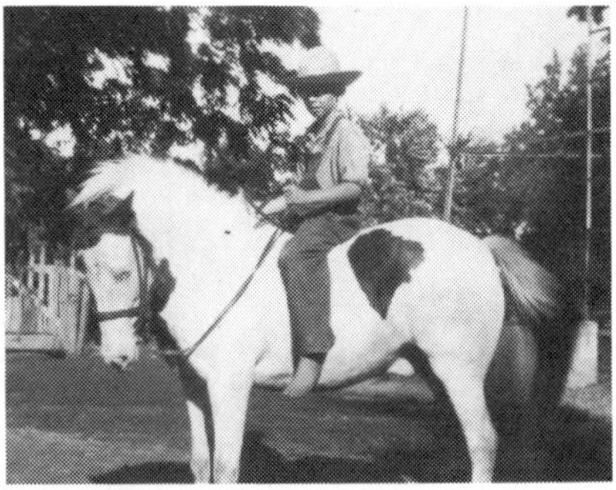

Good guy—white hat!
Photo courtesy of Bernice Sealine Lund

Swede Bend outing at old swimming hole.
Photo courtesy of Helen Nelson

Cutting ice with hand saw.

Photo courtesy of Wallace's Farmer

Conveyor carried ice to ice house.
Photo courtesy of Ruth Passwaters Neese

Cutting ice with gasoline driven saw.
Photo courtesy of Ruth Passwaters Neese

ICE HARVESTING—DELIVERY

Zublin and Garth ice wagons

Photo courtesy of Louis Lovelace

The ice man cometh.

Photo courtesy of Mason City Public Library Historical Collection

Ice truck—Lake Mills Ice Co.

Photo courtesy of Warren Burman

Edgar "Bud" Passwaters delivers ice.

Photo courtesy of Ruth Passwaters Neese

Plowing with horses.

Plowing with tractor.

Discing with horses.

Discing and harrowing with tractor.

Harrowing with horses.

Could a 5-hp car out-pull these horses?

Planting with horses.

Planting with tractor.

All photos in Farming Progress section courtesy of Wallace's Farmer *unless otherwise noted.*

FARMING PROGRESS

Seeding with horses.

Cutting hay.

Windrowing hay.

Pitching hay.

Baling hay with portable baler.

Horse-pulled oats binder

Tractor powered oats binder

Shocked oats

Pitching bundles into hayrack.

Threshing oats.

Combining oats.

Stop! Did you forget to use your manure spreader?

Corn cultivator—left, Nels Hanson, right, Axel Sandberg

Photo courtesy of Ellen Ankrum

Hand picking corn.

Picking corn with corn picker.

Smoking meat.

Morris Stein with hand corn sheller

Photo courtesy of Donald Andrew

No farming progress that day

First Snow/Last Load

Drawing by William Weber. Reproductions of his wonderful art are available from the Webster City, Iowa artist.

Bellville country school—recess play
Photo courtesy of Derald Hanson

Left, teacher Caroline Gerber. Right, students of Mud Hollow School 1925–1926
Photo courtesy of Coleen Whipple

FROM THE PUBLISHER

Readers are encouraged to read Homer R. Ankrum's "Dogfaces Who Smiled Through Tears - In World War II." The book is an extension of "Bittersweet Years - Smiling Through Tears."

CLARK MOLLENHOFF—Pulitzer Prize winning journalist and author calls "Dogfaces Who Smiled Through Tears - In World War II" an outstanding chronicle of heartaches, hardships, heroics and humor of the North African and Italian campaigns. The book also provides an excellent overview of those campaigns.

GENERAL JOHN W. VESSEY, JR., U.S. Army, Retired former Chairman of the Joint Chiefs of Staff: Among other laudatory remarks, General Vessey states, " 'Dogfaces Who Smiled Through Tears' is one of those rare books that not only tells campaign history, but captures the action packed stories of infantry, artillery, armored and other combat units that squared off with the enemy in ground combat. Ankrum has succeeded in capturing the spirit and tenacity of the American combat soldiers, their fabulous sense of humor and unwavering determination to prevail, even against overwhelming odds and adverse conditions."

MINNEAPOLIS STAR TRIBUNE: David Wood states, "Any reader with a taste for heroism and high adventure will enjoy Ankrum's exhaustively researched and crackingly told story."

SIOUX CITY JOURNAL: John Quinlan writes, "Like Ernie Pyle before him, Ankrum does a skillful job of following the average Dogfaces across the battlefields of World War II. Humorous anecdotes, however, lighten what could otherwise be a grim story of heroic men."

OMAHA WORLD-HERALD: George Shestack concludes, "There are enough good stories packed in Ankrum's writings to provide materials for a dozen books!"

COUNCIL BLUFFS NON-PAREIL: Ed McGrath, Managing Editor states, " 'Dogfaces Who Smiled Through Tears' will be read with enthusiasm and relish by military buffs and the general public."

FORT DODGE MESSENGER: Walter B. Stevens, Editor: "Only one who had been part of the action could have written as interesting, graphic and appealing book. His own experience and extensive research are apparent on every page, but so is the faculty to see humor in trying situations and a deep sense of caring which made battle conditions tolerable for the combat soldier."

A comment frequently received from readers is, "Dogfaces Who Smiled Through Tears" is the best book written on World War II. This book should be compulsory reading for high school and college students; it is a book all Americans should read."

"Bittersweet Years - Smiling Through Tears" or "Dogfaces Who Smiled Through Tears" may be ordered from Graphic Publishing Company or through your local book store.

Graphic Publishing Company
P.O. Box 158
Lake Mills, IA 50450
Phone 1-800-458-2922
Mason City, IA 50401
Phone 1-800-247-5986

ABOUT THE AUTHOR

Webster City, Iowa born author, Homer R. Ankrum, has had a widely diversified career. He received a battlefield commission during the Italian Campaign of World War II, retiring from the U.S. Army in 1963 as a Lieutenant Colonel to accept appointment as City Manager of his hometown.

After completing a nearly twenty-year stint as a city manager, Ankrum retired early to pursue a career in writing and authored the successful novel, "Dogfaces Who Smiled Through Tears – In World War II." Ankrum's emotion arousing poetry has drawn high praise from readers. He has also composed the stirring words and music for the "The March of the Red Bull Legions."

Readers encouraged Ankrum to write a prelude to his World War II book embracing the period between the two world wars. Now, after years of extensive research and tireless effort, Graphic Publishing Co., Inc. is proud to announce the publication and release of "Bittersweet Years – Smiling Through Tears (1920-1941)." An outstanding treasure of humor, human interest, and historical events to be enjoyed by young and old alike.